D1458845

Vocational A-level
Travel and Tourism

Ray Youell MSc MTS MSA

Longman

In this book you will find helpful icons showing which Key Skills the Activities can be used for:

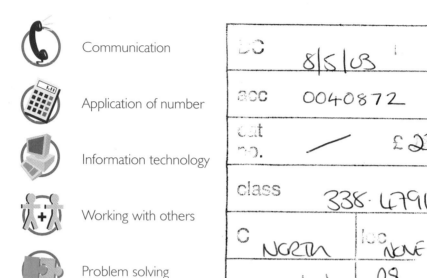

Communication

Application of number

Information technology

Working with others

Problem solving

Improving own learning and performance

Pearson Education Limited
Edinburgh Gate
Harlow
Essex CM20 2JE, England
and Associated Companies throughout the world

This edition published 2000
Second impression 2000

ISBN 0 582 40445 2

British Library Cataloguing-in-Publication Data

A catalogue record for this book is available from the British Library.

Set by 3 in Humanist, Rotis Serif, Caslon
Produced by Pearson Education

Printed in Malaysia, PP

Contents

Foreword

Brent Hoberman, co-founder of the Internet company lastminute.com, offers an interesting insight into how travel, leisure and tourism will develop in the future, and highlights the important role that the Internet will play.

Travel, Leisure and Tourism in the 21st Century

When I came up with the idea for lastminute.com, I was inspired by the Internet's tremendous reach. Literally thousands of people can look at a web site simultaneously regardless of where they are in the world. This makes it a fantastic medium for communicating one idea to lots of people, or lots of ideas to specific groups of people who share similar interests – like travellers.

lastminute.com's concept is all about making quick and spontaneous lifestyle decisions. This can include decisions to travel, see a show, eat at a restaurant, treat someone special or get away for a weekend. Looking at the travel sector of the site as an example, this means we can help both airlines and travel companies to find spontaneous people to take advantage of their unsold tickets and packages. For other travel companies with different criteria, the Internet presents a host of new opportunities to bring information closer to the people who need it – would be travellers and the people who help them make their travel choices.

The technology that makes the Internet a reality can also be used to link all sorts of information together in new ways. Masses of data about flight timetables, information and pictures about resorts, famous destinations and annual tourist events can be amassed in cyberspace and served up in palatable chunks to anyone with an Internet connection. At lastminute.com, we have positioned ourselves at the forefront of new platform development, which, in tandem with personalisation, gives us the opportunity to offer a truly tailored service. It has to be about giving the customer the right deal, at the right time, through the right channel.

Accessing a site like the British Tourist Authority's award winning site, visitbritain.com, can help foreign visitors plan an entire trip from the comfort of their home or office without having to consult a tour guide. The real beauty of the Internet is that it is a virtually limitless source of linked information which allows people to drill down to the subjects which really grab their attention without moving off their PC, TV or other Internet access device.

21st century lifestyle opportunities are becoming more accessible thanks to the Internet's ability to put great deals into the hands of people who want to take advantage of them. The world is getting smaller in the sense that it's easier to find official web sites packed with information, or connect with people in chat rooms who've had first hand travel experiences they want to share. And the travel experience doesn't end with the planning and booking. There are hundreds of websites which can help you research the history, people and language of the places you want to visit to make sure you get more from the experience.

Communities of people from all around the world who share the same interests can communicate via the Internet and group together to get great deals on travel, share experiences and stay in touch after the event. We've even taken bookings for flights to the edge of space on lastminute.com for thrill seekers chasing the ultimate travel buzz. One thing's for sure, the Internet is here to stay and it's already changed the way that many millions of people plan and book their leisure. With this much choice, information and access to great deals, there's no excuse to stay at home.

Brent Hoberman
CEO and co-founder
lastminute.com

Introduction

Vocational A-level Travel and Tourism has been written specifically for the Vocational A-level Travel and Tourism courses starting in September 2000. It follows exactly the structure of the six new compulsory units developed by the QCA (Qualifications and Curriculum Authority) and applies to courses offered by all three awarding bodies – Edexcel, AQA and OCR.

It builds on the success of my previous best-selling Longman books – *Advanced GNVQ Leisure and Tourism* (1994), *Advanced GNVQ Leisure and Tourism* 2nd edition (1995) and *Advanced GNVQ Travel and Tourism Optional Units* (1996). Together, these have set the standard for the study of leisure and tourism at this level in schools and colleges across the UK.

This book includes many of the popular features found in my previous editions – case studies, realistic activities and up-to-date statistics. Most of all, it offers something many of you have told me that you have appreciated in my previous books, namely an **in-depth** study of travel and tourism, the industry that I have been involved with for more than 20 years.

However, just like the travel and tourism industry, nothing stands still for long! So there are extra features in this new book, including links to Internet websites, key skills opportunities and industry examples. You will find these throughout the book, helping to turn theory into practice and giving you ideas for further research.

Included for the first time is a glossary of terms and sources of further information. You will also appreciate the selected bibliography that gives you the chance of investigating particular subjects in greater depth.

I hope you find the book a useful companion in your studies. Good luck with your course and future career!

Ray Youell
Aberystwyth
February 2000

Acknowledgements

Once again I am indebted to many individuals and organisations that have helped with the project. Those who have provided valuable information and illustrations are acknowledged in the relevant section of the text. I am grateful to them all for their co-operation and helpful comments. I would like to pay special thanks to Mike Westaway at the British Tourist Authority, Richard Allen at the English Tourism Council and Chris Gratton at the Leisure Industries Research Centre in Sheffield for their help with the book. Thanks are also due to Ian Little, Caroline Howard and the rest of the team at Pearson Education for their usual professional approach. Peter Carr and Julie Gibson have provided valuable advice throughout the project. As always, Sue, Megan and Owen have been patient in their suffering!

Whilst every effort has been made to trace the owners of copyright material, in a few cases this has proved impossible and we take this opportunity to offer our apologies to any copyright holders whose rights we may have unwittingly infringed.

Investigating travel and tourism

1

Travel and tourism is commonly referred to as 'the world's biggest industry'. This unit introduces you to the reasons why people travel and defines what we really mean by 'travel and tourism'. You will also learn about the different organisations found in the travel and tourism industry, from tourist attractions and tourist boards to accommodation providers and travel agencies. You will discover that travel and tourism has grown dramatically since the end of the Second World War to become one of the world's fastest-growing industries, offering a wide variety of employment opportunities. You will gain an insight into what it is like to work in travel and tourism, with opportunities to develop your own career path into the industry.

This unit is divided into seven main areas:

- **Defining travel and tourism**
- **The development of travel and tourism**
- **Features of the travel and tourism industry**
- **Structure of the travel and tourism industry**
- **Scale of the UK travel and tourism industry**
- **Working in the travel and tourism industry**
- **Pursuing your own progression aims**

We guide you through each of these areas using examples and case studies from the travel and tourism industry. At the beginning of each section you will see a list of key topics to help you fully understand what you need to learn. Look out for the links to websites so that you can learn more about a particular travel and tourism company, organisation or topic.

Defining travel and tourism

Key topics in this section:

- **Introduction – what is travel and tourism?**
- **Defining travel and tourism**
- **The main types of tourism (domestic, inbound, outbound)**
- **The reasons why people travel (leisure, business, visiting friends and relatives)**

Introduction – what is travel and tourism?

A simple answer to this question is that travel and tourism is big business! It is set to become the world's biggest industry in the early years of the new millennium, with more people than ever before travelling in their own countries and exploring new destinations abroad. It covers all aspects of people travelling away from home, whether for leisure, business or visiting friends and relatives, and the industry that supports this activity. The travel and tourism industry is very wide-ranging, covering many different sectors as shown in Figure 1.1.

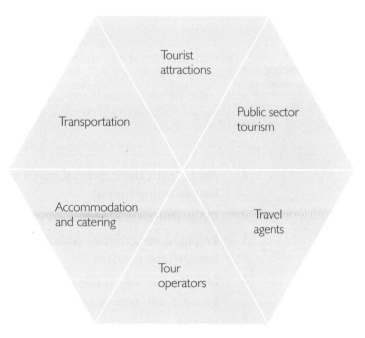

Figure 1.1 *The travel and tourism industry*

Figure 1.1 shows us that there are six main sectors in the travel and tourism industry:

- ✪ **Tourist attractions – e.g. Alton Towers, Warwick Castle, local museums**
- ✪ **Transportation – e.g. airlines, coach operators, rail companies, car hire**
- ✪ **Accommodation and catering – e.g. hotels, villas, apartments, camping**
- ✪ **Public sector tourism – e.g. tourist boards, local authority tourism departments**
- ✪ **Tour operators – e.g. Thomson, Airtours, Superbreak**
- ✪ **Travel agents – e.g. Lunn Poly, Going Places, Thomas Cook**

We will investigate each of these sectors in more detail later in this unit.

Defining travel and tourism

There are many definitions of travel and tourism used throughout the world. The World Tourism Organisation (WTO), affiliated to the United Nations and recognised as the leading international body on global tourism, states that tourism comprises:

browse this website

www.world-
tourism.org

> . . . the activities of persons travelling to and staying in places outside their usual environment for not more than one consecutive year for leisure, business and other purposes (World Tourism Organisation, 1993)

Probably the most widely accepted definition of tourism in use in the UK today is:

browse this website

www.toursoc.org.
uk

> Tourism is the temporary, short-term movement of people to destinations outside the places where they normally live and work, and activities during their stay at these destinations; it includes movement for all purposes, as well as day visits or excursions (Tourism Society, 1976)

Both definitions clearly show that people we would think of as tourists are:

1   **Away from their normal place of residence (although they will be returning home)**
2   **On a visit that is temporary and short-term**
3   **Engaged in activities which would normally be associated with leisure and tourism**
4   **Not necessarily staying away from home overnight; they may be on a day trip or excursion**
5   **Not always away from home for holiday purposes; they could be on business and still qualify as tourists**

However, neither definition mentions the impacts, both negative and positive, that travel and tourism has on the environment and the people who live in destinations. This topic is discussed later in this unit and in greater detail in Unit 2: Tourism Development.

The main types of tourism

It is very important to remember that tourism is not just about going abroad! There is a common misconception in Britain that travel and tourism is only concerned with taking overseas holidays; this could not be further from the reality of the truth. Research shows us that British people take nearly five times as many tourist trips within the UK as they take abroad, but the majority do prefer overseas destinations for their main holidays.

There are three main types of tourism:

Domestic tourism: When people take holidays, short breaks and day trips in their own country

Incoming/inbound tourism: A form of international tourism which deals with people entering another country from their own country of origin or another country which is not their home

Outbound tourism: A form of international tourism which concerns people travelling away from their main country of residence

A few simple examples will help to clarify what can sometimes be a confusing concept.

Domestic tourism: The Smith family from Birmingham enjoying a two-week holiday in a caravan in Scarborough.

Incoming/inbound tourism: M. et Mme Du Pont from Limoges sampling the delights of Cardiff as part of a driving tour of England and Wales.

Outbound tourism: The Smith family from Birmingham deciding to give Scarborough a miss this year and taking a week's holiday at EuroDisney in France.

Activity 1.1

Carry out a small-scale survey of the rest of your group to find out how many people took their last holiday abroad and what proportion stayed in the UK. Find out the main reasons for taking holidays abroad.

The reasons why people travel

Contrary to popular belief, travel and tourism is not just about holidays! Tourism is usually divided into leisure tourism, business tourism and visiting friends and relatives. Figure 1.2 indicates the main purposes under each of these categories.

As you can see from Figure 1.2, leisure tourism includes many of the types of activities which most people think of as 'tourism'. However, business tourism is an increasingly important sector since it is often of high value and earns hoteliers, caterers and transport operators significant income. Indeed, many city-based travel agents operate a separate department geared exclusively to the needs of business clients. Visiting friends and relatives (VFR) is also an important contributor to tourism revenue. You may be wondering how it is that somebody who stays for free with a friend or relative in their home is helping tourism in an area. The answer to this question is that the visitor, although enjoying free accommodation, is likely to spend money on other goods and services in the locality, such as food, entertainment and transport, so contributing to the local economy. Indeed, the very fact that he or she is not paying for accommodation may well be an incentive to spend more on such things as eating out and entertainment.

Some examples from each of the categories shown in Figure 1.2 will help to give a clearer understanding of the meaning of travel and tourism. Leisure tourism examples are shown in Figure 1.3 and different examples of business tourism are given in Figure 1.4.

Figures from the British Tourist Authority (BTA) show that British people made a total of 122.3 million trips in the UK for all purposes in 1998, of which:

- ✪ **65.1 million (53 per cent) were on holidays**
- ✪ **13.7 million (11 per cent) were on business**
- ✪ **38.4 million (32 per cent) were visits to friends and relatives**
- ✪ **5.1 million (4 per cent) were for other miscellaneous reasons**

Tourism

Leisure tourism	Visiting friends and relatives (VFR)	Business tourism
• Holidays • Health and fitness • Sport • Education • Culture and religion • Social and spiritual		• Business meetings • Exhibitions and trade fairs • Conferences and conventions • Incentive travel

Figure 1.2 *Why people travel*

Holidays	• A weekend break in a guesthouse in York
	• A two-week family holiday to the Algarve staying in a self-catering villa
	• A murder/mystery weekend at a hotel in Torquay
Health and fitness	• A cycling tour in France
	• A weekend in a hotel with a fitness room and health suite
	• A walking holiday in Scotland
Sport	• The British team's visit to the Olympic Games
	• Visiting Old Trafford to watch a one-day cricket international match
	• A weekend break to watch the Monaco Grand prix
Education	• A week at an Open University summer school in Durham
	• A weekend sailing course in Plymouth
	• A French student attending a college in Brighton to learn English
Culture and religion	• A week studying Celtic folklore in the West of Ireland
	• A pilgrimage to Mecca
	• A weekend studying the churches of East Anglian villages
Social and spiritual	• A weekend reflexology workshop
	• A one-parent family holiday to Suffolk
	• A week-long meditation course in the Lake District

Figure 1.3   *Examples of leisure tourism*

Business meetings	• A British sportswear manufacturer on a two-week fact-finding tour of the west coast of the USA
	• An advertising executive taking a train journey from her home base for a meeting with a client in Belfast
	• A Member of the European Parliament flying to Brussels for the day for meetings with EU officials
Exhibitions and trade fairs	• A representative of the English Tourism Council visiting the Scottish Travel Trade Fair in Glasgow
	• The Gardeners' World exhibition at the Birmingham NEC
	• Visiting the World Travel Market in London
Conferences and conventions	• Lawyers from EU countries attending a two-day conference on new Directives in Copenhagen
	• Attending the TUC Conference in Blackpool
	• Visiting the ABTA Domestic Conference in Llandudno
Incentive travel	• A weekend golfing break at Gleneagles for achieving top monthly sales for your company
	• Free care hire for one week on your holiday for completing an important project ahead of time
	• Two weeks in Florida for you and your family for clinching a new multi-million pound contract

Figure 1.4 · *Examples of business tourism*

Figures for spending on trips for the same period show a total spend of £14 billion on trips in the UK for all purposes by British people, of which:

- **9.8 billion (70 per cent) was spent on holidays**
- **2.2 billion (16 per cent) was spent on business tourism**
- **1.6 billion (11 per cent) was spent on visiting friends and relatives**
- **0.4 billion (3 per cent) was spent on other miscellaneous purposes**

These figures confirm that business tourism has a higher spend per head than either holiday tourism or visits to friends and relatives.

Industry example

Harrogate Borough Council was one of the first local authorities in the UK to develop business tourism, by targeting the conference trade. A purpose-built exhibition hall was opened in 1959, followed by further halls in the 1970s and, in 1982, a major conference auditorium, exhibition space and modern hotel. By the early 1990s major capital investment was needed to upgrade the facilities to meet changing business clients' requirements. The Council created the Harrogate International Centre to further stimulate conference and exhibition trade. In 1998, the Centre generated a net operating surplus of approximately £1 million and, as a result of its activities, Harrogate hosted more than 2,000 conferences, 27 exhibitions and 29 trade fairs, attracting over 360,000 business visitors who spent over £100 million. The Centre has enabled Harrogate to secure its position as an important conference and exhibition venue, helping to support some 7,000 local jobs.

The development of travel and tourism

Key topics in this section:

● **Background to the development of travel and tourism**

● **Factors that have led to the growth in travel and tourism**

● **Future developments in travel and tourism**

Background to the development of travel and tourism

Throughout history, people have travelled across Britain for purposes of trade, education, religion and to fight in battles. It was not until the eighteenth century, however, that the foundations of what we now regard as the British tourist industry began to be laid (see Figure 1.5).

1752	Dr Richard Russell published *Concerning the Use of Sea Water*, leading to a rise in the popularity of UK seaside resorts
1830	Introduction of the railways
1841	Thomas Cook organised his first excursion from Leicester to Loughborough
1851	Tours were organised to the Great Exhibition in London
1866	Cook organised his first excursion to America
1871	The Bank Holiday Act created four public holidays per year
1901	The Factory Act gave women and young people six days' holiday per year
1903	'Trust Houses' opened a chain of hotels in Britain
1936	The first UK holiday camp was opened by Billy Butlin at Skegness
1938	Introduction of the Holidays with Pay Act
1949	First overseas 'package holiday' by air offered by Vladimir Raitz of Horizon
1965	Lord Thomson took the first step towards the creation of the Thomson Travel Group
1969	Development of Tourism Act established the English, Wales and Scottish Tourist Boards, plus the British Tourist Authority (BTA)
1970	Introduction of the Boeing 747 'jumbo jet'
1974	The UK's number one tour operator Clarksons went into liquidation
1986	The number of UK package holidaymakers topped 10 million for the first time
1991	The Intasun holiday company ceased trading
1994	Channel Tunnel opened
1998	A record 25.7 million overseas visitors came to Britain, spending more than £12 billion

Figure 1.5 *Milestones in the development of UK travel and tourism*

Spa towns such as Cheltenham, Leamington Spa and Buxton were frequented by the wealthy classes who came to sample the health-giving properties of the saline waters. Seaside resorts, including Brighton, Margate and Blackpool, grew in popularity, helped by the introduction of the railways from the mid-nineteenth century onwards; the first passenger train service was opened in 1830 between Manchester and Liverpool. There followed a massive expansion of the rail network, principally to service industrial centres, but with the capacity to bring many of Britain's seaside resorts within easy reach of the centres of population; Brighton was a popular destination with some 132,000 visitors recorded on Easter Monday in 1862.

The Industrial Revolution, which had been the catalyst for the development of the railways, led to improvements in the road and canal networks in the UK. Also at the time of the Industrial Revolution, workers began to want to escape from their normal harsh routines and often dirty environments in favour of relaxation and entertainment in the relative purity of the countryside and coast.

The 1938 Holidays with Pay Act gave a stimulus to mass tourism in the UK, with 80 per cent of workers being entitled to paid holidays by 1945. Holiday camps flourished immediately before the outbreak of the Second World War, the first having been opened by Billy Butlin in 1937 at Skegness. Two years later, there were around 200 camps offering self-contained 'package' holidays to 30,000 people per week. In the early 1950s, two-thirds of all domestic holidays were taken at the seaside and the majority of holidaymakers travelled to their destinations by coach or train. The late 1950s saw the establishment of the British Travel Association, forerunner to the British Tourist Authority (BTA), which was given the role of encouraging the development of hotels and resorts.

The 1960s can be chronicled as the time when UK tourism came of age. The government passed the Development of Tourism Act in 1969, establishing the English, Wales and Scottish Tourist Boards, plus the British Tourist Authority, which was charged with promoting the whole of Britain to overseas visitors. Three important elements of post-Second World War society in the UK, namely the development of jet aircraft, the growth of the overseas 'package tour' and increasing car ownership, were to have far-reaching implications on the UK domestic tourism scene.

Factors that have led to the growth in travel and tourism

The end of the Second World War in 1945 was a watershed in the history of the world, and also in the development of the travel and tourism industry. The industry has grown very rapidly since the 1950s, the result of a number of related factors, including:

- **Changing socio-economic circumstances: increasing car ownership, more leisure time and higher income levels have allowed people to travel more often, particularly on overseas holidays**

- **Developments in technology: developments in jet aircraft and computer technology have contributed to the growth in domestic and international travel and tourism**

- **Product development and innovation: the development of seaside resorts, introduction of holiday camps, package holidays, long-haul destinations and all-weather attractions have all been introduced to meet the growing demand for travel and tourism products and services**

- **Changing consumer needs, expectations and fashions: through exposure to television and other mass media, people are looking for more opportunities to travel in the UK and overseas**

We will now look at some of these developments in more detail.

The rise of seaside resorts

In the early eighteenth century, doctors began to realise that the healing and relaxing minerals that were present in spa waters were also to be found in the sea; Scarborough, with the twin benefits of spa and sea water, was quick to exploit its benefits. It was not, however, until 1752 with the publication of Dr Richard Russell's noted medical work *Concerning the Use of Seawater* that seaside resorts such as Southend, Brighton and Blackpool began increasing in popularity. Accommodation, catering and entertainment facilities were developed in the resorts, some of which benefited from the introduction of steamboat services in the early nineteenth century, a factor that led to the construction of many of the piers still seen at seaside resorts today.

The introduction of holiday camps

The first purpose-built holiday camp (what the industry now refers to as a holiday centre) was opened by Billy Butlin in 1936 at Skegness. Holiday camps worked on the simple principle that if the children were happy on holiday then the parents would be happy as well. To this end, holiday camps provided entertainment and activities for both parents and children at a low, all-inclusive rate with the added bonus of a child-minding service to allow the parents to enjoy themselves. Butlin's and Warners became market leaders in this type of holiday which still survives to this day, albeit in a different form.

Increasing car ownership

The increase in car ownership after the Second World War provided individuals with greater freedom and flexibility in the use of their leisure time. People travelled further afield, exploring new areas of the British coast and countryside. The number of private cars on the roads of Britain rose steeply from 2.3 million in 1950 to 11 million in 1970. In 1999, the figure exceeded 23 million vehicles.

Although this rise in car ownership has brought undoubted benefits to individuals and their families, it has highlighted a number of issues of concern. Firstly, the upward trend in the ownership of cars has resulted in a drop in demand for traditional types of public transport. According to figures published in *Insights*, the use of trains for holiday travel fell from 48 per cent of all journeys in 1951 to just 8 per cent in 1990. Statistics for coach travel for the same period show a similar trend, with a drop from 28 per cent in 1951 to 9 per cent in 1990. This fall in demand for train and coach travel has led to cuts in services and, in the case of the railways, the closure of unprofitable lines. Those living in the remoter rural areas of Britain have been particularly affected by these service reductions and the loss of choice in their travel arrangements.

A second consequence of the growth in car ownership in the UK has been the rise in associated environmental problems, including pollution, congestion and the loss of land to further road building (see Figure 1.6).

These problems are particularly acute in many of Britain's historic cities and most scenic countryside areas. In many National Parks and Areas of Outstanding Natural Beauty, for example, the volume of cars is having a damaging effect on the landscapes and wildlife habitats, often spoiling what the visitors have come to see and enjoy. These problems have led to calls for cars to be banned from some areas or for their use to be strictly controlled. Popular historic cities, including Canterbury, Cambridge and York, have introduced measures such as 'park and ride' schemes, cycle hire and pricing mechanisms to help alleviate the problems. Managers in the Peak District National Park encourage the use of public transport by working in partnership with local bus and train operators.

The development of jet aircraft

One positive outcome of the Second World War was the rapid advance in aircraft technology, which led to the growth of a viable commercial aviation industry in Britain and the USA (see Figure 1.7). The surplus of aircraft in the immediate post-war years, coupled with the business flair of entrepreneurs including Harold Bamberg of Eagle Airways and Freddie Laker, encouraged the development of holiday travel by air. Comet aircraft were used in the 1950s, but it was not until the introduction of the faster and more reliable Boeing 707 jets in 1958 that we began to see the possibility of air travel becoming a reality

Figure 1.6 *Increasing car ownership is causing serious congestion problems*
Courtesy of the Highways Agency

Figure 1.7 *A Virgin Atlantic Boeing 747*
Virgin Atlantic © www.virgin.com

for the mass of the population. The 1960s saw a surge in demand for scheduled and charter flights, the latter being combined with accommodation, transfers and courier services to form the overseas 'package tour' that is so familiar today.

The growth of package tours

Vladimir Raitz of Horizon Holidays is credited with having organised the first modern inclusive tour by air when he carried a party of holidaymakers to Corsica in 1950. The holiday consisted of full-board accommodation in tents and travel in a 32-seater DC3 aircraft. From a modest start with just 300 passengers carried in its first year of operation, Horizon repeated the formula in subsequent years with increasing success. The 1960s saw the beginning of the rapid increase in the number of package holidays sold. Destinations such as the coastal areas of Southern Spain, the Balearic Islands and Greece were favourite locations for British and other European travellers. The convenience of an all-inclusive arrangement, coupled with the increased speed which the new aircraft brought, caught the imagination of the British travelling public. Today, in the region of 15 million package holidays are sold to British tourists each year.

Long-haul destinations

From the British perspective, long-haul destinations are generally considered to be those beyond Europe, for example the USA, Australia, the Far East and India. Advances in aircraft technology, coupled with low prices offered by some of the major holiday companies, have opened up many new long-haul destinations in recent years. Places such as Florida, the Gambia, the Caribbean, Goa, Hong Kong, South Africa and Australia have all become popular with British tourists. Unit 3: Worldwide Travel Destinations looks in detail at a selection of popular long-haul destinations.

Future developments in travel and tourism

We have seen how travel and tourism has developed very rapidly to become one of the world's biggest industries. But what of the future? Will this dramatic growth be sustained or will the bubble burst? Most industry experts agree that travel and tourism will continue to grow, but in different ways. There will be a number of important influences on the way that the industry develops in the future, including:

1   **Social factors:** Demographic trends (those concerned with the characteristics of the population) and social changes will have important

impacts on the future development of the industry in the new millennium. The fact that people are living longer, the fall in the number of young people, the increase in one-parent households, more couples choosing not to have children or to delay having children until later in life, all point to the fact that the type of travel and tourism products and services will change radically.

The chart in Figure 1.8 shows the changes in the age structure of the UK population between 1993 and 2000. It shows the numbers of young adults in the 15–34 age group declining by around 8 per cent. In contrast, the number of middle-aged people is growing (45–64 year olds), with the largest increase in the 35–44 age group (see Figure 1.9).

2 **Political and economic factors:** On a global scale, the late 1980s saw historic world developments with countries emerging from State control and embracing the Western 'market economy'. Events such as the demolition of the Berlin Wall have had profound effects on travel and tourism developments; tourists from Western countries are now more able to visit the former Eastern bloc countries, while those from the former East are curious to sample Western hospitality by travelling further afield. The completion of the Single European Market in 1993, with the easing of border controls, has further increased travel within EU member countries. Closer to home, the buoyant economy will continue to lead to greater demand in travel and tourism.

3 **Cultural and environmental factors:** The 1980s saw the emergence in Britain of a greater environmental awareness and a society that was beginning to take its health and fitness seriously. These factors

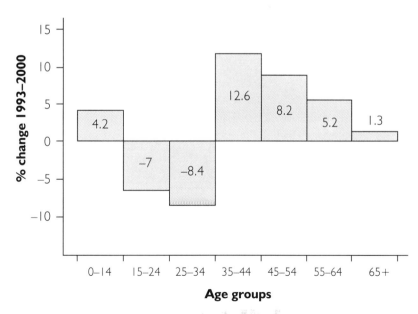

Figure 1.8 *Britain's ageing population*
Adapted from Henley Centre for Forecasting data

Figure 1.9 *Older people are a growing market in travel and tourism*
Courtesy of Magic of Italy

are likely to remain important influences on travel and tourism developments in the future with so-called 'green issues' high on the agenda.

4   **Technological factors:** Travel and tourism has always been an industry that has made extensive use of new technology equipment. Central reservation systems (CRS), the use of computers in travel agencies and sophisticated databases for marketing purposes are now commonplace. Increasing competition within the industry will force organisations to use new technology to the full. New developments in transportation make extensive use of new technology; the Channel Tunnel is a good example of this as are the advances in aircraft design, opening up new long-haul destinations.

The British Tourist Authority estimates that:

✪   **Growth in overseas visitors to the UK is expected to average 4.4. per cent over the next five years, reaching 34.6 million visits in 2005**

✪   **Spending by overseas tourists to Britain is forecast to rise by an annual average of 7.4 per cent, producing £21 billion spend in 2005**

Working with a colleague, draw up a list of the likely effects of Britain's ageing population on the following travel and tourism sectors: hotels, self-catering accommodation, transportation and attractions.

○ **UK residents' tourism in the UK is expected to show an average 2.6 per cent increase in visits and 8 per cent in spending between 1998 and 2003**

The trend towards UK residents taking their main holidays abroad rather than in Britain is also set to continue.

The government's new tourism strategy *Tomorrow's Tourism* includes a series of action points to help Britain develop a world-class travel and tourism industry for the future (see Figure 1.10).

1 A blueprint for the sustainable development of tourism
2 Initiatives to widen access to tourism
3 More money for a more focused and aggressive overseas promotion programme
4 New Internet systems to deliver more worldwide tourist bookings for Britain
5 New computerised booking and information systems
6 A major careers festival and image campaign
7 A hospitality industry programme to sign up 500 employers to work towards *Investors in People* standard
8 A new strategic national body for England
9 A new grading scheme for all hotels and guesthouses
10 New targets for hotel development in London and a further £4.5 million for marketing
11 More integrated promotion of our wonderful cultural heritage and countryside attractions
12 The development of innovative 'niche' markets
13 Encouraging the regeneration of traditional resorts
14 More central government support for the regions
15 A high profile annual Tourism Summit

Figure 1.10 *Action points from the government's National Tourism Strategy document* Tomorrow's Tourism

Features of the travel and tourism industry

Key topics in this section:

- **Introduction**
- **Key features of the travel and tourism industry**

Introduction

We have seen that travel and tourism has grown rapidly since the end of the Second World War to become one of the world's biggest industries. It has evolved over a very short period of time and, as such, sometimes lacks the economic credibility of industry sectors that have existed over a longer period of time. It is a very dynamic industry, continually developing to meet changing customer needs and expectations. When people go on holiday today, they are not prepared to accept standards of accommodation and facilities that are worse than they are used to at home. Travel and tourism companies that are unwilling or unable to meet these changing demands are unlikely to succeed in this highly competitive industry. But what is the industry really like? The next section of this unit explores this question in more detail.

Key features of the travel and tourism industry

We shall see in the next section of this unit that investigates the structure of travel and tourism that the industry is made up of a wide range of separate enterprises, from airlines and hotels to tourist attractions and travel agencies. The industry as a whole has a number of important features, namely:

- ✪ **It is predominantly private sector led**: The great majority of the enterprises that are part of the travel and tourism industry operate in the private or commercial sector. However, public sector bodies, such as tourist boards and local authorities, have an important role to play in tourism planning, regulation, development and marketing

- ✪ **The majority of enterprises are small and medium-sized**: It would be easy to believe that the travel and tourism industry is dominated by large, multinational companies, such as British Airways, Virgin and Holiday Inn. In reality, the bulk of tourism businesses are very small, often just a single person operation or a couple working in partnership. Small and medium-sized enterprises supply the vast majority of travel and tourism products and services.

- ✪ **There is extensive use of new technologies**: Travel and tourism has always used new technology to provide high standards of service to customers. The use of computers and communications technology in all sectors of the industry is now commonplace. With the rapid growth of the Internet, companies are changing the way they communicate with their customers. Many travel and tourism organisations are developing websites to provide customers with information and advice, with some offering on-line reservations.

- ✪ **It is vulnerable to external pressures**: Travel and tourism is a very risky business! A sudden rise in the world price of oil, a terrorist attack at an airport or a spate of attacks on tourists in a resort can have devastating effects on travel and tourism businesses. You only have to think of the former Yugoslavia, a country that once had a thriving tourist industry, to appreciate this fact.

- ✪ **It has positive and negative impacts on host communities**: Unit 2: Tourism Development looks in detail at the impacts of the industry. Although travel and tourism has the potential to deliver substantial economic benefits, it is fair to say that the industry must work towards making its operations more sustainable in the long term.

Structure of the travel and tourism industry

Key topics in this section:

- **Introduction**
- **Commercial and non-commercial organisations**
- **Tourist attractions**
- **Accommodation and catering**
- **Tourism development and promotion**
- **Transportation**
- **Travel agents**
- **Tour operators**

Introduction

Travel and tourism in the UK is a highly fragmented industry, employing some 1.7 million people who help provide a vast range of products, services and facilities to cater for the needs of British residents and visitors from overseas. Tourism in Britain is sustained by thousands of small businesses, a smaller number of large well-known companies and a range of public sector agencies which assist the industry at European, national, regional and local levels. Figure 1.11 shows how the major sectors of Britain's tourist industry interact.

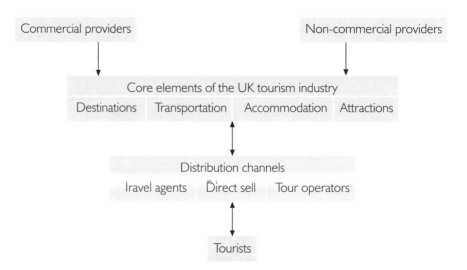

Figure 1.11   *The structure of the UK travel and tourism industry*

Figure 1.11 rightly places the tourist as the focus of tourist activity in the UK, since without tourists there would be no need for an industry, a fact that private and public sector operators ignore at their peril! The core elements of the industry – destinations, transportation, accommodation and attractions – are supplied by a mixture of commercial and non-commercial providers, ranging from multi-million pound companies such as Virgin Holidays and British Midland Airways, to local councils which provide leisure facilities and tourist information services for visitors.

Private sector companies are responsible for supplying the bulk of tourist facilities and services in the UK, with the public sector usually acting in a regulatory or co-ordinating role. The diagram shows that UK tourism 'products' are made available to people in the UK and overseas tourists via three main distribution channels:

1   **'Direct sell' – where operators offer their facilities direct to the paying public**
2   **Through travel agencies**
3   **Through tour operators**

The next section of this unit investigates the different objectives of commercial and non-commercial organisations in travel and tourism.

Commercial and non-commercial organisations

The UK tourism industry is dominated by **commercial organisations** whose aims are primarily financial. Some of the best-known names in the industry are commercial (private sector) companies, for example British Airways, Center Parcs, Thomas Cook, Swallow Hotels, Thomson Holidays, Alton Towers and Stena Line (see Figure 1.12).

The commercial sector of the UK travel and tourism industry consists of large and small organisations owned by individuals or groups of people whose primary aim is to make a profit. Many members of the general public invest in these organisations, relying on the profits generated by tourism companies for a part of their income. Profit maximisation is an important objective for any commercial tourism provider, since it helps provide the capital for future business expansion, thereby enabling staff and management to respond better to the needs of customers by providing the products and services they will buy.

Although profit maximisation is the primary objective of the majority of private sector companies, it is by no means the only objective of all commercial tourism organisations. A lot of small businesses in the UK tourism industry are run by people who used to work for larger companies, but became frustrated with the high level of bureaucracy they encountered. Such people value the

Figure 1.12 *Stena Line's 50 mph HSS*
Photograph courtesy of Stena Line Limited

greater degree of control over their business affairs that self employment can offer and thrive on making their own decisions. The operators of some tourism companies may not seek to maximise profits to the full, but may be content with a level of profit that gives them the type of lifestyle they are happy with; after all, why work in an industry concerned with holidays and travel and have no time to enjoy yourself and have fun!

In addition to their revenue maximisation objectives, even the biggest UK tourism companies have a variety of related aims. These are often concerned with providing high standards of customer service, respect for the environment, providing value for money and being a good employer.

Non-commercial organisations in travel and tourism, falling within the public or voluntary sectors of the UK economy, do not usually have profit maximisation as their primary objective. It may be that they have been developed with wider social or community objectives in mind; the principal aim of a tourist attraction developed at the site of an archaeological dig, for example, may well be to provide an educational and recreational experience for the benefit of local people. There are many examples of organisations working in the UK travel and tourism industry that have non-commercial objectives. Local authorities play a major role in the provision of infrastructure and facilities for tourists, as well as marketing their particular areas both home and abroad (see Unit 2: Tourism Development for more on the role of local authorities in UK tourism). National, regional and local tourist boards exist to encourage tourists and help their members provide high quality products and services to visitors (see British Tourist Authority case study on pages 40–43). Charitable trusts working in travel and tourism range from small, localised groups who may be protecting an endangered natural resource, to large organisations such as the Youth Hostels Association (YHA) and the National Trust (see case study on pages 109–110 in Unit 2: Tourism Development).

Although profit maximisation is not the primary objective of non-commercial organisations operating in the UK travel and tourism industry, those which are part of local government or are agencies of central government are expected to offer value for money and meet targets and agreed performance criteria. Many local authorities have recruited staff from the private sector and have implemented private sector management practices in order to help achieve their objectives. Similarly, all charitable trusts and voluntary groups will aim to keep their costs to a minimum while striving for their wider social or community objectives. The British Tourist Authority (see case study on pages 40–43) is a good example of a publicly funded organisation that has a range of commercial and non-commercial objectives.

Tourist attractions

Attractions are a vital component of the UK tourism scene; indeed, they are often the single most important reason why tourists visit a destination and are, thus, the stimulus for other sectors of the tourism industry, including accommodation, catering, transportation and entertainment. Different people have different ideas about what constitutes an 'attraction'; a person living in the West Midlands may think of Drayton Manor Park as an example of a tourist attraction. People living in the south of England might mention Thorpe Park or Legoland (see Figure 1.13). Those living in Wales may include St Fagans or Powys Castle on their list of attractions, while residents of Scotland are likely to mention Aviemore or the Burrell Collection in Glasgow. The people of Northern Ireland would surely put the Giant's Causeway towards the top of their list of tourist attractions.

browse this website for information on UK attractions

www.visitbritain. com

While all these well-known examples clearly fall within anybody's definition of a tourist attraction, it is important to remember that the majority of attractions throughout Britain are not household names. Small museums, craft galleries, shops, leisure facilities and farm attractions, to name but a few, are crucial to the economic well-being of many areas of the country. Together, they form the 'critical mass' of attractions in a locality that forms the basis for encouraging tourists to explore and perhaps stay overnight. As the following English Tourist Board (ETB) definition of a 'visitor attraction' shows, such places should be promoted to local people as well as to tourists:

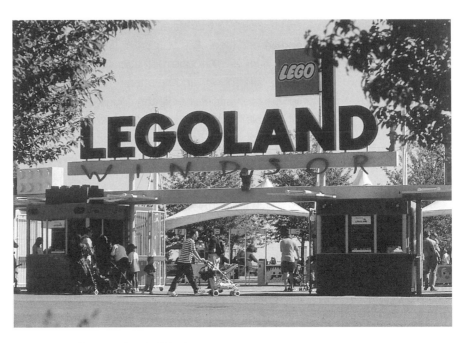

Figure 1.13 *Legoland, Windsor*
Courtesy of Legoland Windsor Park Ltd

> *A permanently established excursion destination, a primary purpose of which is to allow public access for entertainment, interest or education; rather than being a primary retail outlet or a venue for sporting, theatrical, or film performances. It must be open to the public, without prior booking, for published periods each year, and should be capable of attracting day visitors or tourists, as well as local residents.*

Tourist attractions can be either natural or built. The British countryside (and in particular its 'protected' areas including National Parks, Areas of Outstanding Natural Beauty and Heritage Coasts) is a major resource for leisure and tourism. ETB figures estimate that there are in the region of 550 million day visits to the countryside each year, a quarter of which take place in July and August. The Countryside Agency, charged with protecting the countryside and providing facilities for its enjoyment, suggest that some 18 million people visit the English countryside on a fine summer Sunday. In certain parts of Britain, the pressure on the countryside is such that the visitors are in danger of damaging the environment permanently and are certainly guilty of spoiling the very thing which attracted them in the first place.

Natural attractions

Britain has an abundance of fine landscapes, from Land's End to John O' Groats. Visitors are attracted to the beautiful coastline, the rugged mountains and the picturesque dales. Many of these areas have been given special status to protect their environment and provide facilities for their enjoyment by the public. The job of overseeing these 'protected' areas in England lies with the Countryside

Draw up a list of the natural and built attractions in your own local area, adding details of whether each attraction operates in the private, public or voluntary sector.

browse these websites

www.countryside.
gov.uk
(Countryside
Agency)

www.ccw.gov.uk
(Countryside
Council for Wales)

Agency, whose aim is to conserve and enhance the natural beauty of England's countryside and help give people better opportunities to enjoy and appreciate it. The Countryside Council for Wales does a similar job in the Principality.

National Parks

The ten National Parks in England and Wales (see Figure 1.14) were established under the 1949 National Parks and Access to the Countryside Act (the Broads in Norfolk and Suffolk, and the New Forest are not National Parks as such but have equal status). The word 'national' does not mean that the Parks are owned by the government; most of the land within National Park boundaries is privately owned and often under severe pressure from visitors and their vehicles. The Peak District National Park is a good case in point being located between the large conurbations of Sheffield and Manchester. The total number of visitors to the National Parks in England is more than 70 million in a typical year and, when combined with the three Welsh Parks, they cover approximately one-tenth of the land area of England and Wales.

Areas of Outstanding Natural Beauty (AONBs)

Thirty-seven of England's most cherished landscapes are protected as AONBs (see Figure 1.14). They range from the wild open moorlands of the North Pennines to the green belt countryside of the Surrey Hills and the intimate valley of the Wye, which straddles the border with Wales (there are another four AONBs wholly within Wales itself). AONBs can be popular destinations for travel and tourism, although, unlike National Parks, they are not designated for their recreational value. The Countryside Agency has proposed stronger measures for their management and more funding for their upkeep. In total, AONBs in England cover around 15 per cent of the landscape.

Heritage Coasts

There are 44 Heritage Coasts in England and Wales. They are among the most precious assets for wildlife and landscape, as well as for tourism. Concern over the harmful impact of increasing numbers of visitors led to their designation and a plan of action which includes creating and repairing footpaths, cleaning up bathing water and removing litter.

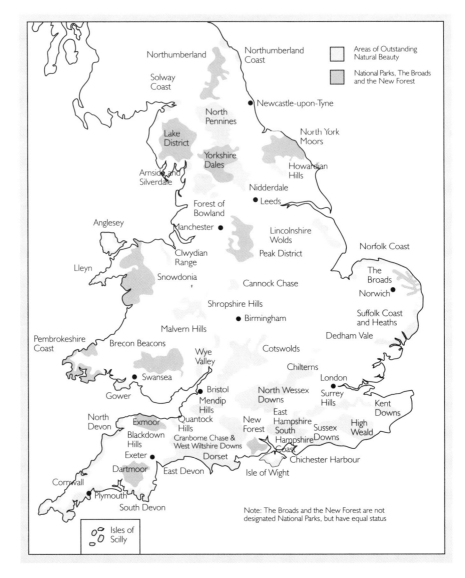

Figure 1.14 *National Parks and Areas of Outstanding Natural Beauty (AONBs) in England and Wales*

Activity 1.2

Visit the website of either the Countryside Agency www.countryside.gov.uk or the Countryside Council for Wales www.ccw.gov.uk and make notes on the organisation's aims and activities.

Built attractions

The term 'tourist attraction' usually brings to mind a purpose-built facility, designed to provide fun and entertainment. If asked to give the name of the first major tourist attraction in Britain which comes to mind, an overseas visitor may well mention the Tower of London or Buckingham Palace, while a UK resident is likely to name the Millennium Dome in Greenwich. Table 1.1 gives 1998 visitor numbers for the top 20 UK attractions charging for admission.

	1998
Alton Towers, Staffordshire	2,782,000
Madame Tussaud's, London	2,772,500
Tower of London	2,551,459
Natural History Museum, London	1,904,539
Chessington World of Adventures	1,650,000
Legoland, Windsor	1,646,296
Science Museum, London	1,599,817
Canterbury Cathedral	1,500,000
Windsor Castle, Berkshire	1,495,465
Edinburgh Castle	1,219,055
Victoria and Albert Museum, London	1,110,000
Flamingo Land Theme Park, Kirby Misperton	1,105,000
St Paul's Cathedral, London	1,095,299
Windermere Lake Cruises, Cumbria	1,060,600
London Zoo	1,052,886
Drayton Manor Park, Staffordshire	1,003,802
Kew Gardens, London	1,000,000
Chester Zoo	920,000
Royal Academy, London	912,714
Roman Baths and Pump Room, Bath	905,426

Source   Insights

Table 1.1   *Visitor numbers for the top 20 UK attractions charging admission, 1998*

Figure 1.15 *The 85 mph Pepsi Max Big One at Blackpool Pleasure Beach*
Courtesy of Blackpool Pleasure Beach. Photographer: Lord Lichfield

Table 1.1 shows that, once again, Alton Towers in Staffordshire was the most popular of all UK attractions that charged for admission, with nearly 2.8 million visitors. What the table does not show is that, when data for free attractions is included, the most popular attraction in the UK was Blackpool Pleasure Beach (see Figure 1.15), which attracted around 7 million visitors in 1998. Other free attractions that welcomed more than 2 million visitors in 1998 include Albert Dock Liverpool, The British Museum, Strathclyde Country Park, Eastbourne Pier and York Minster.

Built attractions created specifically for the enjoyment and education of visitors occur in a variety of different forms throughout Britain, for example:

- ✪ **Historic monuments**
- ✪ **Theme parks**
- ✪ **Heritage attractions**
- ✪ **Entertainment facilities**
- ✪ **Sport and recreation centres**
- ✪ **Cultural attractions**

Historic monuments

Britain is renowned for its wide range of historic monuments, which have great appeal to UK residents and overseas visitors. The majority of historic monuments are in public ownership, with many London properties under the management of the Historic Royal Palaces Agency, a division of the Department for Culture, Media and Sport (formerly the Department of National Heritage). Many castles and stately homes in England and Wales are cared for by the

National Trust, CADW: Welsh Historic Monuments and English Heritage, who manage the sites and provide facilities for visitors.

Theme parks

Theme parks have been a success story in the UK since the first was opened at Thorpe Park in 1979. Based on a concept that was first developed in the USA, theme parks offer visitors a wide range of permanent rides and entertainments in a themed setting or range of settings, with a single entry charge giving access to all facilities. Most large UK theme parks have experienced growth in their attendances since the late 1980s through constant updating of their facilities and visitor services. There is evidence, however, that the theme park market is becoming saturated in some parts of Britain, leading to price discounting by parks and the introduction of other incentives to maintain their market share.

Heritage attractions

The term 'heritage' has been adopted by many visitor attractions that depict life at a particular time in the past. Many existing attractions have attached the word 'heritage' to their facility, in the hope of attracting greater numbers of visitors and widening their visitor base. They are part of a general trend towards themed attractions in the UK, for example the Jorvik Viking Centre in York and the World of Robin Hood in Nottingham. Some parts of Britain have developed attractions that celebrate their industrial heritage, for example Ironbridge Gorge in Shropshire and the Big Pit museum in South Wales.

Entertainment facilities

Entertainment facilities such as nightclubs, casinos, discos, theatres, concert halls, arenas and opera houses all provide entertainment opportunities for visitors to an area and local residents. Indoor arenas, such as the Birmingham National Exhibition Centre (NEC), London Docklands Arena and Sheffield Arena, are major venues for concerts, attracting people from a wide catchment area. Much of the appeal of UK tourist destinations is the wide range of entertainment facilities they offer visitors. Seaside resorts such as Rhyl, Blackpool and Brighton, for example, will attract tourists with a variety of live shows, concert events and 'night life' opportunities. Smaller towns and cities will also attract day visitors from their immediate area to enjoy the entertainment at cinemas, theatres, night clubs and arts centres.

Sport and recreation centres

As well as being popular with local residents, sport and recreation centres also add to the appeal of towns and cities in the UK, helping to attract overnight and day visitors. Swimming baths and leisure centres offer visitors indoor facilities when the weather outside is inclement. There has been considerable investment in sport and leisure facilities in the UK in recent years, with the introduction of wave machines, jacuzzis, health suites, flumes and saunas into centres run by public and private sector operators. On a national scale, sport and recreation facilities are being used to help change the image of certain parts of Britain and attract further inward investment; for example the Don Valley Stadium in Sheffield and the National Cycling Centre in Manchester are both part of urban regeneration projects.

Cultural attractions

Some parts of Britain have a variety of cultural attractions that attract both UK and international visitors. Links with famous people, cultural diversity, associations with the arts and music are all used to build an image of a destination and attract tourists. Shakespeare's birthplace in Stratford-upon-Avon, for example, is a magnet for UK and overseas visitors alike, while historic Bath (see Figure 1.16), the Cardiff Singer of the World competition and the Edinburgh Festival attract tourists from all over the world. Museums and galleries have long been popular places to visit for entertainment and educational purposes. Britain has an abundance of high quality museums of national and international significance, including the British Museum, the Tate Gallery at St Ives in Cornwall, the Burrell Collection in Glasgow, the National Museum of Wales in Cardiff and the National Museum of Photography, Film and Television in Bradford, to name but a few.

browse this website

www.24hourmuseum.
org.uk

Figure 1.16 *The Great Bath and Abbey, Bath*
Courtesy of Bath Tourism Bureau

Case Study
Eureka! The Museum for Children

Eureka! was the first museum of its kind in Britain. It is wholly designed to teach children between the ages of 5 and 12 about the world in which they live using a 'hands-on' educational approach. Visitors to the museum in Halifax, West Yorkshire are encouraged to touch, listen and even smell, as well as look; Eureka! is truly at the forefront of the new breed of 'interactive' museum attractions. It draws on the traditions of the international community of children's museums that are to be found all over the United States and throughout the world.

Since its official opening in July 1992 by HRH The Prince of Wales, the museum has been a runaway success – so successful that it was voted Museum of the Year 1993 in the ETB 'England for Excellence Awards'. Within six months of opening, Eureka! had attracted 250,000 visitors and the figure at nine months had risen to over 375,000. The museum welcomed its one millionth visitor in 1994.

► AIMS

The aims of Eureka! The Museum for Children are as follows:

★ To promote, maintain, improve and advance public education by the creation of an informal learning centre, designed primarily for children up to the age of 12

★ To pay particular attention to children with special needs and the adults who care for them

★ To offer an educational resource for use both in the context of schools and the National Curriculum, and as a leisure facility

★ To encourage dialogue between adults, children and all sections of the community who have an interest in children's development and welfare, such as the family, the school and industry

continued

continued

★ To enable children to become aware of their future importance as citizens, examining the issues and problems of today

★ To help visitors, both child and adult, to discover their unexpected abilities, and to give them a desire to learn new skills

MUSEUM FACILITIES

Eureka! is housed in a futuristic 4500 square metre building designed by Building Design Partnership. This steel, stone and glass structure is intended as the biggest exhibit of all. Development costs for the attraction totalled £9 million, a third coming from private sponsors and the remaining two-thirds from the Clore and Duffield Foundations. Eureka!, a registered charity, was conceived and built without any local or central government funding.

The focus of the museum is the exhibition which has four main areas, entitled:

★ '*Me and My Body*' – where children are encouraged to explore how the body and senses work

★ '*Living and Working Together*' – investigates how the individual fits into an extended family and into society

★ '*Invent, Create and Communicate*' – provides opportunities for children to use their imagination, shared skills and knowledge to solve the problems of today and to open up new perspectives for tomorrow

★ '*Things*' – investigates how and why many of the everyday objects that we take for granted are designed and made

Eureka! also offers an extensive programme of events which, for 2000, includes a Lego challenge, space adventure, wacky races, pirates a'hoy, number fun and masquerade crafts.

continued

continued

THE MARKET

The prime target market for Eureka! are the 8.5 million people who live within a 90-minute travelling distance of Halifax, of whom 2.7 million are in family groups with children under the age of 14. The museum is situated at the centre of a densely populated area, with major conurbations including:

★ Greater Manchester   population 2,500,000

★ West Yorkshire   population 2,053,000

★ Merseyside   population 1,468,000

★ South Yorkshire   population 1,298,000

School groups account for 25 per cent of all visitors and tend to be from within a 50-mile catchment area. Weekends outside the main holiday periods tend to attract family groups from a 50–60 mile radius. Most visitors during peak holiday times tend to be on holiday in the region.

(Information courtesy of Eureka! The Museum for Children)

Case study discussion questions

browse this website

www.eureka.org.uk

1 Why do you think Eureka! has proved to be so popular since it opened in 1992?

2 How does the attraction go about meeting its aims?

3 What do you think the future holds for this type of 'interactive' attraction?

4 Why is it important for attractions like Eureka! to offer a programme of events?

Accommodation and catering

The accommodation and catering sector is an important revenue earner in UK tourism. Often referred to more simply as 'hospitality', it includes all types of accommodation that people use for leisure and business tourism, plus the full range of catering outlets available to visitors, from restaurants to fast-food premises. Data from the BTA shows that spending on accommodation and catering by domestic and overseas visitors to Britain in 1998 was more than £15.5 billion, representing 58 per cent of total visitor spending. This made accommodation and catering the single largest sector of tourist spending in 1998, ahead of shopping (20 per cent), travel within the UK (13 per cent), entertainment (4 per cent) and services (4 per cent). The accommodation and catering sector is also a significant employer in the UK, as the following June 1999 figures from the BTA indicate:

⊘ **Hotels and other tourist accommodation**   **342,500 employees**

⊘ **Restaurants, cafés, etc.**   **408,300 employees**

⊘ **Bars, pubs and nightclubs**   **449,400 employees**

Taken together, employment in accommodation and catering totals more than 1.2 million posts, representing more than 70 per cent of all UK travel and tourism jobs.

The accommodation sector in the UK is dominated by commercial enterprises, providing a wide range of hotels, guesthouses and self-catering accommodation. The main non-commercial suppliers of accommodation are the Youth Hostels Association, universities and colleges, and premises operated by religious groups.

When it comes to taking holidays in the UK, staying in the various types of self-catering accommodation is more popular with the British than serviced accommodation, although the single most popular type of accommodation used in 1998 was hotels, accounting for 25 per cent of all accommodation used. Visiting friends and relatives is another significant category of tourist accommodation, used for 18 per cent of all holidays in Britain by the British in 1995.

Types of accommodation

Visitors to Britain and UK residents can choose to stay in a wide range of establishments, all of which can be classified as 'accommodation'. There are city centre hotels, motels, farm guesthouses, country house hotels and self-catering cottages, to name but a few. For those looking for something a little different, the Landmark Trust specialises in self-catering accommodation in unusual settings, including a lighthouse and a former railway station!

UK accommodation can be classified in a number of ways, for example commercial or non-commercial, static or mobile, urban or rural. However, it is most commonly classified as either serviced or self-catering, depending on the level of service offered. As its name implies, the term 'serviced accommodation' is used when a service is provided along with an overnight stay, for example meals and housekeeping. In this category, therefore, we find:

- **Hotels**
- **Motels**
- **Guesthouses**
- **Bed and breakfast establishments**
- **Youth Hostels**
- **Farm guesthouses**

Self-catering, or self-serviced, accommodation includes:

- **Cottages**
- **Villas and apartments**
- **Chalets and log cabins**
- **Camping and caravan sites**
- **Hired motor homes**
- **Second homes**
- **Timeshare**
- **Canal boats**
- **Educational institutions**
- **Camping barns**
- **Home 'swaps'**

The distinction between serviced and self-catering accommodation is not quite as clear as these lists suggest; for example, it is quite common now for self-catering establishments, particularly if they form part of a complex, to offer visitors the option of buying food and ready-to-eat meals. Some even have on-site restaurants, cafés and snack bars.

Serviced accommodation

Hotels are the most common type of serviced accommodation found in Britain. The annual English Hotel Occupancy Survey (EHOS), commissioned by the regional tourist boards, defines a hotel as:

> *An establishment having 5 or more bedrooms, not calling itself a guesthouse or a boarding house, and not being listed as providing bed & breakfast accommodation only.*

Using this definition, BTA/ETB statistics show that there are in the region of 52,000 hotels in England, Wales, Scotland and Northern Ireland. Although gathering data on accommodation stock is always difficult, since different

Figure 1.17 *Novotel, Sheffield*

regions use different classification criteria, it can be estimated that, in addition to this figure of 52,000, there are around 20,000 guesthouses, farm guesthouses, boarding houses, and bed and breakfast establishments. Most of this combined total of 72,000 establishments are operated by owner-proprietors who usually live on the premises. Many large hotels in the UK are run by hotel groups, such as Swallow Hotels, De Vere Hotels, Holiday Inn and Novotel (Accor Group) (see Figure 1.17), which benefit from 'economies of scale' in terms of purchasing, recruitment and marketing.

One type of serviced accommodation that has grown rapidly in recent years is the budget hotel sector, with brands such as Travelodge and Travel Inn now commonplace in the UK (see Table 1.2).

The figures in Table 1.2 show just how much the sector has grown, from just 200 hotels in 1992 to a forecast of more than 1100 in 2003, offering 71,600 rooms. This growth is a response to the rise in the number of budget-conscious business travellers and the increased demand for leisure breaks.

Self-catering accommodation

Self-catering accommodation in the UK includes all rented premises used for holiday purposes, self-catering holiday centres and villages, all types of caravan accommodation, self-catering youth hostels, second homes and boats (excluding cruises). Using this definition, figures from the BTA/ETB show that

Year	Number of hotels	Number of rooms
1992	200	8,422
1993	222	9,364
1994	264	11,389
1995	322	14,224
1996	400	18,155
1997	484	23,002
1998	554	27,447
2003 (forecast)	1,169	71,600

Source   Deloitte and Touche

Table 1.2   *Growth in UK budget hotels, 1992–2003*

Industry example

Travelodge is one of the best-known budget hotel companies with over 190 locations nationwide, on motorways and 'A' roads, in towns and city centres, near tourist attractions and Areas of Outstanding Natural Beauty. All Travelodges offer the same services, so the customer always knows what to expect. These include en-suite facilities, satellite TV, tea and coffee making facilities, free newspaper and free car parking. The company offers booking via the Internet or from its centralised reservations centre.

browse this website

www.travelodge.
co.uk

self-catering accommodation was used on 50 per cent of all long British holidays in 1998, compared with 31 per cent for serviced accommodation. All holiday-makers like the freedom and value for money that the different forms of self-catering can offer, while families with young children and/or older relatives find it particularly convenient and flexible.

Self-catering accommodation in the UK can take many forms. The former holiday camps, now renamed holiday centres and villages, converted much of their accommodation to self-catering in the 1970s and 1980s in response to customer demand. The market leaders in the UK are Warner's, Butlin's, Haven and Pontin's, which together account for approximately 20 per cent of all UK domestic holidays. Since the mid-1980s, Butlin's has invested £100 million in upgrading its five holiday centres, which between them welcome over 1.5 million visitors every year. The company is currently embarking on a complete refurbishment of its stock of budget accommodation. Center Parcs aims at a more 'up market' clientele at its UK holiday villages in Sherwood Forest, Elveden Forest and Longleat Forest (see Figure 1.18).

Self-catering cottages throughout the UK are popular with the more affluent AB social groups, who appreciate the rural locations of many of the properties and the convenience of booking through one of the many agencies specialising in self-catering accommodation, for example Blakes, English Country Cottages, Hoseasons, Wales Holidays and Country Cottages in Scotland. The National Trust and the Forestry Commission offer self-catering accommodation throughout Britain in houses, cabins, lodges and cottages.

Self-catering is an increasingly popular form of tourism on farms in the UK. Encouraged by advice and grant-aid from the Ministry of Agriculture and other government departments, many farmers and landowners have converted farm buildings into accommodation units. Such accommodation is popular with families and, from the owners' point of view, is less labour intensive than farmhouse bed and breakfast enterprises.

Timeshare is a particular type of self-catering accommodation involving the purchase of time, usually in blocks of weeks, in a holiday property. The

Figure 1.18   *Center Parcs*
With kind permission of Center Parcs Ltd

purchaser is then able to use that property at the specified time period each year, or may be able to swap it for accommodation at timeshare properties elsewhere in the world. Although most commonly associated with overseas resorts, there are many timeshare properties in the UK. One of the first was developed on the banks of Loch Rannoch in Scotland in 1974. Most UK timeshare developments are found in the rural areas of Britain, including the Lake District, North Yorkshire, Scottish Highlands and Cornwall. As well as self-catering villas, cottages and log cabins, apartments in seaside resorts and city centres are also available on a timeshare basis.

Camping and caravanning are excellent choices for those looking for good value self-catering accommodation. Caravans were used on 24 per cent of all long holidays in Britain in 1998, with camping accounting for 3 per cent. The owners of many camping and caravanning sites have invested heavily in recent years, to provide their customers with an enhanced range of facilities, including swimming pools, fitness suites, entertainment and eating facilities, aimed principally at the family and youth market. Touring caravans are particularly popular with older age groups, many of whom are members of the Caravan Club or the Caravan and Camping Club of Great Britain.

browse this website

www.hoseasons.co.uk

Industry example

Hoseasons Holidays is a long established self-catering company, specialising in holiday parks, lodges, country cottages and boating in Britain, plus holiday parks and apartments in Europe. The company also offers boating holidays in France and Belgium. It is the leading independent holiday booking service in the UK. Each year, over one-third of the company's business comes from people who have been with Hoseasons before. A further one-third comes from friends and relatives of those who have booked previously. Hoseasons distributes approximately 650,000 boating holiday brochures and over 1.4 million holiday homes brochures each year. Most holidays are booked by telephone (Hoseasons was the first UK company to develop telesales for holiday bookings). Approximately 200,000 holiday weeks are booked every year; as the average size of each party is 4.8 persons, this means that Hoseasons arranges holidays for more than 925,000 people each year.

Tourism development and promotion

Unit 2: Tourism Development looks in detail at the role of public sector organisations in tourism promotion and development, including the national and regional tourist boards and local authorities (see page 85). Nearly all local authorities in the UK have an involvement in tourism, with many responsible for providing tourist information centres (see Figure 1.19).

browse this website for links to local authority websites

www.open.gov.uk

One of the key organisations that promotes Britain overseas is the British Tourist Authority, the subject of the next case study.

Figure 1.19 *Windsor tourist information centre*
Courtesy of Royal Windsor Information Centre

Case Study
British Tourist Authority

The British Tourist Authority (BTA) works in the non-commercial sector of UK tourism and is responsible for promoting Britain as a tourist destination overseas. Its central role is to help maximise the contribution that

continued

continued

incoming tourism can make to the British economy. It was established under the 1969 Development of Tourism Act, together with the Wales, English and Scottish Tourist Boards (the English Tourist Board became the English Tourism Council in July 1999). The Northern Ireland Tourist Board was set up in 1948. Unlike the national tourist boards, which are charged with encouraging tourism to their own particular country, the BTA is responsible for promoting the whole of Britain to overseas visitors.

THE WORK OF THE BTA

BTA's objectives are:

★   To maximise the benefit to the economy of tourism to Britain from abroad while working worldwide in partnership with the private and public sector organisations involved in the industry and the English Tourist Board, Scottish Tourist Board and Wales Tourist Board

★   To identify the requirements of visitors to Britain, whatever their origin, and to stimulate the improvement of the quality of the product and the use of technology to meet them

★   To spread the economic benefit of tourism to Britain more widely and particularly to areas with tourism potential and higher than average levels of unemployment

★   To encourage tourism to Britain in off-peak periods

★   To ensure that the Authority makes the most cost-effective use of resources in pursuing its objectives

In order to meet these objectives, BTA undertakes a wide-ranging programme of market research and product promotion in the major countries of the world. In many respects it acts as the overseas arm of the national tourist boards, gathering market intelligence via its network of

continued

continued

overseas offices and representatives. This market intelligence is fed back to the home tourist boards, which help generate new products and services to meet the needs of overseas visitors, through liaison with commercial operators and local authorities. Recent BTA initiatives have included the '*Britain – Now is the Time*' campaign to tie in with the new millennium, the launch of its new Internet site at www.visitbritain.com, the publication of the *Rock and Pop Map of Britain* and the development of a new 'brand identity' for Britain.

▶ BTA'S STRUCTURE AND OPERATION

As well as co-operating closely with the British national and regional tourist boards, the BTA also has extensive networks and contacts with the overseas travel trade, media and overseas residents interested in visiting Britain, as shown in Figure 1.20.

In addition to running the British Travel Centre in London, BTA operates a network of 40 overseas outlets worldwide, which act as information points for potential visitors to Britain and pass on information about the market from that particular country to the BTA's headquarters in London.

BTA plays an important role in highlighting areas of concern to the tourism industry, such as Britain's comparatively high VAT rate, which has to be passed on to

Figure 1.20 *BTA networking*

continued

continued

the consumer, and likely effects of the European Package Travel and Distance Selling Directives on UK tourism. It also acts as a catalyst and co-ordinator for the fragmented private sector in UK tourism, helping to develop new partnership arrangements between the commercial and public sectors of the industry.

BTA's principal source of funding is via grant-in-aid from the government. For the financial year 1999/2000 this amounted to £36 million, with further sums being generated from commercial activities, such as selling advertising and space at overseas exhibitions. A record 25.7 million overseas tourists visited Britain in 1998, injecting over £12.6 billion of additional revenue into the economy, a 3 per cent increase on the previous year.

(Information courtesy of the BTA)

Case study discussion points and essay questions

1   What is the prime role of the BTA?

2   What influence does the BTA have on the range of tourism products on offer in Britain?

3   What impact is new technology likely to have on the future work of the BTA?

4   What is the justification for spending government money on funding the BTA?

browse this website

www.visitbritain.com

Transportation

Transportation for UK tourists and overseas visitors to Britain can be divided into land, sea and air travel. Having effective transport networks is essential for a successful travel and tourism industry, whether people are on business or travelling for leisure. Figure 1.21 shows Britain's principal motorways and ports.

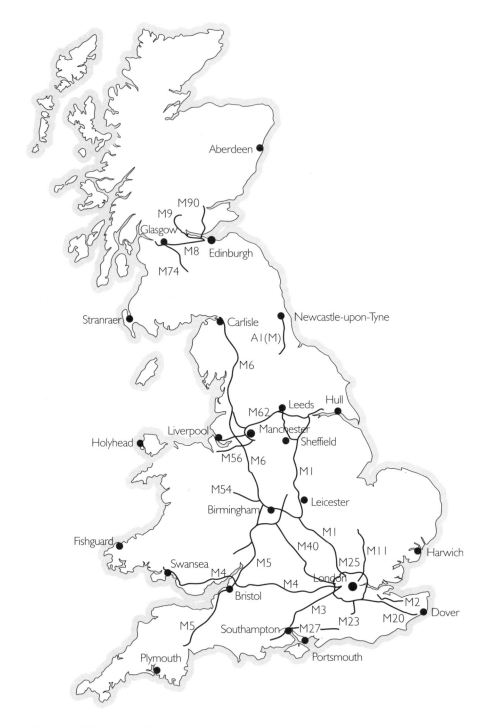

Figure 1.21 *Britain's principal motorways and ports*

Land transport

Land, or surface, transport includes travel by road and rail. Table 1.3 shows that the private car is the main mode of transport used by UK tourists and overseas visitors to Britain.

Year	Car (%)	Train (%)	Coach/bus (%)
1951	28	48	28
1961	49	28	23
1971	63	10	17
1981	72	12	12
1991	78	6	12
1998	71	7	14

Adapted from BTA figures

Table 1.3 *Modes of transport used for holiday travel in the UK, 1951–98*

Increasing car ownership and access to private transport has meant that the use of cars for tourist trips has grown dramatically since 1951, at the expense of rail and coach/bus travel, both of which have experienced dramatic losses in market share.

Although the growth in the use of the private car for tourism has given people the freedom to explore the lesser-known parts of Britain that are not well served by public transport, there is increasing concern about the environmental problems that cars can cause. Congestion and pollution in historic cities, coupled with erosion and congestion in popular countryside areas, has increasingly led to calls for cars to be banned from some areas, or for their use to be strictly controlled. Many historic cities are experimenting with traffic control measures, while the 'honey pot' areas of popular National Parks are piloting 'park and ride' schemes and restrictions on car access.

Rail travel is an altogether more environmentally friendly mode of transport, but one that has lost popularity with UK tourists in recent years. Tourist trips by train are now at only 15 per cent of their 1951 level. There are, however, one or two growth areas in tourist travel by rail, notably short breaks in cities and the popularity of narrow-gauge scenic railways, particularly in Wales. Some operators have successfully exploited the market for 'nostalgia' travel by introducing rail holidays using steam locomotives, e.g. the Venice–Simplon Orient Express, which is sometimes chartered for special excursions in the UK.

Travel by coach consists of holidays offered by companies such as Shearings and Frames Rickards (see Figure 1.22), and networked, timetabled services between major cities and towns operated by National Express, a former state-run enterprise that was bought by its management in 1988 (see Figure 1.23).

Figure 1.22 *Coach operators are an important sector of UK tourism*
Courtesy of Frames Rickards

Industry example

National Express carries more than 15 million passengers every year to around 1200 destinations throughout Britain and a further 400 in Europe and Ireland. The company operates five distinct service brands and is equipped to meet the needs of a wide range of customers:

★ National Express – long distance express coach services and shorter distance inter-urban shuttle services

★ Flightlink – coach services to and from major UK airports

★ Jetlink – services to and from major UK airports

★ Speedlink Airport Services – connecting Heathrow and Gatwick airports

★ Eurolines – European express coach services

browse this website

www.nationalexpress.
co.uk

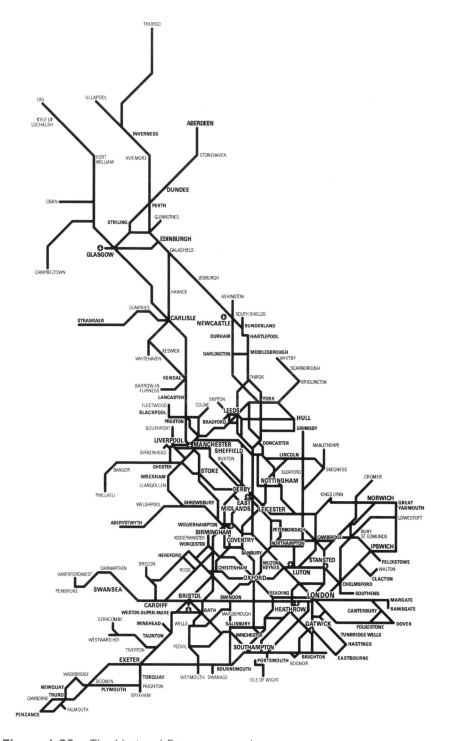

Figure 1.23 *The National Express network*
Courtesy of National Express

Many smaller coach companies also run extensive programmes of tours and excursions for their local markets and visitors on holiday in their area. Flexibility and good value for money make coach travel particularly popular with the youth market and senior citizens. The ageing of the UK population will be an opportunity for coach operators to increase their business to the 'senior' market.

Sea transport

Sea transportation in UK tourism is dominated by the ferry companies which operate services between the UK and Ireland, Scandinavia and the near continent, principally France, Belgium and the Netherlands. Approximately 9 per cent of all overseas visitors to the UK arrive by car using the many seaports around the coast (see Figure 1.21 on page 44). If, however, we concentrate on European visitors to Britain, the figure rises to around 20 per cent. Faster, more frequent and more comfortable cross-Channel services, using new generation 'super ferries', hovercraft and hydrofoils, have given the incoming tourist who wishes to come by car a range of opportunities for travel to the UK. Ferry companies are in fierce competition with Le Shuttle to retain their share of the cross-Channel market.

browse this website

www.eurotunnel.
co.uk

Activity
1.3

Visit the Eurotunnel website and make notes on the Eurotunnel Group and the services it offers for passengers and their vehicles wishing to travel between England and France.

Air travel

The majority of overseas visitors, approximately two-thirds, travel to Britain by air, particularly those from long-haul destinations such as Australia, the Far East and the USA. With the introduction of off-peak and stand-by fare arrangements and new types of aircraft, for example STOL (short take-off and landing), domestic air travel for holiday purposes is being given serious consideration by growing numbers of British travellers.

There has been rapid growth in one particular sector of the airline business, namely budget or 'no frills' airlines, which sell direct to the public and offer a basic service at a very competitive price. Companies such as EasyJet, Go, Ryanair and Buzz (see Figure 1.24) are proving to be extremely popular with leisure and business travellers, posing a serious threat to the more established scheduled airlines. The 'no frills' airlines are at the cutting edge of e-commerce (electronic commerce), offering information and reservations on the Internet, thereby keeping their costs to a minimum. According to Euromonitor's January 2000 budget airlines survey, this sector of the airline business is set to grow 133 per cent by the year 2003.

London is the principal gateway for overseas visitors to Britain arriving by air. The capital is currently served by five airports:

Figure 1.24 *'buzz' – one of the new budget airlines*
Courtesy of buzz airlines

Activity
1.4

Carry out some research on one of the new budget airlines to discover its routes, prices, additional services, fare structures, aircraft fleet, etc.

- ✪ **Heathrow**
- ✪ **Gatwick**
- ✪ **Luton**
- ✪ **Stansted**
- ✪ **London City**

Outside the south-east of England, Manchester Airport ranked third to Heathrow and Gatwick in 1998 in terms of passenger traffic, while Birmingham International Airport was the fifth most popular airport, recording more than 6.6 million terminal passengers (see Table 1.4).

The number of passengers flying by air is predicted to double in the next 20 years, making airport expansion versus conservation of the environment a very important issue. At present, some of the expansion plans being considered in the UK include:

- **A new runway for Manchester Airport to cope with an expected throughput of 30 million passengers by the year 2005**
- **A fifth terminal for Heathrow**
- **Expansion of the runway at East Midlands Airport**
- **A new terminal for Liverpool Airport**
- **A multi-million pound development at Southampton Airport**
- **A new terminal for Bristol Airport**
- **Expansion at Gatwick**

There are likely to be heated debates concerning the economic benefits that airport expansion can bring to an area and the environmental damage such expansion can cause.

Industry example

buzz, one of the UK's newest low cost airlines, was launched in January 2000, and now flies to 14 European destinations: Berlin, Düsseldorf, Frankfurt, Lyons, Milan, Paris, Vienna, Jerez, Montpellier, Toulouse, Helsinki, Marseilles, Hamburg and Bordeaux. The company is a subsidiary of KLM uk and markets itself as a 'pay-as-you-go' airline. It offers extras such as lounge access, speedy security clearance and a choice of meal options and allows travellers to tailor their travelling experience according to their needs. On the first day of operation, the buzz booking lines received 3000 calls, with a further 20 per cent of bookings being taken on its website. Since then, bookings on the website have doubled and now account for 40 per cent of total sales on average.

browse this website

www.buzzaway. com

Activity
1.5

1 Find out the main UK and overseas destinations served by your nearest airport.

2 Locate the 20 airports listed in Table 1.4 on an outline map of the UK.

	Terminal passengers (thousands)	Passengers at all UK airports (%)
Heathrow	60,360	38.0
Gatwick	29,033	18.3
Manchester	17,206	10.8
Stansted	6,830	4.3
Birmingham	6,608	4.2
Glasgow	6,481	4.1
Edinburgh	4,545	2.9
Luton	4,116	2.6
Newcastle	2,920	1.8
Aberdeen	2,652	1.7
Belfast International	2,627	1.7
East Midlands	2,136	1.3
Bristol	1,814	1.1
Leeds Bradford	1,398	0.9
London City	1,360	0.9
Belfast City	1,314	0.8
Cardiff Wales	1,230	0.8
Liverpool	869	0.5
Southampton	725	0.5
Isle of Man	701	0.4

Source CAA

Table 1.4 *Passenger traffic at the top 20 UK airports, 1998*

Travel agents

There are some 7000 travel agencies in the UK that are members of the Association of British Travel Agents (ABTA). Travel agencies in the UK are either independently owned or part of a chain of agencies owned by a single company (often referred to as the 'multiples'). There has been a shift in emphasis in favour of multiple agencies that have carried forward ambitious expansion plans at the expense of independent agents. Three of the biggest multiple agencies in terms of number of branches are:

1   **Lunn Poly (see Figure 1.25)**

2   **Going Places**

3   **Thomas Cook**

Each of these three multiples has a close alliance with a major tour operator, a process known as vertical integration (one company having control of more than one level of the distribution chain). For example, Going Places is part of the Airtours group, while Lunn Poly is owned by Thomson, the UK's largest tour operator, which also runs its own airline (see Figure 1.26).

Figure 1.25 *Lunn Poly – one of the UK's leading travel agents*

Figure 1.26 *Vertical integration in the Thomson Travel Group*

Vertical integration of this sort, when a tour operator controls the sales policy of its own retail travel agencies, is thought by some people in the industry to be against the public interest, as it could lead to an anti-competitive environment. In such cases the Competition Commission can be asked to investigate if the public are indeed being disadvantaged.

Activity 1.6

Working with a colleague make a list of the travel agencies in your area and indicate whether they are independents or part of a 'chain'.

Travel agency functions and products

Travel agencies are the retail arm of the travel and tourism industry. In the same way that a clothes shop sells products to shoppers, so travel agencies retail their 'products' to the general public. Indeed, the term 'travel shop' is commonly used to refer to travel agency premises. The one major difference between these two types of retail outlets, however, is that, unlike the clothes retailer, travel agencies do not buy in 'stock' in advance, but rather react to the wishes of their customers before contacting the holiday companies. The fact that opening a travel agency does not involve a heavy initial capital outlay is an attractive feature to many people who are considering starting up their own business in the service sector.

Travel agencies are generally acting on behalf of two parties when they undertake their work. They are agents for the customer, referred to as the client, on whose behalf they are making the travel arrangements. They are also agent for the company that is supplying the product; this company is sometimes referred to as the 'principal', and may include:

- ✪ **A tour operator**
- ✪ **An airline**
- ✪ **A coach company**
- ✪ **A hotel**
- ✪ **A car hire firm**
- ✪ **A ferry company**
- ✪ **A train company**
- ✪ **A cruise line**
- ✪ **A theatre**

Travel agents earn commission from the principals whose products they sell. The commission payment is usually expressed as a percentage and varies according to the product being sold and the commission policy of the principal. At present, average commission rates are as follows:

Package holidays	*10%*
Airline tickets	*7.5%–9%*
Ferry bookings	*9%*
Travellers' cheques	*1%*
Travel insurance	*35%–40%*
Coach holidays	*10%*
Rail ticket	*7%*
Cruises	*9%*

These figures should only be taken as a guide, since commission levels fluctuate daily in response to competitor activity. Some principals offer incentive commission, where the amount paid increases as the sales volume rises.

Most people associate high street travel agencies with the sale of one particular product, namely overseas package holidays (also known as inclusive tours). An analysis of the work of a typical agency, however, shows that it actually offers a wide range of products and services, including:

- ✪ **Package holidays**
- ✪ **UK short breaks**
- ✪ **'Flight-only' sales**
- ✪ **Theatre bookings**
- ✪ **Car hire**
- ✪ **Cruising holidays**
- ✪ **Rail tickets**
- ✪ **Coach holidays and tickets**
- ✪ **Travel insurance**
- ✪ **Foreign exchange**
- ✪ **Visa and passport applications**

As the market for overseas travel becomes even more competitive, travel agencies will be looking for ways of increasing their income from the sale of products other than the traditional inclusive tours.

Tour operators

Unlike travel agents, who sell holidays and a range of other travel products, tour operators actually assemble the component parts of a holiday, i.e. the means of travel, accommodation, facilities, transfers, excursions and other

Figure 1.27 *The role of tour operators*

services. If we consider that travel agents are the retail arm of the travel business, then tour operators can be likened to wholesalers, since they buy in 'bulk' from the providers of travel services, such as the hoteliers and airlines, break the bulk into manageable packages and offer the finished product, the inclusive tour (package holiday), for sale via a travel agent or direct to the consumer. The package is sold for an all-inclusive price, which is generally lower than if the component parts of the holiday had been booked individually by the holidaymaker. Figure 1.27 shows the role of tour operators and their position as intermediaries between the suppliers of travel products and travel agents.

Figure 1.27 also shows that some tour operators deal direct with their customers rather than selling through travel agents. In the case of foreign package holidays booked by British people, 75 per cent of customers use the services of a travel agent rather than booking direct with the operator. There are, however, a number of high volume 'direct sell' operators, such as Portland Direct, and many smaller, specialist tour operators who prefer to deal directly with their clients, advertising their holidays through newspapers and other media. Direct sell operators stress that, since they do not have to pay a commission to a travel agent, they are able to pass this saving on to the client who should benefit with a cheaper holiday. The more specialist the product on offer, the more likely it is that the customer will deal direct with the operator, for example skiing holidays and mountain exploration tours.

browse this website

www.portland-holidays.co.uk

Types of tour operators

There are approximately 600 UK tour operators, most of which are small companies specialising in a particular destination or type of product. Most operators fall into one of the following four categories:

- ✪ **Mass market operators**
- ✪ **Specialist operators**
- ✪ **Domestic operators**
- ✪ **Incoming tour operators**

Mass market operators

These tour operators include some of the best-known names in the industry, such as Thomson, Airtours and First Choice Holidays. They organise package holidays for around 11 million British people each year, thereby dominating the UK outbound tourism market. As well as offering popular Mediterranean holiday destinations, tour operators are increasingly selling packages to long-haul destinations, such as Florida, the Caribbean and the Far East, as travellers seek out new destinations and experiences.

Exercise 1.3

How do you think that the 'products' offered by mass market tour operators might change in the next 10 years? Is the role of the travel agent likely to change over the same time period?

Industry example

Airtours plc is the largest provider of air-inclusive holidays in the world. The company and its associates carry passengers from 17 countries with:

- ★ 1,613 travel outlets
- ★ 17 telesales centres
- ★ 42 aircraft
- ★ 40+ tour operating brands
- ★ 46 resort properties

continued

browse this website

www.airtours.com

continued

★   10 cruise ships

★   2 vacation ownership resorts

Airtours employs over 20,000 people worldwide and operates a wide range of business units in the UK, including Airtours Holidays, Panorama Holidays, Direct Holidays, Bridge Travel Group, Cresta Holidays, Tradewinds, EuroSites, Jetset and Going Places.

Specialist operators

Although less well-known than the mass market operators, there are literally hundreds of specialist operators in the travel and tourism industry, including:

✪   **Those that offer holidays and other travel arrangements to a particular geographical region or destination, e.g. Paris Travel Service and Magic of Italy**

✪   **Those that cater for a particular segment of the market, e.g. PGL Adventure Holidays for young children and Saga Holidays which specialises in the 'senior' market**

✪   **Those that specialise in a particular type of activity, e.g. walking holidays offered by the Ramblers' Association and Susie Madron's 'Cycling for Softies', which offers all-inclusive packages to France**

✪   **Those that cater for the special interests of their clients, e.g. wine tasting holidays in the Loire and art history tours to Italy**

✪   **Those that specialise in sporting holidays and breaks, e.g. Roger Taylor's tennis holidays in the Algarve and tours to see the motor racing Grand Prix around the world**

✪   **Those that use a specific type of accommodation or form of transport, e.g. EuroSites, part of the Airtours Group, which organises self-drive camping holidays on the Continent, and operators who offer nostalgic tours using steam railways**

A glance at the *Travel Trade Directory* will show that the range of specialist operators is vast, indicating that the travel industry is not afraid to rise to the challenge of meeting the needs of many different types of customers.

Select a small number of activities and special interests, and carry out some research to discover if there are any UK tour operators that sell holidays in your chosen areas.

Domestic operators

browse this website

www.wallacearnold. com

Although, in general, the British tourism product has not been extensively 'packaged', there are a number of UK operators that put together inclusive tours for the home market. Probably the best known are coach operators, such as Shearings and Wallace Arnold, which offer value-for-money products geared mainly to the older age groups.

browse this website

www.superbreak. com

The packaging and marketing of UK short breaks has been something of a success story in recent years. Companies such as Superbreak and Rainbow Holidays have led the development of city and country breaks offered for sale through travel agencies. Some local authorities, keen to boost their visitor numbers, have worked with tour operators to feature their particular destinations in brochures and tour programmes.

Special interest groups are well catered for by domestic operators. Activity holidays are growing in popularity and operators, large and small, are emerging to cater for the demand, for example YHA Holidays and HF Holidays. Companies offering specialist services and facilities, ranging from sketching holidays to ballooning breaks, are being increasingly sought by a public looking for something unusual to do in its leisure time.

Hotel groups and marketing consortia (for example Best Western Hotels) have created and marketed domestic tours for some time, often in conjunction with coach companies. The competitive situation that has arisen in the hotels sector in recent years, however, has forced some hotel groups to widen their customer base by developing themed breaks and activity and special interest tours.

Incoming tour operators

Incoming, or inbound, UK tourism is concerned with meeting the needs of the increasing numbers of overseas visitors who choose to visit Britain; outbound tourism, on the other hand, deals with UK people taking holidays abroad. Just as we would visit a travel agency to book our annual overseas holiday or business trip abroad, so many overseas visitors do the same in their own country when they want to come to Britain. A travel agent in the USA, for example, who has a client wanting to spend a week in Scotland, has to contact a tour operator to make all the arrangements; this operator, who may be based in the USA or in Scotland, is known as an incoming tour operator, since it is providing a service for overseas visitors to Britain.

There are around 300 incoming tour operators in this country that specialise in dealing with the incoming market. Some are little more than handling agents offering a transfer or 'meet and greet' service on behalf of an agent or operator. Others, such as British Heritage Tours, Frames Rickards and Evan Evans Tours, offer complete package tours of the UK, which are sold through overseas agents. The packages are often themed, including tours based on British heritage, gardens or castles. Approximately 100 incoming tour operators in the UK are members of BITOA (the British Incoming Tour Operators' Association). Founded in 1977, BITOA is an independent organisation that aims to provide a forum for the exchange of information and ideas, to follow an accepted code of conduct and to act as a pressure group in dealing with other bodies in the UK with a common interest in tourism matters.

browse this website

www.bitoa.co.uk

Scale of the UK travel and tourism industry

Key topics in this section:

- **Introduction – the significance of the UK travel and tourism industry**
- **Consumer spending on travel and tourism**
- **Employment in the travel and tourism industry**
- **Overseas visitors to the UK**
- **UK residents travelling in Britain and abroad**

Introduction – the significance of the UK travel and tourism industry

Tourism is one of Britain's leading industries, worth more than £61 billion to the UK economy in 1998, categorised as follows:

- ✪ **£14 billion (23 per cent) – spending by UK residents staying overnight**
- ✪ **£12.7 billion (21 per cent) – spending by overseas visitors in the UK**
- ✪ **£31.3 billion (51 per cent) – spending by UK residents on day trips**
- ✪ **£3.2 billion (5 per cent) – overseas visitors' fares to UK carriers**

UK tourism provides jobs for 1.75 million people, some 7 per cent of the total workforce and five times as many as the car industry. Tourism (excluding day visitor spending) accounts for 4 per cent of the UK's gross domestic product (GDP), 6 per cent of all consumer spending, and more than £11 million per day is collected in VAT and excise payments. Quite apart from these economic benefits that tourism brings, it has an important social role to play in rural communities, plays a vital part in urban regeneration and contributes to regional prosperity. As such, tourism plays a major part in enhancing the image of towns, cities and villages throughout Britain, thereby helping to sustain its prominent role in world affairs.

Industry example

In its National Tourism Strategy document *Tomorrow's Tourism* (Department for Culture, Media and Sport, 1999) the UK government stresses that:

Britain's tourism industry is big and growing bigger:

★ *It employs 1.75 million people in 125,000 businesses*

★ *It has accounted for one in six of all new jobs created in the last 10 years*

★ *It is worth £53 billion a year*

★ *It brought in 25.5 million overseas visitors to Britain in 1997 and is expected to attract 27.5 million in 2000*

browse this website

www.culture.gov.uk

Consumer spending on travel and tourism

Spending by British people on travel and tourism is a significant proportion of overall spending by consumers in the UK. According to data from the Leisure Industries Research Centre (LIRC) (see Table 1.5), we spent £134.65 billion on all types of leisure in 1997, with holidays and tourism accounting for £26.25 billion of this total.

The data in Table 1.5 is divided into leisure in the home and leisure away from home (of which holidays and tourism makes up approximately one-quarter of total spending in this category). LIRC forecasts that UK consumer spending on holidays and tourism will top £36 billion in the year 2002.

Exercise 1.4

Working with a few of your colleagues, discuss the main factors that you think will influence consumer spending on holidays and travel in the next five years in the UK.

	1992	1993	1994	1995	1996	1997	1998	1999	2000	2001	2002
In the home											
Reading	5.02	5.32	5.40	5.45	5.45	5.62	5.80	5.95	6.09	6.22	6.35
Home entertainment	9.62	10.53	11.24	12.34	13.22	14.21	14.83	15.27	15.83	16.49	17.09
House & garden	7.65	8.19	8.55	8.81	9.47	10.37	11.18	11.64	12.17	12.79	13.41
Hobbies & pastimes	5.65	5.79	6.01	6.16	6.51	6.96	7.37	7.58	7.81	8.07	8.34
Total	27.94	29.83	31.20	32.76	34.65	37.16	39.18	40.44	41.90	43.57	45.19
Away from home											
Eating out	20.60	22.03	22.82	23.66	25.76	27.82	29.96	31.58	33.28	35.15	37.20
Alcoholic drink	23.48	24.31	25.62	26.08	28.02	28.63	30.15	32.02	33.72	34.99	35.89
Total: *Eating and drinking*	44.08	46.34	48.44	49.74	53.78	56.45	60.11	63.60	67.00	70.14	73.09
Local entertainment	2.76	2.96	3.12	3.13	3.27	3.45	3.69	3.90	4.11	4.32	4.54
Gambling	3.25	3.45	3.77	5.82	5.64	6.15	6.38	6.58	6.80	7.03	7.23
Active sport	4.12	4.26	4.47	4.55	4.79	5.18	5.53	5.77	6.03	6.32	6.61
Total: *Neighbourhood leisure*	10.13	10.67	11.36	13.50	13.70	14.78	15.60	16.25	16.94	17.67	18.38
Sightseeing	0.55	0.59	0.65	0.69	0.74	0.80	0.86	0.92	0.97	1.03	1.09
Holidays in UK	6.01	6.69	7.08	7.32	7.60	8.03	8.62	9.00	9.34	9.72	10.07
Holidays overseas	13.27	13.65	16.62	15.91	15.58	17.42	19.27	20.63	22.16	23.60	24.92
Total: *Holidays & tourism*	19.83	20.93	24.35	23.92	23.92	26.25	28.75	30.55	32.47	34.35	36.08
Total	74.04	77.94	84.15	87.15	91.40	97.48	104.46	110.40	116.41	122.16	127.55
Total: All leisure	101.98	107.77	115.35	119.90	126.05	134.64	143.64	150.84	158.31	165.73	172.74

Source Leisure Forecasts 1998–2002 Leisure Industries Research Centre

Table 1.5 *UK consumer spending (£ billions), 1992–2002*

Employment in the travel and tourism industry

Tourism's ability to create jobs is one of its main economic benefits and often the main reason why public sector bodies invest in UK tourism. Data from the BTA's *Digest of Tourist Statistics* shows that employment in tourism-related industries in Britain in June 1999 stood at 1,783,000, classified as follows:

- ✪ **Pubs, bars and nightclubs** — 449,400
- ✪ **Restaurants, cafés, etc.** — 408,300
- ✪ **Sport and other recreational activities** — 371,500
- ✪ **Hotels and other tourist accommodation** — 342,500
- ✪ **Travel agencies and tour operators** — 122,600
- ✪ **Libraries, museums and other cultural activities** — 88,700

Employment in these categories, plus those self-employed in tourism,

UNIT 1 INVESTIGATING TRAVEL AND TOURISM

accounted for some 7 per cent of all the employed labour force in the UK. It is estimated that for every one direct job in the UK travel and tourism industry, half of an indirect job is created elsewhere in the economy. This can be illustrated if we consider a holiday taken by a family in a caravan at a UK seaside resort. Apart from the direct beneficiaries of the holiday, for example the caravan site owner, other firms in the area not directly associated with tourism will benefit, for example petrol stations, shops, tradespeople and banks.

Overseas visitors to the UK

In spite of increased competition from other global destinations and recent periods of world recession, Britain has been very successful in attracting growing numbers of overseas visitors. As Figure 1.28 shows, a record number of 25.7 million tourists visited Britain in 1998.

Total earnings from overseas tourists to Britain have also risen steadily over the same period, reaching a new high of £12.6 billion in 1998 (see Table 1.6).

As well as contributing vital income to Britain's balance of payments, overseas visitors also bring a variety of other benefits, for example:

✪ **An influx of tourists to an area helps create or sustain jobs, thus increasing the wage-earners' spending in the locality and leading to an improved local economy**

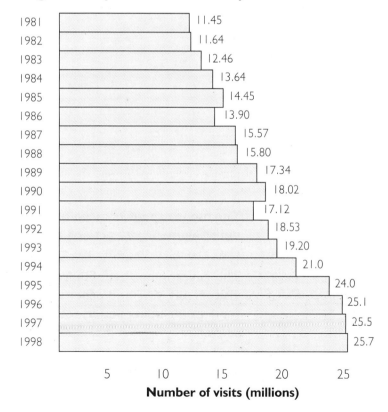

Year	Number of visits (millions)
1981	11.45
1982	11.64
1983	12.46
1984	13.64
1985	14.45
1986	13.90
1987	15.57
1988	15.80
1989	17.34
1990	18.02
1991	17.12
1992	18.53
1993	19.20
1994	21.0
1995	24.0
1996	25.1
1997	25.5
1998	25.7

Number of visits (millions)

Figure 1.28 *Overseas visits to Britain, 1981–98*
Source: BTA/ETB Annual Reports

Year	Total spending (£m)
1981	2,970
1982	3,188
1983	4,003
1984	4,614
1985	5,442
1986	5,553
1987	6,260
1988	6,184
1989	6,945
1990	7,748
1991	7,386
1992	7,891
1993	9,354
1994	9,919
1995	12,092
1996	12,290
1997	12,244
1998	12,671

Sources BTA/ETB Annual Reports; BTA National Facts of Tourism

Table 1.6 *Spending by overseas visitors to Britain, 1981–98*

○ **The money spent on accommodation, food, transport, entertainment, attractions and leisure facilities creates profits that are used to generate more business for companies**

○ **The government benefits from incoming tourism since overseas visitors pay VAT and other taxes on a range of products and services including liquor, tobacco, petrol, accommodation and souvenirs**

○ **Overseas visitors' spending on facilities such as public transport and leisure facilities can help to keep costs down for local people, who may also benefit from a greater range of facilities provided for both tourists and residents alike**

○ **Income from overseas visitors can be channelled into**

improvements to the local environment, thus enhancing the quality of life for everyone

- ✪ **British theatres and the arts in general benefit from spending by tourists from overseas**
- ✪ **Income from overseas visitors may help to preserve historic buildings and conserve areas of special environmental significance**
- ✪ **An international reputation for cultural and sporting events can be maintained if large numbers of visitors are attracted from overseas**

The British Tourist Authority, through its headquarters in London and network of offices and representatives around the world, works hard to ensure that information on the needs of potential visitors to Britain is used to create products and services that they will want. This 'market intelligence' is vital for the continued success of incoming tourism to the UK (see case study on the work of the BTA on pages 40–43).

Why do overseas visitors come to Britain?

The many images of Britain, from the pageantry associated with the great cities of London, Edinburgh and Cardiff to the quaint towns and villages of Wales, England, Scotland and Northern Ireland, paint a picture of a wealth of experiences and adventures for the overseas visitor (see Figure 1.29). Many tourists from overseas put Britain's heritage as the number one reason for their visit; famous buildings such as St Paul's Cathedral, the castles of Stirling and Caernarvon, the Elizabethan architecture in Shakespeare's birthplace Stratford-upon-Avon, rural and industrial heritage, are all focal points for overseas

Figure 1.29 *Overseas visitors enjoy Britain's varied architectural heritage*

visitors. The Royal Family, with their palaces and ancestral homes such as Kensington Palace and Hampton Court, is also an important reason for visiting the UK.

Museums, art galleries, theatres, the ballet, and events such as the Chichester Festival and Cardiff Singer of the World, are all part of Britain's rich and varied culture and customs which attract the overseas visitor. Sporting events, such as Wimbledon, international rugby matches, Henley Royal Regatta and the Open Golf Championship, are popular with tourists from abroad. Some visitors are attracted by the excellent shopping facilities, not only in London's West End, but also in historic cities such as Chester, Cambridge, Oxford, Edinburgh, Bath and York. Many overseas visitors come to Britain to study, perhaps learning English in one of the many language schools that can be found throughout Britain. Business tourism, too, is important to Britain's tourism balance; more than 6.8 million business trips were made by overseas visitors to Britain in 1998, accounting for more than 27 per cent of all trips.

Most first-time visitors to Britain will visit London as part of their stay, or may choose to remain in the capital for the whole of their trip. They may visit the cities and regions most frequented by overseas visitors and become part of what is known as 'the milk run'; this is a round trip which includes London – Oxford – Bath – Cardiff – Chester – the Lake District – Edinburgh – York – Cambridge – London. Increasingly, however, overseas visitors are beginning to explore the parts of Britain located far from London, in search of the 'real Britain', as it is sometimes promoted. In recent years, BTA marketing campaigns have highlighted the attractions of the whole of Britain, rather than just concentrating on the well-known images of London: the Beefeaters, Tower of London, the British 'bobby', Big Ben, etc. Such campaigns have been particularly targeted at visitors on their second and subsequent trips to Britain.

Exercise 1.5

Choose six UK destinations and list the features that you think make them popular with overseas visitors.

UK residents travelling in Britain and abroad

Table 1.7 shows how British people's attitude to taking holidays has changed over the last 30+ years. In 1965, most UK residents took their main holidays

Year	In Britain (millions)	Abroad (millions)	Total (millions)
1965	30.0	5.0	35.0
1970	34.5	5.75	40.25
1975	40.0	8.00	48.0
1980	36.5	12.00	48.5
1985	33.0	15.75	48.75
1990	32.5	20.5	53.0
1995	33.0	26.0	59.0
1998	27.0	29.25	56.25

Adapted from BTA data

Table 1.7   *Number of long (4+ nights) holidays taken by the British, 1965–98*

in Britain, often to traditional seaside resorts. Only 5 million people ventured abroad on holiday. By 1998, this situation had changed dramatically, with 29.25 million holidays overseas. For the first time ever, more main holidays were taken abroad than in the UK in 1998.

Exercise 1.6

Working with a colleague:
1   List the reasons why the demand for overseas holidays has grown so rapidly since 1965.
2   Explain why you think UK destinations are losing popularity with the British for long holidays.
3   Suggest how this situation could be improved.

UK residents taking holidays in Britain

Of the four home countries, England is by far the most popular destination for British people taking domestic holidays, as the following 1998 figures from the BTA demonstrate:

✪ **England**   **52 million holiday trips**
✪ **Wales**   **7 million holiday trips**

| ✪ | **Scotland** | **6 million holiday trips** |
| ✪ | **Northern Ireland** | **0.6 million holiday trips** |

The West Country, with its relatively mild climate and pleasant scenery, was the most popular holiday region with the British, accounting for 12 million holiday trips in 1998. The East of England region was the second most popular (7.3 million trips) and the Heart of England third (6.9 million trips).

Working in the travel and tourism industry

Key topics in this section:

- **The range of employment opportunities in travel and tourism**
- **The nature of travel and tourism employment**
- **Personal and technical skills required**
- **How to find jobs in travel and tourism**
- **Preparing yourself for a career in travel and tourism**

The range of employment opportunities in travel and tourism

We have seen that the travel and tourism industry is made up of a wide range of enterprises of different sizes. As one of the fastest-growing sectors of the UK and global economies, travel and tourism offers a wide variety of job opportunities for people with the right skills, knowledge and personal qualities.

The main employment opportunities in travel and tourism occur in:

- **Airlines and airports**
- **Car hire companies**
- **Coach operators**
- **Ferry and cruise companies**
- **Guiding**
- **Hotels and other accommodation**
- **Local authority tourism departments**
- **Tour operators**
- **Tourist attractions**
- **Tourist information centres**
- **Training**
- **Travel agencies**

Each of these sectors offers a range of jobs at different levels. A travel agency, for example, will need a manager, supervisor, customer service staff and possibly a foreign exchange clerk. If it is part of a large chain of agencies, there is likely to be a regional manager who reports to a senior manager at head office, which in turn will have a variety of employees looking after administration, finance, human resources management, sales and marketing, etc.

Not all jobs in travel and tourism are full-time appointments. Depending on the particular sector, employment opportunities may be full-time, part-time, permanent, temporary or seasonal.

Industry example

Throughout its European villages, Center Parcs employs around 9,500 staff in a wide range of jobs, including marketing and sales, product development, catering, housekeeping, recreation, logistics, finance, human resource management, projects and maintenance. The company offers challenging positions at all levels, in its restaurants, swimming pools, reception areas, shops, sports halls and in recreation generally. Center Parcs looks for employees who will go out of their way to please guests and give them a relaxed, holiday feeling. As such, service is an important quality among staff, along with application, enterprise, well-developed communication skills and the ability to solve problems.

browse this website

www.centerparcs.
com

**Activity
1.8**

Under the direction of your tutor, have a 'brainstorming' session with the rest of your group and write down on a flipchart all the jobs you can think of in travel and tourism. When you have finished, group the jobs into different industry sectors, for example attractions, tour operations, airlines, etc., and transfer the information on to a computer. This will come in handy later in this unit when you are considering your career development in travel and tourism.

The nature of travel and tourism employment

To many people, the thought of working in travel and tourism, in a young, dynamic industry that aims to make people happy and relaxed, seems too good to be true – and it sometimes can be! Like many other jobs, working in travel and tourism is sometimes tedious, often involves long, unsociable hours, and requires personal commitment, patience and an understanding of others. It really is a 'people business' and if you don't enjoy dealing with the public, think again about a career in travel and tourism! However, for those who choose to work in the industry, it offers:

- ✪ **A satisfying job where employees get pleasure from helping others make best use of their leisure time**
- ✪ **Opportunities for travel, both at home and abroad**
- ✪ **Great variety in the work that is undertaken**
- ✪ **Excellent prospects, often at a young age, for those with the talent and determination**

Industry example

The Travel Training Company, one of the leading providers of training for the travel industry, offers the following advice to those thinking of working as an overseas holiday representative.

You will need to be able to work well in a team, have a good standard of general education, be of smart appearance and be able to speak good, clear English. Being able to communicate with people of all ages and backgrounds will be a considerable advantage, as will the ability to speak one or more additional European languages.

You will need to be very flexible, as a tour rep will be on duty around the clock. You will also need to be able to use a word processor for the paperwork and reports.

Early starts and late finishes can be expected, particularly on those days when clients arrive or depart. A degree of stamina is needed and the ability to keep on smiling is essential, as you will be the public face of the company you represent. Being available to give advice and to resolve problems at virtually any time of the day is a major requirement so a pleasant outgoing personality will be a great advantage.

You will need to be a good organiser and a practical person with plenty of common sense. Some companies will look for sporting qualifications or expertise.

browse the Travel Training Company's website for more information on careers in travel and tourism

www.tttc.co.uk

Personal and technical skills required

Anybody thinking of working in travel and tourism should be:

- ✪ **A 'people person' – in other words, like working with the general public and serving their needs**
- ✪ **Prepared to work unsociable hours**
- ✪ **Aware of the importance of high standards of customer care and customer service**
- ✪ **Patient and able to work under pressure at times**
- ✪ **Able to know where to find relevant information in answer to enquiries**
- ✪ **Accurate in their work, particularly when dealing with money matters**
- ✪ **Prepared to learn fast!**
- ✪ **Able to accept responsibility and work with little supervision**
- ✪ **Able to demonstrate basic computer skills**

browse this website

www.careercompass.
co.uk

Figure 1.30 lists the personal qualities needed for a selection of jobs on offer in the travel and tourism industry, demonstrating the range of skills needed.

Exercise 1.7

Using the information in Figure 1.30 as a guide, write down the personal qualities you think would be needed in two other popular travel and tourism jobs.

browse this website

www.airtours.co.uk

Industry example

Airtours, one of the UK's leading tour operators, has developed a set of questions that anybody considering a career in an overseas job with the company should ask themselves:

★ Do you really enjoy working with the general public?

continued

continued

★ Can you make fast decisions, solve problems and keep calm under pressure?

★ Could you cope with and adapt to a complete change to your current life in the UK?

★ Do you thrive on challenges and a busy schedule?

★ Are you ready and willing to join the fast-moving world of travel?

Airtours considers that if you can answer yes to all the above and are aged 19 or over, available for a full season and have previous experience in a customer service or childcare environment, then working in an overseas position may be just for you!

Hotel receptionist
A friendly and outgoing personality is vital and a receptionist must be customer orientated. Reception staff must have a good knowledge of the hotel's facilities and services and of the local area and be able to communicate well with guests and hotel staff. A smart, well-groomed appearance is essential and a uniform is often provided.

Tourism officer
Tourism officers need to be highly motivated and organised. A background in tourism or amenity management would be an advantage, as would experience in publicity and marketing. A good knowledge of the local area and development possibilities is vital.

Tourist attraction staff
In larger tourist attractions the management have to cater for thousands of visitors which involves complex logistical planning. Staff who deal with the public should be friendly and helpful and have good communication skills. They will have to deal with requests and complaints and be able to converse with a wide range of different people.

Travel agent
A real interest in travel and some knowledge of foreign countries is desirable, although not essential. All staff must have excellent communication skills and enjoy dealing with a range of people. Computer literacy is important and experience of using a computer reservation system is an advantage.

Air cabin crew
Cabin crew staff need to have a smart appearance and a pleasant personality; possess excellent communication skills; be able to deal with the unexpected and to work under pressure; be in excellent physical condition with good eyesight and meet age, height and weight requirements.

Figure 1.30 *Personal qualities needed for travel and tourism jobs*
Source: Careercompass website: www.careercompass.co.uk

How to find jobs in travel and tourism

Because the travel and tourism industry covers such a wide spectrum of activities, the range of information sources on employment opportunities is very broad. Each sector, for example airlines, hotels or travel agencies, will have its own specialist sources. As a starting point, you should try the following:

- ✪ **Careers advisers**: There will be specialists in your school, college or local authority who will give you general advice about working in travel and tourism, e.g. the range of jobs available, skills required, training, further contacts, etc.

- ✪ **Libraries**: Your school, college or local library should have books and directories of employment in the travel and tourism industry. One of the most popular is the *Handbook of Jobs in Leisure and Tourism.*

- ✪ **Trade newspapers and magazines**: You should find out what trade publications are available in the sector or sectors that interest you, e.g. *Travel Trade Gazette, Travel Weekly, Leisure Management, Attractions Management, Caterer and Hotelkeeper,* etc.

- ✪ **Make contact with companies**: Direct contact with travel and tourism companies often pays dividends. Your approach should be the same whether you are calling personally, sending a letter or telephoning, i.e. polite, professional, presentable, knowledgeable, confident and friendly. In most cases, writing a letter and enclosing a copy of your CV (see page 78) will be the most appropriate contact method.

- ✪ **The Internet**: Many travel and tourism companies now have Internet sites, some of which carry details of current posts. On some of them you can even fill in an application form on-line. There is an Internet site dedicated to careers in travel and tourism called Careercompass at www.careercompass.co.uk.

- ✪ **Talk to people working in the industry**: This is a good way of finding out what it is really like to work in a particular job in travel and tourism. You could have a chat with staff while you are on holiday or ask friends and relations if they have any contacts in the industry.

- ✪ **Employment agencies**: In major cities there are agencies that specialise in travel and tourism jobs. Local job centres will also hold lists of current vacancies in particular sectors, e.g. hotels and catering.

Preparing yourself for a career in travel and tourism

Whatever job you are considering, whether it is in the UK or overseas, you must be realistic. Setting your sights too high at an early stage will only lead to disappointment. You should ask yourself a series of questions, including:

- ✪ **What are my strengths, weaknesses and interests?**
- ✪ **What sectors of the industry are available to me?**
- ✪ **What job opportunities exist in the short and long term?**
- ✪ **How can I prepare myself to pursue my progression aims?**

Be as objective as possible when answering these questions, to make sure that the job you want in travel and tourism really does fit your personality, skills, experience and expectations.

Exercise 1.8

Working with a partner, carry out a strengths and weaknesses analysis of yourself and each other in preparation for completing your own CV later in this unit.

Pursuing your own progression aims

Key topics in this section:

- **How to plan your own career development**
- **The range of employment, training and education opportunities in travel and tourism**
- **How to obtain the right information and advice**
- **How to produce a CV and complete application forms**
- **How to prepare yourself for interviews**

How to plan your own career development

You should now have a clear idea about job opportunities in the different sectors of the travel and tourism industry. To succeed in your chosen career, it is important to develop a plan of action. In compiling your action plan you must:

- ✪ **Have a clear aim in sight**
- ✪ **Know your own strengths and weaknesses**
- ✪ **Make sure you know where to find relevant facts and information about career prospects**
- ✪ **Seek advice and support from friends, family, tutors and others with an interest in your future**

The range of employment, training and education opportunities in travel and tourism

The last section of this unit looked in detail at the range of employment opportunities in travel and tourism (see page 69). Education opportunities exist at a number of levels and include all the full- and part-time courses on offer in schools, colleges and universities. These range from the GCSE in Travel and Tourism and the Vocational A-level in Travel and Tourism that you are taking to HNDs/degree courses and even postgraduate programmes in higher education. Training opportunities in travel and tourism can be a mixture of on- and off-the-job training as the next two sections of this unit explain.

On-the-job training

As its name implies, on-the-job training is when employees gain and develop their skills and knowledge while carrying out their normal everyday duties. Many jobs in travel and tourism are ideally suited to this type of 'hands on' training, for example operating a VDU in a travel agency, training to be a chef in a restaurant or hotel, or working behind the counter in a tourist information centre, to name but a few. On-the-job training often leads to qualifications such as National Vocational Qualifications (NVQs) and SVQs in Scotland.

browse this website

www.tttc.co.uk

Industry example

The Travel Training Company, a subsidiary of ABTA, is a commercial training organisation that specialises in travel and tourism training. The company develops and provides training courses for school leavers, travel agents, tour operators, transport operators and tourist boards, including the ABTA Travel Agents Certificate (ABTAC), ABTA Tour Operators Certificate (ABTOC), Travel Services and Events NVQs and air fares/ticketing courses.

Off-the-job training

Training that takes place away from the normal place of work is sometimes preferred by staff and employers as a way of achieving a specific training objective. Some travel and tourism organisations make extensive use of 'day release' courses offered by local colleges and private training providers, often leading to industry-related vocational qualifications. Evening classes are also popular in sectors such as travel agencies and tour operations. Some organisations encourage their senior staff to work towards management and supervisory qualifications, either by the traditional route of going on a course, or perhaps by following a distance-learning programme based around home study and a small amount of tutorial support. Many organisations have found that training in selling skills, customer care and foreign languages is particularly beneficial for staff working in travel and tourism.

How to obtain the right information and advice

Page 74 has details of the many sources of information and advice available to people wanting to work in travel and tourism, including careers advisers, the Internet and trade journals.

Activity 1.9

Make a list of Internet sites you have found that give useful advice and information about working in the travel and tourism industry.

How to produce a CV and complete application forms

A curriculum vitae (CV) is a structured, written statement of a person's career history that has one simple aim, namely to get you a job interview! A CV can be used in place of a completed application form when applying for a specific job or can be sent speculatively to employers to persuade them to invite you for interview.

The precise format you choose for your CV is up to you. Remember that your CV is a reflection of you. The CV is more than just a 'selling' document; it must be a 'marketing' document, i.e. one that matches your skills and experience to the needs of the employer. Whatever format you choose, whether it is a CV that focuses on your skills and achievements or one that emphasises your academic and employment credentials, there is certain basic information that must be included (see Figure 1.31).

It is unlikely that you will get the CV right at the first attempt and you may need several drafts. Writing it on a computer will help with this, since you can make and save alterations as necessary. Remember also that your CV is dynamic; it needs updating at regular intervals throughout your personal and professional development to reflect new skills acquired, qualifications gained, etc.

When you are happy with your CV, you may wish to review it by answering the following questions:

○ **Does it look good? Is it well laid out, with a professional appearance?**

- Name
- Address
- Telephone number
- Age
- Date of birth
- Nationality
- Education to date
- Academic and vocational qualifications
- Employment history (most recent first)
- Skills
- Notable achievements
- Interests
- Names and addresses of referees

Figure 1.31 *Minimum information that should be included in a CV*

- **Will the first half-page immediately gain the reader's interest?**
- **Does it include all your vital selling points?**
- **Are the benefits of your achievements noted?**
- **Are there any discussion openers for interviews?**
- **If it is more than two pages, will the reader's effort be rewarded?**
- **Is the contact information clear?**

It may be sensible at this stage to show your CV to a friend or colleague to see if they agree that it does you justice.

Job application forms

Some employers prefer candidates to complete an application form for a job, rather than accepting CVs. Figure 1.32 gives an example of a typical application form for employment.

Exercise 1.9

Copy the application form in Figure 1.32 and complete it as if you were applying for your first job after leaving school or college. You can choose the particular post that you are applying for, but make sure it is at the appropriate level for your skills and experience.

Application for Employment

Strictly Confidential

Position applied for _____

Date free to take up appointment _____

Personal details

Surname _____ First name(s) _____

Mr/Mrs/Miss/Ms _____ Age _____ Date of birth _____

Nationality _____ Marital status _____

Telephone (home) _____ (work) _____

Do you own a car? _____ Do you have a current driving licence? _____

Education

School, college, university	From	To	Qualifications obtained

Present and past employment

Name and address of employer	From	To	Job title and duties

Explain why you have applied for this job (continue on separate sheet if necessary)

References

Please provide contact details for two referees

1 Name _____	2 Name _____
Address _____	Address _____
_____ Tel. _____	_____ Tel. _____
Relationship to you _____	Relationship to you _____

Signed _____ Date _____

Figure 1.32 *Application form for employment*

You will see that the form includes much of the same information that is found in a CV.

Letters of application

Whether you are completing an application form or sending a CV, you will need to include a covering letter. A typical letter would include the following information:

- ✪ **Why you are applying for the job**
- ✪ **What contribution you could make to the organisation**
- ✪ **Your skills and achievements you consider to be relevant to the post**
- ✪ **The capabilities you have developed through education, training and leisure activities**

In writing your letter you should be positive at all times, including the kind of 'action' words shown in Figure 1.33, which can also be included in your CV and any application forms you complete.

It goes without saying that your letter should not include spelling mistakes or grammatical errors. It should be to the point, look uncluttered and be presented in a professional manner. Unless requested to apply in your own handwriting, it is usual to have your letter typed or word processed.

• Achieved	• Introduced
• Planned	• Completed
• Created	• Set up
• Established	• Finished
• Developed	• Reorganised

Figure 1.33 *'Action' words to use in application letters, CVs and application forms*

Activity 1.10

Write your own CV using a word processing package. Write a covering letter in your own handwriting that you could include when sending your CV to a variety of travel and tourism employers looking for a job.

How to prepare yourself for interviews

An interview is the most commonly used selection technique in travel and tourism. It gives an employer the opportunity to assess whether a candidate will fit in well with the organisation and meet the demands of the job on offer. For you as the candidate, it is your chance to 'sell yourself' to the employer while at the same time assessing whether you would be happy to work in the organisation. An interview may be on a one-to-one basis or a panel interview. One-to-one interviews tend to be less stressful for the interviewee. Panel interviews, where you will be asked questions by a number of people, tend to be used for more senior appointments. Whatever the format adopted, there are a number of key points to bear in mind before and during the interview. You need to prepare well **before the interview** by:

- ✪ **Acknowledging the invitation for interview promptly**
- ✪ **Planning your journey in advance and arriving in good time**
- ✪ **Wearing appropriate dress for the interview**
- ✪ **Finding out as much as you can about the organisation**
- ✪ **Rereading the job details, summarising what you consider to be your major strengths**
- ✪ **Anticipating and preparing answers to likely questions**
- ✪ **Listing any questions you wish to ask**

During the interview, you must try to impress the interviewer(s). Introduce yourself on entering the interview room and, if given the opportunity, shake hands with the interviewer. Although it can be difficult, try to smile, relax and stay calm; remember that first impressions count! When answering questions you should:

- ✪ **Pause before you reply to show that you are giving the question proper consideration**
- ✪ **Reply to the question asked, not the one you wish the interviewer had asked!**
- ✪ **Recognise the difference between questions needing short answers and those requiring extended replies**
- ✪ **Be honest and never lie about your qualifications and experience**
- ✪ **Maintain eye contact with the person asking the questions**
- ✪ **Communicate effectively using positive non-verbal communication where appropriate**

When you are given the opportunity to ask questions, do not take up too much time, since the interviewer will have a schedule to keep to. Ask relevant questions from the list you had prepared in advance plus any points of clarification that may have come up during the interview. At the close of the interview, thank the interviewer for the opportunity to discuss your application in detail.

Activity

1.11

Select one job in travel and tourism that best matches your own aspirations, skills and abilities. Carry out some research to discover more information about the job you have chosen.

Tourism
development

2

Tourism is developing rapidly throughout the world, in both developed and developing nations. In this unit you will discover exactly what we mean by 'tourism development' and why it takes place, both in the UK and overseas. You will also learn about the organisations involved with tourism development in the private, public and voluntary sectors. There is little doubt that travel and tourism has considerable impacts on destinations and the people who live there. You will investigate the positive and negative effects of tourism development, investigating how destinations and organisations can get the most out of tourism development while at the same time keeping tourism's negative impacts to the minimum.

This unit is divided into three main areas:

- **The agents of tourism development**
- **The objectives of tourism development**
- **The impacts of tourism development**

We guide you through each of these areas using examples and case studies from the travel and tourism industry. At the beginning of each section you will see a list of key topics to help you fully understand what you need to learn. Look out for the links to websites so that you can learn more about a particular travel and tourism company, destination or topic.

The agents of tourism development

Key topics in this section:

- **Introduction – what do we mean by 'tourism development'?**
- **Organisations involved in the tourism development process**
- **Private sector enterprises**
- **Public sector organisations**
- **Voluntary sector bodies**

Introduction – what do we mean by 'tourism development'?

Tourism development is the process by which a destination area provides facilities and services for visitors, whether on business or at leisure, as a way of securing economic and social benefits. Tourism development has a number of identifiable characteristics, which can be summarised as follows:

- **It takes many forms:** Everything from the building of a resort complex, construction of an airport, hotel developments to the provision of tourist attractions, are different types of tourism development.

- **It has associated infrastructure:** Tourism development can only take place where there is existing or planned infrastructure, i.e. roads, railways, airports, telecommunications, power supplies and other utilities. Commercial developers often rely on the public sector to provide these facilities and services.

- **It occurs on differing scales:** Tourism development can be as small as a local village hall committee organising an exhibition for day visitors or as big as a major tourist attraction such as Disneyland Paris.

- **It occurs at different rates:** Advances in travel and communications technology mean that some tourism development can take place very quickly, e.g. the growth in the development of long-haul destinations has been very rapid in recent years since the introduction of aircraft that can travel greater distances without stopping. Other developments occur at a much slower rate, with more planning and a greater concern for the negative impacts of tourism development, e.g. the controlled tourism policies of countries bordering the Himalayas.

- **It occurs in all countries:** Whether a developed, developing or underdeveloped country, all regions of the world now recognise the important economic benefits that tourism can generate.

- **It takes place in a variety of environments:** From virgin South American rain forests to the hustle and bustle of cities such as Bangkok, New York and Sydney.

- **It has both negative and positive impacts:** Tourism development can add significantly to the economic well-being of regions, but it can also have negative impacts on the people, environment and culture in destination areas. These points are investigated later in this unit (see page 120).

Activity 2.1

Under the direction of your tutor, brainstorm all of the 'tourism development' that has taken place in your local area. Try to find out whether there are any plans for new tourism developments locally. When you have done this, try to think of two or three tourism developments overseas.

Industry example

In its National Tourism Strategy document *Tomorrow's Tourism* (Department for Culture, Media and Sport, 1999) the UK government has stressed that its aim is to:

browse this website

www.culture.gov.uk

...ensure that new tourism development is more sustainable by ensuring that it: is located on public transport routes; offers pedestrian and cycle access; is linked to other infrastructure (for example hotels and restaurants); is aesthetically attractive; is in keeping with the quality of building and identity of the area; and causes the minimum of environmental damage during construction, adaptation and operation.

Organisations involved in the tourism development process

The individuals and organisations that carry out tourism developments are sometimes known as the agents of development. On an international scale,

Figure 2.1 *The agents of tourism development in the UK*

browse this website

www.world-
tourism.org

commercial and government organisations work together to develop and promote their individual countries, in order to reap economic, social and political benefits. They will be guided, and sometimes helped financially, by global organisations such as the World Bank, World Tourism Organisation or the United Nations. In the case of the UK, the agents of tourism development are shown diagrammatically in Figure 2.1.

*browse these Arts
Council websites*

www.artscouncil.
org.uk

www.ccc-acw.
org.uk

Figure 2.1 indicates that the agents of tourism development fall into a number of different categories. Public sector organisations include the English Tourism Council, Wales Tourist Board, Scottish Tourist Board and the Northern Ireland Tourist Board, plus the British Tourist Authority and the regional tourist boards in the various countries. Local authority tourism departments are also public sector agents of tourism development. Private sector organisations include the multitude of commercial companies that run our tourist attractions, hotels, transport operations and other travel and tourism facilities. These may be companies in their own right or part of larger groups or multinationals, for example Holiday Inn or Hertz Rent-a-Car. Quangos (quasi-autonomous non-governmental organisations) are public bodies that are funded from central government, but are not under direct governmental control. Examples that have an interest in tourism include the Countryside Agency, English Heritage and the Arts Councils of England and Wales, plus the new Regional Development Agencies (RDAs). Voluntary sector organisations with tourism interests include the National Trust and the Youth Hostels Association.

*browse these national
tourist board websites*

www.englishtourism.
org.uk

www.visitbritain.
com

www.tourism.wales.
gov.uk

www.ni-tourism.
com

www.holiday.scotland.
net

**Activity
2.2**

Carry out some research to discover who the various agents of tourism development are in your own local area.

Private sector enterprises

Private sector tourism enterprises come in all shapes and sizes, from an individual making a living from taking holidaymakers on guided walks in the foothills of the Himalayas to some of the world's biggest corporations, such as airline companies and hotel groups.

Historically, tourism development in the UK and worldwide has been championed by private sector entrepreneurs, with little direct public sector involvement or support from either central or local government (the names of Thomas Cook and Billy Butlin spring readily to mind). It is the private sector that has been responsible for developing attractions, hotels, transport companies, car hire firms, tour operators and travel agencies, to name but a few. It is only in the last 30 years or so that the public sector has begun to play a significant part in UK tourism development, usually at the strategic level in a promotional and/or co-ordinating role.

It is becoming increasingly apparent to all those with an interest in tourism, both in the UK and further afield, that the most effective way forward is for public, private and voluntary sectors to work together in partnership arrangements, so as to make best use of scarce resources and to pool expertise (see the case study on tourism development in York on pages 113–119). By working in partnership, central and local government can help provide the infrastructure and development funding within which private sector operators can develop facilities for visitors.

Activity 2.3

Find out if there are any tourism development initiatives in your local area that aim to encourage the public, private and voluntary sectors to work in partnership with each other.

Tourism development in the private (commercial) sector involves business units, both large and small, owned by individuals or groups of people whose principal aim is to maximise their profits. Revenue from the sales of their services or goods will hopefully be greater than the costs of operating the business so as to leave a surplus. This can be either taken as profit or reinvested in the business in order to build a solid foundation for future success for owners, directors, employees and any shareholders who may have bought a stake in the business.

The commercial sector provides the majority of the tourism facilities, services and products on offer to visitors, including:

- ✪ **Theatres**
- ✪ **Cinemas**
- ✪ **Hotels and other forms of accommodation**
- ✪ **Restaurants, cafés, pubs and bars**
- ✪ **Discotheques and nightclubs**
- ✪ **Travel agencies and tour operators**
- ✪ **Airlines**
- ✪ **Tourist attractions**
- ✪ **Health and fitness clubs and studios**
- ✪ **Mixed retail and leisure complexes**
- ✪ **Transport operations**

browse these private sector websites

www.british-airways.com

www.fly.virgin.com

www.thomson-holidays.com

www.iflybritish midland.com

www.drivebudget.com

Most of the household names in the UK travel and tourism industry operate in the private sector, for example British Airways, Thomson Holidays, Virgin, Thomas Cook, Legoland Windsor, Cadbury World, British Midland Airways, Budget Rent-a-Car and Britannia Airways (see Figure 2.2).

The biggest tourism enterprises operate as private and public limited companies (plcs), while many providers of support services in tourism are organised as partnerships or sole traders, for example hoteliers, restaurateurs, guides, marketing consultants, travel writers, chauffeurs and ground handlers. This same pattern of private sector ownership of the majority of tourism

Figure 2.2 *A Britannia Airways Boeing 767*
Courtesy of Britannia

enterprises is repeated in overseas countries that have developed, or are developing, their travel and tourism industry.

Activity 2.4

Collect information about the main private sector tourism operators in your area. Make a list of the range of products, services and facilities each provides.

Public sector organisations

Public sector organisations, including central governments, regional bodies and local authorities, become involved with tourism for a number of reasons. It is often tourism's economic benefits, such as job creation, revenue generation, export earnings, urban regeneration and tax revenues, that persuade public bodies to take an interest in the travel and tourism industry. Some countries realise that tourism can also bring with it a variety of political and social benefits, for example improvements in residents' quality of life, a favourable image on the world stage and the fostering of a national identity.

National tourism organisations

Any country that has a significant and established travel and tourism industry is likely to have a separate department of government or public body known as the national tourism organisation (NTO). In the UK, the NTO is the British Tourist Authority, the organisation that promotes Britain to the rest of the world to encourage tourists to visit (see case study in Unit 1 on pages 40–43). Other examples include the National Tourist Organisation of Greece, the French Government Tourist Office and the Spanish National Tourist Office, all of which are responsible for encouraging tourism to their countries. NTOs carry out a wide range of functions, as shown in Figure 2.3.

Figure 2.3 indicates that a typical NTO will have four principal areas of responsibility – namely marketing, development, research/corporate planning and finance/administration – under the direction of a chief executive through a number of departments. The functions undertaken by the NTO and other regional and local public authorities include:

✪ **Establishment of tourism policy:** This is generally the starting point for government involvement in tourism, when its sets out the policies and priorities for tourism development. The UK government has recently published a new tourism strategy called *Tomorrow's Tourism* (DCMS, 1999).

National tourism organisation

↓

Chief executive

Marketing
- Marketing planning
- Advertising & direct marketing
- Promotional print
- Travel trade activities
- Business & conference promotion
- Tourist Information Centre (TIC) networking

Development
- Development strategy
- Product development
- Project financial assistance
- Training liaison
- Trade relations
- Quality assurance & customer care

Research & corporate planning
- Corporate planning
- Research services
- Policy advice
- Planning advice

Finance & administration
- Finance management & control
- Administrative & personnel services
- Corporate press & PR
- Information technology

Figure 2.3 *The functions of a typical national tourism organisation*

○ **Destination promotion:** This is often the most important function of the NTO, which will be responsible for market research, marketing planning, travel trade activities and producing brochures and other promotional materials.

○ **Infrastructure provision:** Either independently or in partnership with the private sector, public bodies provide funding for many infrastructure developments that are directly or indirectly associated with tourism, for example road schemes, railway systems, airports and transport terminals.

○ **Tourism facilities:** Government departments and public agencies sometimes have the responsibility for maintaining tourist attractions and facilities, such as museums, parks, castles, historic houses, ancient monuments, National Parks and forests, coastal areas and galleries.

○ **Tourist information services:** National tourism organisations often co-ordinate the provision of tourist information services for visitors, which may be delivered by regional and local authorities.

○ **Legislation and regulation:** Governments enact a wide variety of legislation and regulation relating directly or indirectly to the tourism industry concerning, for example, health and safety, consumer protection, registration of accommodation and attractions, passport and visa requirements, the licensing of travel agencies, the training of tourist guides and restrictions on transport.

- ✪ **Finance for development:** Some governments provide, for example, grants, loans, tax concessions and tariff reductions, as incentives for tourism development.

- ✪ **Advisory services and training:** Many public bodies at national, regional and local levels provide business advisory services and training as a way of raising standards in the tourism industry.

browse these websites for links to national tourism organisations (NTOs)

www.tourist-offices.org.uk

www.world-tourism.org/tourworl.htm

The precise functions undertaken and degree of public involvement in tourism will depend on the importance attached to the industry by the government concerned. As tourism's contribution to a nation's economy grows and tourist revenues increase, the public funds available for tourism development are likely to increase the range and variety of functions that can be carried out.

Activity 2.5

Carry out some research to find the contact details of a range of national tourism organisations based in the UK. You could co-ordinate your work with other people in your group to produce a very useful information sheet listing the majority of popular overseas holiday destinations.

The following case study on the Japan National Tourist Organisation gives an indication of the responsibilities and activities of a NTO concerned primarily with the promotion of inbound travel to its country.

Case Study
Japan National Tourist Organisation

The Japan National Tourist Organisation (JNTO) was established under Japanese law in April 1959 and subsequently reorganised in 1964, 1979, 1983 and 1985. It is a non-profit making organisation, working under the direction of the Japanese Ministry of Transport, and has two principal aims:

★ The promotion of inbound travel to Japan

★ The provision of information to Japanese nationals on travelling safely overseas

continued

continued

In order to fulfil its principal aims, the JNTO is charged with undertaking the following activities under Japanese law:

★ Conduct publicity in order to stimulate visits by foreign tourists to Japan

★ Operate tourist information centres for overseas visitors

★ Furnish travel safety information to Japanese overseas tourists

★ Conduct investigations and research on pertinent aspects of international tourism

★ Perform activities incidental to those mentioned above

STRUCTURE OF THE JNTO

The organisational structure of the JNTO is shown in Figure 2.4.

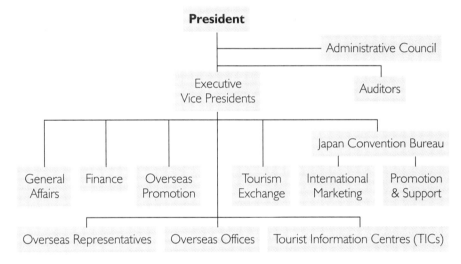

Figure 2.4 *Organisational structure of the Japan National Tourist Organisation*
Source: JNTO

The Organisation's administrative council investigates and deliberates on matters concerning the operation of JNTO's activities. The council consists of 26 members drawn from experts on international tourism in Japan. They are appointed by the president of the JNTO and are subject to the approval of Japan's Minister of Transport. JNTO maintains six departments in its Tokyo head office and 14 overseas offices in the world's key cities (see Table 2.1).

continued

continued

Office	Countries and territories administered
New York Chicago San Francisco Los Angeles	USA, countries in Central America and in Caribbean area
Toronto	Canada
São Paulo	Countries in South America
London	United Kingdom, Ireland, Denmark, Norway, Sweden and English-speaking countries in Africa
Paris	France, Spain, Portugal, Belgium, Luxembourg and French-speaking countries in Africa
Geneva	Switzerland, Italy, Greece, countries in former Yugoslavia and the Middle East
Frankfurt	European countries excluding those covered by other European offices
Bangkok	South-east Asian countries excluding those covered by the Hong Kong office
Hong Kong	Hong Kong, China, Macau and the Philippines
Seoul	Korea
Sydney	Australia and New Zealand

Source JNTO

Table 2.1 *Overseas offices of the Japan National Tourist Organisation*

The responsibilities of the six head office departments are as follows:

★ *General affairs:* responsible for JNTO's administrative functions, including legal matters, personnel, staff training, domestic public relations and general co-ordination of the Organisation. It also manages the long-range marketing plans and priority projects, performance and analysis of market surveys, publishing of periodicals and the collection of statistical data on international tourism.

★ *Finance*: oversees the formulation of budgets, requests for government subsidies, contracting, procurement activities and reporting financial settlements to the Japanese government.

★ *Overseas promotion*: responsible for administering and overseeing the

continued

continued

work of JNTO's overseas offices, providing media assistance to travel journalists, participation in travel trade fairs and exhibitions, and carrying out joint marketing activities in conjunction with the Japanese travel industry.

★ *Tourism exchange*: responsible for improving reception services for foreign visitors to Japan, administering the tourist information centres and conducting the national examination for guide–interpreters. Since the amendment of JNTO law, this department also provides Japanese travellers with information on how to travel overseas in safety.

★ *Japan Convention Bureau*: responsible for convention and incentive travel promotion. The Bureau consists of two departments. The international marketing department administers marketing and promotional activities concerned with the encouragement of convention visitors to Japan, for example the collection and analysis of marketing data, attracting conventions to Japan, advertising and public relations. The promotion and support department manages such activities as training programmes for staff engaged in convention-related duties, providing information and advice for organisers of international meetings in Japan, and supporting tourist programmes for foreign participants attending international conventions in Japan.

Under the direction of the Tokyo head office, the overseas offices implement various tourist promotion activities, including travel information services, media assistance, participation in fairs and exhibitions, and advertising in major consumer and travel trade publications. Areas distant from the JNTO's overseas offices are covered by a network of representatives who provide information on travel to Japan and distribute travel literature. They are stationed in major cities in North America, South America, Europe, Asia and Oceania.

JNTO'S ACTIVITIES

The Japan National Tourist Organisation undertakes a wide-ranging programme of promotional and product development activities, which can be summarised under the following headings:

★ *General promotion*: JNTO engages in a variety of promotional activities targeted at consumers and the travel trade. These include advertising, public relations work, media assistance, travel trade seminars, familiarisation visits,

continued

continued

regional promotion fairs, overseas exhibitions and an information service via its 14 overseas offices and network of representatives. The Organisation has recently established an information service on the Internet.

★ *Convention and incentive travel promotion*: The Japan Convention Bureau, a specialist department of the JNTO, is responsible for marketing Japan as an international convention and incentive travel destination. Members of the Bureau undertake market research studies on how to increase Japan's share of international conventions, attend overseas trade exhibitions and organise training programmes for staff working in this sector of Japan's travel industry.

★ *International co-operation*: JNTO maintains close working relationships with the following major world tourism bodies: World Tourism Organisation (WTO), East Asia Travel Association (EATA), Pacific Asia Travel Association (PATA), American Society of Travel Agents (ASTA) and Confederacion de Organizaciones Turisticas de la Americana Latina (COTAL). It also works with several individual countries on a bilateral basis to increase inbound tourist traffic.

★ *Reception services for foreign visitors*: JNTO continually works to improve, expand and enhance the reception services for visitors from abroad. It aims to improve the quantity and quality of tourist information services, ease any language problems that may arise, promote mutual understanding and friendship between foreign visitors and the Japanese, generate greater international tourism in local areas and reduce the travel costs of overseas visitors.

★ *International tourism exchange project*: This JNTO initiative was started in 1995 and is designed to promote inbound tourism to Japan by supporting and developing people-to-people exchange programmes between Japan and other countries. Specific themes include sister city exchanges, school-to-school exchanges and vocational exchanges.

★ *Japan tour development project*: This project is designed to explore the possibilities of developing new tour products under the co-sponsorship of the JNTO and local tourism bureaux in Japan. The main objective of the project is to stimulate inbound tourism to local regions in Japan, thereby spreading the economic and social benefits of international tourism to as wide an area of the country as possible.

★ *Activities for Japanese overseas tourists*: Since 1979, the JNTO has been

continued

continued

given the responsibility of offering services to Japanese people in order to ensure trouble-free overseas travel. This includes providing advice and assistance with such matters as security, etiquette and customs, for both the Japanese travelling public and the travel industry as a whole.

★ *Research and statistics*: The JNTO has established a Marketing Council to investigate the further refinement of its targeted marketing activities,

Revenues (thousand US$)	1994	1995
Government subsidies	24,500	25,381
Government funds	0	0
Contributions	3,815	4,082
National guide–interpreter examination	364	461
Miscellaneous	4,442	4,698
Total	33,121	34,622
Expenditure (thousand US$)	**1994**	**1995**
Overseas tourism promotion (including overseas personnel expenses)	15,499	16,196
Promotional aids	1,328	1,034
Convention promotion	1,710	1,800
Reception of foreign visitors	2,030	2,359
Services for Japanese overseas tourists	304	325
Statistics and research	120	126
National guide–interpreter examination	371	387
Management (excluding overseas personnel expenses)	11,142	11,683
Reserve	747	749
Total	33,251	34,659

Source   JNTO

Table 2.2 *Annual budgets of the Japan National Tourist Organisation, 1994 and 1995*

continued

continued

particularly partnerships between the public and private sectors of the tourism industry. For this and other promotional work, the Organisation relies heavily on a wide range of statistical data, including surveys of foreign visitors' travel in Japan and the Overseas Visitors Japan Travel Survey, which focuses on impressions and interest before travelling to the country. JNTO also collects and analyses statistical data on worldwide tourism trends and forecasts.

★ *Consignment activities*: JNTO is often commissioned by outside organisations to undertake various types of tourism-related activities, including advising on training programmes, promotional work, the development of information networks and the production of PR materials.

▶ BUDGETS AND REVENUE SOURCES

JNTO's budget for the 1995 financial year was 3.3 billion yen (US$34.7 million), of which 2.4 billion yen (US$25.4 million) was in the form of government subsidies (see Table 2.2).

Contributions of 392 million yen (US$4.1 million) were received from Japanese organisations and enterprises involved with tourism, such as Japan Railways, Japan Airlines, prefectural governments, the Japan Hotel Association and the travel agency sector. JNTO funds for services to Japanese overseas tourists consist of the capital furnished by the government and contributions from the Japanese tourist industry.

Information courtesy of the Japan National Tourist Organisation

Case study discussion questions

1 What does the JNTO do to promote its country abroad?

2 What problems do you think the JNTO is likely to encounter when competing for international visitors on a global scale?

3 What influence does the JNTO have on the development of Japan's tourism products?

4 How is the JNTO working towards improving facilities for incoming tourists?

Public sector tourism in the UK

Public sector involvement in UK tourism can be traced back to before Victorian times when many 'resorts', both inland and on the coast, benefited from investment in tourist facilities by their local councils. However, central government recognition of the economic importance of tourism was not forthcoming until as late as 1969, with the passing of the Development of Tourism Act. This first piece of tourism legislation, now more than 30 years old, still applies today, although the nature and scale of the industry has changed dramatically. The principal outcomes of the Act were:

- ✪ **The establishment of the British Tourist Authority (BTA), English Tourist Board (ETB), Wales Tourist Board (WTB) and Scottish Tourist Board (STB)**
- ✪ **The introduction of 'section 4' grants for tourist developments**
- ✪ **The establishment of a hotel development grants scheme**
- ✪ **Legislation to introduce a compulsory registration scheme for accommodation**

The Northern Ireland Tourist Board was not included in the Act since it had already been established in 1948.

Figure 2.5 shows the relationships between the various public sector organisations with an interest in tourism development in the UK.

While the Department for Culture, Media and Sport (DCMS) can be regarded as the 'lead' government department when it comes to tourism matters, other departments, including the Ministry of Agriculture and the Department of the

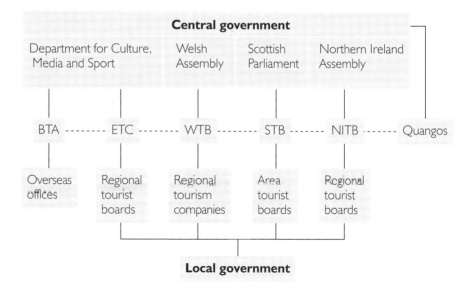

Figure 2.5 *The structure of public sector tourism in the UK*

Environment, Transport and the Regions, undertake activities that are associated with tourism development. Quangos include bodies such as Highlands and Islands Enterprise and the Welsh Development Agency, which have interests in tourism development in their respective regions.

National tourist boards

The UK has four national tourist boards: the English Tourism Council, the Wales Tourist Board, the Scottish Tourist Board and the Northern Ireland Tourist Board. The national tourist boards aim to set the framework and policy for their particular country, within which the private and public sectors can undertake tourism development. For example, the English Tourism Council (ETC), launched in July 1999 as the successor to the English Tourist Board, has the following mission:

> We will drive forward the quality, competitiveness and wise growth of England's tourism, by providing intelligence, setting standards, creating partnerships and ensuring coherence.

The aims of the ETC fall into three distinct areas: quality, competitiveness and wise growth.

In terms of **quality**, the ETC will:

- ✪ **Set, develop and promote the highest standards through the existing schemes for accommodation in England**
- ✪ **Evaluate whether other quality initiatives are needed to improve the product, customer service standards and environment that make up England's tourism experience**
- ✪ **Identify examples of best practice and interpret them for the benefit of the industry**
- ✪ **Champion the development of national initiatives such as resort regeneration in England**

To ensure **competitiveness**, the ETC will:

- ✪ **Provide the industry with relevant market research and forecasts**
- ✪ **Champion and develop standards for common systems and techniques to help businesses and other agencies reach consumers more efficiently**
- ✪ **Publish business advice and information on how legislative change may impact on tourism**
- ✪ **Identify the big issues facing tourism; publicise the opportunities and threats and champion possible solutions**
- ✪ **Research growth sectors in tourism and signal how the industry can take advantage of them**

In terms of **wise growth**, the ETC will:

✪ **Provide the framework for the successful delivery of the government's tourism strategy, *Tomorrow's Tourism*, and fund England's regional tourist boards to deliver their part**

✪ **Raise sustainability on the tourism industry's agenda, set measurable targets and audit progress**

✪ **Champion the value of and interests of English tourism wherever possible, particularly the social, economic and job creation benefits**

✪ **Represent industry interests to advise government and provide advice on policy issues which affect the ability of tourism to flourish**

browse this website

www.englishtourism.
org.uk

✪ **Promote opportunities to make tourism accessible to all**

In order to achieve its aims, the ETC works in partnership with a range of organisations, including the Department for Culture, Media and Sport, local authorities, the tourist industry, other government departments and the British Tourist Authority (see Figure 2.6).

Regional tourist boards

Although partly funded from the public purse, the work of tourist boards at regional level in the UK is altogether more commercial, with close liaison

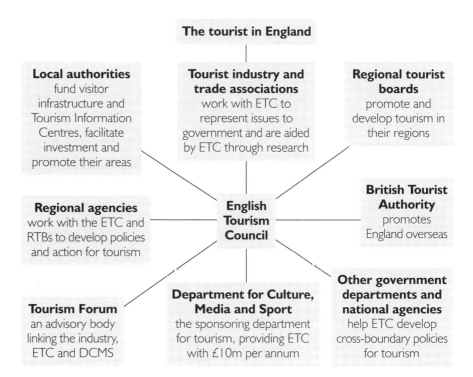

Figure 2.6 *The English Tourism Council's partners*

Figure 2.7 *The regional tourist boards in England*

between public and private sector concerns. A typical regional tourist board will have a wide range of members, from hoteliers, restaurateurs and tourist attractions to local councils, farm guesthouses and education establishments. In order to manage its three designated regions, the Wales Tourist Board has established associated companies, namely North Wales Tourism, Mid Wales Tourism and Tourism South and West Wales. The number of English regional tourist boards is now ten, following the demise of the Thames and Chilterns Tourist Board in the early 1990s and the East Midlands Tourist Board in 1996 (see Figure 2.7).

The commercial nature of regional tourist boards is shown by the ways in which they generate revenue, which include:

✪ **Grants from central government sources via the DCMS, Welsh Assembly, Northern Ireland Assembly or Scottish Parliament**

- Subscriptions from local authorities
- Subscriptions from commercial members
- Revenue from sales, e.g. selling advertising space in regional publications and letting space on exhibition stands

The main responsibilities of the English regional tourist boards are to:

- Have a thorough knowledge of tourism within their region, as well as the facilities and organisations involved in the tourism industry
- Advise the English Tourism Council on the regional aspects of major policy issues and to supply management information
- Service enquiries attributable to nationally developed promotions and to provide literature
- Co-ordinate regional tourist information services as part of the national tourist information centre (TIC) network
- Maintain close liaison with planning authorities on policies affecting tourism
- Carry out a continuing domestic public relations campaign with the local authorities, the travel trade and the public within the region
- Create awareness of the need for tourism to be managed for the benefit of residents as well as tourists
- Promote tourism to the region both from other parts of the country and from overseas

Activity 2.6

Find out which regional tourist board your area falls into and what plans it has for future tourism development.

Local authorities and tourism

At the local level, district, city and county councils in the UK are keen to develop tourism in their areas as a way of injecting income into the local economy and creating much-needed employment. Many will support the establishment of local tourism groups and associations that will bring together the private and public sector. The Local Government Act of 1948 gave local authorities the powers to set up information and publicity services for tourists. This was reinforced by the Local Government Act 1972 which empowered local authorities to publicise their areas for tourism and provide facilities for visitors.

Today, there are few local authorities in the UK that are not actively involved in some way with promoting their areas to tourists; places as diverse as Brighton and Berwick, Newcastle and Nottingham, Scarborough and Shrewsbury, are all competing for a slice of the 'tourism pound'. The scale of involvement is very variable, ranging from authorities with a single person responsible for tourism development and promotion to councils with separate tourism departments under a Director of Tourism. Some local authorities see tourism as a natural extension of their planning function and house their tourism officer and staff in this department; some consider that tourism is an integral part of economic development; while others view tourism, and particularly the marketing and promotion of tourism, as a PR activity which lends itself very well to their press and PR department.

Local authorities use their resources to provide as wide a range of tourism facilities and services that finances will allow. In a typical area, this might include:

- ✪ **Promotional leaflets and brochures**
- ✪ **Parks and gardens**

Figure 2.8 *Tourist information centre, Bath*
Courtesy of Bath Tourism Bureau

- ✪ **Theatres**
- ✪ **Museums**
- ✪ **Tourist information centres (see Figure 2.8)**
- ✪ **Accommodation booking services**
- ✪ **Sports and leisure centres**
- ✪ **Outdoor activity centres**
- ✪ **Art and craft galleries**

Regardless of how tourism development is organised within a particular local council, it is clear that it will remain a vital and increasing part of the work of local authorities in the future (see Figure 2.9).

Activity 2.7

Find out if your local authority is involved in tourism, and, if so, in what ways.

Figure 2.9 *Waveney District Council's Tourism Strategy, 1999*
Courtesy of Waveney District Council

Industry example

In its National Tourism Strategy document *Tomorrow's Tourism* (Department for Culture, Media and Sport, 1999) the UK government estimates that local authorities in England invest £75 million per annum in the development and promotion of tourism.

Voluntary sector bodies

Not all travel and tourism facilities and services in Britain are provided solely by private and public sector organisations. A third important source of provision, the voluntary sector, also plays an important part in the travel and tourism industry.

The voluntary sector includes charities, trusts and non-governmental organisations (NGOs) involved in:

- ✪ **Conservation/environment**
- ✪ **Community activities**
- ✪ **Sustainable tourism**
- ✪ **Play schemes**
- ✪ **Heritage**
- ✪ **Minority groups**
- ✪ **Youth organisations**
- ✪ **Cultural/entertainment organisations**
- ✪ **Clubs and societies**

Voluntary organisations vary enormously in their size and aims. At one end of the scale, a small group of like-minded people may decide to form a volunteer group to manage a nature reserve or clear rubbish from local beaches. At the other end, large organisations such as the National Trust (see case study on pages 109–110), the Youth Hostels Association and the Royal Society for the Protection of Birds fall within the voluntary sector, each with its own objectives. Pressure groups play an important part in highlighting issues and campaigning for change (see the case study on the work of Tourism Concern on pages 130–132). Voluntary organisations at local, national and international level often receive advice and financial help from both the public and private sectors, sometimes in the form of grants or sponsorship.

browse this website

www.yha.org.uk

Industry example

Although it is a charity, the YHA has a turnover of more than £26 million per year, making a major financial contribution to the UK travel and tourism industry with over 2 million overnight stays recorded per year. Total net assets in 1996 were £10.3 million.

The following case study highlights one of Britain's most successful voluntary organisations, the National Trust, which welcomes more than 11.5 million visitors to its properties and land each year.

Case Study
The National Trust

The National Trust – or to give it its full title, The National Trust for Places of Historic Interest or Natural Beauty – is a charity which holds countryside and buildings in England, Wales and Northern Ireland for the benefit of everyone. It was founded in 1895 as an independent charity in response to the spread of industrialisation, which was affecting both town and countryside at the end of the nineteenth century. Today, the Trust is the country's largest private landowner. It protects and opens to the public 165 historic houses, 19 castles, 49 industrial monuments and mills, 48 churches and chapels, 9 prehistoric and Roman properties, 12 farms, 165 gardens and 76 landscape/deer parks. It also protects some 271,000 hectares of countryside and 575 miles of coastline.

Although its name might suggest that it is run by the government, the Trust is jealously independent of the State. It depends on the generosity of those who give it properties and the money to maintain them, on more than 2.5 million

continued

continued

subscribing members and on its friends and supporters everywhere. There is an independent National Trust for Scotland.

STRUCTURE AND ORGANISATION

The Trust employs around 3,000 salaried staff and more than 4,000 seasonal workers. It also relies on the support of over 38,000 volunteers. The day-to-day administration of the Trust is carried out by its executive staff at head office in London and in 15 regional offices covering England, Wales and Northern Ireland. Policy is determined by the Trust's Council, half of whose 52 members are nominated by institutions such as the Ramblers' Association, the British Museum and the Royal Horticultural Society, and half elected by Trust members at the annual general meeting.

ACTIVITIES

The Trust plays host to an immense number of people. Each year, some 11.5 million people visit its 400 buildings and gardens open at a charge, and on a fine summer weekend, untold millions freely enjoy the coastline, hills and woodlands which the Trust preserves for us all. The Trust must ensure the right balance between the often conflicting interests of preservation and presentation to the public. Too great a pressure of visitors could destroy the atmosphere they seek. The Trust runs several special appeals including Enterprise Neptune, launched by the Duke of Edinburgh in 1965, which aims to preserve unspoilt coastline and set itself an initial target of raising £2 million. To date, some £25 million has been raised through Neptune and over 575 miles of unspoilt coastline are now both safe from damaging development and permanently available to the public.

(Information courtesy of The National Trust)

Case study discussion questions

browse this website

www.nationaltrust.
org.uk

1   Why do you think the National Trust is such a popular voluntary organisation with over 2.5 million members?

2   Does the National Trust only protect historic buildings?

3   How does the work of the National Trust help tourism in the UK?

4   How is it that the Trust employs paid staff, even though it is a voluntary organisation?

Activity 2.8

Find out if there are any National Trust properties or protected areas in your locality and, if so, what facilities they have for visitors.

The objectives of tourism development

Key topics in this section:

- **Introduction**
- **Economic objectives**
- **Environmental objectives**
- **Socio-cultural objectives**
- **Political objectives**

Introduction

We have seen earlier in this unit that tourism development is concerned with providing facilities for tourists and that the organisations that make the developments happen are known as the agents of development. These agents have different objectives for their involvement with tourism. Public sector organisations exist to provide services and facilities, and are often associated with creating the infrastructure within which commercial tourism development takes place. The public sector is also keen to exploit the economic benefits of tourism, particularly the creation of new jobs. Private operators are in business to make a profit, while quangos often act as the catalyst for commercial developments, for example Highlands and Islands Enterprise provides advice, grant-aid and business support to tourism companies relocating or developing in their area. The objectives of voluntary sector organisations include conservation and the preservation of our cultural heritage.

Economic
- Employment creation
- Foreign currency
- Income for commercial operators
- Economic development and regeneration

Environmental
- Preserving wildlife habitats
- Environmental education
- Environmental improvements

Objectives of tourism development

Socio-cultural
- Promoting understanding of different cultures
- Improving 'quality of life'
- Providing community facilities

Political
- Enhancing the image of an area
- Creating a regional or national identity

Figure 2.10 *The objectives of tourism development*

Figure 2.10 summarises the main objectives of tourism development, i.e. the reasons why organisations get involved with tourism in the first place. These are explored in more detail when we look at the impacts of tourism development in the next section of this unit.

The following case study considers the objectives of tourism development in York, one of the UK's most popular tourist cities.

Case Study
Tourism development in York

The City of York is one of the leading tourism destinations in Britain, offering UK and overseas visitors a wide variety of museums and other attractions, the historic architecture of the city itself, plus many different shopping and accommodation facilities (see Figure 2.11).

Tourism is vitally important to the economy of York. Research carried out by Touche Ross consultants in 1994 indicated that some 4 million visitors each year are attracted to the city, spending more than £250 million and supporting over 10,000 jobs. Of the 4 million visitors, 600,000 were overnight stay visitors who accounted for more than 1.5 million visitor nights in the city's accommodation. A significant proportion of the tourism

Figure 2.11 *York Minster*
Courtesy of York Tourism Bureau

continued

continued

revenue is accounted for by visitors' spending on shopping, contributing substantially to the continued prosperity of city centre shops in the face of out-of-town retail competition. Other important data from the Touche Ross research showed that, of the 4 million visitors to York in 1993:

★ 199,000 stayed in the main hotels

★ 379,000 stayed in other accommodation

★ 1,125,000 were on day visits primarily for leisure purposes

★ 2,250,000 were on day visits primarily for shopping purposes

★ Average length of stay of overnight visitors was 2.7 nights

★ Of all visitors to York, 67 per cent were day visitors and 33 per cent staying visitors

Although the research highlighted the positive aspects of the York 'product' and the significant economic benefits of

Attraction	Number of visitors
York Minster	2,000,000*
Jorvik Viking Centre	676,935
Castle Museum	428,587
National Railway Museum	399,120
Cliffords Tower	136,289
York City Art Gallery	126,304
Yorkshire Museum	120,000
Archaeological Resource Centre	53,852
Treasurer's House	50,744

*Estimated

Source   Adapted from York City Council data

Table 2.3   *Visitor numbers to selected attractions in York, 1993–94*

continued

continued

tourism to the city, there was also a note of caution, with the comment that 'there is no room for complacency'. There was evidence that some of the attractions in York were experiencing reductions in their visitor numbers (see Table 2.3). Moreover, York faces increasing competition as a regional tourist and shopping destination from places such as Leeds, with the Royal Armouries attraction, Halifax, with its Eureka! Museum for Children, and Bradford, the home of the National Museum of Photography, Film and Television.

SWOT ANALYSIS

As part of their research, the consultants analysed a number of factors that affect the competitiveness of York as a tourist destination. These were set out as a SWOT analysis:

★ *Strengths* – strong national and international identity
– superb built heritage

★ *Weaknesses* – poor market intelligence
– difficulty in identifying growth markets
– lack of reinvestment by leading attractions
– limited exploitation of synergies between attractions

★ *Opportunities* – development of Castle Museum
– potential for further developing inbound markets

★ *Threats* – lack of monitoring methods to assess performance and make adjustments
– environmental damage/capacity constraints
– shopping tourism may 'suffocate' leisure tourism
– fading appeal of Jorvik

continued

continued

The consultants' implications arising from the SWOT analysis for York fell into three distinct areas:

1 There is little need for broad-based destination marketing of York since there is already a strong positive image of the city

2 There is need for comprehensive and continuous market research, given the increasingly competitive and fast-moving market for tourist destinations

3 York will need to develop a flagship tourist attraction in order to maintain its position as a popular leisure destination

► A TOURISM STRATEGY FOR YORK

At the beginning of 1995, representatives of the tourism industry in York met as the York Tourism Forum to discuss the report of the research by Touche Ross. A small strategy group was established and asked to translate the consultants' findings into a strategy and action plan for the city, which would be recommended to the whole of the tourism industry in York. The strategy group included representatives from the following organisations:

★ York City Council
★ Yorkshire and Humberside Tourist Board (now Yorkshire Tourist Board)
★ York Visitor and Conference Bureau
★ York and North Yorkshire Chamber of Commerce
★ North Yorkshire Training and Enterprise Council
★ York Attractions Group
★ York Archaeological Trust
★ GMB trade union

The strategy group reported back to the Forum in July 1995 and the 'First Stop York' tourism initiative was born (see Figure 2.12).

continued

continued

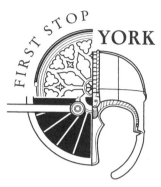

Figure 2.12 *The logo of the 'First Stop York' tourism initiative*
Courtesy of First Stop York Tourism Bureau

The strategic goals of the initiative were to create, through partnership between the public and private sectors, a tourism industry in York where:

★ Economic and employment benefits are maximised

★ The city is recognised as a high quality tourism destination that is continually being enhanced, in terms of both product and customer service

★ A wide range of quality jobs is available, with training and career opportunities

★ The potentially negative environmental and social impacts of the tourism industry are managed so that both the quality of life for residents and the enjoyment of York by visitors are enhanced

★ Local citizens can appreciate the benefits of tourism in York and therefore give it their support

★ Those engaged in the industry in York possess the means to understand and respond to national and international trends in their business

Based on the outcomes of the Touche Ross research, the strategy group identified a number of core principles and objectives of the 'First Stop York' initiative, including:

★ *Intelligence gathering*: the monitoring of local, regional, national and international trends as an aid to informed planning and management

continued

continued

★ *Product development*: including the continuation of a clear image for the city, encouraging reinvestment in attractions and facilities, and improving evening facilities in the city

★ *Product marketing and packaging*: to adopt a highly targeted and co-ordinated approach to marketing the city, particularly the short break opportunities, and adopt a single, clear, high quality brand for the York product; to market York as a year-round destination

★ *Bookability and management*: including the introduction of booking systems that will facilitate easy access to the York product for potential visitors, improving facilities for the arrival of visitors to the city and ensuring equal access to all sections of the community

★ *Centre of excellence*: to improve job quality, training and career prospects for those working in the tourism industry and to develop a high quality and consistent approach to providing services to the visitor

★ *Citizens' support*: increasing understanding of the tourism industry among local people and gaining a greater understanding of residents' concerns about the development of tourism in the city

★ *Partnership*: to develop a co-ordinated partnership framework for the management, implementation and monitoring of all activities resulting from the strategic plan for tourism in York

ACTION POINTS

Building on the initiative's strategic goals, core principles and objectives, members of the strategy group have devised a series of specific action points, published as an action plan, with detailed timing, leadership and cost implications. The action points concerned with the objective of

continued

continued

improving product marketing and packaging, for example, include the establishment of the 'First Stop York' brand, with its associated logo, artwork and displays and a commitment by all partners to corporate, trade-related marketing activities including trade fairs, liaison with tour operators, trade advertising, etc. Further product marketing action points include:

★ A year-round campaign led by the York Visitor and Conference Bureau aimed at UK and overseas visitors

★ An enhanced rail campaign with Regional Railways

★ Targeting of incoming visitors through the exploitation of the Yorkshire Tourist Board's links with the British Tourist Authority

★ Linkages with Eurotunnel and Eurostar

★ Liaison with air operators

★ Development of the incentive travel market

(Information courtesy of York City Council)

Case study discussion questions

1 Why is it important for tourist destinations such as York to have accurate intelligence gathering capabilities?

2 What impacts can tourism development have on local people in destinations such as York and why is it important to involve local residents in future tourism development plans?

3 How might a city such as York devise and implement a year-round short breaks programme aimed at UK and overseas tourists?

4 What particular roles do private sector operators and the different public sector organisations involved with tourism in York play in the implementation of the strategy?

5 How will the members of the initiative know if the strategy has been a success?

The impacts of tourism development

Key topics in this section:

- **Introduction**
- **Economic impacts**
- **Environmental impacts**
- **Socio-cultural impacts**
- **Maximising travel and tourism's positive impacts**
- **Minimising travel and tourism's negative impacts**

Introduction

An industry the size of travel and tourism cannot fail to have impacts on the people, culture, environment and the economies of destination areas and countries. Often these impacts are **positive**, for example providing jobs and incomes, but sometimes tourism has **negative** impacts, such as congestion, pollution and high prices in tourist areas. The following sections of this unit look in detail at the positive and negative effects of tourism development under the following headings:

- ✪ **Economic impacts**
- ✪ **Environmental impacts**
- ✪ **Socio-cultural impacts**

Economic impacts

Positive economic impacts of tourism development

It is often the positive economic impacts that persuade governments, companies and individuals to get involved with tourism development. Tourism has the potential to generate revenue and help provide jobs. Thinking of your own area, there may well be hotels, caravan parks or tourist attractions that produce an income for the people who own them and provide jobs for local people.

At a global level, international tourism has been one of the world's fastest growing industries (see Figures 2.13 and 2.14).

As Figures 2.13 and 2.14 indicate, international tourist arrivals grew from just 25 million in 1950 to a record 625 million in 1998, with total receipts of US$ 445 billion for the same year.

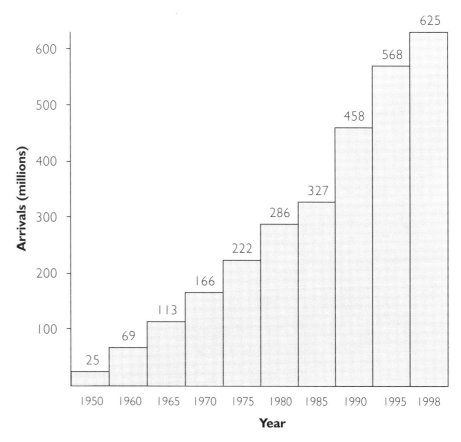

Figure 2.13 *International tourist arrivals, 1950–98*
Source: WTO

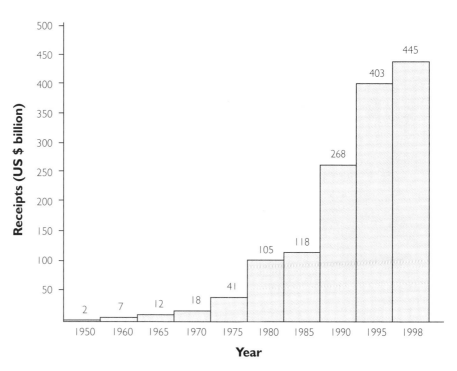

Figure 2.14 *International tourist receipts, 1950–98*
Source: WTO

Estimates from the 1996 Research Report of the World Travel and Tourism Council (WTTC) show that, on a world scale, the travel and tourism industry:

- **Employs 255 million people (10.7 per cent of total jobs)**
- **Generates an output of US$ 3,600 billion (US$ 3.6 trillion)**
- **Contributes 10.7 per cent of total world gross domestic product (GDP)**
- **Represents an investment of US$ 766 billion**
- **Generates US$ 653 billion in total world taxes**

WTTC forecasts that by the year 2006, tourism will employ 385.4 million people worldwide, generate an output of US$ 7.1 trillion and contribute 11.5 per cent of world GDP.

The travel and tourism industry has the ability to provide a variety of positive economic impacts, the most important of which are:

- **Income generation**
- **Employment**
- **Improvements to infrastructure**

Income generation

The travel and tourism industry generates income and wealth for private individuals, local authorities, companies, voluntary bodies and national governments. At the international level, the money that tourists spend in a country can make a considerable contribution to its balance of payments. Spain, for example, earned US$ 29.5 billion from visiting tourists in 1998.

Closer to home, Britain's tourism industry is estimated by the British Tourist Authority to be worth £61.2 billion (1998 figures), broken down as follows:

- **£12.7 billion – spending by overseas visitors in the UK**
- **£3.2 billion – payments in fares to UK carriers (airlines, ferry companies, etc.)**
- **£14 billion – spending by UK residents on overnight stays within the UK**
- **£31.3 billion – spending by UK residents on day visits within the UK**

At a local level, revenue generated by travel and tourism facilities is often vital to the economic well-being of an area and is boosted by an important concept known as the multiplier effect. Research has shown that the amount spent by visitors to an area is recirculated in the local economy (by, for example, the wages of somebody working in a tourist attraction being spent on goods and services in local shops) and is actually worth more to the area than its face value. For example, £200 spent by a couple on a short break in a hotel could be worth £200 x 1.4 (the hotel multiplier effect for that area), i.e. a total of £280.

The actual value of the multiplier (1.4 in the above example is merely an illustration) varies between regions and different sectors of the travel and tourism industry. The multiplier for, say, a farm guesthouse is likely to be greater than for a city centre hotel which is part of a large multinational chain. This is because the owners of the farm guesthouse are likely to spend their money locally, buying food and other services for their business, while the goods and services for the large hotel may well be brought in from outside the area as part of a national distribution contract, i.e. income is lost to the area (in economic terms this is known as a leakage from the local economy).

Activity 2.9

Carry out some research to find out to what extent your local area, or one nearby, benefits from spending by tourists.

browse this website

www.waveney.gov.
uk

Industry example

The overall value of tourism to the Waveney District Council area in Suffolk, centred on the coastal resort of Lowestoft, is estimated at £102.6 million. The tourism expenditure in the district supports more than 4,600 jobs locally.

Employment

Tourism's ability to create jobs is one of the main reasons why governments and other public sector bodies encourage the development of tourism. When compared with creating employment in the manufacturing sector, service sector jobs in tourism are seen as a relatively cheap and easy way of making jobs available, since the associated capital start-up costs are generally considerably lower. **Direct** employment in tourism occurs in hotels and other types of accommodation, transport operators, travel agencies, tourist attractions, government departments and tour operators, to name but a few.

Tourism also has the ability to stimulate the creation of **indirect** employment opportunities in sectors not directly associated with the industry, as the following examples from the World Travel and Tourism Council (WTTC) indicate:

- ✪ **Traditional travel service jobs**: include employment in airlines, hotels, restaurants, attractions, car rental companies, tour operators and travel agents
- ✪ **Government travel service jobs**: include employment in tourism promotion and information offices, National Park or monument guides, air traffic controllers, road safety and maintenance staff, and lifeguards on tourist destination beaches; they also include customs and immigration officials at land borders and airports
- ✪ **Travel and tourism capital investment jobs**: on the public side, these include design and construction of roads, parks and airports; on the private side, they include employment in the conception and construction of aircraft, hotels/resorts, holiday homes, travel company office buildings, cruise ships, and some retail shops and restaurants
- ✪ **Travel product jobs**: these jobs provide goods and services to travellers and travel companies, ranging from film developers to accountants, to dry cleaners, to butchers, to shoemakers, to sign makers

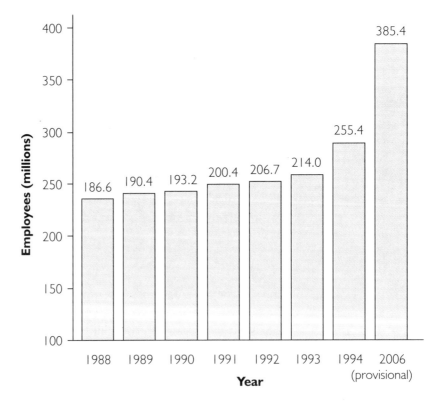

browse this website

www.wttc.org

Figure 2.15 *Employment in world tourism, 1988–2006*
Source: WTTC

At the international level, the forecast growth in tourism in the new millennium will create additional direct and indirect jobs in the industry. The World Travel and Tourism Council estimates that by the year 2006, tourism will generate employment for more than 385 million workers, representing 11.1 per cent of the total global workforce (see Figure 2.15).

Exercise 2.1

Make a list of some of the jobs in your local area that are directly associated with travel and tourism. Are there any other businesses that benefit indirectly from tourism?

Improvements to infrastructure

As well as generating revenue and creating jobs, tourism development also contributes to infrastructure improvements in destination areas, for example road and rail improvements, airport developments, improvements in telecommunications and utilities. In this way, local people can benefit from improved facilities that are provided for tourists. Member states of the European Union can apply for financial help with infrastructure projects from the European Regional Development Fund (ERDF), while developing countries are often supported with funds from the World Bank, United Nations and multinational corporations.

Tourism is often included in multi-purpose regeneration projects, for example the Salford Quays area of Manchester, Albert Dock in Liverpool, developments in Cardiff Bay and the Docklands area of London.

Negative economic impacts of tourism development

Although tourism development has the potential to offer significant economic benefits to destination areas, it can have negative economic impacts, including:

✪ Prices of goods and services in tourist areas are sometimes increased in the peak holiday season in order to maximise tourist revenue. This disadvantages local residents who may have to pay higher prices for food, entertainment, transport services, etc.

✪ Extra charges may be levied on the local community to finance facilities and services for visitors. Through their taxes, local people may have to pay for such facilities as tourist information centres and museums, which are primarily for the benefit of tourists. Some sectors of the community will contribute to the costs of running travel and tourism facilities that they never use.

✪ The price of land and houses may rise as a result of tourism development, making it difficult for local people to buy their own property. In rural areas of Wales, England, Northern Ireland and Scotland, the purchasing of second homes, which may only be used for a small proportion of the year, can inflate house prices and put them beyond the reach of the local population, particularly young couples looking for their first property.

✪ Areas of the country that become particularly popular with tourists may lose their local shops in favour of retail outlets geared specifically to the needs of the tourists, such as gift shops and cafés. This means that local people have to travel further to buy their staple foods, thus incurring extra expense. Rural areas are again particularly at risk; the village of Holmfirth, which has become famous as the location where the TV programme 'Last of the Summer Wine' is filmed, has seen many of its village shops being replaced by facilities for visitors.

✪ Tourism development can lead to the loss of traditional employment opportunities, when workers move from industries such as farming and fishing into service jobs in tourism. This has been particularly apparent in Mediterranean resorts, including Majorca, the Spanish Costas and Greece.

Activity 2.10

Gather information about the positive and negative economic impacts of tourism development in your local area. Work as part of a group to come up with some ideas as to how the positive impacts could be maximised and the negative impacts minimised.

Environmental impacts

Positive environmental impacts of tourism development

Although the tourism industry is often criticised for damaging the environment, it can sometimes be a positive force for environmental change. Tourism to remote areas, such as the rain forests of South America and Papua New Guinea, and hitherto undiscovered Pacific islands, can help expose damaging environmental activities. Pressure groups, such as Tourism Concern (see case study on pages 130–132) and Friends of the Earth, campaign for sensitive tourism development that is respectful of local environments and customs.

Closer to home, tourism development can lead to the improvement of derelict land and waterways, the restoration of redundant buildings, landscaping and environmental improvements linked to schemes such as the Britain in Bloom campaign, co-ordinated by the Tidy Britain Group.

Negative environmental impacts of tourism development

We have seen that tourism can have a positive impact on the environment, but there is much evidence to suggest that the industry could do a lot to improve its negative environmental impacts. On a global scale, tourism can have harmful effects on 'fragile' habitats, such as coral reefs, rain forests and mountain areas. In Britain, the coast, countryside, towns and cities all suffer from the pressures of increasing numbers of visitors and their transportation. Some of the worst problems include:

- ✪ **Physical erosion – the wearing away of soil and vegetation by walkers, horse-riders, cyclists, cars and motorcycles**
- ✪ **Litter – both an eyesore and a threat to safety**
- ✪ **Congestion and overcrowding – in popular holiday areas we all see the effects of too many people and too many cars**
- ✪ **Pollution – of water and air, not forgetting noise pollution**
- ✪ **Loss of habitats for flora and fauna**
- ✪ **Spoiling of the landscape that people have come to see and enjoy**

Better education, improved visitor and traffic management techniques, adjusting prices and better signposting, are some of the possible solutions that are being tried in our towns and countryside to reduce the harmful environmental effects of travel and tourism (see the industry example on traffic management in Cambridge on page 144).

In the UK, the negative environmental impacts of tourism are not confined to countryside areas, but are also to be found in cities and on the coast. Negative impacts in the countryside are most acute in the National Parks, which together accommodate over 100 million visits per year. Parks close to urban centres come under particular pressure; at summer weekends, some parts of the Peak District and Lake District National Parks reach saturation point, with traffic jams for many miles. The large numbers of people visiting the countryside, most travelling by car, put pressure on the physical environment, resulting in erosion by walkers, cars, cycles, horse-riders and motorcyclists. Litter and the pollution of fields and waterways are also a constant problem, resulting in harm to the natural flora and fauna.

Tourism's harmful effects on the urban environment affect many historic destinations that are popular with tourists, such as York, Bath, Chester,

Cambridge, Stratford-upon-Avon and Oxford, as well as our capital cities – Cardiff, London, Belfast and Edinburgh. Congestion, pollution and litter are three of the most common problems concerning tourism in the urban environment. Noise pollution, particularly associated with increased traffic flows, can also affect residents and visitors alike.

On the coast, sensitive areas such as sand dunes and estuaries can be harmed by tourist pressure, while the popular seaside resorts, such as Scarborough, Brighton and Newquay, have to deal with a huge influx of visitors for a relatively short period of time, plus all that they bring with them. In areas of the country that are prone to drought, water supply can be a problem in the peak tourist season, while sewage disposal is a constant challenge to local authorities.

Activity 2.11

Gather information about the positive and negative environmental impacts of tourism development in your local area. Work as part of a group to come up with some ideas as to how the positive impacts could be maximised and the negative impacts minimised.

Industry example

browse this website

www.resort-guide.co.uk/purbeck/

Purbeck in Dorset is one of the most easily accessible and heavily used stretches of coastline in the UK, attracting some 4.5 million visitors each year. By the early 1990s, visitor pressures were intense and the local community began to react negatively to increased numbers of tourists. Congestion and overcrowding also reduced the quality of the visitors' experience. The local authority's response was to develop a management plan to promote more sustainable types of tourism. They established the Purbeck Heritage Committee (comprising environmental groups, the Regional Tourist Board, the National Farmers' Union and local councils) and the Purbeck Forum to oversee the local development of tourism.

Socio-cultural impacts

Positive socio-cultural impacts of tourism development

Given that many of the reasons for visiting tourist destinations are concerned with social and cultural experiences, for example meeting new people and exploring cultural sites, the travel and tourism industry can be said to have positive impacts in this regard. Although tourism development is often criticised for its negative social and cultural impacts on destination areas, it can have positive impacts, such as:

- **The revitalisation for visitors of neglected regions**
- **The rebirth of local arts, crafts and customs**
- **The provision of community facilities**
- **Refurbishment of local architecture**
- **Greater understanding between cultures**

At a local level, the provision of tourism facilities for the enjoyment of visitors gives local people the opportunity to improve the quality of their lives and to take part in community activities for the benefit of all. Also, by helping to maintain a clean and attractive environment for visitors, tourism can instil a sense of civic pride in local residents.

Negative socio-cultural impacts of tourism development

There is a general feeling among those with an interest in tourism development that the negative social and cultural impacts of tourism development are far more harmful in the long run than the environmental problems associated with the industry. This is based on the belief that many of the negative environmental impacts can be easily corrected with the right management and funding. The social and cultural problems, however, can be far more deep-rooted and may take generations to eradicate, for example:

- **Overcrowding may cause a reduction in the quality of life for the 'host community', i.e. those living in the area visited**
- **Traditional activities, e.g. farming, may lose labour to the seemingly more attractive jobs in travel and tourism**
- **Tourists' behaviour can distort local customs**
- **Religious codes may be altered to adapt to the needs of visitors, e.g. Sunday opening of facilities**
- **Local languages may be lost through under-use**

- ✪ Traditional crafts may be lost in favour of mass-produced souvenirs
- ✪ Communities may be lost when tourists buy second homes in destination areas
- ✪ Crime, including public disturbances and burglaries, may increase

Activity 2.12

Gather information about the positive and negative socio-cultural impacts of tourism development in your local area. Work as part of a group to come up with some ideas as to how the positive impacts could be maximised and the negative impacts minimised.

Case Study
Tourism Concern

▶ **WHAT IS TOURISM CONCERN?**

Tourism Concern is a membership organisation established in 1989 to bring together British people with an active concern for tourism's impact on the community and environment, both in the UK and worldwide. The organisation is working for change in tourism and insists that tourism takes account of the rights and interests of those living in the world's tourist areas. Tourism Concern aims to look past the cosmetic 'green issues', such as recycling and energy conservation, to the way that tourism affects the people living in destination areas, their communities and their environments. It seeks to raise awareness of tourism's impacts, informs and influences decision-makers at all levels, and provides a comprehensive information base. Through its membership network, global contacts and resource collection, Tourism Concern is a respected centre for advice and information on tourism's impacts on environment and culture.

continued

continued

▶ WHAT DOES TOURISM CONCERN STAND FOR?

Tourism Concern advocates:

- ★ Tourism that is just, yielding benefits that are fairly distributed
- ★ Tourism that is participatory, recognising the rights of residents to be involved in its development and management
- ★ Tourism that is sustainable, putting the long-term social and environmental health of holiday areas before short-term gain

▶ HOW IS TOURISM CONCERN ORGANISED?

Tourism Concern is made up of a voluntary membership body, led by an elected council, operating to a written constitution. It is supported by membership subscriptions, donations, grants and involvement in joint projects. Tourism Concern's current grant funders are:

- ★ The Joseph Rowntree Charitable Trust
- ★ Christian Aid
- ★ London Borough Grants Council
- ★ University of North London
- ★ Department for International Development
- ★ Network Foundation
- ★ VSO (Voluntary Service Overseas)
- ★ Polden Puckham Charitable Foundation
- ★ CAFOD (Catholic Fund for Overseas Development)

There are links to a global network of like-minded organisations sharing information and occasional joint action. Tourism Concern has a full-time co-ordinator, supported by part-time staff and volunteers. Its base is in north London.

continued

continued

▶ WHAT IS TOURISM CONCERN DOING?

★ *Campaigning* to see that tourism is recognised by governments and development agencies as a key issue for the twenty-first century; to raise issues of injustice, like the harassment of those who speak out against developments in certain countries

★ *Networking* to bring together different sectors to work on local and global projects such as the Himalayan Tourist Code, now distributed by the tourism industry, and Guidelines for Sustainable Tourism Development

★ *Informing* the public, mounting exhibitions and providing literature to heighten awareness of tourism issues; providing speakers and information for the press, broadcasts and conferences

★ *Developing* a resource base of information on the issues

★ *Educating* by contributing to teaching resources on tourism's impact and exploring new ways to integrate tourism issues into education

(Information courtesy of Tourism Concern)

Case study discussion questions

browse this website

www.tourismconcern.org.uk

1 How can Tourism Concern influence the development of tourist resorts and facilities that conform to the principles of sustainable development?

2 What factors will affect Tourism Concern's success in meeting its aims?

3 Do campaigning organisations like Tourism Concern have a role to play in regulating the tourism industry?

4 What measures can Tourism Concern implement to persuade governments of the need for planned tourism development?

Maximising travel and tourism's positive impacts

It is in the long-term interest of the travel and tourism industry for public, private and voluntary sector organisations to work together to maximise industry benefits. This can be achieved by careful attention to a number of factors, including:

- ✪ **Maximising visitor spending**
- ✪ **Investing in public and social projects**
- ✪ **Widening access to facilities**
- ✪ **Staff training and development**
- ✪ **Tourism education**

Maximising visitor spending

All tourism operators seek to maximise spending by visitors, although, for public bodies and voluntary sector organisations, it will not be their prime objective. Effective marketing, human resource management and financial control are the key factors contributing to the success of tourism enterprises. In addition to their primary source of revenue, all tourism operators aim to maximise their revenue from secondary sources. Examples of this 'secondary spend' include:

- ✪ **Catering and retail outlets at tourist attractions and destinations**
- ✪ **Travel agents selling insurance and foreign currency to holidaymakers**
- ✪ **Tour operators offering car hire and excursions to their clients**
- ✪ **Hotels promoting leisure breaks to their business guests**
- ✪ **Airlines and ferry companies selling reduced price goods**

The sale of locally produced food, drink and other items to visitors will help to generate income for local communities, thereby helping the local economy.

Investing in public and social projects

The growth and development of Britain's tourism industry depends on its ability to generate a return on investment. Returns are generally measured through the financial rewards that the investor receives, in the form of interest or a dividend. Capital growth, for example the rise in value of a resort complex, hotel or restaurant, is another way of measuring returns on investment in travel and tourism. Public bodies do not always measure the success of tourism investments in purely financial terms, but assess their significance against wider social, political and cultural objectives.

Individuals, private companies and public agencies invest in tourism development for a number of reasons, including:

- ✪ An obvious commercial reason for investing in a tourism development project is that the investor expects to receive a healthy return on his or her investment, in the same way as if the investment was in any other commercial sector of the economy.

- ✪ Some governments undertake investment in tourism for non-commercial reasons, such as social and community benefit. Investment in leisure centres, parks, tourist information centres, transport infrastructure and visitor attractions may be justifiable on social if not always commercial grounds.

- ✪ A lot of investment in travel and tourism is property-driven, meaning that entrepreneurs who are essentially property developers will invest in capital projects such as hotels, resort complexes and theme parks, as alternatives to shops, factories and offices.

- ✪ Some investments in tourism are made for 'lifestyle' reasons such as an extension of a hobby or as a tax loss. Investment in tourism may also be needed to subsidise an existing enterprise, such as a stately home or family farm. Travel and tourism has an appeal to investors outside the industry who consider that it is an easy sector in which to operate and brings with it significant lifestyle benefits.

- ✪ Some investments in tourism can be justified on the grounds that they are joint-use. Leisure centres are often joint enterprises between a local authority leisure services department and a school or college. Major out-of-town retail developments often include entertainment facilities such as multi-screen cinemas and bowling complexes.

Income from tourists can be 'ploughed back' into a variety of public and social projects. Developing countries, for example, use the proceeds from tourism to help build hospitals, schools and other development projects. In some parts of the UK, money from tourists is used to maintain the areas that they visit, for example car parking charges are used to maintain footpaths and dry stone walls.

Activity 2.13

Try to find out what plans exist in your area for public and private sector investment in tourism development projects and how they are to be funded.

Widening access to facilities

Making tourism developments open to as wide a variety of potential customers as possible will help all travel and tourism organisations maximise the benefits of tourism. Much has been done in the UK since the late 1980s to improve access to tourist facilities as a result of the pioneering work of the Tourism for All Campaign.

Case Study
The Tourism for All Campaign

Launched in 1989, following the publication of the Baker Report, the Tourism for All Campaign aims to encourage the tourism industry to cater for all people regardless of age or disability, and create a genuinely welcoming and accessible environment in all tourist facilities, including visitor attractions. The Baker Report was commissioned initially by the English Tourist Board, in association with the Holiday Care Service, and was expanded to take in Scotland and Wales, with the participation of the Wales and

continued

continued

Scottish Tourist Boards. The Northern Ireland Tourist Board has also joined the other partners in promoting the Tourism for All message. The Campaign believes that by catering for people with special needs, such as people with impaired sight, hearing or mobility, operators can make their premises more accessible to many other visitors. Wide ramps and doorways installed for wheelchair users benefit adults with pushchairs and young children; lifts help elderly people and those carrying luggage. The Tourism for All Campaign recommends that the tourism industry should be aware of the statement:

a person is not handicapped by their impairment, but by the environment and the attitudes of the people they encounter.

CAMPAIGN CO-ORDINATION

The Campaign is co-ordinated by the national Tourism for All Committee, with a membership drawn from the tourist boards, the tourism industry, the Department of Transport and the voluntary sector. The Committee meets regularly to monitor and to advise on the recommendations in the Baker Report on Tourism for All, to promote the development of the principles in that report and to offer advice on any new initiatives relevant to Tourism for All.

THE SIZE OF THE MARKET

The Campaign argues that an accessible tourism industry should benefit from increased business from this 'last untapped market'. Figures from a government survey in 1988 show that there are some 6.2 million adults in Great Britain with some form of disability, plus an estimated 50 million in Europe and 34 million in the USA. If any one disabled person is turned away, the business of their family, friends, work associates or colleagues may also be lost. With an estimated 6 million carers in the UK, the Campaign suggests it is reasonable to assume a doubling of the

continued

continued

effective market size to 12 million people. Furthermore, there is a close relationship between disability and age and in Britain we have an ageing population. By the year 2021 nearly one in five (20 per cent) of the population will be over 65 years of age, compared with only one in ten in 1951. There is also clear evidence of the increasing aspirations of disabled people in their holiday and travel requirements and expectations.

ACCESS EXPLAINED

The Tourism for All Campaign considers that true access, in the widest sense, requires attention to three interlinked aspects:

★ Design or re-design of the physical environment: e.g. the provision of level access, ramps and lifts

★ Provision of reliable information based on agreed standards: e.g. promotional literature should include reference to the level of accessibility

★ Staff awareness: a friendly welcome is essential, as is a knowledge of the facilities on offer, coupled with an understanding of the needs of disabled people; staff training and development should address this issue and seek to integrate customers with disabilities into mainstream provision

INDUSTRY PARTICIPATION IN THE TOURISM FOR ALL CAMPAIGN

Many tourist establishments are already accessible and have applied for accreditation under the National Accessible Schemes for Tourism for All run by the tourist boards and the Holiday Care Service. Operators are further encouraged to include disability awareness training in their staff training programmes and to consider the adoption of a written policy statement expressing their commitment to Tourism for All in all its aspects.

Case study discussion questions

1 What is the overall aim of the Tourism for All Campaign?

2 Which sectors of the tourist industry does it encompass?

3 How does the Holiday Care Service help people with disabilities?

4 Why is it important for the operators of tourist attractions to provide facilities to meet the needs of customers with disabilities?

5 What can the management and staff working in tourist facilities do to ensure that people with disabilities have an enjoyable visit?

Staff training and development

Public bodies and commercial operators alike are beginning to realise that one of the most cost-effective ways of maximising tourism's positive impacts is to invest in staff training and development. Tourism training brings benefits to a range of parties, as shown in Figure 2.16.

Staff working in tourism organisations can benefit from structured training in a number of ways, including:

- ✪ **Enhanced self-esteem**
- ✪ **Greater job satisfaction**
- ✪ **Financial rewards**
- ✪ **Better understanding of the travel and tourism industry**
- ✪ **Higher skill levels**

Travel and tourism organisations can also benefit from training by, for example:

- ✪ **Increased profitability and efficiency**
- ✪ **Reduced staff turnover**

Figure 2.16 *The beneficiaries of staff training and development*

- ✪ **A more motivated workforce**
- ✪ **Reduced costs**
- ✪ **Increased flexibility**
- ✪ **Better identification of business opportunities**

The travel and tourism industry as a whole benefits from better personnel planning, an improved image of the profession and better definition of industry sectors. Tourism training brings benefits to customers as well, such as enhanced levels of customer service, better product standards and higher quality facilities (see also Unit 5: Customer Service in Travel and Tourism).

Activity 2.14

Carry out some research to discover what tourism training opportunities exist in your own area. Consider if there are any gaps in provision and how these could best be filled.

Tourism education

If people are educated about tourism development, they are in a better position to understand the benefits that the industry can offer. Tourism education is not just about people such as you on a tourism course at school or college. It is also concerned with informing local communities about the economic, environmental, social and cultural benefits of tourism. Education can help people to manage tourism development in a way that is sustainable in the long term.

Minimising travel and tourism's negative impacts

The performance of organisations in relation to the impact that they have on the environment and on host communities has become a major issue. No travel and tourism organisation can operate without having positive and negative effects on its immediate natural environment and, in many cases, on the environment thousands of miles away. Western societies are becoming increasingly concerned about the threats to the environment posed by many tourism developments. The 1980s saw the growth of the 'green consumer' who looks not only for environmentally friendly products in the supermarkets, but also for tourism products that are developed in harmony with the environment. Many tourism developments have been criticised for their lack of concern for environmental and socio-cultural impacts, while many argue that the whole of the tourism industry is, by its very nature, environmentally and culturally destructive.

Techniques and practices for minimising the negative impacts of tourism development are many and varied, and include:

✪ **Planning control**
✪ **Using the principles of sustainable tourism**
✪ **Visitor and traffic management**
✪ **Environmental impact assessments**
✪ **Environmental auditing**

Planning control

Planners are responsible for making sure that any tourism development is acceptable to local people and respectful of the local environment. Local authorities have the power to refuse planning permission for tourism developments if they do not meet certain criteria, for example their impact on the landscape, scale and location. Planners are called upon to make judgements about a wide variety of developments in tourism, for example:

✪ **The building of a hotel or holiday complex**
✪ **Signposting of hotels and tourist facilities**
✪ **Change of use of buildings and land for tourism purposes**
✪ **The development of tourist attractions**
✪ **Car parking associated with tourism projects**

In all cases, planning authorities have to balance the economic benefits of tourism projects with the possible damage to the local environment and communities.

The principles of sustainable tourism

Sustainable tourism is an emerging concept that has grown out of increased concern about the negative environmental and socio-cultural impacts of unplanned tourism development. An extension of 'green tourism', which has developed out of concern for the environment, sustainable tourism is part of a much wider global debate on sustainable development, highlighted by the Brundtland Report in 1987 and the first Earth Summit in Rio in 1992. Various bodies concerned with travel and tourism have developed policies on sustainable development, including the English Tourist Board (now English Tourism Council) 'Tourism and the Environment Task Force', whose principles for sustainable tourism developed in 1991 state that:

- The environment has an intrinsic value which outweighs its value as a tourism asset. Its enjoyment by future generations and its long-term survival must not be prejudiced by short-term considerations.

- Tourism should be recognised as a positive activity with the potential to benefit the community and the place as well as the visitor.

- The relationship between tourism and the environment must be managed so that the environment is sustainable in the long term. Tourism must not be allowed to damage the resource, prejudice its future enjoyment or bring unacceptable impacts.

- Tourism activities and developments should respect the scale, nature and character of the place in which they are sited (see Figure 2.17).

- In any location, harmony must be sought between the needs of the visitor, the place and the host community.

- In a dynamic world some change is inevitable and change can often be beneficial. Adaptation to change, however, should not be at the expense of any of these principles.

- The tourism industry, local authorities and environmental agencies all have a duty to respect the above principles and to work together to achieve their practical realisation.

The challenge facing the travel and tourism industry, especially the mass market tour operators, is to implement the principles of sustainable tourism for the benefit of present and future destinations and their host communities. Many communities in the UK and elsewhere have developed action plans, known as Local Agenda 21, to promote the idea of sustainable development locally.

Figure 2.17 *Cycling can contribute to sustainable tourism development*
© Steve Morgan/Sustrans

Activity 2.15

In relation to your own area, carry out some research to find out if the local authority has a policy on sustainable tourism development or a Local Agenda 21 group.

The mainstream travel and tourism industry is slowly waking up to the fact that it needs to give consideration to the potentially damaging effect that its operations can have on the environment and host communities. Pressure from a travelling public that is more environmentally and culturally aware is forcing airlines, tour operators, destination planners and accommodation providers to implement the principles of sustainable tourism. It is no longer uncommon to find statements of environmental policy in the holiday brochures of the mass market tour operators, giving advice to holidaymakers on how to protect local environments and respect local cultures and traditions.

browse this website

www.wttc.org

Industry example

Green Globe is an environmental management programme for the travel and tourism industry, dedicated to improving environmental practices and increasing environmental awareness within the industry. Developed by the World Travel and Tourism Council in 1994 as a direct response to Agenda 21, the programme has the following aims:

★ To increase systematically environmental responsiveness throughout the travel and tourism industry, its suppliers and customers

★ To encourage the widest possible environmental participation from companies of all sizes and sectors

★ To promote and emphasise the synergy between good environmental practice and good business

★ To identify and demonstrate, through the Green Globe logo, the commitment of travel and tourism companies to environmental improvement

★ To highlight leading examples of best practice and outstanding progress through Achievement Awards

continued

continued

As part of its programme of work to advance the cause of environmentally friendly and culturally sensitive tourism, Green Globe produces a leaflet for travellers, with a list of practical tips on holiday preparation and planning, including:

★ Look at the environmental content of brochures and ask companies about their environmental policy

★ Take time to think about your holiday plans

★ Take time to learn in advance about the place you intend to visit

★ Consider what you really need to take with you

★ Only take environmentally friendly detergents and shampoos

★ Choose natural oils

★ Take a camera to record any wildlife you see

★ Take a few small gifts from your home country

While on holiday, the Green Globe 'tips for travellers' leaflet suggests:

★ Look at personal travel options – choose public transport, cycling and walking, where appropriate

★ Ask your hosts where they go in their off-duty hours to enjoy their leisure

★ In rural areas, try to use small, locally owned accommodation

★ If beaches are dirty, let your travel representative know

★ Try out local food dishes and specialities

★ Buy locally made crafts

★ Ask your holiday representative about local environmental issues

★ Try to get to and from the airport by public transport

★ If travelling by car, ensure your vehicle is well maintained and energy efficient

Visitor and traffic management

The pressures on many of Britain's most beautiful landscapes and historic cities from the growth in visitor numbers has led to a range of measures to control the impact of people and their cars on the environment. Initiatives in rural areas, often sponsored by the Countryside Agency, have attempted to persuade visitors to leave their cars at home and use public transport instead, for example in the Peak District National Park. Some of the busiest roads in the National Parks are closed to traffic altogether at peak times, encouraging walkers and cyclists to explore areas free from noise and pollution. Historic cities such as Canterbury, Cambridge and York have developed integrated transport policies aimed at reducing the number of cars in the city centres and encouraging cycling and the use of public transport, including park-and-ride schemes.

browse this website

www.cambridge.
gov.uk/leisure/

Industry example

Cambridge City Council in its draft Local Plan proposes a transport strategy with the following elements:

★ Increasing the role played by public transport, particularly buses, including bus-based park-and-ride schemes and bus priorities

★ Supporting increased investment in local rail services

★ Limiting car use, particularly in the city centre and at the busiest times, by traffic management, parking controls and the investigation of road pricing

★ Providing improved facilities for people with disabilities, pedestrians and cyclists

★ Considering new road building only where this gives clear and sustainable benefits, particularly in terms of environmental protection and improvement

Environmental impact assessments

The rise in the awareness of, and concern for, the environment has meant that travel and tourism organisations are becoming more involved in measuring the environmental effects of their operations. This is often as a direct result of a national or local government regulation linked to the planning and development process. It is now very common for the developers of large tourism projects to be asked to carry out an appraisal of the costs and benefits of the development from an environmental point of view. The most common technique for carrying out such an evaluation is the environmental impact assessment (EIA), which can be applied to a wide range of planned tourism developments. The EIA is a structured process which aims to:

- **Identify the costs and benefits of a particular development**
- **Establish who will lose and who will gain if the development goes ahead**
- **Examine alternative courses of action and their likely impacts**
- **Consider ways of reducing impacts if the project is given the green light**

Environmental auditing

For tourism enterprises already in existence, the technique of environmental auditing is gaining in popularity. An environmental audit is an investigation of an organisation's policies and practices from the point of view of their impact on the local and global environment. Following on from some pioneering work carried out by the Inter-Continental Hotel Group, which produced a manual of procedures on the environmental consequences of all its business activities, many large hotel companies, airlines and tour operators are now investigating their activities and processes from an environmental standpoint. They examine everything from the fuel used in their cars to the type of detergents used for cleaning. Some organisations have used their concern for the environment as a marketing tool, hoping to capitalise on the growing market for tourism products and services that are truly respectful of the world in which we live.

Many major travel and tourism companies, including Thomson Holidays, British Airways and Inter-Continental Hotels, have developed environmental policies and train staff in their implementation. The British Airways 'Tourism for Tomorrow Awards' recognise environmentally responsible tourism developments on a worldwide basis. Recent global winners have included Whale Watch Kaikoura, New Zealand and the Sea to Sea Cycle Route across the north of England.

Case Study
Managing tourism development for the benefit of the community and the environment – the North Pennines Tourism Partnership

Lying across the boundaries of Cumbria, Northumberland and Durham, with the market town of Alston at its heart, the North Pennines is known as 'England's last wilderness'. The natural combination of high, uninhabited moorlands and fertile farming valleys embraces an area that is a haven to plants and wildlife, and provides visitors with a chance to experience life and culture in upland communities. Its conservation is of significant importance to both the local population and the nation as a whole, with its official designation as an Area of Outstanding Natural Beauty.

▶ THE PARTNERSHIP

The North Pennines Tourism Partnership (NPTP) was established in 1991 under the English Tourist Board's Tourism Development Action Programme (TDAP) initiative, which, in collaboration with a range of local authorities and agencies, provided pump-priming funding for an initial three-year period. The Partnership developed and implemented a co-ordinated work programme throughout the 1990s. The members of the Partnership included:

- ★ Cumbria and Northumbria Tourist Boards
- ★ The County Councils of Cumbria, Durham and Northumberland
- ★ Tynedale, Eden, Wear Valley and Teesdale District Councils
- ★ The Countryside Commission
- ★ Cumbria and Durham Training and Enterprise Councils (TECs)
- ★ English Tourist Board
- ★ Rural Development Commission

continued

continued

- ★ Parish councils
- ★ Private and voluntary sector individuals and groups

► **AIMS OF THE TOURISM PARTNERSHIP**

The North Pennines Tourism Partnership exists to help strengthen the rural economy and to care for the countryside. Within this overall aim, the Partnership is working towards the achievement of a number of specific objectives, which are to:

- ★ Increase general awareness of the North Pennines as an area and a visitor destination by co-ordinating appropriate marketing opportunities
- ★ Increase the range of active and informal countryside activities and promote these activities
- ★ Improve existing attractions and provide quality, small- to medium-scale attractions based on the area's heritage and attributes
- ★ Improve the quality and standards of existing accommodation and encourage modest expansion in key market sectors
- ★ Promote the development of rural arts and crafts
- ★ Help conserve the character of the landscape and heritage, and enhance the appearance of the area's towns and villages
- ★ Develop community involvement in, and private sector support for, tourism
- ★ Improve accessibility to business advice and training for the local tourism industry

► **COUNTRYSIDE RECREATION IN THE NORTH PENNINES**

In seeking to achieve its objective of increasing the range of active and informal countryside activities in the North

continued

continued

Pennines, the NPTP has adopted the following set of principles:

1 Encourage activities which draw upon and respect the particular character and attributes of the North Pennines AONB

2 Encourage quiet, non-motorised activities which do not adversely affect the ecology of the area, local communities, the enjoyment of other countryside users, or the interests of land managers

3 In order to minimise damage to the countryside, it will be necessary for some activities to be dispersed to spread the load, while others may need to be focused on adequately robust areas and/or at particular times of the year

4 Activities which simply use the area as a venue and do not depend upon its particular characteristics for full enjoyment of the activity should not be encouraged

5 Ensure that visitors are aware of the opportunities for recreation in the North Pennines and have the confidence, ability and understanding to enjoy it in a considerate way

6 Ensure that visitors are aware of and respect the ecological importance of the area

7 Encourage providers and participants in countryside recreation to recognise the human factors which have shaped and are still shaping the area, and highlight the link between conservation and existing management of the countryside, and its enjoyment by the public

8 Where possible, provision for informal recreation should be linked to public transport and this information highlighted in any promotional literature

9 Activities should be promoted only where the land

continued

continued

and wildlife affected are robust enough to withstand damage and disturbance, and where adequate provision has been made for management and maintenance

10 Promotion of activities should stress the special nature of the area and the need to respect and conserve the countryside

IMPLEMENTATION

In line with the above general principles, the Partnership has developed a number of strategies in order to further 'green tourism' in the area, namely:

★ To promote as visitor activities walking, cycling, riding and cross-country skiing

★ To promote visitor interests such as photography, painting, crafts, bird watching and practical conservation

★ To encourage the development of low impact themed holidays involving these activities and interests

★ To encourage accommodation providers to hire out or lend bicycles, binoculars, waterproofs, etc.

★ To encourage accommodation providers to take an interest in their local footpath network and the overall environment so as to be able to inform and encourage visitors

★ To guide organisers of events to act in accordance with these principles

★ To develop 'green charters' or codes of practice for adoption by outdoor activity centres, riding establishments and all other individuals or organisations who promote the use of the area for any interests

★ To encourage activity centres and establishments to

continued

continued

include practical conservation work in their programmes and develop links with countryside management projects

★ To incorporate the above in the Business and Training Initiative

(Information courtesy of North Pennines Tourism Partnership)

Case study discussion questions

1 What are the aims of the North Pennines Tourism Partnership?

2 How realistic is it to expect the Partnership to achieve each of its objectives?

3 What benefits are there to private sector travel and tourism organisations from being involved with the Partnership?

4 What types of training is such an initiative likely to offer to its members?

5 What techniques should be used to promote the area to visitors?

Worldwide travel destinations

3

Having a sound knowledge of popular destinations and what they offer visitors is very important for anybody working, or hoping to work, in the travel and tourism industry.

In this unit you will learn about the location and key features of travel destinations, investigating major continental European and long-haul destinations that are popular with British tourists. You will learn about the importance of developing your research skills in order to be able to access relevant information about destinations. You will also research main travel gateways and routes to destinations, as well as investigating the factors that affect the popularity of destinations.

This unit is divided into five main areas:

- **Research skills**
- **The location and features of major travel and tourism destinations in continental Europe**
- **The location and features of major overseas travel and tourism destinations**
- **Main travel and tourism gateways and routes**
- **The changing popularity of tourist destinations**

We guide you through each of these areas using examples from the travel and tourism industry. At the beginning of each section you will see a list of key topics to help you fully understand what you need to learn. Look out for the links to websites so that you can learn more about a particular travel and tourism destination, company or topic.

Research skills

Key topics in this section:

- **Introduction**
- **Sources of information**

Introduction

Everybody working in the travel and tourism industry needs to develop effective research skills in order to gather information for their work and to provide accurate and up-to-date information and advice to customers. Developing these skills will help not only in the work situation, but also when it comes to completing activities and assignments as part of your Vocational A-level course. Researching involves:

- ✪ **Being clear about what you are trying to find out:** When responding to customers' enquiries it is important to discover **exactly** what information they need, so as not to waste your time and theirs.

- ✪ **Knowing how to search for information:** Build up lists of useful sources of information, from other work colleagues, your own experiences of destinations, newspapers, magazines, television, the Internet, etc.

- ✪ **Deciding what might be useful:** Match what you find to the customers' needs and discard any information that is not useful (but remember that it may be useful for future enquiries!)

- ✪ **Collecting and presenting relevant information:** Accuracy and reliability are important when collecting travel and tourism information, particularly in relation to timetables, pricing, features of destinations, etc. You should present the information you find in a manner that is appropriate to the customer. This might be in a written letter, included in a brochure, as part of an e-mail, on the telephone, face to face over the counter or via a group presentation, for example at a promotional evening to launch a new range of holidays.

- ✪ **Drawing conclusions about your findings:** Study the information you find and draw conclusions that are valid in consultation with the customer.

- ✪ **Acknowledging your sources:** If you are compiling a written report it is usual to include details of where you found specific information, so that the reader can go back to the original source to check its authenticity or to get further details.

**browse these websites
for information on
worldwide destinations**

www.wtg-online.
com

www.travelocity.
com

www.tourist-offices.
org.uk

www.lonelyplanet.
com

www.oag.com

www.roughguides.
com

Having well developed research skills is particularly important when it comes to advising on travel destinations, since many people will not have visited a particular destination before and will, therefore, be relying on the knowledge and experience of members of staff to provide reliable information. Luckily, you are not expected to know everything about every destination in the world the minute you start a job in travel and tourism! Knowledge and experience of destinations grows over time. However, what you will be expected to know is where to get hold of information, i.e. the sources of information, which is the topic we look at next in this unit.

Sources of information

Staff working in travel and tourism must be able to refer to a wide variety of information sources when dealing with customers. These may be either primary or secondary. **Primary** sources include other people working in travel and tourism, for example a colleague working in the same organisation as you, and even customers! Frequent travellers can be a very valuable source of information on destinations, but you should always check the reliability of their information before acting on behalf of another customer. **Secondary sources** of information in travel and tourism include:

- ✪ **Gazetteers**
- ✪ **Brochures**
- ✪ **Maps**
- ✪ **Atlases**
- ✪ **Guidebooks**
- ✪ **Textbooks**
- ✪ **The Internet**
- ✪ **Computerised information systems**
- ✪ **Newspapers and magazines**
- ✪ **Trade journals**

Some information sources are used primarily by people working in the travel sector, while others are specific to tourism, as the next two sections of this unit demonstrate.

Travel information sources

Although much of the information used by travel professionals is computer-based, most staff will refer to a range of travel manuals and timetables in the course of their work. Manuals provide travel staff with general information on resorts, hotels and travel requirements. Some of the most common in use in agencies are:

- *Guide to International Travel*
- *Official Hotel Guide* (OHG) – formerly *Official Hotel and Resort Guide* (OHRG)
- *Travel Trade Directory*
- **Columbus Press *World Travel Guide* and *World Travel Atlas* (see Figure 3.1)**
- *ABC Guide to International Travel*
- *Hotel and Travel Index*
- *Agents' Hotel Gazetteer*
- *Apartment Gazetteer*
- *ABC Summer Holiday Guide* and *Winter Holiday Guide*

Access to timetables is very useful for staff putting together itineraries for customers and can save the time of contacting a number of individual transport operators. A basic set of timetables used by travel staff should include:

- *Thomas Cook European Rail Timetable*
- *Thomas Cook Overseas Timetable*
- *ABC Rail Guide*
- *British Rail Timetable*
- *ABC Shipping Guide*
- *ABC World Airways Guide*
- *Official Airline Guide* (OAG)
- **Individual airline timetables**

Figure 3.1 The *World Travel Atlas*
Courtesy of Columbus Press

Tourism information sources

Information specific to tourism is available from a wide range of commercial and public bodies, and includes:

- ✪ **Annual reports of the Scottish, Northern Ireland and Wales Tourist Boards, and the English Tourism Council**
- ✪ **BTA (British Tourist Authority) Annual Report**
- ✪ **The International Passenger Survey (IPS)**
- ✪ **The United Kingdom Tourism Survey (UKTS)**
- ✪ **The British National Travel Survey (BNTS)**
- ✪ *Business Monitor MQ6 – Overseas Travel and Tourism,* **published by The Stationery Office**
- ✪ **Annual reports of commercial travel and tourism organisations including British Airways, Thomson Holidays, Airtours, Thomas Cook, etc.**
- ✪ **Reports from consultants such as Mintel, Leisure Industries Research Centre, MORI, etc.**
- ✪ **Trade associations such as ABTA, AITO and IATA**
- ✪ **The Statistical Office of the European Communities (EUROSTAT)**
- ✪ **Professional bodies such as the Tourism Society, Institute of Travel and Tourism, and the Hotel, Catering and Institutional Management Association (HCIMA)**

Electronic information

The use of computers for accessing information is growing very rapidly in travel and tourism (see Figure 3.2).

Figure 3.2 *Computers are a valuable source of information*
Courtesy of Airtours

Companies such as travel agencies, tour operators, hotel groups and airlines have used centralised computer systems for many years to check availability, make bookings and search for information. Computer reservation systems (CRS), such as Galileo, Sabre and Worldspan, provide travel professionals with a wealth of information on airline services, destinations, accommodation, car hire and even passport and visa requirements. Travel agents use viewdata computer systems, for example Istel and Fastrak, to provide customers with up-to-date information on a wide range of holidays and other travel services.

The growth of the Internet has revolutionised the collection of information about travel and tourism products and services. Today, anybody with a computer and Internet connection can access a wealth of information on travel destinations, transport, accommodation and attractions, as well as making bookings direct with travel and tourism companies.

Industry example

Worldspan is a computer reservation system (CRS) that provides global communications and electronic distribution of information for the world's leading travel service providers. The Worldspan CRS supplies nearly 18,000 travel agencies with information on more than 455 airlines, 200 hotel companies, 44 car hire companies, 27 tour operators and 49 special travel service suppliers. The system is used in more than 60 countries worldwide, covering the USA, Africa, Canada, the Caribbean, Europe, Mexico, Asia Pacific and the Middle East.

browse these CRS websites

www.sabre.com
www.worldspan.com
www.galileo.com

Activity 3.1

Carry out some research of your own and make a list of specific information sources that a couple wanting a holiday in the Greek Islands could look through before contacting a travel agency to make a booking.

The location and features of major travel and tourism destinations in continental Europe

Key topics in this section:

- **Introduction**
- **Popularity of European destinations**
- **Spain – location, main tourist areas, climate, transport routes**
- **France – location, main tourist areas, climate, transport routes**

Introduction

Continental Europe has a wide variety of travel and tourism destinations that can be grouped as follows:

- ✪ **Towns and cities, e.g. Paris, Vienna, Madrid, Prague, Athens, Berlin, Rome – see Figure 3.3**
- ✪ **Seaside resorts, e.g. Benidorm, Nice, St Tropez**
- ✪ **Purpose-built resorts, e.g. Disneyland Paris, Center Parcs**
- ✪ **Countryside areas, e.g. forests, mountains, lakes·**
- ✪ **Historical/cultural destinations, e.g. Pompeii, Pisa, Madrid**

Each of these destination types has its own particular features, which can appeal to visitors in different ways. These features include:

- ✪ **Climate, e.g. sunshine hours, rainfall, humidity**
- ✪ **Topography, e.g. mountains, lakes, coastline**
- ✪ **Natural attractions, e.g. waterfalls, cliffs, forests**
- ✪ **Built attractions, e.g. stately homes, ancient monuments, theme parks**
- ✪ **Events, e.g. carnivals, music festivals, sporting events**
- ✪ **Food, drink and entertainment, e.g. cafés, restaurants, bars, nightclubs**
- ✪ **Types of accommodation, e.g. self-catering, serviced**
- ✪ **Types of transport, e.g. buses, ferries**
- ✪ **Accessibility to travel and tourism gateways, e.g. airports, seaports, land border crossings**

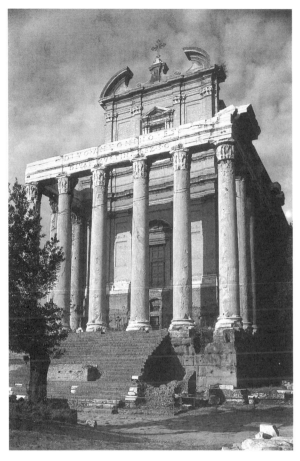

Figure 3.3   *The Forum in Rome*
Courtesy of the Italian State Tourist Board

Activity 3.2

Find out the capital cities of each of the countries shown in Figure 3.4.

It is important for anybody working, or wanting to work, in travel and tourism to understand the different features that give a destination its particular appeal to visitors. You must also appreciate that different destinations will be popular with different types of visitors. For example, a lively resort with lots of night life is unlikely to meet the needs of older people, who may prefer a quieter resort. Similarly, the needs of a backpacker travelling independently on a limited budget will be different from those of someone on an expensive, all-inclusive holiday.

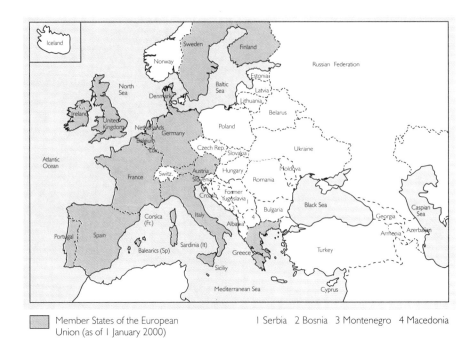

Member States of the European
Union (as of 1 January 2000)

1 Serbia   2 Bosnia   3 Montenegro   4 Macedonia

Figure 3.4   *Europe*

Popularity of European destinations

Europe is the world's number one destination for international travel. More people choose destinations in Europe for their holidays than any other world region. Continental Europe is very popular with British holidaymakers, as the data in Table 3.1 demonstrates.

Country	Visits (thousands)	% of overseas visits
Spain (incl. Balearic Islands)	8,513	32
France	3,246	12
Greece	1,706	6
Italy	1,142	4
Irish Republic	1,137	4
Portugal	988	4
Turkey	946	4
Cyprus	848	3
Malta	416	2
Germany	397	2

Source   BTA

Table 3.1   *Top ten European holiday destinations for the British, 1998*

Table 3.1 shows that Spain is the number one overseas holiday destination for British tourists, accounting for nearly one-third of all holidays abroad. France is the next most popular destination with more than 3.2 million visits in 1998.

Activity 3.3

Locate the ten countries listed in Table 3.1 on an outline map of Europe.

The remainder of this section looks in detail at these two destinations, concentrating on location, main tourist areas, climate and transport routes.

Spain

Location

Spain is situated in south-western Europe and has borders with Portugal, France and Andorra. Its northern coastline fronts the Bay of Biscay, while the southern coastal resorts are bathed by the warmer waters of the Mediterranean Sea (see Figure 3.5).

Spain is the most popular holiday destination with British tourists, who enjoy the warm climate and attractions of its Mediterranean coastline at resorts along

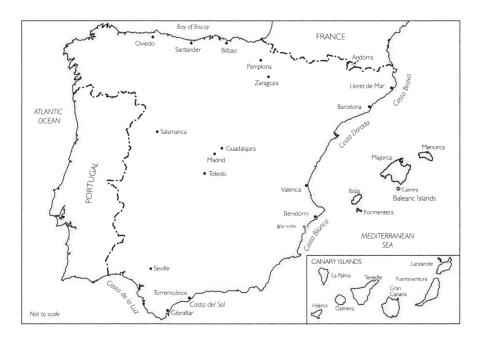

Figure 3.5 *Mainland Spain and its islands*

the Costa Brava, Costa Dorada, Costa Blanca and Costa del Sol, as well as its other coastal areas. Interior Spain is also gaining in popularity, with Madrid, the country's capital, attractive to both long-stay tourists and those on short breaks from the UK. Spain's northern coastline is relatively undiscovered, but extra promotion of regions such as Asturias, Galicia and Cantabria (see Figure 3.8 on page 164) is opening up their tourist potential to visitors.

The Canary Islands and the Balearic Islands are Spain's two principal island destinations (see Figure 3.5). Majorca, the largest of the Balearics, is the number one Spanish destination for UK tourists, while the Canaries attract visitors all year round, particularly in the winter season.

The main tourist areas in Spain

Spain can be divided up into a number of different holiday areas:

- ✪ **Mediterranean Spain – resorts along the east-facing Mediterranean coast**
- ✪ **Southern Spain – areas along the country's southern coastal strip**
- ✪ **Green Spain – northern regions bordering the Bay of Biscay and the Atlantic Ocean**
- ✪ **Inland Spain**
- ✪ **The Balearic Islands – Majorca, Menorca, Ibiza, Formentera and Cabrera**
- ✪ **The Canary Islands – Gran Canaria, Lanzarote, Fuerteventura, Tenerife, La Palma, Gomera and Hierro**

Mediterranean Spain

Mediterranean Spain stretches from the French border to the north to the Costa Calida in the south, and includes the well-known tourist areas of the Costa Brava, Costa Dorada and Costa Blanca (see Figure 3.6). All the major mass market tour operators, and many smaller specialist companies, offer package holidays to the most popular resorts in these areas, including Lloret de Mar, Tossa de Mar, Salou, Sitges, Benidorm, Calpe and Javea.

Southern Spain

This region includes the well-known resorts of the Costa del Sol, such as Torremolinos, Marbella, Fuengirola and Nerja, stretching east along the Mediterranean from Gibraltar, and the Costa de la Luz on the Atlantic shores of southern Spain (see Figure 3.7).

Green Spain

This is the name given to the region in the north-west of the country fronting the Bay of Biscay (see Figure 3.8). Its name derives from the nature of the

Figure 3.6 *Mediterranean Spain*

Activity
3.4

Carry out some further research to discover which tour operators feature the regions of Green Spain in their programmes. Don't forget to investigate the ferry companies' brochures.

Figure 3.7 *Southern Spain*

landscape, with wooded valleys and lush meadows. The Spanish National
Tourist Office promotes the area as a 'green tourism' destination, in contrast to
the mass tourism in the south of the country.

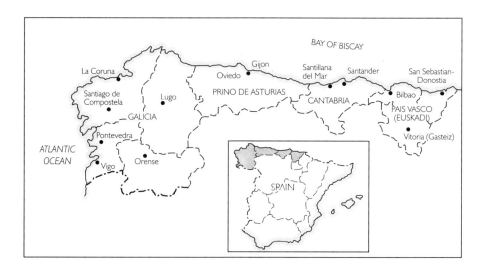

Figure 3.8 *Green Spain*

Inland Spain

The Spanish National Tourist Office has been working in partnership with cities, town and rural areas to increase the marketing and promotion of Spain's interior, as a way of spreading the economic benefits of tourism. Madrid occupies the geographical centre of the Iberian peninsula and is a popular leisure and business travel destination. Other important tourist centres include Toledo, Zaragoza, Seville, Pamplona, Salamanca and Guadalajara (see Figure 3.5 on page 161). The introduction of paradores – state-operated tourist accommodation in a variety of historic buildings – has helped many parts of inland Spain to develop their tourist potential. Visitors to the interior are attracted by the dramatic scenery, rich cultural heritage and regional customs.

The Balearic Islands

The Balearic Island chain is located in the Mediterranean Sea off Spain's eastern shore, some 240 kilometres from Valencia (see Figure 3.5 on page 161). With its warm climate, picturesque beaches and excellent facilities for visitors, the Balearics is one of Spain's foremost tourist areas. The four principal Balearic Islands are Majorca, Menorca, Ibiza and Formentera (see Figure 3.9).

Palma de Majorca (known to the British simply as Palma) is the capital of the archipelago and an important port in the Mediterranean. Among its architectural treasures are the Gothic cathedral, the fourteenth-century Bellver Castle and the ancient market area. The island as a whole is the most popular overseas holiday destination for British tourists, who frequent a number of resorts in the south and north of Majorca, including Magaluf, Palma Nova, Santa Ponsa, Cala d'Or, Alcudia and Puerto Pollensa.

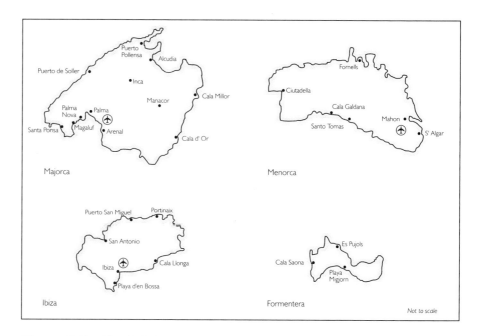

Figure 3.9 *The Balearic Islands*

Menorca is regarded as a quieter holiday island than Majorca, boasting a variety of resorts used by the major tour operators, such as Cala Galdana, S'Algar and Santo Tomas. Mahon is the capital of Menorca and has a layout and architecture that combines typical island features with British characteristics, the result of a long relationship with the UK dating back more than 250 years. Ibiza is the capital of the island of the same name, with resorts ranging from the lively San Antonio in the west of the island to quieter, more sophisticated areas in the north and south, including Playa d'en Bossa and Puerto San Miguel. Formentera is a small, uncrowded island with access from Ibiza by ferry.

The Canary Islands

Volcanic in origin, the Canary Islands are a popular winter sun destination for the British, including those on cruises. The islands are located some 1500 kilometres south-east of the Spanish mainland in the waters of the Atlantic Ocean. There are seven islands in the chain and they are divided administratively into two provinces:

⊛ **Las Palmas – which includes the islands of Gran Canaria, Fuerteventura and Lanzarote**

⊛ **Santa Cruz de Tenerife – governing the four islands of Tenerife, La Palma, Gomera and Hierro**

Figure 3.10 shows the position of the seven islands and a selection of popular resort areas. Tenerife is the biggest of the Canary Islands and boasts a number of resorts used by the major tour operators, including Puerto de la Cruz and Playa de las Americas. It has two international airports, one in the south and one in the north of the island.

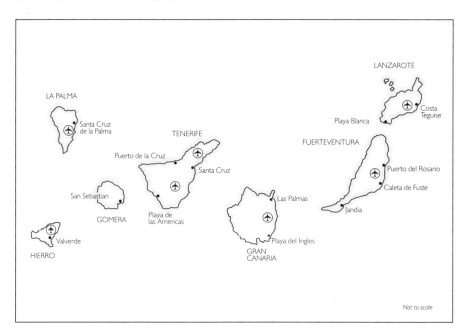

Figure 3.10 *The Canary Islands*

Activity
3.5

Analyse the brochures of a range of tour operators that feature the Canary Islands. Identify the products they offer and illustrate how these relate to the needs of different sectors of the market.

Climate

The climate in mainland Spain varies from temperate in the north to dry and hot in the south. The warmest months are from April to October. It can become excessively hot in the peak summer months of July and August throughout the country, except for the coastal regions. The Balearic Islands enjoy a temperate, Mediterranean climate throughout the year. The cooling influence of the sea ensures that, even in high summer, temperatures do not become excessive. Mild winters make the island resorts, and the south of the Spanish mainland, popular off-season destinations. The climate in the northern Canary Islands is sub-tropical, while the southern islands tend to be hotter and drier, although rainfall is generally low throughout the islands. Table 3.2 shows the annual temperatures throughout mainland Spain and the islands.

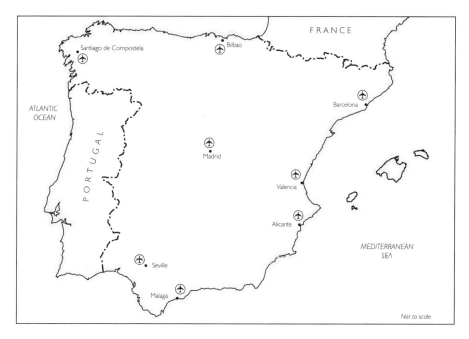

Figure 3.11   *Principal airports of mainland Spain*

Town and area		Jan	Feb	Mar	Apr	May	Jun	Jul	Aug	Sep	Oct	Nov	Dec
Cape Bagur:	Max.	14	14	16	17	20	23	27	26	25	21	16	15
Costa Brava	Min.	6	6	8	9	18	16	18	21	17	13	9	7
Barcelona:	Max.	13	14	16	18	21	25	28	28	25	21	16	13
Costa Dorada	Min.	6	7	9	11	14	18	21	21	19	15	11	8
Valencia:	Max.	15	16	18	20	23	26	29	29	27	23	19	16
Costa del Azahar	Min.	6	6	8	10	13	16	19	20	18	15	10	7
Alicante:	Max.	16	17	20	22	26	29	32	32	30	25	21	17
Costa Blanca	Min.	7	6	8	10	13	15	19	20	18	15	10	7
Murcia:	Max.	15	16	18	19	23	25	29	29	27	24	20	17
Costa Calida	Min.	5	5	8	9	13	17	20	20	18	14	10	7
Malaga:	Max.	17	17	19	21	23	27	29	30	29	23	20	17
Costa del Sol	Min.	9	9	11	13	15	19	21	22	20	16	12	9
Cádiz:	Max.	15	14	18	21	23	27	29	30	29	23	20	17
Costa de la Luz	Min.	8	7	11	12	15	18	20	20	19	15	12	9
Santander:	Max.	12	12	15	15	17	19	22	22	21	18	15	12
Cornisa Cantabria	Min.	7	7	8	10	11	14	16	18	15	12	10	8
Pontevedra:	Max.	14	15	16	18	20	24	25	26	24	20	16	14
Galicia	Min.	3	4	5	7	10	12	13	13	12	9	6	5
Madrid:	Max.	9	11	15	18	21	27	31	30	25	19	13	9
Castilla	Min.	1	2	5	12	10	14	17	17	14	10	5	2
Seville:	Max.	15	17	21	23	26	32	35	36	32	26	20	16
Inland Andalucia	Min.	6	6	9	11	13	17	21	20	18	14	10	7
Majorca:	Max.	14	15	17	19	22	26	29	29	27	23	18	15
Balearic Islands	Min.	6	6	8	10	13	17	19	20	18	14	10	8
Las Palmas:	Max.	21	21	22	23	23	24	25	26	26	27	24	22
Canary Islands (East)	Min.	16	16	16	17	18	19	21	22	22	21	18	17
Tenerife:	Max.	20	21	22	23	24	26	28	29	28	26	24	21
Canary Islands (West)	Min.	14	14	15	16	17	19	20	21	21	19	17	16

Source Spanish National Tourist Offfice

Table 3.2 *Average temperatures in Spain (°C)*

Transport routes

The great majority of British tourists travelling to Spain go by air, arriving at one of the principal airports shown in Figure 3.11. The Balearic Islands and the Canary Islands are also well served by airports, as shown in Figures 3.9 and 3.10 respectively, making them particularly accessible to UK tourists.

Travel from the UK to Spain by ferry is possible, using either the 24-hour Plymouth to Santander Brittany Ferries service or the slightly longer Portsmouth to Bilbao service operated by P&O. For those visitors wishing to drive from the UK to Spain, the route is via France. If using autoroutes, access to the north of Spain is via Toulouse or Bordeaux, while travellers to eastern Spain should head for Toulouse or Barcelona. Rail travel to Spain is again via France, with direct routes from Paris to both Barcelona and Madrid. Some coach operators, for example Eurolines, operate scheduled coach services to Spain from London, with connections elsewhere in the UK.

France

Location

France is the largest country in Europe, lying on the western edge of the European land mass and has boundaries with Belgium, Luxembourg, Germany, Switzerland, Italy, Andorra and Spain. It also has jurisdiction over the Mediterranean island of Corsica. France has more than 3,000 kilometres of coastline, fronting the Atlantic Ocean to the west, the English Channel to the north and the Mediterranean Sea to the south (see Figure 3.12).

Figure 3.12 also shows a selection of the most popular holiday regions in France, although some might say that the whole of the country is the perfect holiday destination given the variety of its scenery, climate, gastronomy and cultural attractions. France is the second most popular holiday destination for British people, and with the opening of the Channel Tunnel and the introduction of the Eurostar rail service from London to Paris, its popularity is growing.

The main tourist areas in France
Brittany

Occupying the north-western tip of France, Brittany is a popular destination for British tourists who want to be near the coast. The landscape is not dissimilar to England's west country, with its rugged coastline and rocky headlands. Inland lie lush, green fields that support Brittany's agricultural economy, as well as reminders of the area's Celtic traditions. Fishing ports are found all round Brittany's coastline, from St Malo in the north to Concarneau on the Atlantic coastline. The area is popular with British campers and caravanners, who do not have to venture too far from home to experience the French way of life. Important tourist resorts include Quimper, Benodet and Carnac.

Figure 3.12 *Holiday regions in France*

The Loire Valley

The Loire river rises in the Massif Central and flows in a westward direction to meet the Atlantic Ocean at La Baule. This is one of the most popular tourist regions in France, noted for its châteaux, vineyards and gently undulating valleys. The main concentration of châteaux, often located in prominent hill top positions overlooking the river, lies between Angers and Orléans. The Loire is also popular with garden lovers, with many châteaux and country houses with landscaped gardens open to the public. The region of Western Loire, where the river flows into the Atlantic, marks the boundary between the temperate climate of the north and the warmer maritime climate of the south of the country.

The French Alps

The highest point in the French Alps is Mont Blanc in the Savoy Alps, rising to 4,807 metres above sea level. From this high point in the Alpine region the mountains slope gently to the south, terminating in the Basse Alps in Provence close to the Mediterranean coastline. Thus the area welcomes visitors all year round, attracting skiers in the winter and tourists in the summer months to the coastal resorts and hinterland. Popular ski resorts in the French Alps include Courcheval, Chamonix, Val d'Isère, Meribel and Alpe d'Huez.

The Mediterranean coast

France's Mediterranean coastline stretches from its border with Italy in the east to the boundary with Spain in the west. It includes the famous Côte d'Azur located between the Italian border and Marseille, with its sophisticated resorts such as Cannes, Nice and St Tropez. Further west along the coast near Marseille is the Camargue, an area known throughout the world for its wild horses, bulls and flocks of pink flamingos. The coastline west of Marseille is less popular with foreign tourists, although French people enjoy its landscape of marshy lowlands and shallow lagoons. The whole of the Mediterranean coastline of France is a haven for the sailing fraternity, from the multi-million pound craft found in the up-market resorts of the Côte d'Azur to the small pleasure boats found in the western area.

The Pyrenees

The Pyrenees is a 400-kilometre chain of mountains running along the border between France and Spain. The area is important for summer tourists, who are attracted by the landscape of deep gorges, wooded valleys and fast-flowing streams. The mountains rise to over 3,000 metres and have sufficient snow cover in the winter to support a healthy winter ski market. Popular ski resorts in the Pyrenees include Font Romeu, Cauterets, Luchon and La Mongie. The area also benefits from hot thermal springs, a fact that is reflected in many of the place names, e.g. Les Eaux Bonnes, Aulus-les-Bains and Ax-les-Thermes.

Main cities

Paris is one of the world's finest cities, famed for its variety of attractions including the Arc de Triomphe, Eiffel Tower, Pompidou Centre, the Louvre and Notre Dame, to name but a few. Paris is a very popular short break destination for UK tourists who have the choice of travelling by air, rail, ferry, coach or taking their own car. Many large and small tour operators feature a range of accommodation in the capital. Twenty miles east of Paris is Disneyland Paris, accessible by air, autoroute and rail services. Other cities in France popular with UK tourists include Bordeaux, Calais, Dijon, Lyon, Marseille, Nantes, Nice, Perpignan, Poitiers, Rennes, Strasbourg and Toulouse.

Activity 3.6

Carry out some further research and list the principal attractions of the main French tourist cities listed above.

Climate

France's climate varies between cool temperate in the north of the country to a Mediterranean climate in the south. The Jura Mountains have an alpine climate, while Lorraine is relatively mild due to its sheltered position. In the

	Jan	Feb	Mar	Apr	May	Jun	Jul	Aug	Sep	Oct	Nov	Dec
Paris/Ile-de-France	7.5	7.1	10.2	15.7	16.6	23.4	25.1	25.6	20.9	16.5	11.7	7.8
Alsace	5.5	5.3	9.3	13.7	15.8	23.0	24.1	26.3	21.2	14.9	7.6	4.7
Aquitaine	10.0	9.4	12.2	19.5	18.0	23.7	27.2	25.7	24.2	19.7	15.4	11.0
Auvergne	8.0	6.4	10.1	15.9	17.1	24.2	27.0	24.5	23.3	17.0	11.0	8.3
Brittany	9.3	8.6	11.1	17.1	16.0	22.7	25.1	24.1	21.2	16.5	12.1	9.3
Burgundy	6.1	5.9	10.3	15.3	15.8	23.8	25.8	26.1	21.2	15.5	9.1	6.2
Champagne-Ardenne	6.2	5.6	8.9	13.8	15.1	22.5	23.8	24.9	19.3	15.0	9.6	6.2
Corsica	12.9	12.2	14.1	16.5	21.0	25.5	28.1	27.9	25.7	21.5	18.1	14.5
Franche-Comté	5.4	4.8	9.8	14.6	15.5	23.0	25.0	26.5	21.8	15.2	9.6	5.8
Languedoc-Roussillon	12.4	11.5	12.5	17.6	20.1	26.5	28.4	28.1	26.1	21.1	15.8	13.5
Limousin	6.1	6.1	9.6	16.1	14.9	22.1	24.8	23.6	21.0	16.2	12.8	8.5
Lorraine	5.5	5.3	9.3	13.7	15.8	23.0	24.1	26.3	21.2	14.9	7.6	4.7
Midi-Pyrenees	10.0	9.0	12.3	18.3	19.1	26.4	27.6	27.2	25.0	19.3	15.5	9.8
Nord/Pas-de-Calais	6.6	5.6	8.3	13.7	14.9	21.5	22.7	24.0	19.3	15.3	8.3	6.9
Normandy	7.6	6.4	8.4	13.0	14.0	20.0	21.6	22.0	18.2	14.5	10.8	7.9
Picardy	6.6	5.6	8.3	13.7	14.9	21.5	22.7	24.0	19.3	15.3	8.3	6.9
Poitou-Charentes	10.0	8.7	11.7	18.2	16.4	22.4	25.3	24.6	22.0	18.4	14.0	9.8
Provence	12.2	11.9	14.2	18.5	20.8	26.6	28.1	28.4	25.2	22.1	16.8	14.1
Rhône Valley	7.4	6.7	10.8	15.8	17.3	25.6	27.6	27.6	23.5	16.5	10.4	7.8
Riviera/Côte d'Azur	12.2	11.9	14.2	18.5	20.8	26.6	28.1	28.4	25.2	22.2	16.8	14.1
Savoy & Dauphiny Alps	3.1	3.7	7.9	13.8	15.7	22.4	26.8	25.7	22.7	15.9	10.7	6.3
Loire Valley	7.8	6.8	10.3	16.1	16.4	23.6	25.8	24.5	21.1	16.2	11.2	7.0
Western Loire	9.9	8.6	11.3	17.7	16.7	23.3	25.7	24.6	21.8	16.9	12.4	9.5

Source   Direction de la météorologie de France, courtesy of the French Government Tourist Office *Traveller in France* Publication, London

Table 3.3   *Average temperatures in France (°C)*

south, the mountainous areas are cooler with heavy snow in winter in the Alps. The climate of the western coastal regions is influenced by the Atlantic Ocean, giving relatively mild, temperate conditions with rainfall distributed throughout the year. Summers can be very hot and sunny. The holiday regions in the French Riviera and Provence enjoy a Mediterranean climate, although strong winds can occur throughout the region, the most famous being 'the Mistral'. Table 3.3 shows the average temperatures during the year throughout a number of French regions.

Transport routes

There are a number of ferry companies competing on the cross-Channel routes between England and France, including Sea France, Brittany Ferries, Hoverspeed and P&O Stena. Add to this the vehicle shuttle service operated through the Channel Tunnel (*Le Shuttle*), and the permutations of date and time of travel for those travelling to France in their own cars are seemingly endless. The main Channel ferry points of entry into France include:

- **Roscoff**
- **St Malo**
- **Cherbourg**
- **Caen**
- **Le Havre**
- **Dieppe**
- **Boulogne**
- **Calais**
- **Dunkirk**

France has an excellent internal rail service, including the TGV (*train de grande vitesse*) linking major cities, plus a network of provincial services. Access from the UK is via the Channel Tunnel on the Eurostar service from Waterloo to either Paris or Lille. Motorail services carry cars, motorbikes and passengers overnight from Calais, Lille and Paris to all the main holiday areas. Bicycle and car hire is available at many stations in France.

Principal international airports for those flying from the UK on charter or scheduled services include:

- **Bordeaux**
- **Lille**
- **Lyon**
- **Marseille**
- **Nantes**
- **Nice**

- **Paris (Charles de Gaulle)**
- **Paris (Orly)**
- **Toulouse**

A scheduled coach service between the UK and France is offered by Eurolines, operating over 70 services to Calais, Amiens, Perpignan, Strasbourg, Toulouse and Tours. Hoverspeed also operates a London to Paris coach service as part of its hovercraft operation.

Activity 3.7

Draw the location of the main French Channel ports on an outline map of the country and indicate alongside each port which ferry company services the route. Locate also the principal international airports of France on the same map.

Activity 3.8

Using the same format as in the examples of Spain and France above (i.e. location, main tourist areas, climate, transport routes), carry out some research into one other European country that is popular with the British. Make your choice from the list in Table 3.1 (see page 160) and use the sources of information mentioned at the beginning of this unit (see page 154) as the starting point for your research.

The location and features of major overseas travel and tourism destinations

Key topics in this section:

- **Introduction – the growth in long-haul destinations**
- **USA – location, main tourist areas, climate, transport routes**
- **The Caribbean – location, main tourist areas, climate, transport routes**
- **Australia – location, main tourist areas, climate, transport routes**

Introduction – the growth in long-haul destinations

Advances in aircraft technology, coupled with low aircraft charter prices from the major tour operators, have led to a steep rise in the demand for package holidays to long-haul destinations. The USA is the number one long-haul destination for UK holidaymakers, due in no small part to the popularity of Florida as an all-year-round holiday destination (see Table 3.4). The Caribbean is also growing in popularity, with new destinations such as Cuba and the Dominican Republic attracting many British tourists for the first time. The Far East is an increasingly popular long-haul destination, not only with package holidaymakers but also for those travelling independently; Thailand, Malaysia and Singapore are particularly popular with British tourists. Goa, on India's west coast, has long been a favourite destination for independent travellers, but its popularity with package holidaymakers looking for winter sunshine is growing steadily. On the African continent, Kenya and the Gambia are following suit, while the change in political climate in South Africa has meant that many UK holidaymakers are eager to explore the country for the first time. The USA and Canada are both emerging as attractive ski-ing alternatives to the pistes of Europe. As for cruising, the Caribbean remains a firm favourite with UK tourists, and the west coast of America is the third most popular fly-cruise destination with the British.

Locate the ten countries listed in Table 3.4 on an outline map of the world.

Country	Visits (thousands)	% of overseas visits
USA	2,214	8
Caribbean	577	2
Canada	340	1
Tunisia	329	1
India	235	1
Australia	165	1
South Africa	165	1
Mexico	157	1
Thailand	140	1
Egypt	94	<1

Adapted from BTA data

Table 3.4 *Top ten long-haul holiday destinations for the British, 1998*

The remainder of this section looks in detail at three of the most popular long haul destinations with the British – the USA, the Caribbean and Australia – investigating the location, main tourist areas, climate and transport routes of each.

USA

Location

The United States of America is one of the largest countries in the world, covering the greater part of the North American continent, and has borders with Canada to the north and Mexico to the south. Its eastern seaboard fronts the Atlantic Ocean, the west coast faces the Pacific Ocean, while the southern shores are bathed by the warm waters of the Gulf of Mexico (see Figure 3.13). The state of Alaska is separate from the rest of the USA, being located adjacent to Canada in the north-west corner of the continent. The island state of Hawaii is found more than 2,000 miles from mainland USA in the Pacific Ocean. The total population of the USA is more than 250 million.

The country has a wide diversity of terrain, including the gentle landscape of the New England states, the grandeur of the Rocky Mountains, the deserts and canyons of Arizona, the Everglades in Florida, the Great Lakes on the northern border and the fertile plains of the Mid West. As well as the country's natural attractions, tourists from all over the world are drawn by such famous cities as New York, Las Vegas, San Francisco, New Orleans, Boston, Los Angeles and

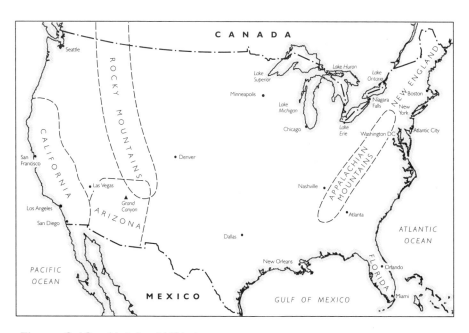

Figure 3.13 *Mainland USA*

Washington DC. Popular built attractions include Walt Disney World, Universal Studios, the Golden Gate Bridge, the Statue of Liberty and the White House, to name but a few.

The main tourist areas in the USA

Florida

The popularity of Florida with British tourists has contributed greatly to the USA becoming the number one long-haul destination for UK travellers. Located in south-eastern USA, 100 miles north of the Tropics, Florida's east coast borders the Atlantic Ocean, while its western shores are bathed by the waters of the Gulf of Mexico. Tourism is the state's largest industry, generating more than $30 billion in 1992 and employing 657,000 people across a range of sectors including accommodation, attractions and transportation.

Florida offers visitors a blend of natural, scenic beauty coupled with an array of tourist attractions that any country in the world would find hard to beat. Orlando is the centre of the state's tourist attractions and is home to the world famous Walt Disney World, attracting more than 20 million visitors every year. Some of Florida's best-known tourist attractions are shown in Figure 3.14.

Florida offers visitors a variety of terrain, including more than 10,000 freshwater lakes, over 1,800 miles of coastline, swamps, hills, forests, countless small islands and 1,000 miles of sandy beaches. Miami and Miami Beach are twin gateways to the Florida peninsula, as well as being the world's biggest cruise port. They offer tourists year-round attractions, including the nearby

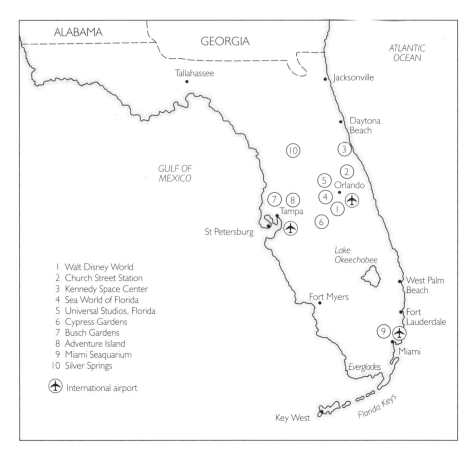

ALABAMA

GEORGIA

ATLANTIC OCEAN

Tallahassee

Jacksonville

Daytona Beach

⑩

③

GULF OF MEXICO

②

⑤ Orlando

④

✈

①

⑦ ⑧

Tampa

⑥

✈

St Petersburg

Lake Okeechobee

West Palm Beach

Fort Myers

Fort Lauderdale

⑨ ✈

Miami

Everglades

Key West

Florida Keys

1 Walt Disney World
2 Church Street Station
3 Kennedy Space Center
4 Sea World of Florida
5 Universal Studios, Florida
6 Cypress Gardens
7 Busch Gardens
8 Adventure Island
9 Miami Seaquarium
10 Silver Springs

✈ International airport

Figure 3.14 *Florida's best-known tourist attractions*

Everglades National Park. The world famous Florida Keys stretch for nearly 200 miles, terminating in Key West with its unique wildlife and architecture.

Sometimes referred to as 'the sunshine state', climate is a key feature of the state's popularity, with long summers and mild winters. Average annual temperatures in summer are around 27°C and in the winter approximately 12°C. It is, however, affected by hurricanes and less severe tropical storms, giving heavy rainfall during the months of July and October.

Activity
3.10

Investigate which major UK tour operators and airlines offer programmes to Florida and draw up a comparative chart outlining price, features, resorts used, departure/arrival airports and accommodation offered.

The eastern seaboard

The cities and states on the east coast of the USA are important destinations for UK visitors for long holidays and, increasingly, short breaks. The area includes the New England states of Maine, Vermont, New Hampshire, Massachusetts, Connecticut and Rhode Island, and the cities of New York, Boston, Philadelphia, Washington DC, Baltimore, Pittsburgh, Cleveland and Newport. Inland, the area has a wealth of natural attractions, including the Great Lakes, Niagara Falls, the Appalachian Mountains, the Adirondacks and Catskill ranges, plus a number of National Parks (see Figure 3.15).

New York is the largest city in the USA and third largest in the world. Among its numerous attractions are the Statue of Liberty, the Empire State Building, Broadway, the World Trade Center, the Lincoln Center, the United Nations and Greenwich Village, to name but a few. The city is famous for its ethnic quarters, including Chinatown and Little Italy in Lower Manhattan, and Germantown along 86th street. Boston is the state capital of Massachusetts and the gateway to New England. It is the cradle of American democracy; the Boston Tea Party began the move towards the declaration of independence in 1776. It is the oldest of US cities and has a distinctly British atmosphere. Washington DC (District of Columbia) is the capital of the USA and offers a variety of tourist attractions, including the White House, the Lincoln Memorial, Arlington Cemetery, the Capitol Building, the Washington Monument, Potomac Park, the Smithsonian Institute and the Jefferson Memorial.

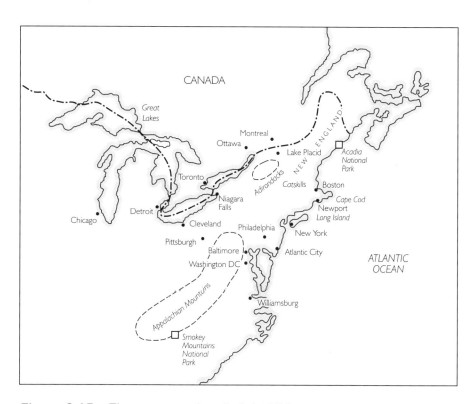

Figure 3.15 *The eastern seaboard of the USA*

The climate of the eastern seaboard and its hinterland provides opportunities for both coastal, summer tourism and winter sports activity in the mountains. Much of the region experiences warm, sunny conditions from May to October, with average temperatures peaking at 22° C in July and August. Winters are cold, with temperatures generally below freezing between December and March.

The west coast

The west coast of the USA runs from the border with Canada in the north to the Mexican boundary in the south (see Figure 3.16).

The region includes the state of California, the most populous state in the USA

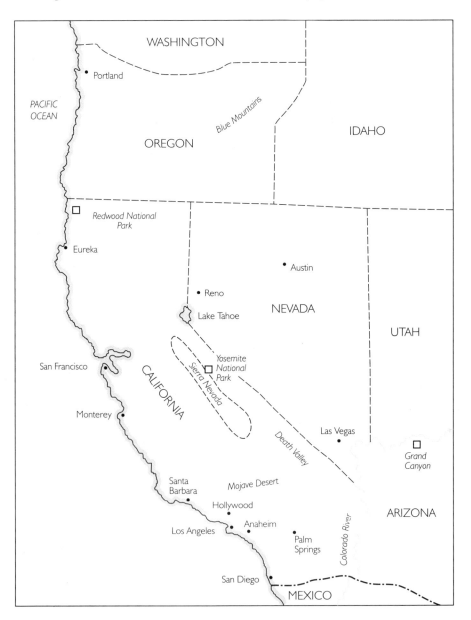

Figure 3.16 *West coast states*

and the country's leading tourist area, famous for its sunny climate, excellent beaches, cosmopolitan cities, wine growing areas, mountain ranges and National Parks. Known as the 'golden state', on account of its sunny climate and links with pioneering for gold, California is also synonymous with glamour and the film industry, being the home of Hollywood, the location of the most famous film studios in the world. The west coast also has some of the world's leading cities, including Los Angeles, San Francisco, Las Vegas and Seattle.

Los Angeles is the principal gateway to southern California and has the second highest population of any city in the USA. It is best known for the Hollywood film studios, exclusive Beverly Hills community and the original Disneyland theme park at Anaheim, some 25 miles south-east of Los Angeles centre. The city also has a number of excellent swimming and surfing beaches, including Laguna Beach, Long Beach, Malibu Beach and Redondo Beach.

San Francisco acts as the main gateway to northern California, Nevada and Oregon. The city has developed on a peninsula, with the Pacific Ocean to the west and San Francisco Bay to the east, the entrance to the Bay being spanned by the famous Golden Gate Bridge. The Chinatown district of the city has the largest Chinese community outside Asia, with a variety of theatres, museums and authentic eating places. The former prison island of Alcatraz in San Francisco Bay has been transformed into a major attraction for visitors. There are a number of natural attractions close to the San Francisco metropolis, including Sequoia, Kings Canyon and Yosemite National Parks, each with a mixture of pine forests, glacial valleys and waterfalls.

Las Vegas is the largest city in Nevada and one of the major gambling and entertainment centres in the world. Hotels, casinos, restaurants, nightclubs and entertainment venues are found on 'the Strip', a section of Las Vegas Boulevard South. Lake Tahoe spans the state boundary between Nevada and California, and is located in one of the USA's main mountain resort areas, with year-round attractions and activities.

Seattle, in the north-west corner of the USA, is the principal international gateway to the state of Washington and the Pacific north-west region of the country, as well as being close the city of Vancouver in British Columbia, Canada. The city is surrounded by the waters of Lake Washington and Puget Sound, with a backdrop of the Cascades and Olympic Mountains. The Seattle Center is the cultural heart of the city, the home of opera, ballet and theatre. Seattle is also well known for its associations with the sea, with harbour tours and fishing trips available to visitors.

Climate

The size of the US land mass, and its varied topographical structure, results in wide variations in the country's climate. The north-east of the country, including the New England states, has warm winters, with temperatures close to 30°C in the summer months, but experiences cold winters with freezing temperatures. Rainfall in this area is spread evenly throughout the year and humidity is generally high in August and September. The southern states of the USA, including Florida, Georgia and Alabama, have hot summers and mild winters. Heavy rainfall in the summer months is not uncommon and the area can be very humid at this time of year. California and other south-western states have hot summers and mild winters, with rainfall generally confined to the winter months. Humidity is high in the summer months, especially in May, June, July and August. The desert regions of the interior are hot and dry throughout the year, while mountain regions, including the Rockies, experience very low winter temperatures.

Transport routes

The great majority of UK visitors travelling to the USA arrive by air. There are currently 20 international 'gateway' airports spread throughout the country, located in or close to the following cities:

✪ **Atlanta**	✪ **Baltimore**
✪ **Boston**	✪ **Chicago**
✪ **Dallas/Fort Worth**	✪ **Denver**
✪ **Detroit**	✪ **Houston**
✪ **Los Angeles**	✪ **Miami**
✪ **Minneapolis/St Paul**	✪ **New York/Newark**
✪ **Orlando**	✪ **Philadelphia**
✪ **Phoenix**	✪ **San Francisco**
✪ **Seattle**	✪ **St Louis**
✪ **Tampa**	✪ **Washington**

Activity
3.11

Locate the international airports listed above on an outline map of the USA, including the full name and three letter code of each airport.

The network of internal air services in the USA is very comprehensive and competition between airlines has kept prices low for domestic travel. The size of the country and often long distances between major population centres has meant that air travel has become the accepted way to travel for Americans, whether for business or leisure purposes. The US passenger rail network is not extensive across the whole country, but there are good services in the densely populated north-east of the country.

Activity 3.12

Using the same format as in the example of the USA above (i.e. location, main tourist areas, climate, transport routes), carry out some research into Canada as a tourist destination. Use the sources of information mentioned at the beginning of this unit (see page 154) as the starting point for your research.

The Caribbean

Location

The Caribbean is one of the fastest growing long-haul destinations for UK tourists, who are attracted by its warm climate, unspoilt beaches and relaxed lifestyle. The major tour operators now offer cut-price package holidays and charter flights to the Caribbean, which is a major centre for cruising. The area also has a significant VFR market from the UK.

The Caribbean islands are located along a 2500-mile long arc in the Caribbean Sea in the western Atlantic Ocean, sweeping eastwards from Florida to the

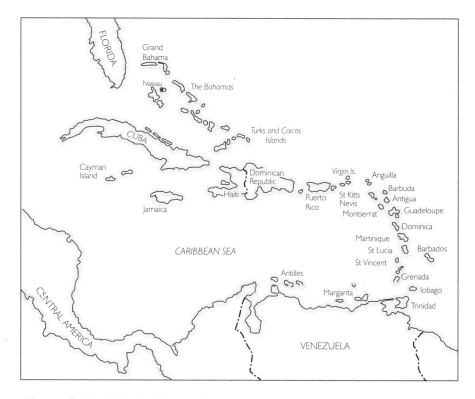

Figure 3.17 *The Caribbean islands*

coast of Venezuela in South America (see Figure 3.17). The islands were colonised from the sixteenth century onwards by a number of European countries, including Britain, France, Spain, Portugal and the Netherlands. Many of the islands retain the character and customs of their colonising countries, making visitors feel immediately at ease when on holiday. Each island is very different in character, from bustling destinations to undiscovered island paradises well away from the pressures of modern life. As well as their natural attractions, the Caribbean islands offer visitors a variety of water-based sports and activities, including scuba diving, sailing, wind surfing and fishing.

The main tourist areas in the Caribbean

The Bahamas

The Bahamas are a group of more than 700 islands spread across a 750-mile stretch of the Atlantic Ocean between Florida and Haiti. Many are low lying and are covered with lush vegetation. The beaches in the Bahamas are among the finest in the world, attracting tourists throughout the year from all parts of the globe. Most visitors to the Bahamas stay in the main resort areas on New Providence and Grand Bahama Islands, including the capital Nassau. The islands are also a magnet for cruises, being the first port of call for many ships that set sail from Florida. Watersports are well catered for in the Bahamas, with sailing, parasailing, powerboat racing, diving, swimming, snorkelling and water skiing all widely available.

Barbados

Barbados is the most easterly of the Caribbean islands and is part of the Windward Islands chain. The western coast of Barbados has sheltered, coral beaches of fine, white sand, while along the east of the island there is a lively surf that pounds a rocky shoreline. It is a predominantly flat island with fertile plains supporting a variety of crops including sugar cane (see Figure 3.18).

Bridgetown, the capital of Barbados, has a decidedly English appearance and character, the result of its former British sovereignty. There is even a miniature Trafalgar Square with a statue of Lord Nelson! The island is equally popular with staying tourists and cruise visitors, who enjoy its fine beaches and crystal clear waters that offer a wide range of water-based activities such as swimming, scuba diving, jet-skiing and water skiing. Other sports on offer include cricket, golf, tennis, horse riding and horse racing.

Jamaica

Jamaica is the third largest island in the Caribbean, located to the south of Cuba and west of Haiti. Most of the island is forested and mountainous, rising from 1,000 metres in the west to the Blue Mountains in the east reaching 2,256 metres in height. Most of the beaches are found on the north and west coasts of the island where the principal resorts of Montego Bay, Ocho Rios, Negril

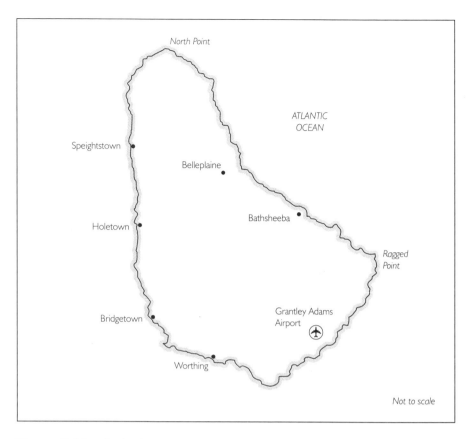

North Point

ATLANTIC
OCEAN

Speightstown

Belleplaine

Bathsheeba

Holetown

Ragged
Point

Grantley Adams
Airport

Bridgetown

Worthing

Not to scale

Figure 3.18 *Barbados*

and Port Antonio are located. Montego Bay is one of the world's great resorts and is the jewel in the crown of Jamaica's tourism industry (see Figure 3.19). The island's capital, Kingston, is on the south coast and is the site of one of Jamaica's two international airports. It is the largest English-speaking city in the Caribbean and an important business and administrative centre (see Figure 3.20).

Like many Caribbean islands, Jamaica welcomes both staying and cruise tourists, who enjoy its varied nightlife, relaxed way of life and numerous sporting opportunities.

Activity 3.13

Carry out some further research to investigate which UK tour operators and airlines offer tour programmes to either Jamaica or Barbados. Make detailed notes on the tourist attractions of the most popular resorts featured in the programmes of your chosen country.

Figure 3.19 *Montego Bay, Jamaica*
Courtesy of the Jamaica Tourist Board

The Dominican Republic

The Dominican Republic occupies the eastern part of the island of Hispaniola, which it shares with Haiti, and is the second largest of the Caribbean states (after Cuba). Its popularity with visitors from the UK is growing rapidly, with many of the larger tour operators promoting the Dominican Republic as an all-year-round destination, with package holidays and regular charter flights. Its main tourist attractions are its unspoilt beaches, for example around Puerto Plata with the popular resort of Sosua and along the Samana Peninsula, both on the north coast (see Figure 3.21). Inland, the landscape is forested and mountainous, with many valleys, plains and plateaux. The capital, Santo

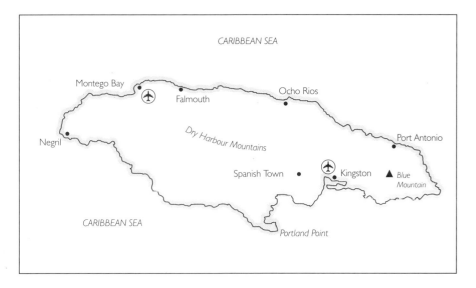

Figure 3.20 *Jamaica*

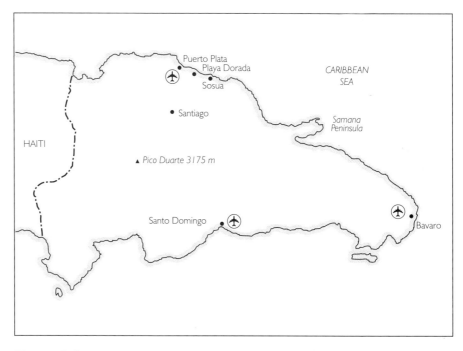

Figure 3.21 *The Dominican Republic*

Domingo, was founded in the fifteenth century and the old, colonial part of the city has been restored to its former glory. The modern part of the capital is a bustling port city, offering visitors a variety of nightlife and cultural experiences.

Tourism has developed much later in the Dominican Republic than in other Caribbean destinations. Consequently, many of its tourist facilities and tourism infrastructure are not fully developed.

Trinidad and Tobago

Trinidad and Tobago are sister islands situated off the coast of Venezuela in the southern Caribbean. Trinidad is the larger of the two islands with its capital, Port of Spain, dominated by mountainous terrain. Elsewhere, inland Trinidad has a relatively flat, agricultural landscape with unspoilt beaches on its north and east coasts. Tobago is a very small island with quiet, sandy beaches and a mountainous interior with lush, tropical vegetation. The islands, particularly Trinidad, are renowned for their carnivals and music festivals, and boast a good selection of restaurants serving local delicacies. The islands are also noted for their flora and fauna, with more than 600 species of butterfly and 700 varieties of orchid. Hummingbirds are found in abundance in Tobago.

St Lucia

St Lucia is the second largest of the Windward Islands (after Dominica), located in the eastern Caribbean between St Vincent and Martinique. It is rich in tropical vegetation and has a mountainous interior. One of its main attractions is its unspoilt, palm-fringed beaches surrounded by the warm, clear Caribbean Sea. The island has a great variety of plant and animal life, including orchids and parrots. The mountains are intersected by rivers that form broad fertile valleys in some parts of the island. The capital, Castries, is a busy, land-locked harbour surrounded by hills. It is a major port of call for cruise ships, which dock at Pointe Seraphine. St Lucia has two international airports, Vigie and Hewanorra, 2 and 42 miles respectively from Castries.

Climate

The Caribbean enjoys a tropical climate that is dominated by the easterly trade winds that blow from the mid-Atlantic towards Mexico. Temperatures throughout the Caribbean generally average over 25°C, peaking at more than 30°C in mid to late summer. The islands in the east experience the greatest cooling effect of the prevailing wind. Elsewhere, relative humidity is high at more than 70 per cent. The so-called wet season varies across the islands, but is generally between the months of June and November. Hurricanes are a problem in the Caribbean, particularly affecting the northern and eastern islands. The incidence of hurricane activity is greatest in the wet season, notably between July and October. Given these climatic conditions, it is not surprising that the main tourist season in the Caribbean is in the winter, between January and April, although there is a summer peak in July and August despite the threat of adverse weather.

Transport routes

Tourism in the Caribbean is dominated by two types of transportation, air travel and cruise ships. Travel by air dominates the staying visitor market in the Caribbean; indeed the growth of tourism in the Caribbean islands has occurred as a direct result of the development of aircraft routes and their associated infrastructure. All the popular island destinations have at least one international airport, generally offering direct scheduled flights from the UK with British Airways or the national airline of the country concerned, for example Bahamasair, Air Jamaica, British West Indian Airways, etc. Charter flights are increasingly on offer to a number of popular Caribbean destinations with the major UK tour operators, including Thomson (Britannia Airways), Airtours (Airtours International) and First Choice Holidays and Flights (Air 2000).

Miami and Puerto Rico tend to be the principal centres of cruise tourism in the Caribbean, attracting mainly US-based tourists. The majority of UK cruise visitors to the Caribbean buy a fly-drive holiday and start their cruise at an island port such as Bridgetown in Barbados, San Juan in Puerto Rico or Montego Bay in Jamaica. Alternative starting points include Miami and Fort Lauderdale in Florida.

Activity 3.14

Carry out some further research and draw up a list of which Caribbean islands have an international airport. Plot these airports on an outline map of the Caribbean and include the appropriate international three letter codes.

Australia

Location

Australia is a huge continent, as big as the whole of Europe and only slightly smaller than the USA. From Sydney in the east to Perth in the west is a distance of nearly 2,500 miles, while a journey from Darwin on the north coast to Adelaide in the south covers more than 2,000 miles. Australia is located in the southern hemisphere, with the Pacific Ocean to the east and the Indian Ocean to the west. To the north are the Timor Sea and the Torres Strait, which separates Australia from Papua New Guinea. Tasmania is located off the south-east tip of Australia, separated from the mainland by the Bass Strait (see Figure 3.22).

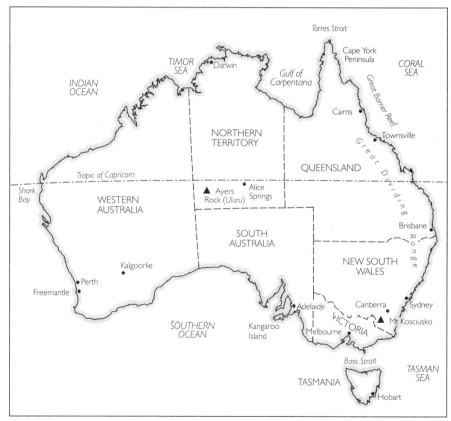

Figure 3.22 *Australia*

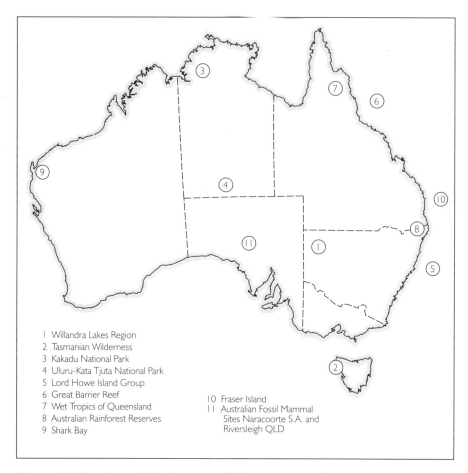

1 Willandra Lakes Region
2 Tasmanian Wilderness
3 Kakadu National Park
4 Uluru-Kata Tjuta National Park
5 Lord Howe Island Group
6 Great Barrier Reef
7 Wet Tropics of Queensland
8 Australian Rainforest Reserves
9 Shark Bay

10 Fraser Island
11 Australian Fossil Mammal
   Sites Naracoorte S.A. and
   Riversleigh QLD

Figure 3.23   *Australia's designated World Heritage Sites*

Australia's terrain is extremely varied, ranging from the wilderness and deserts of the west and central plains to lush green rain forest in the east. The landscape consists mainly of a low central plateau skirted with coastal mountain ranges, the highest being the Great Dividing Range in the east of the country. Its beaches and surfing are world-renowned, and other natural attractions, such as Ayers Rock (Uluru) and the Great Barrier Reef, are magnets for overseas and domestic tourists. The country boasts eleven World Heritage Sites, as shown in Figure 3.23. Australia also has snow fields to rival many Alpine resorts. The ancient cultural history of the Aboriginal people, plus the vibrant way of life found in its bustling cities, also serve to attract visitors to Australia from all over the world. The VFR market from the UK is important, with many British people combining visits to friends and relatives with a tour of the most popular regions of the country.

Australia's share of world tourist arrivals is increasing, due to its natural attractions and favourable climate, backed up by effective marketing and promotion. Although travel times from the UK to some parts of Australia can exceed 24 hours, it is an increasingly popular destination for the British, who are tempted by low-cost package holidays now offered by a variety of tour operators in the UK. The growth in the number of Australian television programmes shown in Britain has also increased the country's appeal.

Activity 3.15

Investigate which UK tour operators and airlines feature Australia in their programmes. Carry out a comparative analysis of the companies in terms of price, product features, resorts used, quality of accommodation, special offers and convenience of travel arrangements.

The main tourist areas in Australia

Queensland

Queensland is located in the north-eastern corner of Australia and is bisected by the Tropic of Capricorn. The state's terrain is a mixture of vast inland, fertile plains, long stretches of sandy beaches, coral reefs, rain forests, forested mountains and expanses of wilderness. It is known as the 'sunshine state' and boasts probably the best beach area in the country at the Gold Coast, close to Brisbane, the state capital. The Gold Coast is made up of 26 miles of white surfing beaches, including the world famous Surfers' Paradise beach, now a lively, sophisticated resort. Queensland has within its borders one of the world's foremost natural wonders, the Great Barrier Reef. The Reef stretches for more than 1,200 miles along the Queensland coast, from the Cape York Peninsula to the Tropic of Capricorn, and supports a unique animal and plant life.

Brisbane is the economic hub of Queensland and is the gateway to the tourist resorts of the Gold Coast and the Sunshine Coast. The city has grown rapidly in recent years, due to the popularity of the region with home and overseas visitors. Further north along the Queensland coast are Townsville and Cairns, both with international airports forming gateways to the Great Barrier Reef.

Western Australia

Western Australia is the largest of the country's states, covering one-third of Australia's land area. It is larger than Western Europe, yet has a population of less than 2 million. It is bordered in the east by South Australia and the Northern Territory. Its northern shores are surrounded by the Indian Ocean, while the south coast fronts the Southern Ocean. The terrain of Western Australia is predominantly desert and the state has rich oil and mineral deposits, including iron, diamonds and gold; Kalgoorlie in the south of the state is well known to tourists as a gold mining ghost town. The only significant concentration of population is in the south-west corner around the capital, Perth, which has a number of fine beaches, including Port, Cottesloe, City and Scarborough. All-year-round sunshine makes Perth Australia's sunniest capital. Western Australia has several National Parks and wildlife reserves, including

Kalbarri, Yanchep and Nambung to the north of Perth. Shark Bay, at the western tip of the state, is one of Australia's eleven designated World Heritage Sites.

Northern Territory

The Northern Territory is a true wilderness area and is closest of all states to the popular image of the Australian 'outback'. It covers one-sixth of the Australian landmass and can be divided topographically into the tropical north, with the capital Darwin as its hub, and the southern red desert ranges dominated by Ayers Rock in the Uluru National Park. This ancient monolith is steeped in Aboriginal mythology and is one of Australia's most important tourist attractions. The starting point for tours to Ayers Rock is the nearby town of Alice Springs, a popular base for exploring the outback, which is located in the geographic centre of the continent. Darwin, found on the north coast, is a modern, provincial city and a good base from which to explore the area's many natural attractions, including the Kakadu National Park.

Victoria

Victoria is Australia's second smallest but most densely populated state and the country's principal producer of agricultural and industrial products. It is located in the south-east of the country, bordered by South Australia to the west and New South Wales to the north, along the route of the famous Murray River. Its mild, temperate climate has given rise to the title 'the garden state', with a varied landscape consisting of mountains, rain forests, deserts, snow fields, market gardens and agricultural plains. Melbourne, the capital, is located in the south of the state at the mouth of Port Philip Bay. It is a modern, cosmopolitan city of some 3 million people and is the home of the National Gallery, which houses Australia's greatest collection of fine art. As well as its cultural heritage, Victoria has a variety of natural attractions, including fine beaches, snow-covered mountain ranges and a number of National Parks.

South Australia

South Australia is the country's driest state, sparsely populated apart from around its capital, Adelaide. It is a region of rocky plains and desert landscape, broken by the fertile wine growing area of the Barossa Valley. The terrain ranges from the beach resorts of the Adelaide suburbs to the expanses of desert outback, from the lush banks of the Murray River to the craggy mountains of the Flinders Range. Offshore from Adelaide is the popular resort of Kangaroo Island, a natural wildlife sanctuary noted for its fishing and colony of seals. Adelaide itself is a modern, coastal city nestling in the foothills of the Mount Lofty Ranges.

New South Wales

New South Wales is located in the south-eastern corner of Australia and has borders with Queensland to the north, South Australia to the west and Victoria

Figure 3.24 *Sydney Opera House and Harbour Bridge*
© ATC

to the south. Its eastern boundary is bathed by the waters of the South Pacific Ocean. The terrain ranges from the sub-tropical north of the state to the Snowy Mountains in the south, home of Australia's highest peak, Mount Kosciusko at 2,230 metres. The interior of the state is typical Australian outback and there are more than 800 miles of coastline with fine, sandy beaches, plus the famous Darling and Murray Rivers. New South Wales attracts visitors throughout the year, whether for skiing in the season between June and September, swimming off Sydney's beaches, including the world famous Bondi Beach, or exploring the natural attractions of the interior at places such as the Blue Mountains, the vineyards of the Hunter Valley or the Warrumbungle National Park. Sydney, the capital of New South Wales, is best known for its Opera House and Harbour Bridge (see Figure 3.24).

Canberra

Canberra is located in the Australian Capital Territory (ACT) in the south of New South Wales. Canberra was conceived in the early 1900s in order to create a capital city in a federal state separate from any of the other states of Australia. It is built around Lake Burley-Griffin and has many fine attractions, including the National Library, Parliament House and the Royal Australian Mint.

Tasmania

Tasmania is located off the south-east corner of Australia, separated from the mainland by the Bass Strait. It is an island of rugged mountains that are snow capped in winter, dense bush land, farmland plains, fine beaches and sand dunes. The more sheltered eastern coastline offers a variety of water sports opportunities, including swimming, surfing, sail boarding and fishing. Hobart, the capital of Tasmania, is Australia's second oldest city after Sydney and is found on the south side of the island. It is characterised by strong links with the sea, still maintaining much of its colonial architecture and ambience.

Climate

Australia's location in the southern hemisphere means that its seasons are the opposite of those in the UK, i.e. the winter in Australia takes place during our summer season, their summer is our winter, and so on. The climate varies from tropical, humid and wet in the north of the country, with a dry season between May and October, to hot, dry desert conditions in the central area. The southern states generally have milder weather than those in the north, enjoying a Mediterranean style climate. The west coast spans a wide range of climatic conditions, but is generally drier than the east of the country. Table 3.5 gives an indication of the seasonal variations in temperature and rainfall in a selection of cities and towns throughout the country.

Transport routes

Air travel dominates travel to and within Australia. The size of the country means that air travel is as common as travel by train and bus in the UK. International airports are located in the following cities and towns:

- ✪ **Canberra**
- ✪ **Sydney**
- ✪ **Adelaide**
- ✪ **Melbourne**
- ✪ **Darwin**
- ✪ **Perth**
- ✪ **Brisbane**
- ✪ **Hobart**
- ✪ **Townsville**
- ✪ **Cairns**

Activity 3.16

Locate the international airports listed above on an outline map of Australia. Include also the main resort areas discussed in the state descriptions given above, plus the state boundaries and capitals.

Area	Summer		Autumn			Winter			Spring		Summer	
	Jan	*Feb*	*Mar*	*Apr*	*May*	*Jun*	*Jul*	*Aug*	*Sep*	*Oct*	*Nov*	*Dec*
Adelaide												
Max.	29	29	26	22	19	16	15	17	19	22	25	27
Min.	17	17	15	12	10	8	7	8	9	11	14	16
Rainfall	19	8	33	47	68	75	84	67	58	44	28	28
Rainy days*	4	4	5	9	13	15	16	15	13	11	8	6
Alice Springs												
Max.	36	35	32	28	23	20	19	22	27	31	33	35
Min.	21	21	17	13	8	5	4	6	10	15	18	20
Rainfall	36	42	37	14	17	15	16	12	8	21	26	37
Rainy days	5	5	3	2	3	3	3	2	2	5	6	5
Brisbane												
Max.	29	29	28	26	23	21	20	22	24	26	28	29
Min.	21	21	19	17	13	11	10	10	13	16	18	20
Rainfall	171	177	152	86	84	82	66	45	34	102	95	123
Rainy days	13	14	15	11	9	8	7	7	8	9	10	12
Cairns												
Max.	31	31	30	29	28	26	26	27	28	29	31	31
Min.	24	24	23	22	20	18	17	18	19	21	22	23
Rainfall	413	435	442	191	94	49	28	27	36	38	90	175
Rainy days	18	19	20	17	14	10	9	8	8	8	10	13
Canberra												
Max.	28	27	24	20	15	12	11	13	16	19	23	26
Min.	13	13	11	7	3	1	0	1	3	6	9	11
Rainfall	59	58	53	49	49	38	40	48	52	68	62	53
Rainy days	8	7	7	8	9	9	10	12	10	11	9	8
Darwin												
Max.	32	31	32	33	32	30	30	31	32	33	33	33
Min.	25	25	24	24	22	20	19	21	23	25	25	25
Rainfall	409	353	311	97	21	2	1	7	19	74	143	232
Rainy days	20	20	19	9	2	1	0	1	2	6	12	17
Hobart												
Max.	22	21	20	17	14	12	11	13	15	17	19	20
Min.	12	12	11	9	7	5	4	5	6	8	9	11
Rainfall	48	40	47	53	50	56	54	52	52	63	56	57
Rainy days	11	10	11	13	14	14	15	15	15	17	14	13
Melbourne												
Max.	26	26	24	20	17	14	13	15	17	20	22	24
Min.	14	14	13	11	8	7	6	7	8	9	11	13
Rainfall	48	47	52	57	58	49	50	59	59	66	60	59
Rainy days	8	7	9	11	14	14	15	15	14	14	12	10
Perth												
Max.	30	30	28	25	21	19	17	18	20	21	25	27
Min.	18	18	17	14	12	10	9	9	10	12	14	16
Rainfall	8	12	19	45	123	184	173	136	80	54	21	14
Rainy days	3	3	4	8	14	17	18	17	14	11	6	4
Sydney												
Max.	26	26	25	22	19	17	16	18	20	22	24	25
Min.	18	19	17	15	11	9	8	9	11	13	16	17
Rainfall	103	113	134	126	121	131	101	81	69	79	83	78
Rainy days	13	13	14	13	13	12	11	11	11	12	12	12

*Rainy day = min. 0.2 mm
Source Australian Tourist Commission

Table 3.5 *Australia's temperatures (°C) and rainfall (mm)*

The major airlines operating scheduled services between the UK and Australia include Qantas, the national carrier, Singapore Airlines and British Airways. Britannia Airways and Airtours International also operate charter flights at certain times of the year. Australia has an internal airline network of more than 95,000 miles, covering the whole continent. The major domestic airlines include Ansett, Qantas and East West, serving the major resorts and cities throughout Australia.

Australia has only one rail service running from coast to coast, although there is an extensive network across the country. The Indian Pacific service runs between Sydney in the east and Perth in the west, covering the 2,500-mile journey in three days. Bus companies, including Greyhound Pioneer, offer a network of services between all major destinations.

Activity 3.17

Using the same format as in the example of Australia above (i.e. location, main tourist areas, climate, transport routes), carry out some research into New Zealand as a tourist destination. Use the sources of information mentioned at the beginning of this unit (see page 154) as the starting point for your research.

Main travel and tourism gateways and routes

Key topics in this section:

- **Introduction – transport types**
- **Road transport**
- **Rail transportation**
- **Air travel**
- **Travel by sea**

Introduction – transport types

The transport sector of the travel and tourism industry covers a variety of water-, air- and land-based services, including travel by coach, train, private car, taxi, hired car, bicycle, aircraft, cruise ship, ferry and canal craft. We saw in Unit 1: Investigating Travel and Tourism that throughout history the growth of tourism has been synonymous with developments in transportation. This still applies today, with advances in aircraft technology, passenger shipping, road improvements and high-speed rail travel offering faster, more comfortable and more convenient travel. Travel by air dominates the international tourism scene, whereas travel by private car is the most popular form of transportation for domestic tourism, offering flexibility, freedom and good value for money.

As domestic and international tourists become more experienced and sophisticated in their travel habits, the transport sector is having to respond by offering a wider variety of travel options, using the latest passenger-carrying vehicles and providing the highest standards of customer care. Competition between and within the different forms of tourist transportation is also contributing to the emergence of an international transportation sector that is becoming more customer-centred in its approach. It is important to remember that transportation is often an integral and pleasurable part of a total travel experience and not merely a means of getting from home to a holiday destination. The excitement felt by young children on a charter flight to a summer sun holiday destination or the pleasure given to senior citizens on a coach tour serve to illustrate this point well.

The transportation sector includes not only the services provided for tourists but also the related infrastructure that supports the means of travel, such as roads, motorway service areas, ferry terminals, railway stations and airports (see Figure 3.25).

Figure 3.25 *Stansted Airport terminal building*
Courtesy of British Airports Authority

Much of this infrastructure is provided by public agencies or through public/private sector partnership arrangements. As demand for travel has grown, many transport terminals have developed into large, integrated complexes offering a range of catering, currency exchange, business, retail and entertainment facilities.

In summary, tourists have a choice of transport types when deciding how to travel to their destination. They can choose to travel by:

- ✪ **Road**
- ✪ **Rail**
- ✪ **Air**
- ✪ **Sea**

We will now look at each of these in detail.

Road transport

Road transport includes travel by private car, bus and coach, taxi and hired car. The private car is an important form of travel for tourist purposes, especially for domestic tourism and intra-continental travel. It offers a degree of flexibility, comfort and convenience that cannot be matched by other forms of transport, but it does bring with it considerable environmental impacts. The high levels of car ownership in the densely populated industrialised regions of the world, particularly in Europe, some Far East countries, South America and the USA, have resulted in sharp increases in the use of cars for long holidays, short breaks and recreational day trips. This has led to problems of pollution, physical

Figure 3.26 *An Airtours transfer coach in Majorca*
Courtesy of Airtours

erosion, loss of land to car parks and congestion in many popular tourist destinations, especially historic cities, coastal resorts and National Parks, where vehicles often spoil the very ambience that attracted the tourists in the first place. Central and local governments are attempting to minimise the impact of vehicles by introducing a variety of schemes, including public transport initiatives, road pricing and pedestrianisation.

Travel by coach is an altogether more environmentally friendly form of tourist travel, transporting large numbers of tourists on scheduled services, coach holidays or on transfer journeys as part of a package holiday (see Figure 3.26).

Deregulation of coach travel, which occurred in the USA in 1982 and more recently in Europe, has liberalised the market for travel by coach and offered travellers a wider choice of operators. In the case of Europe, EU legislation allows a coach operator from any member state of the Union to offer coach services in any other EU country.

Rail transportation

Given that the railway was the dominant form of mass transportation in western industrialised societies until the rise in car ownership of the early twentieth century and the later introduction of air travel services, it is surprising that the demise in the use of rail services has been so swift. It is true that passenger and freight rail transportation still has an important role to play in some developed nations and is the principal form of long-distance travel for people living in the developing countries of the world. In western societies, travel by rail still occupies a small share of most countries' domestic tourism transportation statistics. From an international tourism viewpoint, however, rail travel finds itself unable to compete with other travel modes for the mass movement of tourists to their holiday destinations.

The general fall in demand for tourist travel by rail is not just a consequence of the rise in popularity of the private car and the introduction of travel by air. It is also a function of government approaches to rail travel, which vary considerably in different regions of the world. If we compare rail travel in the United Kingdom and France, for example, we see a UK rail transport network that has suffered from insufficient investment in rolling stock, signalling and track upgrading. As such, demand for tourist travel by rail has fallen sharply. The French government, on the other hand, has invested considerable public funds in the rail system, with its 'flagship' TGV (*train de grande vitesse*) network offering a high-speed service across the country. The French rail system is used extensively for tourist travel and the TGV is regarded as a viable alternative to domestic air services for business travel within the country. A similar situation exists in Japan, where the so-called 'bullet' trains link major centres of population. One notable exception to the poorly developed UK rail network is the Eurostar service linking London with Paris, Brussels and other major European cities via the Channel Tunnel, offering a high-speed service to business and leisure travellers (see Figure 3.27).

As yet, however, the high-speed line between London and the Channel Tunnel is only at the planning stage and is unlikely to be operational for some time. The European Union has recently agreed plans to develop an integrated transport network throughout the continent by the year 2010, including a trans-European rail network.

Figure 3.27   *Eurostar train at Waterloo International Station*
Courtesy of Eurostar

Activity 3.18

Carry out some research into the planned trans-European high-speed rail network and produce an outline map of the main routes. A good starting point is the European Union's Internet site at *www.europa.eu.int*

Despite the best efforts of countries such as France, international tourist travel by rail has become a 'niche market' product, serving the needs of two particular categories of travellers, namely young people travelling on cheap discount tickets often over a long period of time and older people who can afford the luxury of nostalgic trips on the great railway journeys of the world, for example the Venice–Simplon Orient Express, the trans-Siberian route and tourist trains operating in the North American Rocky Mountains.

Air travel

The rapid growth in international tourism since the end of the Second World War has been closely allied to the expansion of air travel services (see Figure 3.28). Advances in aircraft technology have led to increases in aircraft capacity and the development of planes with a far greater flying range. These two factors, coupled with increased demand for air travel generally, have enabled airlines to reduce prices and provide the stimulus for the growth of scheduled services and inclusive tours to medium- and long-haul destinations. Deregulation of air travel has increased competition between airlines and helped to keep fares low on an expanding network of routes. Allied to the growth in air services has been the rapid expansion of the associated infrastructure needed to cope with business and leisure tourists as well as freight traffic, including airport terminals and runways.

Types of air travel services

For statistical purposes, the International Air Transport Association (IATA) classifies air travel services into one of three categories:

1 **Domestic**
2 **International scheduled**
3 **International chartered**

Domestic services refer to air travel within a country, while international

Figure 3.28 *Air travel dominates the international tourism scene*
Virgin Atlantic © www.virgin.com

represents travel between different countries. Scheduled services are those that operate to a published timetable, on defined routes and under government licence. These services must run regardless of the number of passengers and are used primarily by business travellers who are prepared to pay a premium for the extra convenience and flexibility offered. Many governments still fund their national airlines, for example Air France, although there is a general move away from state ownership towards private sector operation, or at least private–public sector partnerships.

Chartered air services evolved to serve the expanding package holiday industry and now represent a significant proportion of passenger traffic in many countries with established outbound tourism sectors. Indeed, seat-only sales are one of the fastest growing products in air travel. Although some package holidays do incorporate scheduled air services the majority include a charter flight, known as an inclusive tour by charter (ITC). Charter services are generally cheaper than scheduled flights since their operators aim to fill as many seats as possible, often only offering the flight if they can be guaranteed a minimum number of passengers, known as the break-even load factor. Often this figure will be as high as 85 or 90 per cent, after which the operator begins to make a profit on the flight.

Travel by sea

In the same way that rail transportation was the dominant mode of surface travel up to the time of the twin developments of the growth in car ownership and the introduction of air travel services, so the ocean-going liners were the most popular form of sea transport for long-distance international travel up to

Activity 3.19

Working with a colleague carry out some research into the scheduled air services operating between the UK and the 20 European/worldwide destinations listed in Tables 3.1 (page 160) and 3.4 (page 176). Find out the main airports in each country and a selection of the airlines that offer scheduled services. Use the sources of information mentioned at the beginning of this unit (see page 154) as the starting point for your research.

the middle of the twentieth century. Passenger shipping services suffered badly when air travel services were introduced from the 1950s onwards. Companies such as P&O, Union-Castle Line and Cunard withdrew their services to the USA, South Africa and the Far East; such routes were to be serviced by the more accessible and affordable scheduled air travel services.

The demise of the ocean-going liners forced the passenger shipping industry to diversify into cruise shipping. Today, cruising is enjoying something of a revival, with the Caribbean, Mediterranean, the Baltic, the Far East and Australasia among the principal cruise destinations of the world. Paradoxically, the introduction of the very same air services that signalled the demise of the international passenger shipping industry has boosted cruising, with the development of the fly-cruise holiday, where tourists combine a charter or scheduled flight to and/or from a port with their sea cruise. Whereas in the past cruising tended to be the preserve of rich and famous senior citizens, today's cruising industry has products geared to all ages and budgets. The arrival of mass market tour operators and new generation vessels onto the cruising scene has heralded a new era of packaged cruises at bargain prices.

In many parts of the world, ferries offer inexpensive and reliable services on short sea crossings. Places as diverse as the Greek islands, Hong Kong harbour, the Scottish Highlands and Islands, the Adriatic Sea and the Baltic coastline all rely on ferry services for everyday travel and tourist business. In places where there is strong competition between ferry operators, such as on the short sea crossings in the English Channel, there have been considerable advances in vessel technology, with the introduction of hovercraft, hydrofoils and jet-foils to compete with the fast, new generation of passenger ships. The opening of the Channel Tunnel in 1994 increased competition on cross-Channel services still further (see Figure 3.29).

In addition to operating the faster vessels, ferry companies have responded to this challenge by offering price reductions, enhanced levels of customer service and greater on-board shopping and entertainment facilities on their ferry services.

Figure 3.29 *Ferries are in competition with Channel Tunnel services for passengers*
Courtesy of Stena Line Limited

Activity
3.20

Make a chart of the main ferry ports in the UK, the ferry companies that operate out of these ports and the destinations they serve. Use the sources of information mentioned at the beginning of this unit (see page 154) as the starting point for your research. See also Figure 1.21 on page 44, which is a map of the main ports in the UK.

The changing popularity of tourist destinations

Key topics in this section:

- **Introduction**
- **The popularity of destinations**

Introduction

In many respects destinations are the external face of the travel and tourism industry, benefiting from tourism's positive economic and social effects, while at the same time being the location for many of the negative environmental and socio-cultural impacts of the industry. They are also of prime importance in tourism since it is often the destination and its image that attracts a tourist in the first instance, thereby acting as a catalyst to the many sectors of the tourism industry, as shown in Figure 3.30.

Figure 3.30 indicates that a destination can be considered the 'umbrella' under which the diverse sectors of the tourism industry work in partnership to provide facilities and services for leisure and business travellers. A typical destination will have a variety of commercial and non-commercial tourism organisations operating in tandem. Public bodies will generally supply the infrastructure, planning and regulatory frameworks, tourist information services and destination promotion, while private operators provide the bulk of the facilities for visitors, such as accommodation, catering, attractions and entertainments.

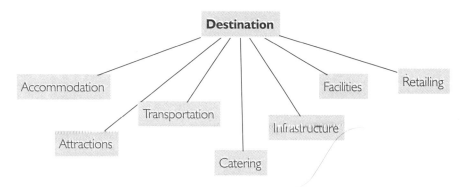

Figure 3.30 *The components of tourist destinations*

The popularity of destinations

The popularity of tourist destinations fluctuates in response to a number of demand and supply factors. For example, the development of a wide range of high-quality tourist attractions and facilities in Florida, coupled with targeted promotional activities, has stimulated demand for holidays in the state in the 1980s and 1990s. Tourism is Florida's largest industry, generating more than US$ 30 billion per year and employing some 657,000 people across all sectors of the industry, including accommodation, catering, attractions and transportation. Spain, on the other hand, experienced a slowdown in tourist demand during the latter half of the 1980s from its dramatic annual growth rates of the 1960s and 1970s, culminating in a fall in tourist numbers in 1990 (see Table 3.6).

The statistics in Table 3.6 show that Spain's popularity as a tourist destination has begun to rise again, the result of increased levels of investment in tourist facilities, improved infrastructure and a 'repositioning' of the destination from one offering just sun, sand and sea attractions to one that also has an important cultural and artistic heritage in its coastal areas and interior regions. Visitor numbers rose sharply after the hosting of the World Expo in Seville and the 1992 Olympic Games in Barcelona.

There are many influences on a destination's popularity, including economic, social/political and environmental/geographical factors, as the next sections of this unit explain.

Economic factors

You will have learned in other units on your Vocational A-level course that

Year	Total visitors (millions)	Receipts from tourism (US$ billions)
1985	43.2	8.1
1986	47.4	12.0
1987	50.5	14.8
1988	54.2	16.7
1989	54.0	14.2
1990	52.0	18.0
1991	53.5	19.0
1992	55.3	21.0
1993	57.3	23.5
1994	61.4	26.8
1995	63.3	29.0

Source   Adapted from Spanish National Tourist Office data

Table 3.6   *Total visitors to Spain, 1985–95*

travel and tourism is primarily a commercial industry, where making a profit is the name of the game. There are many companies competing to offer customers a wide variety of products and services. When **economic conditions** are favourable, people have more money to spend on non-essential items, such as leisure activities and tourism. When the economy is struggling, for example when unemployment figures are high and incomes low, travel and tourism suffers. The money that people have is spent on essential items such as clothing, food and fuel. The competitive nature of the travel and tourism industry means that **cost** is an important consideration to both customers and tourism companies. Customers will often choose their holidays on the basis of the lowest price offered by a tour operator. Prices in the destination are also an important consideration. Changes in exchange rates mean that the cost of living in different countries will fluctuate; sometimes this will be in favour of the UK tourist, sometimes against.

Social and political factors

As well as economic influences, there are a number of social and political factors that can influence the popularity of tourist destinations, including:

- ✪ **Promotion**: The amount of effort and money spent on promoting a destination is likely to have an impact on its popularity. This promotion may be carried out by the tourist boards and other destination agencies or by tour operators and airlines to encourage business.

- ✪ **Exclusivity**: Throughout history, from the development of spa towns to the growth of the French Riviera, people have always sought out new, exclusive destinations. This is still the case today for those who can afford it. Islands in the Pacific and the Caribbean play host to exclusive resort complexes for the rich and famous.

- ✪ **Over-commercialisation**: A resort that becomes too commercialised will not appeal to tourists who are looking for a quieter, more relaxing and more authentic holiday.

- ✪ **Crime**: Busy resort areas can become targets for criminals, who exploit vulnerable visitors. A serious crime wave is likely to have a negative impact on a destination's popularity with visitors.

browse this website

www.fco.gov.uk/ travel

- ✪ **Political instability/unrest**: Tourists will sometimes avoid countries that are experiencing political problems. The Foreign Office offers advice to travellers on the current position in such destination areas.

- ✪ **Media coverage**. This can be either positive or negative. Positive media coverage of a destination, for example favourable articles in newspapers and coverage on the TV or radio, can have quite an impact on popularity. Destinations that are featured in television series or in films can attract large numbers of visitors.

- ✪ **Tourism management**: Destinations that are well managed are likely to

Figure 3.31   *Eurostar train at speed*
Courtesy of Eurostar

be popular with visitors, who will appreciate their clean surroundings, wide range of facilities and respect for the environment.

✪ **The growth of independent travel**: Increasing interest in independent travel, as opposed to package holidays, has widened the range of destinations that tourists are visiting. Previously undiscovered long-haul destinations are becoming increasingly popular with independent travellers.

✪ **The growth of short break holidays**: The way that many people are using their leisure time is changing rapidly. Rather than the traditional two-week holiday, there is a growing demand for short breaks at different times of the year. This is leading to the growth in travel to overseas destinations that are within a couple of hours' travel time from the UK, for example Paris, Brussels, Milan, Barcelona, Amsterdam and Bilbao. Many of the new 'budget' airlines offer very competitive fares to these short break destinations and the introduction of the Eurostar passenger rail service from London has expanded the market for short breaks on the continent (see Figure 3.31).

Environmental and geographical factors

Factors to do with the environment and geography that influence the popularity of destinations include:

✪ **Accessibility**: If a destination is not easily accessible, it is not likely to be popular with the masses of tourists. Some tourists, however, are attracted to the remoteness of a destination in order to experience that 'get away from it all' feeling.

- ✪ **Climate**: This is probably the single most important factor that affects the popularity of tourist destinations. Tourists from the cool northern European countries are tempted by the warmer weather to be found in the Mediterranean resorts.

- ✪ **Pollution**: Pollution on land, in the air or on water will detract from a destination's appeal with visitors. Those responsible for the management of tourism in destinations must have measures in place to minimise the risk of pollution and to deal with any alerts efficiently.

- ✪ **Natural disasters**: Severe flooding, hurricanes, eruptions of volcanoes, forest fires and earthquakes will have short-term effects on the popularity of a tourist destination.

Marketing travel and tourism

4

In this unit you will investigate the subject of marketing and how it operates in the travel and tourism industry. You will discover that marketing is a continuous process that involves identifying customers' needs and then supplying holidays and other travel services to meet their needs. You will learn about the marketing mix (often referred to as 'the 4 Ps') and you will also investigate the important part that market research plays in identifying customer needs. Finally, you will focus on marketing communications, learning about the many techniques that travel and tourism organisations use to tell customers about their products and services.

This unit is divided into four main areas:

- **Marketing travel and tourism**
- **The marketing mix**
- **Market research**
- **Marketing communications**

We guide you through each of these areas using examples and case studies from the travel and tourism industry. At the beginning of each section you will see a list of key topics to help you fully understand what you need to learn. Look out for the links to websites so that you can learn more about a particular travel and tourism company or topic.

Marketing travel and tourism

Key topics in this section:

- **Introduction – what is travel and tourism marketing?**
- **The marketing process**
- **Setting marketing objectives**
- **Internal influences on the business environment (including SWOT analysis)**
- **External influences on the business environment (including PEST analysis)**
- **Needs and expectations of customers**
- **The marketing mix**
- **Evaluating progress in marketing**

Introduction – what is travel and tourism marketing?

We see the results of travel and tourism marketing around us every day – holiday adverts in newspapers, magazines and on TV, brochures in travel agencies, promotions on packets of breakfast cereals, local radio adverts, to name but a few. All travel and tourism companies must market their products to their customers in order to be successful in business.

Marketing is all about:

- **Getting the right product**
- **To the right people**
- **In the right place**
- **At the right time**
- **At the right price**
- **Using the right promotion**

An airline, for example, will invest a lot of time and money finding out exactly what its customers want from the company, for example when they want to travel, what facilities they would like, which destinations they want to travel to and how much they are willing to pay. It will then try to provide services geared to its customers' needs, using a whole host of ways of letting them know what is on offer, for example through brochures, advertisements, mailshots and posters.

Marketing is a very important part of travel and tourism, but it is not always correctly understood, sometimes even by people working in the industry! There are many myths about marketing, such as:

- ✪ **Marketing is advertising – false!** Advertising is a very important part of marketing and the one that we see most often in our daily lives. Millions of pounds are spent on TV and press adverts every year, so it is understandable that people sometimes confuse marketing with advertising.
- ✪ **Marketing is the same as selling – false!** It is true that selling is a vital part of marketing, particularly in travel and tourism, but it is just that, a part of a much wider process.
- ✪ **Employing staff with lively personalities will make your company a marketing success story – only partly true!** A lively personality is a good starting point for working in promotion and sales, but activities such as market research, while perhaps not so glamorous, are just as vital to successful marketing.
- ✪ **Marketing is only for private sector companies – false!** It is now widely accepted that marketing is just as important in the public and voluntary sectors of travel and tourism, e.g. a local museum or the National Trust; like private sector operators, they too have 'customers'.
- ✪ **Marketing is a 'one-off' activity – false again!** You will learn that the key to success is to treat marketing as a continuous process that changes over time and must be constantly reviewed.

browse this website

www.cim.co.uk

For a more formal definition we turn to the Chartered Institute of Marketing, a UK professional body, which defines marketing as:

The management process for identifying and satisfying customer needs profitably.

Let us look at this definition in a little more detail:

1   **Being a management process means that marketing ranks alongside personnel, health and safety, finance and other management functions in terms of the structure of an organisation. The importance given to marketing within an organisation will depend in part on the nature of the business and the attitude of the management.**

2   **Identifying customer needs is absolutely crucial for any travel and tourism organisation that is serious about what it is trying to achieve. Different types of market research can be used to find out the likes and dislikes of existing and future customers.**

3   **Satisfying customer needs is all about developing products and services that the customer will want to buy and the various techniques that can be employed to promote sales.**

4   **Carrying out points 1–3 profitably will ensure that the organisation can survive and indeed grow. As we have seen in Unit 1, private sector travel and tourism companies are primarily concerned with making a profit, whereas the public and voluntary sectors have wider social aims. Marketing must be carried out with the objectives of the organisation very much in mind.**

The marketing process

The marketing process can be explained with the help of Figure 4.1.

Figure 4.1 shows us a number of important points, for example:

✪ The marketing process starts with identifying customer needs. Knowing the facts about your customers, such as whether they like your holidays, how much they are willing to pay, whether they are satisfied with the service you offer, where they live, and so on, provides essential information when marketing decisions are being made. Market research is used to find out this sort of information.

✪ Once you know your customers it is much easier to develop products and services that they will want to buy. By giving attention to such matters as price, location, access and features, you will be able to give your customers what they want.

✪ Having developed your products, you must decide the best way of promoting them to your customers, which could include advertising, direct mail, sponsorship or any one of a wide range of techniques.

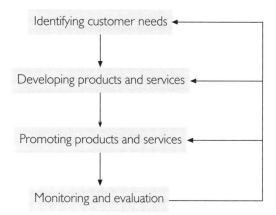

Figure 4.1   *The travel and tourism marketing process simplified*

✪ Evaluation is an important part of the process since marketing is a dynamic activity that must adapt to changes in people's tastes and fashions. It is essential, therefore, for all travel and tourism organisations to reflect on what they are doing at each stage of the marketing process by asking questions such as:

1 **Are our customers the same as they were three years ago?**

2 **Does our product range meet their needs?**

3 **Are our prices competitive?**

4 **Is our promotional work meeting its targets?**

It is only by constantly monitoring and evaluating its marketing process that a travel and tourism organisation can make best use of its resources.

Industry example

The marketing activity at the Tower Bridge Experience, one of London's most famous tourist attractions, is divided between consumer and travel trade marketing. Consumer marketing (aimed at the general public) includes:

★ Market research

★ Leaflet distribution

★ Public relations (PR)

★ Internet

★ Signage

★ Consumer promotions, e.g. voucher schemes, joint tickets

★ Print production

★ Limited consumer advertising

The attraction's travel trade marketing covers:

★ Workshops and travel trade fairs

★ Database management

★ Familiarisation visits

★ Sales calls

continued

browse this website

www.towerbridge.org.uk

continued

- ★ Print production
- ★ Education
- ★ Corporate hospitality

Staff at the Experience have found that there has been an enormous growth in the number of visitors who use the services of a retail agent to make travel arrangements. Their marketing strategy targets these agents directly, by identifying and contacting ground handlers, tour operators, ticket wholesalers, language schools, coach operators and UK schools/colleges.

Setting marketing objectives

We all need objectives or targets to work towards to be successful. You may be saving up for driving lessons or perhaps a holiday with friends and have set some targets of your own. The same applies to marketing in travel and tourism organisations. Marketing objectives are the specific aims or goals that an organisation sets itself when deciding on its marketing activity. It is important for all travel and tourism organisations to be clear from the outset what they are trying to achieve from their marketing. Examples of marketing objectives for an expanding holiday company could be to:

- ✪ **Increase sales by 10 per cent in the next 12 months**
- ✪ **Identify the needs of its customers aged over 50**
- ✪ **Carry out more market research**
- ✪ **Develop a new range of holidays to the West Indies**
- ✪ **Analyse what its competitors are offering**
- ✪ **Introduce a new set of brochures**
- ✪ **Set up a website on the Internet**
- ✪ **Open 20 new sales outlets within two years**

Every travel and tourism organisation will have its own specific marketing objectives which will reflect its overall business aims. Private sector operators, such as travel agencies and hotels, operate in the commercial world and will gear their marketing towards maximising their sales. The public and voluntary sectors, including local tourist attractions and youth groups, will be seeking to fulfil their wider community and social objectives by providing facilities for local people or perhaps helping disadvantaged groups in society.

Whatever marketing objectives an organisation sets itself, they must be SMART, in other words:

Specific: It is no use having 'woolly' ideas that are not well thought through or clearly defined

Measurable: Objectives must be capable of being measured so that you know if you have achieved your targets

Achievable: Setting objectives that are wildly optimistic wastes everybody's time

Realistic: Objectives must fit in with the organisation's overall business aims

Timed: It is important to set time deadlines to review progress

Remember also that setting objectives is not a 'one off' activity; they must be constantly monitored and updated in the light of changing circumstances.

browse this website

www.bestwestern.
co.uk

Industry example

The management of the Queen's Hotel in Southsea, a member of the Best Western Hotel Consortium, has set itself the following clearly defined business objectives:

★ To achieve a minimum room occupancy of 70%

★ To keep to budgets set by the Board of Directors

★ To continue to improve the image of the hotel

★ To achieve 2 AA Rosettes in the restaurant

★ To achieve a 4* rating

★ To improve training for staff and implement training for all staff

★ To achieve Investors in People status

All staff in the hotel work as a team in order to achieve these objectives.

Activity
4.1

Working in small groups, imagine that you are helping a relative to set up a travel and tourism business in your local area. It could be a new travel agency, a cycle hire scheme or perhaps a series of guided walks for visitors. Write down a list of the marketing objectives that the company will need to achieve if it is to be a success. Remember that they must be SMART!

Internal influences on the business environment

Some people say that the only constant thing in life is change! The same applies to the travel and tourism industry where companies operate in very complex business conditions that can change every day. This is often referred to as the business environment. From time to time, a travel and tourism organisation needs to establish exactly where it stands in the wider business environment. One of the most common ways of doing this is to carry out a SWOT analysis, namely:

Strengths – what it feels are its 'plus' points

Weaknesses – the points that could be improved

Opportunities – ways that business could be expanded

Threats – points that need to be guarded against

One example from each of these categories for a typical holiday centre might be:

- ✪ **Strength – the only centre in the locality with a wave machine**
- ✪ **Weakness – only half of the staff have had formal training in customer care**
- ✪ **Opportunity – a brewery wants to buy a stake in the company to help it expand**
- ✪ **Threat – a rival company has planning permission to build a holiday centre nearby**

A SWOT analysis will indicate where an organisation stands in the market and can start the process of deciding the future direction it must take in order to be successful. Figure 4.2 shows a SWOT analysis for the Waveney District Council area centred on Lowestoft in Suffolk.

waveney tourism strategy

Strengths

- *The Beaches:*
  quality - award winning
  variety - sandy resort & shingle rural beaches
  safe - excellent life guard service

- *The Broads:*
  - southern gateway to the National Park
  - excellent for water sports, canoeing, sailing and pleasure cruising
  - nationally recognised as a tourism and leisure destination

- *Natural Beauty:*
  - area of outstanding natural beauty
  - largely unspoilt by development
  - gently undulating landscape (excellent for cycling and riding)
  - rivers and inland waterways
  - variety of landscape: woodland, marshes and coastland
  - peaceful and uncongested country roads
  - strong images of rural Suffolk (corn flowers, poppies, waterways and windmills)
  - impressive skyscapes

- *Built Environment*
  - major attractions (Pleasurewood Hills & Suffolk Wildlife Park)
  - theatres, galleries and museums
  - sports facilities, bowls & bowling
  - attractive towns and villages
  - large selection of restaurants & pubs

- *Local Heritage:*
  - strong maritime connections (both Merchant & Royal Navy and fishing industry)
  - the district is rich in historical links from across the centuries
  - industrial heritage (including boat-building, porcelain and brewing)
  - historic buildings: eg. Somerleyton Hall, Bungay Castle, Lowestoft Scores and churches

- *Range of Accommodation:*
  - good selection of accommodation types (serviced and self-catering) providing for different visitor needs

- *Weather Conditions:*
  - the driest regional climate in the UK
  - above average hours of sunshine

- *General:*
  - good base for touring the region
  - comparatively little congestion
  - high degree of customer loyalty
  - Most Easterly Point.

Weaknesses

- Lack of all-weather facilities
- Limited tourist season
- Limited public awareness of Waveney as a tourist destination
- Tourist experience is vulnerable to bad weather
- High proportion of unclassified accommodation

Opportunities

- European & Other External Funding
  Tourism development in much of the district is eligible for this support.

- Marketing potential
  Opportunity to upgrade marketing of the district to overcome indistinct image

- Partnerships
  Opportunities for improved working relationships between sectors

- Growth of activity holidays
  The district is well-resourced to capitalise on the increase of cycling and other activity holidays.

- Sites available for development
  'Brown' sites are available for tourism (and related) development particularly in the Lowestoft area

- Growth of overseas tourism
  Building on increased number of visits to the district's ports and marinas as well as development of Norwich Airport

Threats

- Cheap, overseas packaged holidays
  - easy to book, affordable and with more reliable weather.

- Image of the British holiday
  - sea-side resorts in particular have received much negative publicity
  - traditional sea-side holiday is no longer fashionable with many people.

- Weather
  - unpredictable
  - recent poor/indifferent summers

- Access
  - poor transport links with major centres of population
  - poor access discourages inward investment
  - the district is by-passed by most overseas visitors to the UK

Figure 4.2 *SWOT analysis for Waveney District*
Courtesy of Waveney District Council

Activity 4.2

Carry out a SWOT analysis on a local travel and tourism company or facility of your choice, for example a coach operator, tourist attraction, hotel or caravan park. Working in small groups, discuss how the weaknesses could be overcome and the threats minimised.

External influences on the business environment

Whereas a SWOT analysis looks mainly at internal factors that affect organisations, a PEST analysis is used in the travel and tourism industry to analyse the external business environment, i.e. the factors over which a company has little direct control. PEST stands for **p**olitical, **e**conomic, **s**ocial and **t**echnological, the main factors that influence organisations.

The PEST analysis will vary between different organisations, but is likely to include information on the following influences:

✪ **Political** – central/local government and European Union policy on travel and tourism, taxation, local authority constraints, regional development, legislation, regulation/deregulation

✪ **Economic** – disposable incomes, exchange rates, inflation, levels of unemployment

✪ **Social** – demographic trends, lifestyle changes, community involvement, education, changing work practices, holiday entitlement, retirement, environmental awareness

✪ **Technological** – global communications, growth in home leisure, reservations systems, payment methods, transport developments

Travel and tourism organisations must also keep abreast of what their competitors are doing in terms of products, pricing and standards of service. This competitor analysis is vital if they are to be successful.

Needs and expectations of customers

We saw earlier in this unit that effective marketing must start with identifying the needs and expectations of customers. It is essential for any travel and tourism organisation to put the customer at the centre of all its activity by developing what is known as a customer-orientated or customer-focused approach to business. Companies that fail to understand this concept are unlikely to flourish in the highly competitive travel and tourism industry. In order to be able to put the customer as the hub of all activity, the organisation will need to have certain basic information on the characteristics of its customers, such as:

✪ **How many are there?**
✪ **What ages are they?**
✪ **Are they male or female?**
✪ **How far do they travel to get to you?**

- ✪ **What level of income do they have?**
- ✪ **What is their attitude to your facility?**
- ✪ **How long do they spend at the facility?**
- ✪ **How much money do they spend at the facility?**

Without this basic data, any travel and tourism organisation, be it a farm guesthouse, museum, art gallery, country house hotel or visitor attraction, will be basing its management decisions purely on guesswork. Decisions on matters such as pricing, design of promotional material, advertising media used and choice of menus, can only be carried out effectively with accurate knowledge of present and future customers.

It is important to appreciate that customers' needs and expectations are always changing. For example, what was acceptable on a package holiday 25 years ago is unlikely to meet the needs of today's customers. Today, we demand speedy travel to our holiday resorts, fine food, wines and service when we get there, plus a standard of accommodation that is no worse (and sometimes better!) than we have in our own homes. Higher standards of living, greater freedom to travel, advances in technology and transport developments all combine to raise our expectations of travel and tourism.

Activity 4.3

Working as a member of a small group, carry out a simple survey of three people of different ages. Ask them what they look for when choosing a holiday abroad and how their needs have changed over the years. Log their answers on a sheet and discuss with other members of your group the similarities and differences of the three people interviewed.

In order to fully understand customer needs and expectations, companies must carry out market research and may decide to subdivide their many customers into different groups, a process known as market segmentation. These two important topics are introduced in the next two sections of this unit.

Market research

Companies use many types of market research to find out about their customers' likes and dislikes. It is quite common to be asked to fill in a questionnaire on the return flight from a holiday abroad or to answer some questions in your resort hotel. The information gathered by companies is invaluable to them when deciding what products or services to offer their customers. Since customers' needs and expectations are constantly changing, travel and tourism companies must review their market research at regular intervals so as to build an accurate picture of their customers.

Market research is covered in greater detail in the third section of this unit (see page 253).

Market segmentation

Market segmentation is the process of subdividing the total market for a product or service into different target groups, each with broadly similar characteristics. Markets can be segmented in a number of ways, including by:

- ✪ **Region, e.g. all the people living in a particular postcode area of a city could be sent a company's holiday brochure**
- ✪ **Age, e.g. designing holidays to meet the needs of the 18–30 age group**
- ✪ **Social class, e.g. targeting all the people in an area in the C2 (skilled working class) social group**
- ✪ **Gender, e.g. developing holidays for women**
- ✪ **Life style, e.g. introducing new holidays for young people who live adventurous life styles**

One of the main benefits of segmenting the market is that it allows an organisation to target particular individuals within the segment. These people then become the focus of all the marketing effort, with the design and promotion of products and services geared to their needs.

Market segmentation is, therefore, a tool that a travel and tourism organisation can use to satisfy the requirements of its particular customers. Being concerned with the needs and expectations of customers, however, does mean that segmentation relies heavily on market research to help match the product exactly to the clients' needs.

The marketing mix

You may have come across the term 'marketing mix' before in your studies. It applies to all industries, but is particularly important in travel and tourism. It is sometimes called the 'four Ps', since it is concerned with **p**roduct, **p**lace, **p**rice and **p**romotion, four of the most crucial aspects of marketing. Organisations aim to strike a balance between the four Ps when deciding on their marketing activity. They must match their product or products to customers' needs, make them available in the right places, offer them at a

Industry example

The Hotel Piccadilly in Bournemouth has been very successful in targeting its marketing activity. A few years ago, in line with the approach of many other hotels, it was considering converting its little-used ballroom into a leisure facility. Concerned about the cost of the conversion, the owner decided to look again at the market for the ballroom in its existing format. He realised that he had a facility that many hotels had lost and that there was an unfulfilled market of ballroom and sequence dancers. Now the hotel specialises in dance holidays and has built up a substantial database of clients. Advertising is limited to inexpensive specialist magazines. More importantly, the hotel now enjoys higher occupancy levels than many similar hotels and has few competitors.

competitive price and promote them successfully to their target customers. You will find more in-depth information on the marketing mix later in this unit (see page 230).

Evaluating progress in marketing

Since travel and tourism is a dynamic industry, companies must regularly evaluate progress in their marketing activity. If they have set themselves clear marketing objectives (see page 217) it will be easier to measure whether or not they have developed a successful marketing mix that meets their customers' needs and expectations. There are many ways that can be used to evaluate progress, including:

- ✪ **Questionnaire surveys and customer comment forms to get feedback from visitors**
- ✪ **Electronic counters to measure visitor numbers and/or cars at an attraction**
- ✪ **Analysis of coupons from sales promotions in newspapers and magazines**
- ✪ **Comparison of financial data before and after a particular marketing promotion**

On the basis of these types of techniques, alterations can be made to an organisation's marketing mix to achieve a successful outcome.

Exercise 4.1

Choose one local and one national travel and tourism company or facility and list the techniques it might use to check on how successful its marketing activity has been.

Case Study
Superbreak's 1999/2000 marketing programme

Superbreak Mini-Holidays was founded in 1983. In 1989 the company took over the Goldenrail brand, which had been operating under British Rail since 1970. In July 1995 both Superbreak and Goldenrail were acquired by Eurocamp plc, a company quoted on the London Stock Exchange with a market capitalisation of over £100 million. As market leaders in the provision of UK short breaks, Superbreak's aim is to constantly grow its business by offering its customers the widest choice and the highest levels of service backed by a guarantee of quality, satisfaction and value for money. Superbreak is the preferred UK short break supplier for the UK's five largest retail travel agency chains and its brochures have guaranteed racking exposure in all their outlets. The company enjoys a turnover of more than £40m per year, carrying in excess of 500,000 customers and distributing over 6 million brochures.

SUPERBREAK MINI-HOLIDAYS – THE PRODUCTS

★ **Superbreak** is the market-leading short break brochure featuring a selection of over 650 hotels throughout the UK. Superbreak features most major UK hotel brands and has been voted number one by

continued

continued

> travel agents in every major survey for over 10 consecutive years.

★ Goldenrail: second in the marketplace only to Superbreak. Goldenrail features 420 UK hotel and holiday villages. Voted number one in the 1997 England for Excellence Awards by the English Tourist Board, Goldenrail complements Superbreak and offers opportunities for a budget break.

★ The Luxury Hotel Collection: a new programme for those that wish to experience the finest hotels in Britain. This four and five star selection has been chosen for the exemplary standards of accommodation, service and cuisine.

★ Theatrebreak: promoted as 'your passport to the performing arts', offering the UK's widest selection of quality hotels together with guaranteed ticket allocations to the top shows in London's West End and beyond. Includes packages to suit all tastes, such as theatre, rock, pop, opera and ballet.

★ Airport Hotels: economical rates at a wide selection of hotels at every major UK air and ferry port, many offering free car parking. Promoted as 'the first choice for take-off/touch-down accommodation'.

★ http://www.superbreak.com: Superbreak has the UK's largest hotel website. In addition, the Superbreak product is distributed electronically around the world through strategic alliances with major marketing partners.

▶ INCLUSION IN SUPERBREAK BROCHURES

Selected hotels get exposure in nearly 3 million Superbreak brochures and/or 2.5 million Goldenrail brochures. Three editions a year enable the company to change or introduce new features on selected pages, such as Christmas and New Year offers, winter and summer savers, etc. Superbreak also

continued

continued

produces a series of brochures for travel agents incorporating hotels which service the main UK airports. This product enables agents to sell UK airport hotels as a stop-over at either the beginning or the end of a client's overseas holiday. In addition, there is a London Theatre and Concert Breaks brochure, a Luxury Collection programme and a Family Breaks programme.

▶ GUARANTEED EXPOSURE IN TRAVEL AGENCIES

Superbreak's brochure distribution strategy supplies brochures to between 6,000 and 7,000 retail travel agents in the UK. The company is guaranteed racking year round with the six major retail multiple and independent consortia to the extent that the Superbreak product is currently selected for 'overprints' and 'own branding' by Thomas Cook, Going Places, Carlson, ARTAC, Worldchoice, American Express and NAITA (National Association of Independent Travel Agents), the consortium of other major independent retailers. Goldenrail is also 'over-branded' by NAITA. No other UK short break operator delivers close to this level of racking penetration.

▶ SALES AND MARKETING TEAM SUPPORT

This team is responsible for stimulating sales through all retail outlets. They ensure not only that the brochure is racked and displayed, but that the range and quality of the product and the various sales options are fully understood. The company's sales representatives are backed up by a head office team dedicated to Sales and Marketing. Over 18,000 sales visits have been made in the past 12 months to make agency staff better informed and more proactive in selling the Superbreak and Goldenrail products.

▶ THE INTERNET

Superbreak also provides a comprehensive Internet site for

continued

continued

people wishing to use this increasingly popular information provision service. Hotels featured in any of the Superbreak brochures are automatically given exposure via the Internet site.

▶ EXPOSURE ON VIEWDATA

Viewdata is the electronic communication system which allows a travel agent direct access into Superbreak/Goldenrail's computer. The travel agent can check availability and make a booking without the need to telephone. There is no additional charge for hotels to be included on this system, which now accounts for over 50 per cent of Superbreak bookings. In addition to allowing travel agents to make a quick and direct booking, Viewdata also provides them with information, so that any special promotions or tactical price reductions a hotel may wish to offer can be featured instantly. This is a very powerful vehicle for moving last minute availability since it is accessed by most agents on a daily basis. The system also allows agents to access hotel information, get directions to the hotel and calculate costings as well as the re-ordering of brochures. No other UK short break operators' systems are achieving similar usage figures.

▶ PUBLIC RELATIONS OPPORTUNITIES

Both programmes are supported by a year-round public relations programme within the trade and public media. You can therefore expect to read about Superbreak and Goldenrail in many newspapers and magazines. Participating hotels have the opportunity to be involved in press facility visits, reader competitions, voucher promotions, etc.

▶ TRAVEL AGENCY STAFF VISITS

It is vital to longer-term sales development that travel

continued

continued

agency staff likely to sell particular hotels have the opportunity to sample the product quality first hand. This is done in a variety of ways, including:

★ Complimentary educational weekend breaks – for individual high-selling agency staff on weekends predetermined by the hotel

★ Familiarisation visits – hotels may be approached to host stays by groups of agents, usually 6 to10 rooms, on familiarisation visits

★ Travel staff concessions – discounted staff rates to encourage agents to visit particular hotels

★ Business meetings – co-hosting meetings with Superbreak/Goldenrail for groups of travel agency management

▶ TACTICAL PROMOTIONS

Where major retail travel agency groups are looking to give additional tactical exposure to the UK short break sector, they will normally look to Superbreak/Goldenrail to provide product offers.

(Information courtesy of Superbreak)

Case study discussion questions

browse this website

www.superbreak.
com

1 What is 'racking' and why is it so important to companies such as Superbreak?

2 In what ways does a hotel benefit from being included in any of the Superbreak brochures?

3 Why does Superbreak have a range of different products?

4 What role do you think the Internet will play in the future for Superbreak and its marketing activity?

The marketing mix

Key topics in this section:

- **Introduction to the marketing mix**
- **Product (types, characteristics, branding, life cycle)**
- **Place (location, chain of distribution)**
- **Price (price determination, pricing policies)**
- **Promotion (advertising, direct marketing, public relations, personal selling, sales promotion, sponsorship)**
- **Mission and objectives**

Introduction to the marketing mix

The term 'marketing mix' is used to describe the key elements that an organisation offers in order to meet its customers' needs and expectations. As we saw earlier in this unit, it is one of the most important concepts in today's travel and tourism industry and is commonly referred to as the 'four Ps', namely:

- ✪ **Product**
- ✪ **Place**
- ✪ **Price**
- ✪ **Promotion**

Just as the ingredients must be in the correct quantities to make a successful cake, so the four elements of the marketing mix must be in the right proportions to make an organisation's marketing a success (see Figure 4.3).

To see how the marketing mix works in practice, we can look at an example of a small specialist tour operator offering villa holidays to Majorca. To be successful, the company must be sure that the **product** it is offering meets its customers' requirements, in terms of quality, availability, features and benefits. The **place** component of the marketing mix refers both to the location of the villas and resorts in the tour operator's programme and to how the holidays are made available to the public, i.e. either sold through a travel agent or direct to the customer. The company must also be sure to offer its holidays at a competitive **price**, giving value for money regardless of the price paid. How the tour operator **promotes** its products will depend on a number of factors, such as its promotional budget, whether it sells direct or through an agent, the size of its operation and the type of customers it is trying to attract.

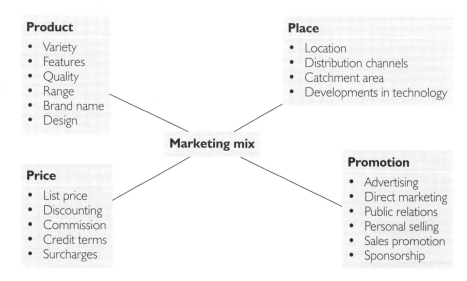

Product
- Variety
- Features
- Quality
- Range
- Brand name
- Design

Place
- Location
- Distribution channels
- Catchment area
- Developments in technology

Marketing mix

Price
- List price
- Discounting
- Commission
- Credit terms
- Surcharges

Promotion
- Advertising
- Direct marketing
- Public relations
- Personal selling
- Sales promotion
- Sponsorship

Figure 4.3 *The marketing mix in travel and tourism*

Activity 4.4

Working in small groups, discuss how some of the travel and tourism companies in your local area (travel agencies, tourist attractions, tourist information centres, hoteliers, etc.) put together their marketing mix. On a flipchart, identify how their activities fall into each of the four components of the marketing mix (product, place, price, promotion).

We will now look in more detail at the four components of the marketing mix.

Product

Travel and tourism products are very different from many other products that we buy and use. Even using the term 'product' is rather misleading, since travel and tourism is a service industry offering a variety of holiday experiences and travel services, rather than providing consumer goods such as cars, CDs or hi-fi systems. In fact, travel and tourism is often thought of as an industry that succeeds by 'selling dreams', perhaps a Caribbean cruise or a weekend break in Amsterdam – but we still have to pay for it!

Types of products

Travel and tourism products are sometimes sold separately, for example a return flight from Birmingham to Paris, or they may be combined with other products to make a package, e.g. hotel accommodation, charter flight and coach transfer all combined to make an overseas package holiday.

Below are a few examples of travel and tourism products:

- **Short breaks**
- **Airline flights**
- **Tourist attractions**
- **Car hire**
- **Coach travel**
- **Package holidays**
- **Hotel accommodation**
- **Cruises**

The range of travel and tourism products offered for sale is very wide, since there are many specialist companies satisfying the needs of a wide variety of customers. In reality, anything that can be sold by a travel and tourism company can be thought of as a product, even a cycling trip in the Himalayas or a balloon flight over the Grand Canyon. The important part is that somebody is willing to pay for the experience and that the company can offer a safe, reliable and efficient standard of service.

Characteristics of travel and tourism products

Travel and tourism products have a number of important characteristics that affect how they are marketed. Unlike many other everyday products that we buy, they are:

- **Intangible**: You cannot, for example, see or touch a short break holiday or a visit to an attraction in the same way that you can a new car or washing machine. The travel and tourism industry is in the business of selling 'experiences'.
- **Perishable**: An airline seat, ticket for an event or room in a hotel not sold today cannot be stockpiled and resold at a later date. It is therefore a lost sales opportunity for the company concerned. Price reductions and discounts can be offered to stimulate sales.
- **Inseparable**: Tourists often experience travel and tourism products as they happen, making the role of the staff who serve them crucial to a pleasurable experience.

- ✪ **Non-standardised**: The experience that a person gets on the same holiday from one year to another could be very different depending on, for example, the weather, attitude of staff, etc. This highlights the importance of quality control in travel and tourism products.

- ✪ **Unpredictable**: Customers who are not treated well may take their custom elsewhere. Training in customer care is, therefore, essential for a successful organisation.

Branding

Many travel and tourism companies use brand names, for example Thomson, Harvester, Going Places, Holiday Inn and Virgin (see Figure 4.4).

A brand name gives a product a certain identity, which, when coupled with promotional activities such as advertising and direct mail, helps persuade the customer to buy or use that particular product. Many customers show brand loyalty, meaning that they will only buy a particular brand above all others; it is not uncommon for clients to use the same travel agent and holiday company year after year. Branding is often linked to the concept of market segmentation (see page 223), with brands being developed to meet the needs of different segments of the market. One of the best examples of this is the wide range of products on offer from Thomson Holidays. Their brands range from 'Small and Friendly', through 'Thomson Cities' to 'A la Carte'.

Figure 4.4 *Virgin is a very well-known brand*
©Virgin Atlantic www.virgin.com

Industry example

The Rank Organisation operates some of the best-known brands in travel and tourism. Its Holiday Division includes Haven, Butlins, Warner, Resorts USA and the Oasis Holiday Village in the Lake District. Popular brands in the group's Leisure Division include Mecca Bingo, Grosvenor Casinos, Odeon Cinemas and Tom Cobleigh pubs. The company also operates the Hard Rock café brand and has a share in Universal Studios in the USA. Each brand is associated with a specific product aimed at a particular sector of the market.

Product life cycle

All products, whether they are in the travel and tourism industry or the consumer goods market, have an identifiable lifespan. There will come a time when the product is no longer in demand at all, or needs remodelling in some way to keep its customers. We are all familiar with the rise and fall of products such as skateboards and ten-pin bowling. The product life cycle concept argues that all products go through similar stages during their useful life, as shown in Figure 4.5.

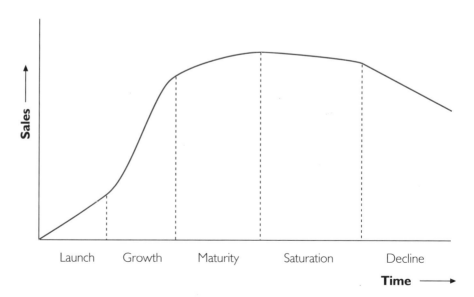

Figure 4.5 *The product life cycle in travel and tourism*

Figure 4.5 shows us that the five stages in the product life cycle are:

1 **Launch**: The product is launched with a lot of promotion, which hopefully results in encouraging sales (or encouraging use in the case of a non-commercial activity).

2 **Growth**: Sales grow steadily with increasing profits.

3 **Maturity**: Sales begin to decline. Perhaps competitors are offering a product with greater benefits. It is often at this point that the organisation will need to decide to either let the product die, remodel it or increase marketing support to generate more sales.

4 **Saturation**: Sales have reached a plateau.

5 **Decline**: Sales are dropping off quickly.

By studying the following example of Majorca you will see how the product life cycle works in practice in the travel and tourism industry.

Industry example
The product life cycle – holidays to Majorca

The way that the number of visitors to Majorca has evolved since the mid-1970s is often thought of as a classic example of the product life cycle concept. After 15 years of steady growth, Majorca began to see a drop in its number of overseas visitors in the late 1980s, with a 6 per cent fall between 1988 and 1989 and smaller decreases in the early years of the 1990s. Many people thought that the island had reached 'maturity' on the product life cycle. The main reasons for this were given as:

★ An overdependence on UK and German markets, which accounted for 70 per cent of all overseas visitors

★ Greater competition from Eastern Mediterranean and long-haul destinations, e.g. the Caribbean, Far East and Australia

★ An overdependence on the package tour market (high volume/low yield)

★ Lack of investment in infrastructure in the resorts

★ An excess of one- to three-star accommodation when people were demanding four-star facilities

continued

continued

★ Poor image, e.g. overcrowded, too British, 'lager louts', noisy, etc.

★ Deterioration of the environment, particularly through unplanned hotel development

The public and private sectors have put forward a number of solutions to try to hold on to the visitors they have and begin to tempt new customers. Among these are the following:

★ Widening the 'customer mix' by extra promotion in countries such as the Netherlands, Scandinavia, Italy and Spain itself

★ Advertising campaigns highlighting 'the other Majorca'; the island is more than one or two lively resorts and can offer a relaxing holiday in natural surroundings, with activities such as walking, cycling, water sports and bird watching

★ More controls on hotel development

★ Improving the quality of the product; £8 million has been spent in Palma Nova and Magaluf alone on environmental improvements

★ Development of new golf complexes aimed at high-spending tourists

The next five to ten years will show whether these improvements will have the desired effect of halting the drop in overseas visitors to Majorca, but early signs are encouraging.

Exercise 4.2

Thinking of British seaside resorts, where do you think they are on the product life cycle curve? Explain the reasons for this and suggest solutions to any problems you have identified.

Place

Place, in the context of the marketing mix, is concerned not only with where travel and tourism activities are undertaken, but also with how they are made available to the customer, sometimes referred to as the chain of distribution. We shall look at each of these in turn.

Location

The right location can often mean the difference between success and failure for a travel and tourism company or facility. A farm guesthouse, for example, which is deep in the countryside and well off the beaten track, will not benefit from 'passing trade' and, unless the proprietor is skilled in marketing, will struggle to attract guests. A travel agency, on the other hand, in a busy high street location should attract a constant stream of clients. For a tourism company looking for a suitable site for a new theme park, the prime location is likely to be close to a major centre of population. Location, therefore, is closely linked to accessibility, at the local, regional and national level. In the public and voluntary sectors of travel and tourism, accessibility is not just about physical access to buildings, although this is important when it comes to catering for those with special needs. In these sectors, accessibility is also about providing facilities for the whole community and giving everybody equal access.

Chain of distribution

When we think of the distribution of products, images of huge container lorries full of chilled food or fashion garments driving up and down the motorway come to mind. However, this has little to do with how travel and tourism products are bought and sold, since they are very often consumed at the point of production, so there is no need for distribution channels of any sort. For example, a round of golf takes place on the golf course, just as a holiday abroad takes place in a hotel, self-catering apartment or some other type of accommodation. In cases such as these, the important point is to make sure that the facilities are made accessible to the customers and that they are promoted effectively to the intended audience.

The way that holidays are sold in Britain is a good example of distribution channels in the service sector. Figure 4.6 shows the different stages in the process.

Figure 4.6 shows us that the tour operator assembles the 'raw materials' of a typical package holiday by buying in bulk such items as hotel rooms and airline seats. Taking on the role of the wholesaler, these are then divided into smaller proportions, the package holidays themselves, and are offered for sale through travel agents (the retailers) to the customers. While this is the usual method of selling holidays, there are certain holiday companies which specialise in selling

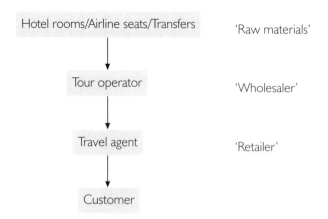

Hotel rooms/Airline seats/Transfers 'Raw materials'

Tour operator 'Wholesaler'

Travel agent 'Retailer'

Customer

Figure 4.6 *The channels of distribution in selling holidays*

direct to the customer without using the services of travel agents. One of the best known of these 'direct sell' operators is Portland Holidays, which claims to offer the public cheaper holidays because the company does not pay commission to travel agents.

Price

The pricing of products and services is a crucial aspect of the marketing mix. Price is just as important as place, product or promotion; if the price is wrong, no amount of advertising or other promotional work will make the customer buy the product. Getting the price right in travel and tourism is no easy task, given that they are service industries and that most products are intangible. It is common to charge different amounts for the same product at different times of the year and even different times of the day. An all-inclusive family French camping holiday with Eurosites, for example, will cost nearly £500 more in August than the same package in late September. Similarly, the admission charge to a theme park may well be higher at the weekend than on a weekday. Pricing in travel and tourism, therefore, often varies in relation to demand.

Price is also closely allied to value, a concept that is notoriously difficult to define since it varies so much between individuals. Some people will put a very high value on a particular type of holiday, for example, while others will not be interested at all and it is clearly of little value to them. Value will also fluctuate according to particular circumstances; staying in a Mediterranean resort in high summer may have greater value than the same holiday spent in the cooler temperatures of February.

Pricing is clearly a far more complex subject than simply adding up all the costs associated with providing a product or service, then adding a small amount of profit. The idea of what something is worth to the individual comes into play, a feature that will influence the amount he or she is willing to pay.

Price determination

Before we look at some of the methods used to price travel and tourism products, we will investigate some of the factors that influence pricing:

✪ **Costs**: It is important for an organisation to be aware of the costs of providing a particular product or service when deciding on its price. This may, however, only be the starting point of a much more complex pricing policy involving many of the points discussed above.

✪ **Demand**: We have shown that the same product can command a higher price at different times according to customer demand. People will often pay high prices for exclusivity, e.g. a trip on the Orient Express or a flight on Concorde.

✪ **Competition**: In the highly competitive travel and tourism industry, an organisation will need to be aware of what competitors are charging and adjust its own prices accordingly.

✪ **The state of the economy**: In times of recession, products may be reduced in price in order to gain revenue, e.g. prices for hotel rooms may be heavily discounted on the assumption that it is better to get a little income for the rooms rather than nothing at all if they are left empty.

✪ **Objectives of the organisation**: Clearly a private sector company will need to maximise revenue and will try to set prices that help achieve this objective. Public sector and voluntary bodies may be able to offer more concessionary prices to achieve their social aims.

Pricing policies in travel and tourism

From the many different pricing policies used by travel and tourism businesses, the following are some of the most common:

✪ **Skimming**: A high price is charged initially for a new product that is unique and that attracts people who are willing to pay the high price for status reasons. The pricing of exclusive hotels is an example of market skimming.

✪ **Cost plus pricing**: Sometimes known as 'accountant's pricing', this is the rather simplistic approach that totals all fixed costs (buildings, machinery, etc.) and variable costs (wages, energy costs, telephone, etc.) and adds a small profit margin to arrive at the price to charge. It assumes that an organisation can calculate its costs accurately, something which a large travel and tourism organisation may find difficult.

✪ **Penetration pricing**: This is used by organisations wanting to get into a new market where there are existing suppliers of the same product or service. The price will be set sufficiently low to persuade customers to switch their allegiance (sometimes known as a 'loss leader'). Many of the new low-cost airlines, such as Go, Ryanair and Easyjet, use this technique to win customers from traditional airlines. It is important that this pricing method is seen as a long-term strategy since customers will resent an early rise in price.

- ✪ **Competitive pricing**: Sometimes referred to as 'the going rate', competitive pricing assumes that where products or services are similar, the organisation will charge the going rate, i.e. will match the price of its competitors. This method often leads to very low profit margins and, in the long run, can lead to the collapse of some organisations, e.g. tour operators, who find that they cannot generate enough profit to survive.

- ✪ **Variable pricing**: Different prices are charged according to season, time of day, types of customers (groups, young people, senior citizens, single parents, etc.) and facilities on offer. Last-minute discounts can also be offered to stimulate demand, for example standby tickets on airlines and trains.

Activity 4.5

Examine the pricing structure of a nearby tourist attraction with which you are familiar. Analyse the factors that have influenced the prices charged and discuss with your colleagues whether there is any evidence of skimming, penetration, competitive or variable pricing.

It is becoming common for larger travel and tourism companies to offer price guarantees to reassure customers that they are getting the best deal for a holiday or other travel product. The following is a good example of this.

browse this website

www.superbreak.
com

Industry example

Superbreak Mini-Holidays, the UK's leading short break company, offers its customers a price guarantee. Clients know that when they book with Superbreak they are getting the best value for money at the most competitive rate. The guarantee, which is published in the company's brochures, states:

continued

continued

> *We guarantee that should a hotel offer directly to our customers a like-for-like package (i.e. with no minimum stay, our children's policy, etc.) at a lower rate than we publish, and for a duration of one of our seasons, then we will refund the difference.*

This type of price matching is commonplace in many high street shops and is now spreading to the travel and tourism industry.

Promotion

Once a travel and tourism product has the right features, is correctly priced and offered for sale in the right place, the fourth element of the marketing mix, namely promotion, comes into play. In the dynamic world of travel and tourism, promotion is used to:

- **Make customers aware of the availability of travel and tourism products**
- **Inform customers of the benefits of one product over another**
- **Stimulate demand for products**
- **Provide incentives to purchase or use products**
- **Remind customers of the existence of a product**

Businesses in the travel and tourism industry use a number of different promotional techniques, sometimes referred to as 'the promotional mix'. The most important are:

- **Advertising**
- **Direct marketing**
- **Public relations**
- **Personal selling**
- **Sales promotion**
- **Sponsorship**

We will now introduce you to these topics, which are covered in more detail in the last section of this unit when we investigate marketing communications.

Advertising

Advertising is the most obvious of all the promotional techniques in use today. We are all subjected to advertising on our TV screens, on buses and trains, on commercial radio, at the side of the road and in newspapers and magazines (see Figure 4.7). These are known as advertising media; the precise choice of media will be dictated partly by cost (a 30-second commercial on TV in peak viewing time can cost more than £40,000) and partly by the type of product and its intended audience. A new museum aimed at local people is unlikely to use national TV advertising but will rely on advertisements in the local press.

Figure 4.7   *A travel advertisement from the national press*
Courtesy of Go

Advertising in travel and tourism is directed either at the customer (consumer advertising) or at those working in the industry (trade advertising). *Travel Trade Gazette* and *Travel Weekly* are two examples of travel and tourism trade magazines that carry advertisements.

Many people believe that travel and tourism organisations spend nearly all of their promotional budgets on advertising, over and above other types of promotional activity. This is far from the case, since many small and medium-sized organisations find it hard to justify the expense of advertising campaigns. They rely much more on methods such as direct marketing and public relations, which can be just as effective with less investment.

Direct marketing

While advertising is sometimes criticised for not always hitting its intended audience (for example, a TV advertisement featuring a product geared specifically to the needs of men will be of little interest to women watching), direct marketing is able to target particular customers very successfully. Direct mail is the best-known method of direct marketing, a technique used extensively in the travel and tourism industry. Using a mailing list, which may have been bought, borrowed or compiled from its own records, a company can mail existing and prospective customers with a personalised letter or brochure giving details of its facilities. If planned carefully, a direct mail campaign can bring excellent results for a wide range of travel and tourism organisations and facilities, ranging from hotels, holiday centres and travel agencies to tour operators, visitor attractions and art galleries. Direct mail is one of the fastest-growing types of promotional activity in travel and tourism today.

Telemarketing (direct selling over the telephone) is a growing method of direct marketing in the UK. Already widespread in the USA, its use in this country in travel and tourism is fairly new, and is limited to activities such as selling timeshare and selling services to businesses.

Public relations

Public relations, or PR as it is often known, is used a great deal in travel and tourism. Organisations sometimes think of it as 'free publicity', particularly when associated with a newspaper or magazine article that features its facilities. In reality, there is usually a price to be paid for this coverage, even if it is just the cost of entertaining the journalist who wrote it!

Public relations is more than just keeping the media informed about your organisation, however, although this can undoubtedly pay dividends. PR is also about making sure that all staff and functions of an organisation which come into contact with the public – for example staff at reception, promotional literature, telephone technique, uniforms, etc. – are well managed so as to gain maximum publicity and goodwill. PR is also about travel and tourism organisations helping in the local community and getting involved in work for local and national charities.

Personal selling

Being a service industry, travel and tourism relies heavily on the selling skills of staff in order to achieve success. Selling is all about helping people to buy rather than selling them something they do not really want. Training in selling techniques is important for travel and tourism staff, particularly in the commercial sector. Planning prior to a sales interview is essential, as is being able to recognise buying signals, such as nodding of the head and signs of agreement from the customer. Closing the sale can be achieved by the taking of a deposit, credit card details or simply noting the customer's name and address. Unit 5: Customer Service in Travel and Tourism has a section on selling skills (see page 340).

Sales promotion

There are many different sales promotion techniques used in the travel and tourism industry. Some of the most common are:

- **Discount vouchers and coupons (often in newspapers and magazines)**
- **Brochures and leaflets**
- **Price cuts and 'sale' offers, e.g. 10 per cent off all brochure prices of summer holidays**
- **Extra product, e.g. a 'three for the price of two' offer at a restaurant**
- **Free gifts, e.g. a free T-shirt with every group booking at a theme park**
- **Prize draws**
- **Competitions**
- **'Giveaways', e.g. free carrier bags, pens, balloons, hats, stickers, etc.**
- **Free membership of a new leisure club attached to a hotel**
- **Displays and exhibitions**

The important point about all sales promotion techniques is that they are temporary and aim to stimulate demand in the short term. The fast-moving nature of travel and tourism means that managers are constantly having to react to fluctuations in demand from customers on a daily, weekly or seasonal basis. Unlike advertising, direct marketing and public relations activities, which are essentially long-term promotional tools, sales promotion gives an organisation the flexibility needed to be able to respond quickly to such changes.

Sales promotion techniques are not only targeted at members of the general public; it is common for many staff working in travel and tourism, especially in the private sector, to be offered incentives and rewards for achieving sales targets. Travel agency counter staff, for example, may be given shop vouchers by tour operators or airlines in return for selling a certain number of holidays or flights. Indeed, incentive travel is a growing sector of travel and tourism. Started in the USA, incentive travel is the reward of, say, a fortnight's holiday in Florida for an employee who has achieved sales success within his or her organisation.

Activity 4.6

Choose three travel and tourism organisations or facilities, local or national, and make a list of the sales promotion techniques each uses to stimulate sales. Discuss with your colleagues which techniques you believe are the most and least effective and explain your reasons.

Sponsorship

Sponsorship is another technique that some travel and tourism companies use to publicise their products, services and events. It varies enormously in scale, from a company such as Virgin Holidays sponsoring a series of outdoor music events to a local coach company providing the cost of the kit for a local football team. Either way, the principle is the same: both Virgin Holidays and the coach company will expect a return on their investment in the form of wider publicity in the national and local media, leading to increased levels of business.

Mission and objectives

It is currently very fashionable for travel and tourism organisations, whether in the public, private or voluntary sector, to develop a mission statement, which is a brief explanation of its primary purpose. The mission statement is intended to convey to all those with an interest in the organisation, be they staff, shareholders or the public in general, what business it is in and where it sees itself going. Some mission statements introduce an element of the organisation's philosophy and values.

Mission statements vary enormously in their complexity; some are very short and to the point, while others go into great detail about how an organisation intends to develop in the future. It is generally thought that a short, concise mission statement is the most useful in giving a clear indication of a company's intentions. A good example is the Tower Bridge Experience in London whose mission is:

To be recognised as one of the world's unique heritage working sites, by delivering excellence in all the services which we provide.

Another company that has spent considerable time on developing its mission statement is British Airways (BA), formerly a state-owned airline and now a public limited company (plc). In 1986, Sir Colin Marshall, then its Chief Executive, set out the mission for British Airways:

To be the best and most successful company in the airline industry.

At the time this seemed an impossible dream for an airline which was considered very poor by its customers. However, by improving customer service and by redefining its marketing, sales and managerial approach ready for life in the private sector, the company transformed its reputation and its finances. Customers were impressed by a new-found focus on service. Investors, including most employees, also benefited from the growth in the value of its shares.

Ten years on, British Airways faced new and different challenges. To continue to improve, it had to reinvent itself again. In May 1997, it redefined its mission, values and goals (objectives) to address four key areas:

✪ **The global economic climate**
✪ **The challenge of competition**
✪ **What customers were asking for**
✪ **What employees wanted**

Helped by a cross-section of employees, it redefined its mission, set out the values by which it would work, and developed long-term goals (objectives) fundamental to achieving its mission.

The new mission, values and goals aimed to drive British Airways forward for the next ten years, with better customer service, financial and operational targets, and improved ways of working between employees and management. The mission and values set its long-term course and define how it will behave. The goals (objectives) are the individual steps which will turn the mission into tangible operational and financial targets, the steps British Airways needs to take to make a real difference to its competitive performance.

BA's new mission is:

To be the undisputed leader in world travel.

Its new values are:

- *Safe and secure*
- *Honest and responsible*
- *Innovative and team-spirited*
- *Global and caring*
- *A good neighbour*

The new goals are:

browse this website

www.british-
airways.com

- *Customers' choice – Airline of first choice in key markets*
- *Strong profitability – Meeting investors' expectations and securing the future*
- *Truly global – Global network, global outlook and recognised everywhere for superior value in world travel*
- *Inspired people – Building on success and delighting customers*

Some people are very sceptical about the value of mission statements and see them as nothing more than a public relations tool. What the mission statement can do is set out in very broad terms the direction in which an organisation is hoping to progress in the future and provide a framework for the development of its more specific business objectives.

Mission statements were first developed in private sector companies, principally in the USA, but are now to be found in public and voluntary sector travel and tourism organisations. Some local authorities, however, have chosen not to follow the trend of developing a mission statement and prefer to continue to summarise their work in a policy statement. A policy statement for a typical, progressive borough council leisure and tourism department is shown in Figure 4.8.

Blueridge Borough Council
Leisure & Tourism Department

Blueridge Borough Council takes pride in the standards of service it delivers to the residents of the Borough and visitors to the area. Our primary responsibilities are to promote services of the highest possible quality within the resources we have, at a cost acceptable to Council Tax payers, tenants and users of our leisure and tourism services. We, therefore, place great emphasis on caring for the needs of our customers and on being cost-conscious and efficient.

We aim to deliver services through an effective partnership of councillors and employees. We endeavour to ensure that our staff are well trained and are aware of the aims and objectives of the Council.

The Council's belief is that the residents of the Borough and visitors from outside expect a high level of efficiency in the services they use, and are looking for a dynamic and forward looking approach towards building on its services for a growing population, thus enhancing the quality of life for all.

Figure 4.8   *Policy statement of a local authority leisure and tourism department*

Activity 4.7

Write down the mission statements of one local and one national travel and tourism organisation and analyse whether each gives a good idea of the philosophy of the organisation. Try to think of some specific objectives that the organisations would need to achieve in order to be successful.

Case Study
Marketing the Queen's Hotel, Southsea

The Queen's Hotel was built in 1860 and was originally known as Southsea House, the home to Sir John and Lady Morris. It became the Queen's Hotel in 1861 when it was rented to William Kemp Jnr. The building was destroyed by a major fire in 1901 and rebuilt as close to its original form as possible. The Queen's Hotel has been owned by the same family since 1962. In 1990 a major refurbishment was undertaken to update facilities. It currently has a three-star rating from the RAC with many of the facilities required to upgrade to a four-star hotel. The Queen's holds a five-crown rating from the English Tourist Board. The Princess Restaurant has been awarded an AA Rosette.

The present General Manager has been with the Queen's since 1993 and has done a great deal to improve working conditions and facilities at the hotel, including the introduction of IT to all working areas. The hotel currently has 100 bedrooms and employs 43 full-time staff and 40 part-time staff. These numbers increase when demand is high, by anything between 10 and 50 casual staff. In comparison to the industry as a whole, the staff turnover at the Queen's is low. The hotel has increased revenue by an average of 14 per cent each year for the last five years.

In 1994 the Queen's became part of Consort Hotels, but in 1997 joined the much larger consortium of Best Western

continued

continued

Hotels. To maintain membership of the group the Queen's Hotel is inspected and must score 68 per cent overall. Best Western recommend striving for 70 per cent, which is difficult to achieve when 1 per cent is lost if dust is found in just one bedroom!

► BEST WESTERN HOTELS

Best Western is the world's largest consortium of independent hotels, with over 3,600 properties in 2,200 cities and in 66 countries. In Britain, more than 200 hotels carry the Best Western label. The consortium has been the country's leading group of independent hotels for well over a quarter of a century. Member hotels are found in all sorts of locations, ranging from city centres and market towns, to country estates and seaside resorts, to off-shore islands such as the Isle of Man and the Channel Islands. All hotels retain their individual style and take pride in maintaining their unique charm and character.

Best Western has an international reputation for providing guests with consistently high standards of service and accommodation coupled with excellent value for money. In Britain, standards have traditionally been monitored through an annual hotel inspection scheme, operated by the Automobile Association (AA) on behalf of Best Western. However, in January 1997 a new Global Quality Assurance Scheme was introduced, although the UK continues to use the AA's star classification and percentage rating system for its own membership and marketing purposes. The new scheme is mandatory for all Best Western properties throughout the world and will provide the customer with the security of consistent global minimum standards.

Membership of Best Western gives independent hoteliers the strength to succeed in an increasingly competitive marketplace. Indeed, one of the greatest strengths of Best Western is that of being the most extensive network of properties in the world. This unprecedented exposure for relatively small individual units is available through no

continued

continued

other channel. Furthermore, the consortium is able to provide central resources and professional skills which give the benefits normally enjoyed only by hotels within large, company-dominated groups.

Best Western does not own hotels; it is a consortium of independently owned properties which have joined together to maximise marketing, reservations and other aspects such as bulk buying power.

Best Western UK is now a buoyant company truly competing with all the major hotel groups. The operation is funded through two major sources: firstly through an annual subscription from the hotels, which varies according to the number of bedrooms at each property, and secondly by levying a commission on bookings made through Central Office.

Best Western members enjoy all the benefits of being part of a major worldwide hotel group, such as international reservations, exposure in over three million pieces of print each year, a national sales team linked to international sales initiatives, press and media exposure, advertising, marketing and sales, research, national and international representation and purchasing power. Inevitably, to negotiate successfully on a corporate basis on behalf of a group of independent owners requires considerable discipline. To this end it is vital that the Best Westerners always work to ensure that the membership as a whole conforms to the requirements of a unitary body, thus endorsing its marketing credibility in terms of its ability to negotiate corporate rates and corporate deals. For the individual hotelier the rewards are clear to see: they benefit from real business growth and market acceptance by the major buyers and agencies. The potential long-term benefit of these arrangements is self-evident, particularly since the true value of being independent is also the core strength of the competitive quality of the consortium, i.e. individual, non-standardised service and hospitality to the customer.

continued

continued

BEST WESTERN MARKETING ACTIVITIES

Marketing activities take many different forms and occur internationally through the Best Western group. Every year six international exhibitions, such as the World Travel Market in London, are attended by representatives of Best Western.

Annual publications that include the Best Western group are:

- ★ *UK Hotel Guide*
- ★ *European Atlas and Hotel Guide*
- ★ *Getaway Breaks*
- ★ *Christmas and New Year Breaks*
- ★ *Meetings and Conference Directory*
- ★ *Group Tours Manuals*

Best Western offer incentives and gift vouchers such as the Pleasure Cheque available in various sterling values. They work in the same way as store vouchers and can be used to settle part or all of a hotel account. Bonus Bonds are an incentive scheme which are exchangeable in outlets such as Debenhams, H. Samuel and all Best Western hotels in the UK.

Employees of Best Western hotels can enjoy a scheme called 'Best Friends', which allows discounts of 50 per cent or more on Best Western accommodation in Europe and between 10 and 50 per cent at selected hotels in the USA and Canada. It is possible to qualify for additional discounts at the proprietor's/manager's discretion. Employees can also receive a 20 per cent discount on car rental with Avis Rent-a-Car.

QUEEN'S HOTEL MARKETING ACTIVITIES

- ★ The hotel is listed in the AA and RAC Hotel and Restaurant Guides

continued

continued

★ Brochures are placed in every tourist information centre in the English Tourist Board's southern region from Hastings to Torquay

★ Advertising occurs in the local press of cities such as Portsmouth, Southampton, Chichester, London, Guildford, Winchester, Basingstoke and Brighton

Events such as Christmas and New Year are additionally advertised by direct mailing of previous seasonal guests and anyone who made enquiries about Christmas and New Year.

Businesses are directly contacted by telephone and letter to publicise the conference facilities and are invited to lunch or dinner with a tour of the hotel.

(Information courtesy of the Queen's Hotel, Southsea)

Case study discussion questions

1 What specific marketing and promotional activities does the Queen's Hotel undertake?

2 How does the Queen's Hotel benefit from being a member of the Best Western Consortium?

3 How does Best Western ensure high standards in its member hotels?

4 What incentives does Best Western offer its employees?

Market research

Key topics in this section:

- **Introduction – what is market research?**
- **The market research process**
- **Classifying customers**
- **Primary research**
- **Secondary research**
- **Survey design and analysis (sampling, questionnaire design, data analysis, reporting on the survey results)**

Introduction – what is market research?

Market research is the collection and analysis of data about customers and its use for management purposes. Market research data, from whatever source, is invaluable to travel and tourism businesses as it provides a sound base on which effective marketing decisions can be made. All organisations need feedback from their existing customers about whether they are happy with the products on offer, whether the prices give value for money and how best they can be promoted. They also need information such as where their customers come from, how often they travel, their ages and so on. In addition, many will want to know why people are not using their facilities but prefer what a competitor is providing. It is the job of market research to provide this sort of data in as objective a form as possible, in other words with no bias. This is why many companies in travel and tourism employ outside specialists to carry out the research on their behalf.

Not all marketing research activity is a costly or elaborate affair. The proprietor of a small hotel, for example, will constantly get informal feedback from guests on their opinion of the hotel's facilities or standards of service and will make the necessary adjustments. What he or she does not always know, of course, are the opinions of the people who say nothing; the British are notoriously reticent about complaining so that an anonymous questionnaire or suggestions form may provide more reliable and honest information!

We saw at the beginning of this unit that successful marketing in travel and tourism is founded on an effective market research base. All organisations need to have detailed information on their existing customers and users, as well as data with which to plan for the future – a concept known as forecasting.

Identifying customer needs is an essential first stage in the marketing process, from which products and services geared to customer needs can be developed and their success monitored. Without the structured, objective and focused approach to the collection of data, which a well-designed market research study can offer, decisions taken by managers in travel and tourism are unlikely to be wholly effective.

Research may be required at any stage of the marketing process, perhaps linked to a feasibility study to investigate the expansion of an existing theme park or to consider alterations to the pricing levels at a holiday centre. Most managers would agree that market research is very important since it can help their organisations remain buoyant in the increasingly competitive travel and tourism industry. More specifically, market research can:

- **Identify problems and suggest solutions, e.g. whether the council of a Victorian spa town, which is keen to expand tourism, should spend its budget on improving facilities at its tourist attractions or on marketing the town**
- **Allow an organisation to plan for the future with confidence**
- **Identify new market opportunities or sales outlets**
- **Monitor the reaction of customers and users to a product, service or facility**
- **Help pinpoint specific business problems, e.g. why there has been a steady drop in sales for a particular product or at a particular facility**
- **Monitor trends in the industry and its constituent sectors**
- **Project an image of an organisation that cares about its customers and respects their views and comments**
- **Reduce costs by highlighting ineffective practices and systems**

Industry example

browse this website

www.warwick-castle.co.uk

Warwick Castle, one of the Tussauds Group of visitor attractions, makes extensive use of market research to maintain its customer-led approach to management. Market research allows the managers of the attraction to have more understanding of their customer markets, monitors consumer behaviour and helps strategic development and

continued

continued

planning for the future. It helps the company to make important decisions on what marketing activity to carry out, what will work most effectively for which customers and when to plan it.

Warwick Castle uses market research techniques to discover more about both existing and potential customers. Once you know the 'profile' of your existing customers, you can target other potential customers in the same categories.

The attraction uses a mixture of primary and secondary market research. Primary research involves surveying customers face to face, for example asking questions as they arrive at or leave the castle. Secondary research involves the analysis of existing data, for example independent surveys and statistics. There are many reasons for carrying out the market research, which can be very specific or quite general, for example gathering the opinions of customers before launching a new product, testing a product or monitoring customer satisfaction levels once they have purchased a product/visited the castle.

The market research process

Although the type of market research carried out will vary between different travel and tourism organisations, depending on such matters as the size of the organisation, the sector in which it operates, its turnover and the importance it attaches to the process, Figure 4.9 shows us that there are a number of clearly defined stages that any market research process needs to go through:

1 **Identify the objectives of the market research**: An example might be 'to seek the views of the visitors to a tourist information centre to help further development of the products and services on offer'. A process with a clearly defined purpose is far more likely to provide information that is useful for decision-making purposes. Aims that are non-ambiguous, identifiable and measurable will not only provide a focus for the research activity, but also allow those who have commissioned the research to evaluate whether or not it has been successful in meeting its objectives.

Stage one
Identify research objectives

Stage two
Develop a research strategy

Stage three
Carry out the strategy

Stage four
Analyse data

Stage five
Report on the findings

Figure 4.9 *The market research process in travel and tourism*

2   **Develop a research strategy**: Once the purpose of the market research has been agreed, it will be necessary to draw up a plan of how the objectives are to be met, in other words, to devise a strategy indicating which research methods are most appropriate; this is known as the methodology. The strategy will need to answer such questions as:

- ✪ Is any (or all) of the information required to meet the objectives already available from other sources?
- ✪ What emphasis will be placed on secondary and primary research sources?
- ✪ If secondary research is needed, which sources will be consulted?
- ✪ What primary research method or methods will be used?
- ✪ Who will carry out the research?
- ✪ What will it cost?
- ✪ What is the timescale for implementation?

3   **Implement the chosen strategy**: It may be, for example, that a major travel agency chain that is considering opening a new city centre travel shop decides to carry out a small-scale interview survey of shoppers in the city and a telephone survey of major businesses as its primary research, together with an analysis of economic and demographic data published by the local council planning department and local chamber of trade. It might also refer to the *Travel Trade Directory*, as its secondary research.

4   **Analyse the data**: Once collected, the information will need to be collated into a form that is easily interpreted. Depending on the size of the market research project, this may be carried out manually or by computer.

5   **Report on the findings of the study**: In nearly all cases, a written report will be produced for distribution to those who have commissioned the study. It is helpful if the main elements of the study and its recommendations are summarised as 'an executive summary'. Nowadays, it is becoming increasingly common to supplement this written document with a formal presentation, where the people who carried out the study can be questioned in more depth on their findings and recommendations. Such an event will normally take place a short while after the distribution of the final report, so as to allow time for the readers to look in detail at the document.

A decision will also have to be made on whether qualitative or quantitative data (or both) is to be collected as part of the market research. Qualitative data is concerned with people's opinions, for example what improvements holidaymakers thought could be made to their accommodation, whereas quantitative data refers to objective statistics, such as the number of visitors to a tourist attraction or total number of holidays sold to a particular destination. In practice, most market research studies involve both types of data.

Classifying customers

If we start from the point of view that everybody is unique, then the number and range of customers who buy travel and tourism products are immense. The characteristics of customers, for example their age, social class and income level, will be different at different travel and tourism facilities, while their habits, tastes and even moods will change over time and in different locations, for example generally most British people feel better when in a sunny climate. Customers' expectations will also differ depending on, for example, their education, religion and cultural background. An important group of customers are those with special needs, including the elderly, young children and people with disabilities.

Because customers are all so different, a number of attempts have been made to classify them or put them into different categories in order to simplify the market research process. We saw earlier in this unit when we investigated market segmentation (see page 223) that classifying customers into particular groups allows a company to focus its marketing more precisely on the people in the group, thereby increasing the chances of marketing success.

Three of the best-known classification techniques used in travel and tourism are:

✪ **Socio-economic classification**

- ✪ **Life cycle classification**
- ✪ **Lifestyle classification**

We will look at each of these in a little more detail.

Socio-economic classification

For many years, this JICNARS (Joint Industry Committee for National Readership Surveys) classification based on 'social class' was the only one available to marketers. Individuals were placed into one of six categories according to the occupation of the head of the household (see Table 4.1).

The underlying principle of the socio-economic classification is that those in each category will have similar interests, display similar patterns of buying behaviour and have similar income levels. It is assumed, also, that those at the top of the scale will have the highest level of disposable income, i.e. money left over when all household and other commitments have been met. Clearly, there are a number of anomalies in this classification system:

- ✪ It is too much of a generalisation to expect all those in a particular category to act in the same way. For example, a surgeon (social grade A) may choose to read the *Daily Mirror*, a newspaper read mostly by working-class people (social grade D).
- ✪ If the managing director of a large public limited company loses his or her job, he or she will immediately move from social grade A to social grade E.
- ✪ Many skilled manual workers (C2) may well have a higher disposable income than those in the C1, B or A social grades when payment for

Social grade	Social class	Typical occupations
A	Upper middle	Higher managerial, admin. and professional (e.g. judges, surgeons)
B	Middle	Intermediate managerial and admin. (e.g. lawyers, teachers, doctors)
C1	Lower middle	Supervisory, clerical, junior management (e.g. bank clerk, estate agent)
C2	Skilled working	Skilled manual workers (e.g. joiner, welder)
D	Working	Semi- and unskilled manual workers (e.g. driver, postman, porter)
E	Those at lowest level of subsistence	Pensioners, widows, casual workers, students, unemployed people

Table 4.1 *Socio-economic classification*

items such as private education and private health care are taken into account.

✪ When the whole social fabric of the nation is changing so rapidly, it is even questionable who the head of the household is. Today, the heads of many households may be unemployed and in receipt of state benefits.

Life cycle classification

The shortcomings of the socio-economic classification led marketers to investigate if there wasn't a better way of categorising segments of the population. The life cycle concept puts an individual into one of nine categories which are based, not on income, but on where that person is in his or her life cycle. The categories, with an indication of their likely demand for travel and tourism products, are:

1   **Bachelor stage**: young single people with few ties and a reasonable level of disposable income. Likely to frequent clubs in the UK and take adventurous holidays abroad.

2   **Newly-wed/living together**: possibly a higher disposable income with leisure pursuits such as going to the cinema, eating out, going to clubs, taking short breaks and holidays abroad.

3   **Full nest 1**: young marrieds/living together with youngest child less than six. Beginnings of family-orientated leisure including visits to the park, tourist attractions and family holidays.

4   **Full nest 2**: as above but youngest child over six. Falling disposable income, less spending on travel, but some holidays taken in the UK.

5   **Full nest 3**: older couples with dependent children, perhaps still studying. Disposable income low. Leisure centred on the home, with some holidays in the UK and cheaper overseas holiday options.

6   **Empty nest 1**: older couples, childless or children all left home. Level of disposable income likely to be restored. Demand for short breaks, overseas travel and active leisure.

7   **Empty nest 2**: older couples, chief breadwinner retired. Income again restricted. Avid watchers of the television and listeners to the radio with holidays again centred on the UK.

8   **Solitary survivor 1**: single/widowed person in work. Home and garden likely to provide most leisure activity, with few holidays taken.

9   **Solitary survivor 2**: as above but retired. Little spare cash for travel. Television, radio and other home entertainment are important leisure activities.

Lifestyle classification

A further refinement of the process of categorisation came with the introduction in Britain during the 1980s of the concept of lifestyle classification, a technique that had previously been used in the USA. One of the first British companies to test the concept was Young and Rubicam, a well-known advertising agency, who developed a lifestyle classification known as the '4 Cs': four classes of people who were categorised according to their lifestyles as follows:

1   **Mainstreamers**: These are people who are looking for security and who live a conventional lifestyle. They usually buy well-known brands of products, such as Heinz, Daz and Fairy Liquid, rather than 'own brands'. Mainstreamers do not want to 'stick out from the crowd'. They are by far the largest of the four groups, accounting for around 40 per cent of the British population. Their travel preferences are rather conventional, choosing well-known holiday companies, such as Thomson and British Airways Holidays, and familiar overseas destinations, such as Spain and Portugal.

2   **Aspirers**: These are people looking for status and who like to be thought of as being 'at the cutting edge' of society. They buy status symbols such as fast cars and expensive jewellery and generally like the good things in life. They are risk-takers and many aspirers run their own businesses. Holiday interests include hang-gliding, motor sports, power boating and expensive overseas holidays to long-haul destinations.

3   **Succeeders**: These are people who have already achieved status and who ultimately like to be in control of their lives. They have no need for status symbols but value quality in all that they purchase. Travel interests include gardening, taking short breaks, cultural holidays and playing golf.

4   **Reformers**: These are people who consider that 'quality of life' is more important than status and status symbols. They are the best educated of all four groups and tend to join groups to influence decision-making in society. They buy many natural products and 'own label' products; they are sometimes referred to as 'the Sainsbury shoppers'! Travel is often family-orientated and includes camping, walking and cycling, both in the UK and overseas in countries such as France and Holland.

Primary research

Once a travel and tourism organisation has identified the need to carry out some market research, it has to decide whether to conduct primary research, secondary research or both. Primary research is the collection and analysis of

**Activity
4.8**

Divide your group into four equal teams, each
choosing to investigate one of the lifestyle
classification categories (mainstreamers, aspirers,
succeeders or reformers). Working with others in your
team, carry out some detailed research on two holidays that
you think would appeal to people in your category. Include
full details of the holidays (cost, destination, mode of travel,
etc.) and explain your reasons for choosing the holidays and
why you think they would be of appeal.

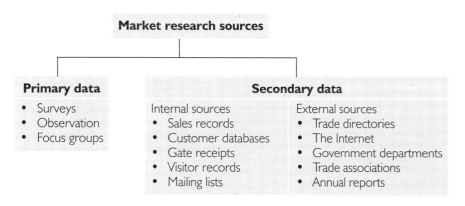

Figure 4.10 *Market research sources in travel and tourism*

new data that is not currently available from published sources, for example an
interview survey of visitors to a tourist attraction at a particular time.
Secondary research is the analysis of data that is already available, either from
public sources or from an organisation's own records. Figure 4.10 shows the
main sources of primary and secondary research data used in travel and
tourism.

Although there is a good supply of relevant and up-to-date secondary data
available on the travel and tourism industry (see page 269), it is highly likely that
an organisation, at some stage in its development, will need to carry out
primary research to collect information that is specific to its own operations and
is not already available.

Methods of collecting primary research data

An organisation wanting to collect primary data has three main options available
to it:

- ✪ **Surveys**
- ✪ **Observation**
- ✪ **Focus groups**

Surveys

By far the most common method of collecting primary data in travel and tourism is by conducting a survey. This involves the collection of data from a proportion of a total 'population' which researchers refer to as the 'sample'. In this context, 'population' means the total number of people who could be interviewed. For example, the manager of a tourist attraction may decide to interview a 10 per cent sample of all visitors to the attraction on a particular day during the season. If the total number of visitors is 5,000 (the population), 500 interviews (the sample) will need to be undertaken. Sampling is carried out because it is usually impractical to interview the whole 'population'. It is a very precise technique which we will investigate later in this section.

There are three main types of survey that can be used to collect primary data:

- ✪ **Face-to-face interview survey**
- ✪ **Self-completed questionnaire survey**
- ✪ **Telephone survey**

Face-to-face interviews

A face-to-face interview survey involves an interviewer asking questions of a member of the general public, known as the respondent, and recording the answers and comments on a questionnaire. This type of survey is very common in all sectors of the travel and tourism industry, from tourist attractions to holiday resorts. The face-to-face interview is a very good way of obtaining both quantitative and qualitative data. Quantitative data refers to factual information such as:

- ✪ **Age of respondents**
- ✪ **How far they have travelled**
- ✪ **Their occupation**
- ✪ **Mode of transport used to reach the facility**
- ✪ **Amount of money spent**
- ✪ **How many times a respondent has visited**
- ✪ **How the respondents had heard about a facility**

Qualitative data refers to a person's opinion or attitude to a particular facility, product or service, and provides managers with direct feedback on the views of their customers. Typical questions that would produce qualitative data are as follows:

- ✪ **Which feature of the theme park did you like the most?**

- **How would you rate the standard of service you received at the hotel – excellent, average or poor?**
- **How could the facility be improved for disabled people?**
- **If the company was to introduce a discount scheme, would you use it?**
- **What is your opinion of the food in the hotel?**
- **What was your general impression of the resort?**

Face-to-face interviews can be carried out in a number of different locations, such as:

- **At the respondent's home – more in-depth interviews tend to be carried out in the comfort and privacy of the home**
- **In the street – busy high street locations are often used to interview a cross-section of the general public on general issues related to travel and tourism**
- **On site, for example, at a leisure centre, tourist attraction, hotel, resort, airport, fitness centre, etc. – on-site surveys have the advantage that customers can be interviewed while they are actually taking part in the activity**
- ***En route* – for example, at a frontier post, a toll booth, on a ship or at a motorway rest area**
- **At work – organisations wanting information on business and conference tourism may choose to interview respondents at their place of work**

Face-to-face interviews have a number of advantages when compared with other survey methods:

- **The interviewer is able to explain difficult questions**
- **Visual aids can be used**
- **The interviewer can prompt the respondent for further detail**
- **Initial interest on the part of the respondent is aroused**

The principal disadvantages of the face-to-face interview are that it is expensive, since the interviewers have to be fully trained and the administrative load is high, and that it is time-consuming when compared with other techniques, for example telephone interviews. It does, however, continue to be employed very widely in travel and tourism as a means of providing valuable information that can be used by management to improve its products and services.

Self-completed questionnaire surveys

A survey that requires respondents to fill in a questionnaire themselves has the benefit of being cheaper than a face-to-face interview survey, since there is no

THOMSON

Customer Satisfaction Questionnaire

The best way to find out what a hotel or apartment is really like is to ask the people who stayed there. That's why we have included Your Opinion charts throughout the brochure. Each chart shows four distinct categories: holiday overall, accommodation, location and food quality. Each was rated either excellent, good, fair or poor by Thomson customers. The figures shown in the chart are percentages of Thomson customers who rated the above aspects of their holiday good or 'excellent'.

Your Opinion
Customers rating good or 'excellent' as a % of those surveyed

HOLIDAY OVERALL
ACCOMMODATION
LOCATION
FOOD QUALITY

Win Thomson Holiday Vouchers worth £1500

Please take a few minutes to complete this questionnaire. If you fill in your name and address you could win Thomson Holiday Vouchers worth £1500

Skytours Portland DIRECT

Please [X] the appropriate box, or write in as requested.

1. Your details

Title

First name

Other initials

Surname

Address

Postcode

Date of birth
Day / Month / Year

Today's date
/ /

Daytime telephone number

2. Your holiday details

A Which holiday company are you with?

Thomson ☐   Portland Direct ☐

Skytours ☐

Other ☐ ➡ write in

B The name of your hotel(s)/villa/apartments (name all accommodation stayed in)

C The name of your resort (s) or the name of your tour/safari/cruise

D Board arrangements:

Bed and breakfast ☐   Self catering ☐

Full board ☐   Half Board ☐

Room only ☐

Flexible dining ☐
(combining B/B & H/B)

All Inclusive ☐
(all meals, drinks etc. included).

E Number of nights abroad:

6 or less ☐   8 - 13 ☐   15 - 20 ☐

7 ☐   14 ☐   21 or more ☐

F If accommodation not included in your holiday price, was this:

Airfare/flight only ☐   Flydrive ☐
(flight & car rental only)

2. Your holiday details cont.

G If accommodation not specified until you arrived in resort, was this a:

Late deal [ ]   Price Breakers [ ]

H I am travelling (indicate all that apply):

Alone [ ]   With other adult(s) of same sex [ ]   With an organised group of 10 or more [ ]

With spouse/partner [ ]

With other adult(s) of opposite sex [ ]

I Was this a Young at Heart or Magic Moments holiday?   Yes [ ]   No [ ]

J How many children in each of the following age groups are you travelling with?

	None	1	2	3+
a) Under 4 years	[ ]	[ ]	[ ]	[ ]
b) 4 - 7 years	[ ]	[ ]	[ ]	[ ]
c) 8 - 12 years	[ ]	[ ]	[ ]	[ ]
d) 13 - 16 year	[ ]	[ ]	[ ]	[ ]

3. Flights

	Excellent	Good	Fair	Poor
A UK airport check-in	[ ]	[ ]	[ ]	[ ]
B Overseas airport check-in	[ ]	[ ]	[ ]	[ ]
C In-flight comfort	[ ]	[ ]	[ ]	[ ]
D In-flight food	[ ]	[ ]	[ ]	[ ]
E Cabin crew: service and assistance	[ ]	[ ]	[ ]	[ ]
F In-flight audio/visual entertainment	[ ]	[ ]	[ ]	[ ]

4. In-resort service

	Excellent	Good	Fair	Poor
A On arrival: assistance at overseas airport	[ ]	[ ]	[ ]	[ ]
B Transfer journey to and from your accommodation	[ ]	[ ]	[ ]	[ ]
C On departure: assistance at overseas airport	[ ]	[ ]	[ ]	[ ]
D Welcome Get-Together: presentation and content	[ ]	[ ]	[ ]	[ ]
E Excursions: choice	[ ]	[ ]	[ ]	[ ]
F Excursions: value for money	[ ]	[ ]	[ ]	[ ]
G Excursions: commentary and knowledge of guide	[ ]	[ ]	[ ]	[ ]

5. Your accommodation

Please give an average rating of all accommodation stayed in:

	Excellent	Good	Fair	Poor
A Representatives: service and assistance	[ ]	[ ]	[ ]	[ ]
B Location	[ ]	[ ]	[ ]	[ ]
C Reception service	[ ]	[ ]	[ ]	[ ]
D Bar service	[ ]	[ ]	[ ]	[ ]
E Cleanliness	[ ]	[ ]	[ ]	[ ]
F Public areas: furnishings and decor	[ ]	[ ]	[ ]	[ ]
G Bedroom comfort	[ ]	[ ]	[ ]	[ ]
H Food quality	[ ]	[ ]	[ ]	[ ]
I Waiter service/buffet efficiency	[ ]	[ ]	[ ]	[ ]
J Daytime activities and leisure facilities	[ ]	[ ]	[ ]	[ ]
K Evening entertainment	[ ]	[ ]	[ ]	[ ]
L Villa/Apartment kitchen equipment	[ ]	[ ]	[ ]	[ ]

6. Overall

Taking everything into account:

	Excellent	Good	Fair	Poor
A Flights	[ ]	[ ]	[ ]	[ ]
B Holiday weather	[ ]	[ ]	[ ]	[ ]
C Resort	[ ]	[ ]	[ ]	[ ]
D Accommodation	[ ]	[ ]	[ ]	[ ]
E Representatives	[ ]	[ ]	[ ]	[ ]
F Holiday overall	[ ]	[ ]	[ ]	[ ]
G Holiday company service in resort	[ ]	[ ]	[ ]	[ ]
H Holiday company overall	[ ]	[ ]	[ ]	[ ]
I Value for money	[ ]	[ ]	[ ]	[ ]

7. Other features

Did you yourself:

	Yes	No
A Go to the Welcome Get-Together	[ ]	[ ]
B Go on any Thomson company excursions	[ ]	[ ]
C Ask your Representative for any help or advice during your holiday	[ ]	[ ]

	Excellent	Good	Fair	Poor
D Children's facilities for 0-12 year olds	[ ]	[ ]	[ ]	[ ]
E Children's club for 4-7 year olds	[ ]	[ ]	[ ]	[ ]
F Children's club for 8-12 year olds	[ ]	[ ]	[ ]	[ ]
G Children's Representatives	[ ]	[ ]	[ ]	[ ]

Figure 4.11 *An extract from a self-completed questionnaire*
Courtesy of Thomson Holidays

need to recruit and train interviewers. Self-completed questionnaire surveys are used extensively in travel and tourism as a relatively low cost method for obtaining both qualitative and quantitative data on customers. Many tour operators carry out a postal survey of returning holidaymakers, asking them to complete a questionnaire related to their holiday experience (see Figure 4.11).

The information contained in these questionnaires gives valuable feedback from clients and is often the starting point for changes to products or services. It is common to find self-completed questionnaires at visitor attractions and leisure facilities for customers to complete and either return by post, or leave behind before they depart. Some travel and tourism organisations provide an incentive, such as a free gift or discounted product, in order to increase the number of completed questionnaires. Although self-completed questionnaire surveys are undoubtedly cheaper than face-to-face interviews, there are disadvantages, such as lower response rates, which can sometimes be improved by sending a reminder to the respondent. Also, if a respondent does not fully understand a question, there is no interviewer to ask for clarification.

Telephone surveys

Telephone surveys are gaining in popularity in travel and tourism, as a way of getting a fast response to an event, facility or service. They are used widely in the USA, but are largely restricted in UK travel and tourism to business-to-business activities, for example following up enquiries from buyers who have attended trade shows such as the World Travel Market in London. Companies specialising in selling timeshare also use telephone surveys to target likely customers. Conducting a survey by telephone can certainly give a speedy response and, if trained operators are used, many interviews are possible in a given time period. Disadvantages include the fact that it is not possible to use visual stimulus materials and the likelihood that people will feel that they have had their privacy invaded and will not co-operate.

Observation

As well as formally requesting information from respondents by way of a survey, some travel and tourism organisations make use of observation as a method of collecting primary research data. It is particularly suitable for visitor attractions such as theme parks, art galleries and museums. Observation is practised in many large attractions with the help of sophisticated techniques such as closed-circuit television (CCTV) and time-lapse photography, and can produce valuable information on the flow of people and traffic. Electronic tally counters are used in attractions, leisure centres and tourist information centres to monitor usage. On occasions, staff may be asked to 'mingle' with visitors or customers and to eavesdrop on their conversations without revealing their identities. People are often far more honest about their true feelings when talking in private than they would be when asked questions as part of a survey.

Observation has an important role to play in researching competitors' products. There are very few products, services and facilities in travel or tourism that are truly unique, most having been based on an idea seen elsewhere. It is not uncommon for hoteliers, travel agents and airlines, for example, to use the facilities of competitors in order to pick up new tips and improve their own products. They sometimes employ 'mystery shoppers' to report on their competitors (and even their own!) facilities and standards of service.

Focus groups

Focus groups, or panel interviews as they are sometimes called, give organisations an opportunity to discover what influences an individual's purchasing decisions; for example, why does somebody prefer to fly with airline A rather than airline B? This in-depth information is not easy to obtain from questionnaire surveys or observation, but focus group sessions give respondents the time to reflect and consider in detail why they make the decisions they do. A focus group usually consists of up to ten consumers under the guidance of a skilled interviewer. The interviewer will use a number of techniques to explore the innermost thoughts and values of the members of the group. The sessions are generally tape-recorded for future analysis and will often signal changes of direction in terms of product range or promotional activities. Given the intensive nature of the focus group, it is an expensive method of gaining primary research material and tends, therefore, to be used mainly by larger travel and tourism organisations.

browse this website

www.firstchoice.co.uk

Industry example

First Choice Holidays is undertaking a major market research campaign, investigating people's experiences and expectations of package holidays. The campaign, called 'people make a difference', involves gathering information from more than 200,000 First Choice customers. A team of researchers is spending time in Majorca interviewing people while they are actually on holiday – on arrival, at welcome parties, in the departure lounges and in a wide variety of holiday accommodation. In addition, the holidaymakers are being asked to keep a detailed diary of their holiday experiences, including why they booked, their feelings before their holiday and their reactions during their time

continued

continued

away. First Choice will carry out a detailed interview on their return. A series of bi-monthly focus groups around the country is also underway, with senior First Choice personnel sitting in on the sessions and asking questions of the customers. A questionnaire will also be sent out in November asking a series of detailed questions not normally covered in traditional customer satisfaction questionnaires (CSQs).

Secondary research

Secondary data is information that is already available, usually in written form, but increasingly via computers and other electronic sources such as the Internet. Research that uses secondary sources is sometimes also known as 'desk research'. The main advantage of using secondary research material is that it can save both time and money when compared with primary market research. In reality, most market research studies undertaken for and by travel and tourism organisations involve a combination of both primary and secondary methods.

There is a wealth of secondary data available to travel and tourism organisations, some available from internal sources and much which exists outside its immediate environment (external sources).

Secondary research data from internal sources

It is often surprising what little use many travel and tourism organisations make of their own internal information. A 'trawl' through existing files, databases and records to see if the information contained in them can help with the market research should be the first priority, before external sources are consulted. The following data, held by most travel and tourism organisations, may reveal useful information:

- ✪ **Past and present usage or attendance figures**
- ✪ **The results of any recent initiatives to record visitor attitudes and behaviour, e.g. visitor surveys**

- Lists of names and addresses of customers
- Details of customer profiles, e.g. age, sex, interests, etc.
- Details of any business or corporate clients and their interests
- Formal and informal feedback from customers, e.g. customer comment forms
- Analysis of spend per head on catering and retail

The advent of computer management information systems makes this sort of data much more accessible and useful for market research purposes.

External sources of secondary data

A great deal of data is available to travel and tourism professionals from published information widely available through public libraries and on subscription from specialist organisations. The government produces a large amount of general data, which, although not always specific to travel and tourism, can be very useful in helping to forecast changes in society and the economy. This includes the Family Expenditure Survey, General Household Survey, Social Trends, the Census of Population carried out every ten years, and data published in the Employment Gazette.

Data specific to the UK travel and tourism industry is available from a wide range of private and public bodies, and includes:

- Annual reports of the Scottish, Northern Ireland and Wales Tourist Boards, and the English Tourism Council
- BTA Annual Report
- The International Passenger Survey (IPS)
- The United Kingdom Tourism Survey (UKTS)
- The British National Travel Survey (BNTS)
- *Business Monitor MQ6 – Overseas Travel and Tourism* published by HMSO
- Annual reports of commercial travel and tourism organisations including British Airways, Thomson Holidays, Airtours, Thomas Cook, etc.
- Consultants such as Mintel, Leisure Industries Research Centre, MORI, etc.
- Trade associations such as ABTA, AITO and IATA
- The Statistical Office of the European Communities (EUROSTAT)
- Professional bodies such as the Tourism Society, Institute of Travel and Tourism, and the Hotel, Catering and Institutional Management Association (HCIMA)

The Internet is also proving to be a very useful source of information on the travel and tourism industry, with up-to-date statistics, company profiles and destination information.

Activity 4.9

Working with a partner, investigate what sources of secondary data on travel and tourism are held in your school or college library. If you have access to the Internet, investigate the information available on one travel and tourism company of your choice. It could be a hotel, tour operator, airline, car hire company, etc.

Survey design and analysis

There are a number of important points that need to be considered when designing and carrying out a market research survey, including:

- ✪ **Sampling**
- ✪ **Questionnaire design**
- ✪ **Data analysis**
- ✪ **Reporting on the survey results**

We will now look at each of these in more detail.

Sampling

It is usually impractical for a travel and tourism organisation to interview all its existing or potential customers to gather information from them. Unless the 'population' is very small, for example interviewing all 12 members of a party of tourists on a Himalayan trekking holiday, the organisation must rely on the responses of a proportion of the total number, known as a sample. If the selection of the sample is fair, accurate and based on proven statistical methods, the responses of the people interviewed should mirror those of the total 'population' within known limits of accuracy. The sampling method chosen must reduce bias to a minimum. For example, if a local authority tourism department wanted to collect data on customer attitude to its three tourist information centres, but carried out 80 per cent of the interviews at its 'premier' centre, the results would clearly be biased and not representative of all three facilities.

Sampling may be either random or quota. For a random survey, individuals are pre-selected from a sampling frame, such as the electoral roll. The interviewer is asked to carry out interviews at selected households chosen at random. Many government surveys are carried out in this way. When using the quota sampling method, the interviewer is given instructions as to the number of respondents he or she must interview in certain categories, for example defined by age, sex or social class.

The size of the sample will determine the level of accuracy of the data. Large samples provide more accurate results than small ones, but the increase in accuracy becomes less significant as the sample size is increased. Provided that proven statistical methods have been used to select the sample, a survey made up of around 2,000 interviews will give an accurate reflection of the public's view of general matters to a 95 per cent confidence level (in other words, 19 out of 20 surveys will fall within a stated 'margin of error'). It would be rare for a market research agency to carry out a survey with a sample size of less than 100, even if only broad impressions were needed.

Questionnaire design

As any student will tell you, designing a questionnaire is not difficult! Designing a good questionnaire that will achieve its intended aim, however, is a skilled operation. It is also a very time-consuming process, with constant checks to see that the questions are easily understood and in an appropriate order. Specialists in the design of questionnaires suggest the following sequence to ensure an effective finished product:

1 **With reference to the objectives of the survey, make a list of expected 'outcomes'**

2 **Formulate the questions that will achieve these 'outcomes'**

3 **Produce a first draft of the questionnaire paying attention to question order, language style and overall layout**

4 **Carry out a 'pilot' survey with a small number of respondents to check understanding and suitability of the questions**

5 **Amend the first draft as necessary to produce a final version**

6 **Use the final version in the survey, but be prepared to make minor adjustments if they will better achieve the 'outcomes'**

The following guidelines should be followed when designing questionnaires:

✪ **Always put 'sensitive' questions, e.g. concerning age, occupation, marital status, etc., at the end of the questionnaire; respondents will feel more comfortable about giving answers to such questions than if they appear at the beginning**

✪ **Avoid ambiguous questions (questions with 'double meanings')**

- ✪ **Avoid using jargon**

- ✪ **Make the questionnaire as short or as long as it needs to be; don't be tempted to include questions that, although interesting, will not help achieve the 'outcomes'**

- ✪ **Simple, objective, pre-coded (agree/neutral/disagree) questions will provide clearer answers than open-ended questions**

- ✪ **Avoid 'leading questions', e.g. 'don't you agree that the hotel is comfortable?' is a question that invites a positive response**

- ✪ **Do not include questions that are an impossible test of the respondent's memory, e.g. 'how much did you spend on drinks per day for the first week of your holiday?'**

- ✪ **Use language that is appropriate to the respondent**

Exercise 4.3

Working with a partner, design a self-completed questionnaire that could be used in a local tourist attraction to provide basic information on visitors to the facility.

Data analysis

Once data has been collected by the most appropriate means, it will need organising into an easily usable form, which is known as collating. In the case of questionnaires, this may involve a process known as coding. Each response is given an appropriate numerical code to simplify the analysis, for example a question may have three possible answers and be coded as follows:

Yes   (code 1)

No   (code 2)

Don't know   (code 0)

Simple factual questions requiring answers such as this are relatively easy to code and may well have been pre-coded, i.e. given a code number when the questionnaire was designed. 'Open' questions, to which there could be an infinite number of possible responses, can still be coded as there are usually five or six 'popular' answers which arise more often. Some market research agencies use a technique known as optical mark reading (OMR). OMR equipment 'reads' the pencil marks made on the questionnaires by the interviewers, so speeding up the process considerably.

The data from the questionnaires is then analysed either manually or with the help of a purpose-designed computer program. Computer software has the advantage of speed and the ability to examine the relationships between a wide range of answers.

Having coded the responses, counts of responses can be made and expressed as percentages, for example 46 per cent of those interviewed were male, 24 per cent lived within a 12-mile radius of the facility, etc. An often more relevant, and interesting, analysis of the data can be found in cross-tabulations, when the responses to questions can be cross-referenced with, for example, the interviewees' age, sex, social class, employment, income, etc. For example, a cross-tabulation of data from a visitor survey may reveal that 45 per cent of men visiting a museum were satisfied with the standard of customer service, but only 34 per cent of women gave the same response. Similar analysis in another survey may indicate that males between the ages of 25 and 34 were twice as likely to visit a tourist attraction than males in the 35–44 age category. Detailed analysis of this type is often more useful for management purposes than simple analysis of numbers of responses.

The collated data will next need interpreting for the eventual reader of the market research study. With the availability of sophisticated computer graphics software and laser printing, it is now possible to present data with excellent style and clarity, using a variety of tables, charts, graphs, histograms, pictograms and pie charts.

Reporting on the survey results

The results of the market research will be included in a written report, which should follow the following guidelines:

- ✪ **It should be written in a tone and style appropriate for the intended audience**
- ✪ **Jargon should be avoided wherever possible so that the report can be easily understood by a non-specialist**
- ✪ **There should be an executive summary of the main points and recommendations of the report**
- ✪ **Items such as blank questionnaires and interview schedules should be included where relevant, but are best put as appendices**
- ✪ **Any critical comments must be fully justified**
- ✪ **Any tables, maps, diagrams, charts, etc., should be reproduced to a high quality, and referred to in the main body of the report**
- ✪ **Where appropriate, references and a bibliography may be included**
- ✪ **Above all, any market research report that is to influence**

management decision making should not be written in an 'academic' style, but should be regarded as a working 'tool' that has practical applications

The format in which the report is presented should include:

- ✪ **Title, date, name of the organisation commissioning the research and name of the individual or organisation contracted to carry out the study**
- ✪ **Executive summary (list of the key research methods and findings)**
- ✪ **Details of the brief, terms of reference, objectives of the study and acknowledgements**
- ✪ **Details of the methodology used, to include reasons for selection of methods, how samples were drawn, number of interviews undertaken, etc.**
- ✪ **The findings of the study**
- ✪ **Conclusions and recommendations**
- ✪ **Appendices**
- ✪ **References and bibliography (where appropriate)**

By following closely the five stages of the market research process (see pages 255–257), the report should summarise the key points of the study and make realistic recommendations that management should be able to put into practice for the good of their organisation.

Marketing communications

Key topics in this section:

- **Introduction – what is marketing communications?**
- **Advertising**
- **Brochures**
- **Direct marketing**
- **Public relations (PR)**
- **Sales promotion**
- **Sponsorship**
- **Marketing communications and the law**

Introduction – what is marketing communications?

Travel and tourism organisations use a wide variety of communication techniques to inform their customers and persuade them to buy. Advertising is the most obvious, but you will discover in this section that there are many other methods that are just as effective. Whatever techniques it chooses, it is essential that a travel and tourism company gets its communication right. A holiday centre, for example, may have the latest state-of-the-art sports, leisure and catering facilities, but if it cannot promote itself effectively it is unlikely to succeed.

There are a number of communications techniques that travel and tourism organisations can use to inform and influence their existing and potential customers. The most important are:

- ✪ **Advertising**
- ✪ **Brochures**
- ✪ **Direct marketing**
- ✪ **Public relations (PR)**
- ✪ **Sales promotion**
- ✪ **Sponsorship**

You may come across the terms 'above the line' and 'below the line' marketing activities. 'Above the line' refers to advertising in the various media, for which an advertising agency earns a commission. 'Below the line' activities include direct mail, public relations and sales promotion, which do not attract a commission but are charged on a 'fee' basis, i.e. an agency may charge £5,000 to devise, implement and monitor a small direct mail campaign for a particular organisation.

Whichever communication technique is chosen, it is likely to follow the principle known as AIDA, which stands for:

- **A**ttention
- **I**nterest
- **D**esire
- **A**ction

AIDA is equally applicable whether an organisation is developing an advertising campaign, writing a direct mail letter, designing an exhibition stand or selecting sales promotion materials. In the case of a newspaper advertisement for a newly opened theme park, for example, the person responsible for writing it may choose to:

- Attract **attention** to the advertisement by using colour, bold headlines, a picture of a famous personality or striking graphics
- Maintain the readers' **interest** by keeping the wording of the advertisement as brief as possible, including language and images that the reader can easily relate to
- Create a **desire** to visit the theme park by perhaps offering a discount voucher or other incentive as part of the advertisement
- Trigger **action** on the part of the reader by clearly letting him or her know what to do next, e.g. by including a simple map or directions to the park, printing the address and telephone number clearly, or displaying the opening times.

Activity 4.10

Research a range of local and national newspapers and magazines that include travel and tourism advertisements. Choose one advertisement that best meets the AIDA principle and one that fails to capture your attention. Explain in detail why each advertisement was chosen.

Advertising

Although advertising in general is very widespread in the UK, its use in travel and tourism is fairly restricted. This may seem hard to understand, particularly if we think of the number of travel advertisements on the television, in the newspapers and on commercial radio, particularly around Christmas time every year. This is the peak advertising time for most travel operators when organisations try to persuade potential holidaymakers to book early. It is only the larger travel companies that have the financial resources to be able to mount expensive nationwide television advertising campaigns. Smaller operators rely on selective advertising in the classified pages of newspapers and in specialist magazines. In an industry dominated by small operators, travel and tourism organisations have to make every promotional pound count and so devote their attention more to 'below the line' activities such as PR and sales promotion, rather than spending their limited budgets on expensive advertising campaigns.

The two main types of advertising in travel and tourism are:

✪ **Consumer advertising – when an organisation such as a tour operator or airline advertises direct to the public, e.g. Hoseasons Holidays placing an advertisement in the *Daily Mirror*, or British Midland advertising in the *Daily Mail***

✪ **Trade advertising – sometimes known as business-to-business advertising, e.g. when a tour operator advertises its products in the *Travel Trade Gazette* which is read by travel agents, or an exhibition company places an advertisement in a magazine aimed at hoteliers, such as *Caterer and Hotelkeeper***

The choice of advertising media

The term 'media' is used in marketing to mean the various channels of communication an organisation can use to advertise its products or services (a single channel is known as a 'medium'). It is important for travel and tourism organisations to seek the advice of professionals before deciding which media to choose. Smaller operators may not have the experience to know which medium will be the most effective for their particular products and may, therefore, be wasting their money. As well as working within budget limits, media selection will also depend on the target audience, i.e. the number and type of potential customers that the organisation is trying to reach (the coverage), as well as the number of times the advertiser wishes the message to be communicated to the audience (the frequency). All types of media will provide detailed data on their coverage and circulation, as well as detailed demographic and 'lifestyle' information on their readers/listeners/viewers. This information is usually presented in the form of a rate card.

The more an organisation knows about its existing and potential customers, the better the chance it has of selecting the right choice of media. Market research, therefore, is crucial to effective media selection.

Types of advertising media

The principal media used most frequently by travel and tourism organisations are:

- ✪ **Newspapers and magazines, including trade newspapers and journals**
- ✪ **Television**
- ✪ **Radio**
- ✪ **Cinema advertising**
- ✪ **Outdoor advertising**
- ✪ **Internet advertising**

Figure 4.12 summarises the advantages and disadvantages of each of these media, which are covered in more detail in the following sections of this unit.

Newspapers and magazines

The printed medium is by far the largest group in the UK in terms of the amount spent by advertisers. The British are avid readers and buyers of

Media type	Advantages	Disadvantages
Newspapers and magazines	• Relatively inexpensive • Segmentation possible • Flexibility • Use of colour possible	• Can be poor production quality • 'Static' medium • Smaller advertisements may have little impact
Television	• Access to a large audience • High degree of creativity • Sound, vision and colour • Repetition easy	• Expensive medium • High production costs • Difficult to target market segments
Radio	• Immediacy • Relatively inexpensive • Segmentation possible • Repetition easy • Low production costs	• 'Background' medium • Limited audience numbers • Can be poor production quality • Lack of visual impact
Cinema	• 'Big screen' impact • Segmentation possible • Access to young audience • Local and regional coverage	• High production costs • Limited market
Transport and outdoor advertising	• Low 'cost per site' • Flexibility	• Localised coverage • High production costs
Electronic media (e.g. Internet, teletext, fax shots)	• Novelty value • Speed • Use of graphics and images • Segmentation possible	• Expensive initial investment • Limited market currently

Figure 4.12 *Advantages and disadvantages of selected advertising media*

newspapers and magazines, which is why they are extensively used by organisations wishing to promote their products and services. The total average daily sale of newspapers in the UK is in the region of 15 million copies, with *The Sun* and the *News of the World* being the most popular daily and Sunday newspaper respectively at the present time. Advertisers have a choice of over 9,000 different magazines from which to choose. The main advantages of newspapers and magazines from the advertisers' point of view are:

- ✪ **They are relatively cheap when compared with other media**
- ✪ **Messages can be sent nationally, regionally or locally, depending on which publication is chosen**
- ✪ **Specific segments of the market can be targeted, e.g. readers with an ABC1 social classification are more likely to read the 'quality' newspapers such as *The Times* or *The Guardian***
- ✪ **Readers with specialist interests can be targeted, e.g. an organisation specialising in offering garden tours can advertise in magazines devoted entirely to the subject of gardening**
- ✪ **Reply coupons can be included in an advertisement as a way of compiling a database or mailing list**
- ✪ **Advertisements can normally be placed at very short notice so giving the medium great flexibility**

As far as disadvantages are concerned, some people point to the static nature of a newspaper or magazine advertisement, poor quality printing (although new technologies have meant that excellent results are now achievable) and the poor impact some advertisements can have, particularly if they are included among many hundreds selling very similar goods and services. An example of this would be the classified advertisements in the travel sections of the 'broadsheet' Sunday newspapers, which at certain times of the year are very crowded.

Trade newspapers and journals, such as *Travel Trade Gazette, Travel News, Leisure Management, Travel Weekly* and *Caterer & Hotelkeeper*, allow travel and tourism organisations to communicate with their fellow professionals in the industry and to inform them of new developments in products and services.

Television

Television is the most powerful advertising medium available, which is why it is the most expensive! Approximately 98 per cent of British households have a television set and audiences in the UK can exceed 20 million viewers for a single programme. With the developments in satellite technology, worldwide audiences of hundreds of millions are easily achievable. Advertisers will pay anything up to £40,000 for a 30-second 'slot' at peak viewing time across all ITV regions, and even more when the advertising is linked to a major feature, such as a British athlete running in the 100 metres final in the Olympic Games, which will guarantee a larger than average audience. These costs only represent the 'air time' that the advertiser buys; costs of producing the advertisements themselves are extra and can sometimes be as expensive, second for second, as producing a Hollywood feature film. With costs of this magnitude, it is not surprising that many travel and tourism organisations are not able to budget for TV advertising. Only companies such as British Airways, the Rank Organisation, Thomson Holidays, Alton Towers and Thomas Cook have the financial resources available for national television advertising. Regional TV advertising is within the reach of some smaller travel and tourism operators, such as tourist attractions, resorts and destinations, hotel groups, leisure centres and regional airports.

When travel and tourism organisations have the resources to be able to use TV advertising, the advantages include:

✪ **Access to a large audience**

✪ **High degree of creativity possible**

✪ **Maximum impact with the use of colour and sound**

✪ **The message is dynamic**

✪ **The advertisement can be repeated**

In addition to cost, another disadvantage levelled at TV advertising is that it is difficult to broadcast to a particular market segment, i.e. the message will not be relevant for many of the viewers. Targeting specific segments is becoming more possible with the introduction of 'themed' satellite channels, such as MTV and SkySports, and with new developments in digital television.

Industry example

Warwick Castle, one of the Tussauds Group of visitor attractions, uses television advertising as part of its promotional strategy. Television channels are selected on the basis of the geographical areas from which it is hoped to attract visitors. Central TV is the area that covers Warwickshire. Other areas used include Meridian TV in London and HTV West covering the south-west of England.

browse this website

www.warwick-castle.co.uk

Teletext

As well as being an up-to-date news and information service for viewers of ITV and Channel 4, teletext is also a fast-growing medium for advertisers. Indeed, its operators, Teletext Limited, claim that it has become the UK's leading classified holiday advertising medium, bigger than any of the leading national newspapers. Over 12.6 million homes in Britain have access to the service through their television sets, representing 57 per cent of all households. Teletext is particularly suitable for last minute bookings and latest offers from the airlines and travel companies. There are sections dedicated to, for example, overseas tours, flights only, skiing, cruising, short breaks and motoring holidays. There is also a regionalised page for local airport departures and a complete section dedicated to different holidays in the UK. The use of teletext is set to grow steadily, with sales of new teletext TV sets currently at 1 million per year.

browse this website

www.teletext.co.uk

Activity 4.11

Make a list of the different travel products advertised on teletext. What are the advantages to tour operators and other travel companies of advertising on teletext?

Industry example

Text Direct is the direct sales force of Airtours Holidays, one of the UK's biggest tour operators. They publish Airtours products on teletext throughout the UK and have recently expanded into selling other tour operators' products, along with their sister company Go Direct, which is based in Manchester. Additional advertising appears in the national newspapers on a regular basis. The public view the holidays on the teletext pages or in the newspapers and call direct to Text. They have different telephone numbers for the public, each linked to a particular advertising medium or type of holiday so that responses can be monitored. Teletext direct sales have proved to be so popular that the company felt the time was right for further development and expansion. Due to space restrictions and exhausted resources at Airtours' head office in Helmshore, they opened Go Direct in May 1997 and relocated their Helmshore base to new premises in Accrington in December 1998.

browse this website

www.airtours.co.uk

Radio

Commercial radio is an important outlet for local news and events. It is also a useful advertising medium for travel and tourism organisations that want to communicate with a local audience. Travel agents will use local radio at certain times of the year to publicise their services, and private and local authority tourism operators will advertise their facilities. Local radio is an obvious choice for events such as a local holiday show or a sports match, and tourist attractions will make extensive use of the medium. Its main advantages are:

- ✪ **It is relatively cheap when compared with other media**
- ✪ **The message can be repeated many times**
- ✪ **Audiences can be targeted geographically**
- ✪ **Production costs are low**
- ✪ **It has the advantage over printed media in that voice and sound can be used**

The main disadvantage of advertising on commercial radio is that it is often seen as a 'background' medium, meaning that messages are not always conveyed to the audience effectively.

browse this website

www.warwick-castle.co.uk

Industry example

Warwick Castle uses a number of radio stations for advertising according to the characteristics of the 'typical listening audience', for example where they live, their age, social class, etc. Stations that have been used include Heart FM, BRMB, Mercia, Fox FM, Northampton 7 Sound, Leicester Sound and Radio Wyvern. Radio advertising is also used for tactical marketing activity, such as promoting special events at the castle on specific days throughout the year and marketing the 'Kingmaker's Feast' at Christmas.

Cinema advertising

The introduction of 'multi-screen' cinemas and the general improvements in levels of quality and customer service led to a revival in cinema going in the mid-1980s. This renewed interest means that advertisers are looking again at the cinema as a means of conveying messages to the general public. Cinema advertising has all the advantages of commercial radio, namely the ability to promote local facilities and services, plus the impact and movement associated with the 'big screen', but it does have the disadvantage of high production costs. Cinema-goers are predominantly in the younger age groups, making it a particularly suitable medium for advertising products and services to a sector of the population which, in general terms, has a high disposable income and is motivated to buy travel and tourism products.

Outdoor advertising

Outdoor advertising includes a much wider variety of media than just posters and billboards: flashing signs, tube trains, delivery vans, representatives' cars, taxis, advertisements on buses, sports ground advertising and fascia signs are all part of the communications process in travel and tourism marketing. Outdoor advertising is often part of a larger advertising campaign involving many different media, acting as a reminder of a message that may already have been shown on television or included in a newspaper advertisement. Some local authorities advertise their leisure and tourism facilities at poster sites in their locality and may co-ordinate this activity with a mailing of leaflets to local residents or advertising on local buses. The London Underground is a particularly popular medium for travel and tourism organisations, which use clever and evocative images to appeal to a 'captive' audience of commuters. The Highlands and Islands of Scotland has featured in a very successful campaign on the tube for a number of years, extolling the virtues of clean air and breathtaking scenery (two features that the Underground is not noted for!).

While production costs are high for outdoor advertising, overall costs per site are lower than comparable coverage by television advertising.

Internet advertising

browse this website

www.lastminute.
com

The Internet is very well suited to the travel and tourism industry. Customers can get up-to-date information on a wide range of travel services from flight schedules to train timetables, compare costs of similar products and find the latest information about worldwide holiday destinations. It is even possible to book on-line using secure credit card facilities and to request travel information by e-mail.

It is also an obvious medium that travel and tourism organisations can use to advertise their products and services. With estimates ranging between 30 million and 100 million worldwide users, the Internet is now firmly established as an important part of many travel and tourism companies' advertising strategies. Its advantages over other advertising media include speed of access, targeting of particular market segments and the ability to include colour graphics and images.

Activity 4.12

Choose one national and one local travel and tourism company and list the different advertising media each chooses to promote its products and services. With the use of examples, explain why you think certain media are more effective than others.

Brochures

Brochures are used to sell a wide range of travel and tourism products and services, from hotels and tourist attractions in the UK to holidays and flights abroad. The importance of the brochure in selling overseas package holidays cannot be overstated. It is the tour operator's main promotional and selling tool when hoping to persuade clients to book with the company rather than go with one of its competitors. Given the crucial role that brochures play in marketing holidays, it is small wonder that UK based tour operators produce more than 100 million copies every year! In addition to the general aim of persuading potential holidaymakers to make a booking, holiday brochures have a number of distinct functions, including:

- ✪ **To accurately present products and services to the reader**
- ✪ **To convey an image of the company**
- ✪ **To convert an enquiry into a sale**
- ✪ **To offer a means of booking a holiday**
- ✪ **To explain booking and contractual conditions**
- ✪ **To present the information within the bounds of current UK and European Union legislation**

Accuracy of the information contained in any tour operator's brochure is essential, since there are now strict legal sanctions for failure to comply with relevant legislation, including the EU Package Travel Regulations and the Trade Descriptions Act. Tour operators that are members of the Association of British Travel Agents are further bound by the Association's Tour Operators' Code of Conduct, which includes detailed regulations concerning the content and presentation of brochures. The Code states that:

Every brochure published by or in the name of any ABTA member shall contain clear, legible, comprehensive and accurate information to enable the client to exercise an informed judgement in making his choice.

The law affecting marketing communications is covered in greater detail later in this unit (see page 299).

Effectiveness of brochures

Brochures from travel and tourism operators have one principal aim: to sell their products and services (see Figure 4.13). How well they achieve this objective will depend on a number of interrelated design features, including:

⚙ **The appeal of the front cover**

⚙ **The quality of the photographs used**

⚙ **The effectiveness of the artwork**

⚙ **The quality of the paper**

⚙ **The use of colour**

In addition to these specific design factors, brochure effectiveness will also depend on a number of 'product' factors, such as:

⚙ **The price of the holidays**

⚙ **The availability of child discounts**

⚙ **The timing of flights**

⚙ **The destinations featured in the programme**

⚙ **The quality of accommodation used**

⚙ **The availability of flights from regional airports**

If you add to this factors such as the speed of brochure distribution, image of the operator, selling skills of the agent's or tour operator's staff, after-sales service, promotional support and product knowledge, you can begin to see that, although the brochure has crucial importance in the selling of holidays, other factors come into play when considering its overall effectiveness.

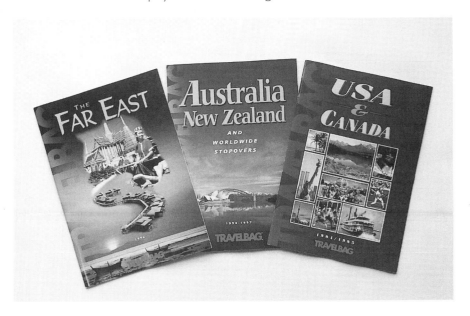

Figure 4.13 *Effective travel and tourism brochures*

Brochure production and distribution

Most mass market overseas holiday brochures are distributed to travel agents in the August or September of the season before the one to which they relate, e.g. brochures for the 2001 summer season will be available in August or September 2000. Winter sun and winter sports are scheduled to be distributed in April or May for holidays taking place in the following winter period, e.g. a February 2001 winter sun holiday will be featured in a brochure distributed in April or May 2000. The brochure production process, however, begins well in advance of these dates, with only the details of pricing being left as late as possible so as to match or beat competitors' prices, or change prices in response to other unforeseen circumstances, for example fluctuations in currency rates. Research for a new tour programme can begin as much as two years before the final brochure is published, while detailed work on brochure preparation generally begins 12 months before the publication date.

Figure 4.14 shows the main stages in the brochure production process, which applies equally well to mass market tour operators and smaller, specialist holiday companies.

Design brief

As Figure 4.14 shows, the first stage in the brochure production process is the formulation of the design brief, which for major tour operators will involve the

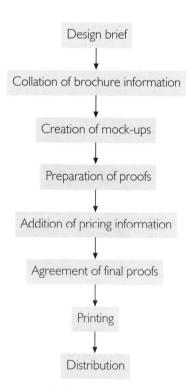

Figure 4.14 *Main stages in the brochure production process*

various product managers and relevant staff from the marketing department, together with in-house or agency designers. The written brief will set out:

- ✪ **The brochure's content**
- ✪ **The style to be adopted**
- ✪ **Extent, i.e. the number of pages**
- ✪ **Illustrations and photographs**
- ✪ **Details of the tour programmes, i.e. which resorts and accommodation are to be included**

It will also explain what other general information needs to be included, such as booking conditions, lists of contents, airport information, etc. The brief may also include details of the total budget for the production of the brochure, although this is sometimes the subject of a separate process.

Collation of brochure information

Once the design brief has been agreed by all parties, work on collating the information to go into the brochure can begin in earnest. This will involve:

- ✪ **Writing the brochure copy**: Specialist copywriters will be responsible for the text of the brochure, mixing factual information on resorts and accommodation with language that will tempt potential holidaymakers to make a booking.
- ✪ **Choosing photographs**: Some may already be available from previous brochures or an in-house library. Other sources of photographic material are specialist commercial libraries, airlines, tourist boards and even holidaymakers themselves! The important point about photographs is to include only good quality material that the target market can readily identify with, and which gives a true representation of the accommodation, resorts and facilities.
- ✪ **Adding ancillary information:** This includes details of insurance, car hire, booking conditions, discounts, health, visa and passport requirements.

While specialists are working on these three tasks, attention will also be paid to the design of any necessary artwork for inclusion in the brochure, plus the all-important front cover. Since the cover is what the customer will see first of all, it must be striking and appealing, while at the same time projecting an image that the prospective holidaymaker can immediately relate to. You would not normally expect to see, for example, a picture of a group of teenagers relaxing by the side of a pool on the front of a brochure targeted at the family market. Tour operators will spend a considerable amount of time with their design agency to select the most suitable front cover image. Nowadays, many of the pictures on front covers are swamped by a mass of other sales messages, such as 'free child places', 'early booking discounts' and 'price guarantees', all designed to appeal to today's cost-conscious holidaymakers.

Creation of mock-ups

Working to the agreed brief, designers will next make a mock-up of what the finished brochure will look like, leaving out detailed information and photographs at this stage. This is presented to the product managers and marketing staff at the tour operating company for their agreement. Changes can still be made to the overall design and layout at this stage if the client is unhappy with something.

Preparation of proofs

Once the mock-ups are agreed, the text is typeset and the photographs and artwork added to produce a first proof of the brochure. These are checked by staff at the tour operator, including the legal department, to ensure accuracy of the text.

Addition of pricing information

While the design process has been underway, the contracting staff at the tour company will have been finalising the prices of the holidays ready for insertion into the pricing panels left by the designers.

Agreement of final proofs

Once inserted, the tour operator will agree a final set of full colour proofs before the brochure is sent for printing.

Printing

Depending on the number of copies to be produced, the brochures may be printed in the UK or overseas, where preferential rates are sometimes available. Small, specialist operators may produce a complete brochure in-house using a desktop publishing (DTP) system, which can offer greater flexibility and reduced cost. Once printing is completed, the brochures are ready to be distributed to travel agents or direct to the public.

Brochure distribution

The precise nature of brochure distribution will depend on whether the holiday or other product is being sold direct to the public or through a travel agent. Since the majority of package holidays are booked through travel agents, distributing the brochures quickly to agents is of paramount importance to the tour operator. An operator's top agents, i.e. those who have sold the most holidays in the past, will receive preferential treatment when it comes to receiving brochures. The tour operator will arrange bulk distribution, either through its own system or on a contract basis with a specialist company such as BP Travel Trade Services (see case study on pages 289–291). Agents with fewer sales will receive smaller numbers of brochures and fewer visits from the tour operator's sales representatives. Point-of-sale (POS) materials, such as posters, window displays and stickers, may also be sent out with brochure supplies for use by the agents in raising awareness of the launch.

Where the holiday company sells direct to its customers, in response to advertising in the consumer press and other promotional techniques, individual copies of the new brochure will be mailed direct to clients who have already made a request. It is common practice to send brochures to clients who have previously booked a holiday with the company in the hope of retaining their custom. The tour company will store the names and addresses of enquirers on a database and use this information for future mailings and for management purposes, for example calculating the number of enquiries that turn into firm bookings or the number of brochures distributed to generate one booking, known as the conversion ratio. Some tour operators will use the services of specialist mailing and distribution companies to distribute brochures to clients rather than carrying out this function themselves, thereby allowing staff to concentrate more fully on the job of selling holidays, as the following case study explains.

Case Study
Brochure distribution – BP Travel Trade Services

Established in 1972, BP Travel Trade Services is a commercial operation that provides a range of marketing and distribution services to the travel industry in the UK. With a purpose-built 68,000 cubic metre warehouse and distribution facility at Ashford in Kent, close to the UK end of the Channel Tunnel, BP offers travel and tourism organisations a number of specialist services, including:

★ *Bulk brochure and literature distribution:* Probably the best known of BP's services, this computerised service offers clients an effective means of distributing brochures, timetables, late availability and special offer sheets, promotions, display materials and commercial information. The service is used extensively by tour operators wishing to service the needs of travel agents.

★ *Brochurebank:* This on-line brochure ordering system for travel agents is accessible via viewdata

continued

continued

systems including Fastrak and Istel. Also now available to the general public via the Internet.

★ *Mailing services:* Frequent mailings to coach operators, UK and European travel agents and numerous other mailings are made by post, courier or fax. Includes 'Mailbag', a twice weekly mailing to UK high street travel agencies, and 'Mailbag Coach World', meeting the needs of more than 3,000 coach operators.

★ *Field marketing services:* Through its sister company 'The Network', BP offers audits of brochure displays in travel agencies, checking of brochure stock levels and reordering, briefings for travel retailers on product benefits, roadshow management, market research and 'mystery shoppers'.

★ *Database management:* A range of services related to direct marketing includes mailing list management, list enhancement, updating and manipulation, plus mailshot production.

★ *On-line services:* Used extensively by travel agents, these include Holidayfinder, Flightfinder and Brochurebank.

★ *Telecommunications:* BP operates a computer integrated call centre servicing its consumer marketing operation (see below).

★ *Printing services:* These provide in-house newsletter printing with a same day despatch option for urgent news.

CONSUMER MARKETING

In addition to its travel trade services, BP also offers a professional fulfilment service to support a company's own promotional or advertising campaign. It operates a call centre that is open seven days a week throughout the day

continued

continued

and evening to answer calls from prospective travellers. Whether enquirers telephone, fax or write, BP undertakes to despatch brochures and other promotional materials promptly.

(Information courtesy of BP Travel Trade Services)

Case study discussion questions

1 What are the main benefits to a travel agency of using the services of a company such as BP Travel Trade Services?

2 What problems might a small travel company encounter when it offers its own enquiry and brochure distribution service to prospective travellers?

3 What changes in brochure distribution techniques are likely to occur in the future?

4 What role is new technology likely to play in helping holidaymakers choose between different destinations and holiday products in the future?

5 Does the location of BP Travel Trade Services give it an advantage over its competitors?

Direct marketing

One of the disadvantages levelled at advertising in the printed and broadcast media is that it is not always effective in reaching its intended audience. For example, an advertisement on local radio may be missed since it is often considered as a 'background' medium. Similarly, a small classified advertisement in the travel columns of a Sunday supplement may be hard to see among many hundreds of others. Direct marketing, however, is rarely criticised for failing to reach its target audience.

Direct marketing is the term used to describe the various techniques that an organisation can employ to sell its products and services on a personalised basis direct to the consumer, without the need for an intermediary. The most common direct marketing methods used in travel and tourism are:

- ✪ **Direct mail**
- ✪ **Telemarketing**
- ✪ **Door-to-door distribution**
- ✪ **Direct response advertising**

Direct mail

Direct mail is the best-known direct marketing method used by UK travel and tourism organisations. It can be very cost-effective when compared to advertising and is, therefore, ideally suited to smaller organisations. It is flexible in terms of timing, budgets and targeting. A direct mail campaign can be actioned quickly and aimed at particular target markets. Its uses in travel and tourism are many and varied, including:

- ✪ **A seaside hotel that sends all its past guests a Christmas card**
- ✪ **The conference officer for a major tourist city who sends a letter and leaflet featuring conference facilities in the city to the top 100 companies in the region**
- ✪ **A travel agency that sends all its previous clients a regular newsletter with details of latest discounts and special offers**
- ✪ **A local authority that sends out a leaflet with its council tax bills giving details of its leisure and tourism services**
- ✪ **A specialist tour operator that automatically sends previous enquirers a copy of its new brochure**
- ✪ **A top tourist attraction that mails details of group rates and facilities to the major coach companies in the UK every year**

One of the most important aspects of a good direct mail campaign is the mailing list, which can either be created from existing information on customers or bought in from a specialist list broker or mailing house. Lists covering all parts of the country and every conceivable interest and lifestyle category are freely available. Larger direct mail campaigns can make use of sophisticated computer-based systems such as ACORN, PIN or MOSAIC, to target by postcode areas the individuals or families most likely to want to buy a particular product or service. The use of these systems will ensure the best possible results and cost efficiency by avoiding wastage by mailing to consumers who are not in the target group.

The basic steps needed for a successful direct mail campaign are:

1 **Decide on the objectives of the campaign – for example, do you want to promote a new attraction; increase off-peak use of a hotel's leisure club; promote your tour packages to overseas travel agents?**

2 **Determine the budget**

3   **Agree the timescale for the campaign**

4   **Create the mailing list**

5   **Devise the direct mail package (see below)**

6   **Carry out the mailing**

7   **Do a follow-up mailing (optional)**

8   **Evaluate the results**

A typical direct mail package will consist of:

✪ **A personalised letter**

✪ **An envelope, which may be overprinted to match the letterhead**

✪ **A 'reply device', such as a freepost address or freefone telephone number**

✪ **An insert, which would usually be a brochure, leaflet or discount voucher**

It takes considerable skill and experience to produce an effective direct mail letter, which will both inform and persuade the reader to buy or use the product or service on offer. As with advertising, the AIDA principle (see page 276) applies to the wording of the letter.

Activity 4.13

Working as a member of a group, devise a direct mail campaign for a local tourist attraction that is aiming to increase its corporate hospitality business, following the eight steps outlined above.

Telemarketing

Telemarketing is growing in importance in travel and tourism, particularly in the business-to-business sector, where one company will provide services and facilities for another. Its use in the consumer sector of the industry is restricted to such products as timeshare and the sale of leisure products.

Door-to-door distribution

Door-to-door distribution is popular with hotels, restaurants, attractions and leisure facilities that want to capture a local market. A certain amount of market segmentation is possible, with particular postcode areas being targeted in terms of social class, family composition, age, etc.

Direct response advertising

Direct response advertising is widely used by travel and tourism organisations that want to create a mailing list at the same time as distributing brochures and other promotional materials. Any advertisement, whether it is on the television, on local radio, in a newspaper, in a magazine or on a billboard, that asks the customer to respond in some way falls within the category of direct response. Some organisations use freefone numbers such as 0800 and 0500, reduced rate 0345 numbers or a freepost address, in order to stimulate more responses.

Public relations

browse this website

www.ipr.org.uk

The Institute of Public Relations (IPR) defines public relations as:

> ... the planned and sustained effort to establish and maintain goodwill and mutual understanding between an organisation and its publics.

The last word of this definition is deliberately used in the plural, since an organisation actually has to deal with many different publics, of which its customers are only one. A travel and tourism organisation, for example, must also maintain goodwill with suppliers, trade unions, the press, councillors (if in the public sector), shareholders (where appropriate), members, distributors, neighbours and voluntary helpers. Public relations is important at all levels and in all departments within an organisation and is not just the concern of the PR department or public relations officer (PRO).

The fact that travel and tourism is a service industry often means that the reputation of an organisation and its products hinges on the attitude of its staff when dealing with customers. The highly competitive nature of travel and tourism makes it vital that all organisations make every effort to develop and maintain a friendly and personal image. PR can play an important role in supporting and publicising this image and presenting to its customers the face of a caring and professional organisation.

As a marketing tool, PR can be far more cost effective than either advertising or direct mail. This makes it a particularly attractive medium for travel and tourism organisations that have small promotional budgets. In fact, the smaller the promotional budget the stronger the case for PR.

If used effectively, PR in travel and tourism can:

- ✪ **Assist in the launch of new products, services and facilities**
- ✪ **Help to 'reposition' existing products, services and facilities**

- ✪ **Generate interest in an organisation**
- ✪ **Help publicise an event**
- ✪ **Influence specific target groups**
- ✪ **Defend an organisation when things go wrong**
- ✪ **Build a favourable image with the outside world**

Although public relations can take many forms and is important at all points where an organisation interfaces with its publics, it is most often associated with press or media relations. It is in the interest of every travel and tourism organisation to build a relationship with the media, whether it be personal contact with key reporters on local, regional or national newspapers, feature editors on appropriate trade and consumer magazines, or TV and radio stations. Familiarisation ('fam') trips are frequently used in travel and tourism as a way of giving a journalist first-hand experience of the product or service that is being promoted. Liaison with the relevant media will not only help the organisation gain publicity for its achievements and success stories, but also improve the chances of putting its side of the story when the news is bad. Good PR can help when a tragedy strikes or unfavourable stories begin to circulate.

The most usual method of informing the media about current news and events is by issuing a press release (see Figure 4.15). These can be sent to local radio and television stations as well as to newspapers and magazines. Editors may be inundated with press releases on a whole range of subjects every day, so the chances of gaining some 'free publicity' are limited. If the release is used, however, the information it contains appears far more credible to the reader than the same message conveyed in an advertisement. The disadvantage of press releases, however, is that the organisation has no control over what the editor chooses to include or exclude. Parts of the news release may be printed out of context and give a negative image of the organisation and its activities.

There are some basic guidelines that will increase the chances of a press release being used:

- ✪ **Keep it crisp, factual and informative**
- ✪ **Write from the point of view of the journalist**
- ✪ **Write to suit the style of the publication**
- ✪ **Answer the basic questions of who?, what?, when?, where?, why?, as early as possible in the release, preferably in the first two paragraphs**
- ✪ **Get the main news point into the first paragraph**
- ✪ **Do not make it any longer than it needs to be**
- ✪ **Give a date to the release and indicate clearly if there is an embargo (a date or time before which it cannot be used)**

Press release

24 January 2000

BUZZ SELLS 100,000 FLIGHTS IN JUST THREE MONTHS

Following the publication of Euromonitor's* 'Budget Airlines' survey estimating that the low cost airline market would grow 133% by 2003, buzz, the newest low cost airline, announces sales of 100,000 seats just twelve weeks after booking lines opened on 31 October, and only two weeks after it took to the skies on 4 January 2000.

buzz is a direct sell airline and flights can be booked over the internet at www.buzzaway.com or by telephone on 0870 240 7070. Internet bookings currently account for, on average, approximately 40% of seat sales on buzz, with the most popular destinations being Milan, Berlin and Paris.

The seat sales figures come just as buzz's introductory price offers ends and the airline's standard fares begin. From 25 January 2000 Done deal fares** to Paris start at £60; Frankfurt, Dusseldorf, Lyons, Milan and Hamburg from £80; Montpelier and Toulouse from £90; Berlin, Bordeaux, Marseilles and Jerez from £100; and Vienna and Helsinki from £120. All prices are for return flights including all government and airport taxes.

buzz begins flights to Helsinki, Hamburg, Bordeaux and Marseilles on 26 March 2000. buzz will also begin flying to its summer sun destinations – Toulouse on 26 March and Jerez and Montpelier on 1 April 2000.

- Ends -

For further information, please contact Jocelyne Simpson or Joanna Cotton at Consolidated Communications

Notes to editors:
*Euromonitor is a market research company that published its 'Budget Airlines' market report on 19 January 2000

**Done deal is the cheaper of the two buzz fare types. It is a return deal, which includes taxes, and flyers must be away for at least two nights. Bookings cannot be changed or refunded. No advance purchase is necessary and seats are subject to availability. Within the Done deal fare there are four pricing tiers with £20 difference between each tier. Approximately 30% of total seat sales will be offered at the lowest Done deal fare – excluding promotional fares.

Open deal is a more expensive but extremely flexible fare. Both return and one-way fares are available. Flying plans can be changed and a credit will be held for six months should a booking be cancelled. Within the one way Open deal fare there will be three pricing tiers with £10 difference between each tier.

Figure 4.15 An effective press release
Courtesy of Consolidated Communications

- ✪ **Respect copy deadlines (the date by which it must be with the editor)**
- ✪ **Include full details of a contact person at the end of the release**
- ✪ **Use double spacing to allow for editing**
- ✪ **Include a picture if it will help tell the story (18 × 13 cm black**

and white for preference, captioned on the reverse to explain who is doing what)

It is important to monitor PR coverage by organising the collection of press cuttings either through an agency or in-house. The PR specialist within the organisation should be encouraged to organise visits by journalists and VIPs to see facilities first hand. Also, the relevant people within the organisation should go out and speak to local groups, clubs and schools, to let them know what you are doing and why.

Exercise 4.4

Write a press release for a forthcoming event taking place in your area or a new travel and tourism facility that has recently opened.

Sales promotion

Sales promotion describes a range of techniques designed to encourage customers to make a purchase. They usually support advertising, direct mail, personal selling or public relations activity and, in travel and tourism, include activities such as:

✪ **Price reductions**: It is common for travel and tourism companies to offer price discounts to encourage more business, e.g. a 'happy hour' in a bar when all drinks are half-price, a leisure centre offering discounted rates at off-peak times, tour operators advertising cut-price holidays if bookings are made before a certain date. National and regional newspapers often join forces with airlines, tourist attractions and hotel groups to run promotions offering discounts on UK and overseas holidays and travel products.

✪ **Free gifts**: A travel agent may provide a free travel bag or item of clothing to all clients booking a holiday; a tourist attraction may give free badges and hats to all children who visit. In 1993, Hoover offered free flights to anybody who bought one of their vacuum cleaners. Unfortunately, the promotion was too successful and Hoover were unable to completely fulfil their promise to every purchaser.

✪ **Exhibitions**: These are a good way of showing both the general public and the trade what's new in travel and tourism. They are also a good PR activity, helping staff to cement relationships and make new contacts.

- ✪ **Competitions**: Some organisations run competitions to encourage the public to buy their products and services. The prizes on offer may include holidays, short breaks or leisure/sports activities.

- ✪ **'Extra product'**: This is when a customer is given additional benefits without having to pay any more. For example, a hotel may provide free newspapers for all guests, a leisure centre may offer vouchers for a free beauty treatment to ladies who attend their aerobics classes, or an airline may provide a chauffeur-driven car from home to the airport for business travellers. 'Three weeks for the price of two', an offer commonly made by holiday companies, is also an example of 'extra product'.

- ✪ **'Passport' or 'loyalty' schemes**: Some travel and tourism organisations offer loyalty schemes to encourage people to stay with them and use their services in the future. Frequent flyer programmes operated by airlines are one of the best-known loyalty schemes; passengers are given points for each trip made and, when they have collected a particular number, can cash them in for free flights. Similar programmes are operated by hotel companies and car hire firms. Visitor attractions sometimes offer a 'passport' which can give free or discounted entry to the site.

- ✪ **Point-of-sale (POS) materials**: These range from window displays, posters and merchandising units to brochure racks, hanging cards and special demonstrations.

The essential feature of sales promotion is that it is a short-term inducement to encourage customers to react quickly. Many sales promotions are undertaken in response to the activities of competitors to ensure that an organisation retains its share of the market.

Although the examples of sales promotions given above are targeted at the consumer, sales promotion techniques can also be aimed at staff working in travel and tourism in order to persuade them to sell or recommend the products or services of a particular company. Travel agency sales clerks, for example, are offered many different incentives by airlines, tour operators and hotel companies. Staff working in travel and tourism may be offered a bonus payment, free training, the use of facilities at discounted rates, social events or entries to a prize draw, to retain their loyalty to a particular company.

As with other forms of marketing activity, it is important to evaluate the effectiveness of the sales promotion against its objectives. It is a relatively easy matter to measure sales or usage before and after a sales promotion and calculate a percentage increase or decrease in activity. The aim of some sales promotions is to clear current stock, for example unsold package holidays or seats for a concert. It is difficult to measure whether a customer who has taken advantage of a special offer may well have paid the full price at a later date. In many respects, the answer to this question is irrelevant as long as the sales promotion fulfils the original objectives.

Activity 4.14

Choose a leading travel and tourism company with which you are familiar and list the various sales promotion techniques it uses.

Sponsorship

In many respects sponsorship is just another type of public relations, since the organisation that sponsors an event or product is looking to gain a return on its investment through increased public exposure. Sponsorship is very common in the sports industry, but less so in travel and tourism. One sector that does attract a considerable amount of sponsorship, however, is museums and the arts in general.

Marketing communications and the law

The various ways that a travel and tourism organisation communicates with its customers are controlled under a number of legal and regulatory provisions, which include:

- ✪ **The Trades Description Act 1968**
- ✪ **The Package Travel Regulations 1992**
- ✪ **The Consumer Protection Act 1987**
- ✪ **The Data Protection Act 1984 and 1998**

We will now look at each of these in detail, plus the work of the body that regulates UK advertising, the Advertising Standards Authority (ASA).

Trades Description Act 1968

This Act protects customers against false descriptions made knowingly or recklessly by those who are selling or providing services, including holiday companies' products and services. Any description of, for example, a hotel or resort must be truthful at the time it was written (if circumstances subsequently change, then the operator must inform the customer of the nature of the changes). This places a duty on owners and operators of travel and tourism facilities to produce brochures and other promotional materials that are not intended to deceive the customer.

Package Travel Regulations 1992

The Package Travel Regulations came into operation on 23 December 1992 in the then 12 Member States of the European Union (the number of countries in the EU rose to 15 in 1995). Its main aim is to give people buying package holidays more protection and access to compensation when things go wrong. The Regulations place a number of duties on the organisers of packages, namely:

- ✪ **Providing information to customers on who is responsible for the package they have booked – that person or organisation is then liable in the event of failure to deliver any elements of the package**
- ✪ **Providing clear contract terms**
- ✪ **Giving emergency telephone numbers**
- ✪ **Providing proof of the organiser's security against insolvency and information on any available insurance policies**
- ✪ **Giving immediate notification with explanation of any increase in prices permitted within the terms of the contract**
- ✪ **Providing a variety of compensation options if agreed services are not supplied**
- ✪ **Producing accurate promotional material including brochures**

The Package Travel Regulations have come as something of a shock to the UK tourist industry since they cover domestic as well as outbound packages. This means that hotels, tourist information centres, resorts, conference organisers, coach operators and even school trip organisers have found that they may well fall within the scope of the Regulations. There has also been much debate about what exactly constitutes a 'package', with Trading Standards Officers, the people given the job of policing the Regulations in the UK, appearing to have different views depending on in which part of the country they are located. The travel industry generally fears that the extra insurance needed by tour organisers to cover against claims under the directive is bound to put up the cost of holidays.

Consumer Protection Act 1987

The Consumer Protection Act makes it a criminal offence for an organisation or individual to give misleading price information about goods, services, accommodation or facilities they are offering for sale. The Act defines a 'misleading' price as one which:

- ✪ **Is greater than the price given in promotional material**
- ✪ **Is described as being generally available, but in reality is only available in certain circumstances**
- ✪ **Does not fully state what facilities are included in the price and the fact than surcharges will be payable after booking**

The Act has special significance for travel and tourism operators who must ensure the accuracy of any price information in their brochures and other publicity material. This is because it is an offence to include incorrect price information even if the inclusion was innocently undertaken, but is later shown to be misleading.

Data Protection Act 1984 and 1998

This government legislation was introduced in 1984 to safeguard the public from problems relating to the inaccuracy of any information held about them on computer records. Under the terms of the Act, all organisations that hold data about individuals on automated systems must register with the Data Protection Registrar and comply with a series of Data Protection Principles, which are a set of good practice guidelines. Individuals who have computer data held on them have a number of rights in civil law, including right of access to the data, rights to compensation for inaccuracy of data or its wrongful disclosure, and rights to have any inaccuracies in the data rectified. Travel and tourism organisations that hold client details on computer databases are likely to fall within the scope of the Act and must abide by the Data Protection Principles. One of the Principles states that the information held on computer must not be disclosed to third parties. This means that a travel agent who holds information on clients on a computer cannot sell the data to another company without being in contravention of the Act.

New data protection legislation came into force on 1 March 2000 with the implementation of the Data Protection Act 1998, which updates and reinforces the Data Protection Principles included in the 1984 Act.

The Advertising Standards Authority (ASA)

The ASA was set up in 1962 to make sure that non-broadcast advertisements appearing in the UK are legal, decent, honest and truthful (TV commercials are under the scrutiny of the Independent Television Commission). The Authority protects the public by ensuring that the rules in the British Codes of Advertising and Sales Promotion are followed by everyone who prepares and publishes advertisements. These are the rules that the industry has written and agreed to follow. Enforced by the ASA, they are there to protect the consumer by helping advertisers, agencies and the media to produce advertisements which will not mislead or offend consumers.

The basic principles of the Codes are that advertisements should be:

- ✪ **legal, decent, honest and truthful**
- ✪ **prepared with a sense of responsibility to consumers and to society**
- ✪ **in line with the principles of fair competition generally accepted in business**

All advertisements and promotions in non-broadcast media are covered by the Codes and are therefore regulated by the ASA. These include:

- ✪ **Press – national, regional, magazines and free newspapers**
- ✪ **Outdoor – posters, transport, aerial announcements**
- ✪ **Direct marketing – direct mail, leaflets, brochures, catalogues, circulars, inserts and facsimiles; as well as the content of such material, the use of mailing lists for targeting consumers is also covered by the ASA**
- ✪ **Screen – cinema commercials and advertisements in electronic media such as computer games, video, viewdata services, CD-ROM and the Internet**
- ✪ **Sales promotions – on-pack promotions, front-page promotions, reader offers, competitions and prize draws**

The ASA will investigate complaints and carry out research for advertisements and promotions in all the media listed above. Independent of both the advertising industry and government, the ASA's work is funded by a small levy on display advertising and direct mail expenditure. In order to preserve the ASA's independence from the industry the levy is collected by a separate body, the Advertising Standards Board of Finance.

browse this website

www.asa.org.uk

The ASA aims to promote the highest standards in advertising. It does this by a programme of industry information and training through some 70 presentations and seminars each year. It actively promotes its work and role through a co-ordinated media relations strategy to the advertising industry and consumers.

Customer service in travel and tourism

5

In this unit you will explore the very important subject of customer service, learning why it is vital to look after customers well. Travel and tourism is a very competitive industry, with many companies offering broadly similar products, for example holidays, short breaks and airline flights, and it is often how well they treat their customers that separates the best from the rest. You will learn about the part that personal presentation, selling and communication skills play in dealing successfully with customers. You will also investigate how to handle customers' complaints and to measure customer service in action.

This unit is divided into eight main areas:

- **Why excellent customer service is important**
- **Personal presentation**
- **Types of customers**
- **Dealing with customers**
- **Selling skills**
- **Customer service situations**
- **Handling complaints**
- **Assessing the quality and effectiveness of customer service**

We guide you through each of these areas using examples and case studies from the travel and tourism industry. At the beginning of each section you will see a list of key topics to help you fully understand what you need to learn. Look out for the links to websites so that you can learn more about a particular travel and tourism company or topic.

Why excellent customer service is important

Key topics in this section:

- **Introduction – what do we mean by 'customer service'?**
- **The benefits of excellent customer service for travel and tourism organisations**
- **What happens when standards of customer service are poor**

Introduction – what do we mean by 'customer service'?

Customers are the most important part of any travel and tourism business. Quite simply, without customers there would be no business! So it is vitally important that customers are looked after well and given the highest standards of service, so that they come back again and also tell their friends about the good time they had. These days, customer service is not just about **meeting** customers' needs, but **exceeding** them. It is also important to stress giving **excellent** and not just **good** customer service.

browse this website

www.centerparcs.
com

Industry example

Staff at Center Parcs, the holiday company with UK villages in Nottingham, Elveden (Suffolk) and Longleat, are fully trained in all aspects of excellent customer service. The company's customer service aim is:

to give our guests a truly unique short break holiday experience which far exceeds their expectations.

(See Center Parcs case study on pages 355–357.)

But, in travel and tourism, customer service is much more than just being nice to your customers. It is about **all** staff in an organisation working towards a positive approach to customers, which involves:

⚙ **Identifying customer needs:** Knowing what your customers want is fundamental to the success of any business. In Unit 4: Marketing Travel and Tourism, we looked in detail at the various techniques that can be used to gather customer information. It is important to remember that the gathering of data is often relatively easy; what can be more difficult is putting into practice the actions that are recommended.

⚙ **Developing the right products and services:** Having found out what its customers want, the organisation can begin to develop products and services that match these requirements to make sure that they are offered at the right price, in the right place, at the right time and, in the case of the commercial sector, at a profit.

⚙ **Measuring customer satisfaction:** Customer service is a constant process to strive to be as successful as possible in satisfying customer needs. The products and services will need careful monitoring and adjustment to meet any changes that the customers are demanding.

⚙ **Developing internal systems**: Customer service is not just about satisfying the customers 'on the other side of the counter'. Many travel and tourism organisations, particularly large employers, will need to give attention to the needs of the 'internal customer', i.e. the staff working within the organisation. Mechanisms to improve internal communications, including regular meetings, social events and staff newsletters, are all part of improving the overall level of service to customers.

⚙ **Staff training:** Training in excellent customer service skills is vital for all staff in travel and tourism organisations, not just those whose work brings them into daily contact with customers. Staff working 'behind the scenes', perhaps in kitchens or on maintenance duties, need to appreciate that they too have an important role to play in keeping customers happy.

Exercise 5.1

Working with a partner, write down ten reasons why all travel and tourism organisations should train their staff in giving excellent customer service. When you have finished, compare your list with others in the class.

Customers are changing!

You have no doubt heard the phrase 'the customer is always right'. While not always strictly true (as staff working in travel and tourism will often tell you!), customers can be very demanding and are often willing to complain when they receive poor standards of service. In Britain today, customers have far greater expectations of service quality than was the case even 10–15 years ago. In the

Figure 5.1 *Customers expect high standards of service*
Courtesy of Eurocamp Travel

travel and tourism industry it is very much a 'buyers' market' where organisations have to compete not only on price but also on quality of service in order to win their share of customers' spending. Service is no longer seen as peripheral, as was often the case in the past (see Figure 5.1).

There is considerable evidence to show that customers, although not always willing to complain openly about poor standards of service, will take action to show their disapproval. The US Office of Consumer Affairs, for example, quotes the following:

- **96 per cent of dissatisfied customers never complain**
- **But 90 per cent of them will not return in the future**
- **One unhappy customer will tell at least nine others**
- **13 per cent of unhappy customers will tell at least 20 others**

Changes in customer expectations have been brought about by such influences as:

- **Exposure to lifestyles from around the world via TV and other mass media**
- **More foreign travel giving greater experience of foreign customer service standards**
- **Increased educational opportunities**
- **Changing work patterns**

The outcome of these influences is a new breed of customer who, in travel and tourism, is demanding improvements in standards of customer service and the products on offer; for example, customers who want to be able to make their travel arrangements 24 hours a day from the comfort of their own home, who are looking for interesting menus and en-suite facilities in their hotels, who want to be able to play a game of squash at 9.30 in the evening, who want a particular newspaper with their freshly ground coffee at breakfast, who want to party until the early hours of the morning and who want to see the latest movies in plush surroundings. In a word, customers who want service excellence.

Industry example

British Airways (BA) is the world's largest international passenger airline with a scheduled network covering some 155 destinations in 72 different countries. It serves more leading international markets than any other European airline. Its mission is:

To be the undisputed leader in world travel.

Its new values are:

- ★ *Safe and secure*
- ★ *Honest and responsible*
- ★ *Innovative and team-spirited*
- ★ *Global and caring*
- ★ *A good neighbour*

The new goals are:

- ★ *Customers' choice – Airline of first choice in key markets*
- ★ *Strong profitability – Meeting investors' expectations and securing the future*
- ★ *Truly global – Global network, global outlook and recognised everywhere for superior value in world travel*
- ★ *Inspired people – Building on success and delighting customers.*

continued

continued

BA's customer service approach was started in earnest in the mid-1980s under the direction of Sir Colin Marshall, then Chief Executive of the airline. To create a clear competitive advantage, the company recognised the importance of adopting a more customer-centred approach to its activities. In 1984 a new corporate identity was introduced across all aspects of the airline, from the colour and design of staff uniforms, through changes to stationery and promotional material to the aircraft themselves. Market research was carried out with a view to establishing both customer expectations of the standard and level of service, and the staff's perception of their role within the company.

The outcome of the market research was the development of a corporate training programme under the banner 'Putting the Customer First – if we don't someone else will'. The programme was launched with a series of corporate events for staff entitled 'Putting People First' aimed at fostering a spirit of teamwork and co-operation among employees. A parallel programme for managers was introduced at the same time, with the title 'Managing People First' which encouraged a more open management style. Subsequent advertising highlighted the excellence in customer service offered to all who chose to fly with BA.

Quality in customer service has now become an essential part of the working practices of all British Airways management and staff. Individual departments have begun to introduce their own quality initiatives and individual members of staff are encouraged to put forward new ideas for improving the level of customer service. One of the major themes of BA's current work in this area is the need to sustain high levels of customer service and provide consistency throughout the company.

browse this website

www.british-airways.com

Travel and tourism is a very competitive industry

Travel and tourism is a fiercely competitive industry. Organisations survive and prosper by having a competitive edge over their rivals and by winning customers from the competition. Because travel and tourism is such a diverse industry, there is competition across a wide range of sectors, for example holiday centres in the UK are competing with villa complexes abroad, different airlines compete with each other on the same routes and high street travel agencies compete for holiday business. In such a competitive environment, excellence in customer service is vital for the survival and development of many companies.

Some travel and tourism organisations have realised that they cannot compete on price alone. A number of holiday companies, for example, have seen their profit margins reduced to such a level that their long-term survival is put in serious jeopardy. Many have decided to develop superior standards of customer service to help single them out from the competition. The race to attract and retain business customers in the airline industry has led to emphasis being placed on such factors as in-flight catering, attention to personal service and even free limousine transfers from airports to hotels!

Activity 5.1

Study the brochures of two well-known, competing holiday companies and list what extra features each includes in its holidays and standards of service to make it more competitive.

We're all consumers now!

Following hard on the heels of customers from across the Atlantic, British consumers are becoming more vocal in their opinions of product and service quality (indeed many British people will have picked up the habit of speaking their mind in such places as the USA where customer complaints are not frowned on but used as a form of market research to be built upon). The introduction of television and radio programmes devoted to the cause of travel and consumerism, for example 'Watchdog', 'Wish You Were Here', 'BBC Holiday Programme' and 'You and Yours', is evidence that people are no longer willing to accept poor service and will 'vote with their feet'.

The increase in consumerism has given rise to customers who place quality of service above all other factors when buying holidays and other travel products. People are, of course, still sensitive to the price of the products they are buying. There is, however, a growing belief that customers will pay a higher price for a higher quality product, delivered with the highest levels of customer service.

The benefits of excellent customer service for travel and tourism organisations

Excellent standards of customer service not only bring benefits to customers, but also to the organisations themselves. Staff working in the organisation will also reap rewards, with increased job satisfaction and maybe even a bonus! The main benefits to the organisation of providing excellent customer service are shown in Figure 5.2.

Figure 5.2 shows that the benefits of offering excellent customer service are part of a cycle, starting with more customers, a better public image and an edge over the competition. Staff will be happier and work more efficiently, resulting in satisfied customers generating customer loyalty and repeat business. Ultimately, the cycle ends with increased sales and profits for the company.

Other benefits to an organisation of introducing excellence in customer service are likely to include:

- ✪ **Fewer complaints**
- ✪ **Improved co-operation between departments**
- ✪ **Reduced absenteeism by staff**
- ✪ **Lower turnover of staff**
- ✪ **Improved security**
- ✪ **Less waste (of materials, time, money, etc.)**
- ✪ **Improved quality in other aspects of the organisation's work**
- ✪ **Reduction in marketing budget (through retaining existing customers)**

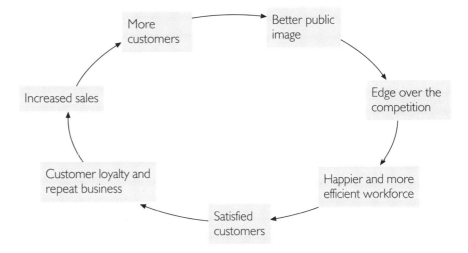

Figure 5.2 *The benefits of excellent customer service in travel and tourism*

Most of all, following a policy of customer service excellence will help to ensure that the organisation achieves its objectives and that all who have a stake in the business, whether they are owners, shareholders, staff, managers or council tax payers, will benefit.

Industry example

Doormen at the Hilton Hotel Belfast are trained in the importance of a warm welcome being offered to guests arriving at the hotel. They greet the guest as follows: 'Good morning/afternoon, sir/madam, welcome to the Hilton Belfast' (or 'welcome back' if the guest has stayed before). They assist the taxi driver/guest with luggage from the car and try to identify the guest's name from the luggage tags, thus giving the personal touch.

browse these websites

www.hilton.com

www.hilton.com/
hotels/BFSHITW/

What happens when standards of customer service are poor

We saw on page 311 that high standards of customer service can bring benefits to travel and tourism organisations. There are times, however, when customers experience poor service, although defining exactly what is 'good' and 'bad' service is not an easy matter. One person's idea of good service in a restaurant, for example, may be thought of by somebody else as merely average. Whether a person is happy or unhappy with the service is essentially a personal experience; no two people have the same perception of good or bad service.

The very personal nature of the customer service experience needs to be accepted by staff working in travel and tourism organisations right from the outset. If customers are not treated as individuals, they will become disenchanted with the service they are getting and may choose to take their business elsewhere.

Although it is not always easy to define exactly what constitutes good service, we are all familiar with circumstances when the level of service we have received is either very good or very bad. In travel and tourism, the following examples give a flavour of what excellent customer service is all about:

✪ **In a restaurant:** An example of good service would be when the management remembers that an evening booking is for a couple's first wedding anniversary and provides a complimentary bottle of champagne. Bad service is when you telephone in advance to make a booking, only to find when you arrive that the waiter has no record of the booking and all the tables are taken.

- **In a hotel:** Good service would be when the receptionist remembers the name of a guest's child and provides a box of toys for the child to play with. Bad service would be not attending to a broken shower in a guest's room as soon as possible after the fault is reported.

- **In a health club:** An example of good service would be providing free use of armbands for all the under 5s in the swimming pool. Bad service would be the temporary receptionist telling a telephone caller that he (the receptionist) is not sure of the cost of hiring the indoor bowls hall for the day as he is new to the job and only comes in on Saturdays.

Activity 5.2

Carry out a small-scale survey of a mixture of people to find out their recent experiences of good and bad service in travel and tourism facilities (hotels, tourist attractions, airports, ferry terminals, villa complexes, travel agencies, tourist information centres, etc.). Record what they say on a sheet and analyse the results with the rest of your group. Suggest how the examples of poor service standards could be put right.

Why are customer service standards sometimes poor?

Providing excellent customer service is a highly skilled task requiring motivation, effort and commitment from the staff involved and support from senior management. However, even the most experienced staff can have bad days! There are many, many reasons why a member of staff may not deal with customers in his or her usual, friendly manner, some personal and some professional. Four of the most common are:

- **Lack of commitment**
- **Insufficient knowledge**
- **Poor communication**
- **Lack of training**

Lack of commitment

We are all familiar with the 'take it or leave it' attitude that is still evident in certain sectors of the travel and tourism industry today, for example the restaurant waiter who gives the impression that he would rather be at home watching the

TV or the hotel receptionist who is less than helpful when you are trying to make a booking. Thankfully, this negative attitude is being tackled in many organisations through management and staff training. It is the job of management to:

✪ **Discover any underlying problems that are causing the lack of commitment**
✪ **Arrange staff training sessions to help deal with the problems**
✪ **Provide a supportive environment in which staff can flourish**
✪ **Involve all staff in customer service improvement**

We will see later in this unit that a positive attitude and commitment are important qualities that anybody wanting to work in travel and tourism needs to develop, particularly those working in front-line customer service jobs.

Insufficient knowledge

Some staff, particularly those new to their job, will take time to settle into their role and gain the knowledge and experience necessary to work to their full

---

BRITISH MIDLAND
QUALIFICATIONS AND REQUIREMENTS FOR CUSTOMER SERVICE STAFF

The following is for information only and does not form part of a Contract of Employment.

Education: 4 GCSE/O Levels including English Language and Mathematics.

Desirable qualifications: Experience in dealing with the general public, as well as being able to relate to other members of staff, as team spirit is a necessity. Own transport is essential.

Appearance and personality: Smart personal appearance with weight in proportion to height. Applicants should be able to work calmly and effectively under pressure, and to maintain a friendly and reassuring manner when dealing with passengers and members of the public.

Hours of work: Basic hours of work average 37.5 per week, consisting of shift work on a rota basis. Overtime may be worked as and when required.

Holiday entitlement: Permanent staff are entitled to 18 salary days, increased by one day for each year of service, to a maximum of 23 days per annum. In addition to holiday entitlement, staff will be granted 8 bank/public holidays, with pay, during the year.

Duties: Customer Service Staff are employed for the assistance and benefit of our customers and, whilst on duty, they may be called upon to carry out many varied tasks, which may include, all, or any, of the following: completion of customer documentation, i.e. airline tickets, baggage labels, excess baggage charges; escort customers to and from the aircraft, through airport controls, Immigration and Customs; assist customers with all enquiries which may be by telephone or in person. It is occasionally necessary to provide relief staff cover at other bases.

Salary: Will be paid in accordance with the Company's current salary scales.

Figure 5.3 *Qualifications and requirements for customer service staff at British Midland Airways*
Courtesy of British Midland

potential. In travel and tourism, staff must have good 'product knowledge', i.e. knowing all the details, prices and features of the products or services they are describing and selling. Induction training when they first start a job, followed by detailed training on the services, products and systems of the organisation, should give these staff members the confidence needed to offer a high level of customer service and feel a valued member of the team. Figure 5.3 gives details of the qualifications and skills that British Midland Airways looks for when recruiting customer service staff.

Product knowledge is vital in any travel and tourism organisation since it can help staff to:

- ✪ **Inform customers of product prices and features**
- ✪ **Suggest alternatives if the client's first choice is not available**
- ✪ **Give detailed information of particular services; in travel and tourism it is often 'the little things' that either make or break the total experience for the customer**
- ✪ **Raise the general level of awareness of other services and facilities that the organisation can offer**
- ✪ **Create the impression of a professional and caring organisation**

Exercise 5.2

Choose two local travel and tourism companies and write down the types of 'product knowledge' that a member of staff working in each would need to have to be able to deal efficiently with a wide range of customers.

Poor communication

Communication problems between staff are often the biggest single barrier to successful customer service in travel and tourism organisations. It causes resentment among staff, frustrates managers and is often picked up by customers who are sometimes put in embarrassing situations. Managers can help to break this vicious circle by:

- ✪ **Briefing all staff fully on their job roles and responsibilities**
- ✪ **Using simple language and communications methods that everybody can understand**
- ✪ **'Walking the job', i.e. taking the time and trouble to talk to staff about their jobs, concerns and hopes for the future**

An organisation that looks after its staff is likely to be one that looks after its customers as well.

Lack of training

Many of the problems associated with poor standards of customer service in travel and tourism are the result of a lack of training. Staff must be trained in the skills needed to provide an excellent service to customers, not just when they start a job but throughout their working life.

browse this website

www.englishtourism.
org.uk

Industry example

The Welcome Host customer service training programme was introduced in the UK by the Wales Tourist Board in 1991. It is based on the successful Superhost initiative begun in British Columbia, Canada. Already over 150,000 people have completed Welcome Host training in the UK, including tourist information centre staff, tourist guides, coach drivers, hotel and tourist attraction staff.

The one-day training course covers a number of important issues, including:

★ Making the right impression

★ Remembering names and making conversation with customers

★ Understanding the vital contribution of tourism to economic success – both locally and nationally

★ Communicating effectively and listening actively

★ Helping with special needs

★ Handling complaints and treating customers with care and consideration

★ Guiding visitors to local services and attractions

★ Through personal responsibility, preparing to provide a warmer welcome

The English Tourism Council (ETC) has extended the Welcome Host concept by developing Welcome Management (specifically designed for managers and supervisors in the tourism industry), Welcome Host International (designed to improve the skills and abilities to deal with overseas

continued

continued

visitors) and Welcome All (examining the needs of disabled and special needs customers). Collectively, these are known as the 'Welcome Family' (see Figure 5.4).

INTRODUCING THE POPULAR
WELCOME FAMILY

Result-orientated courses for staff and management
that develop skills, service and revenue

English Tourist Board accredited Customer Service Training
offered by England's Regional Tourist Boards.

Figure 5.4 *The 'Welcome Family' of customer service training
schemes*

Reproduced by permission of the English Tourist Board Awarding Body

Personal presentation

Key topics in this section:

- **Introduction – the importance of personal presentation**
- **Appropriate dress**
- **Personal hygiene**
- **Personality**
- **Attitude**

Introduction – the importance of personal presentation

First impressions count in any business, particularly in the travel and tourism industry where dealing with people is such an important part of the work. It is vital to understand that the way you present yourself to customers has a direct influence on their enjoyment, your job satisfaction and the future success of the organisation that is employing you. In particular, you need to appreciate the importance of the following when dealing with customers:

- ✪ **Appropriate dress**
- ✪ **Personal hygiene**
- ✪ **Personality**
- ✪ **Attitude**

Time and again, employers in travel and tourism stress the crucial importance of these four topics when recruiting and promoting staff, whether you deal with customers face-to-face, on the telephone, in writing, by fax or e-mail.

Industry example

GNER (the Great North Eastern Railway Company) lists the following personal attributes for the post of Customer Service Manager on its network:

★   Excellent personal presentation

continued

continued

- ★ Warm and welcoming
- ★ Shows empathy with people
- ★ Honest and trustworthy
- ★ Resilient
- ★ Willingness to learn and develop
- ★ Team player
- ★ Proactive
- ★ Flexible
- ★ Enthusiastic
- ★ Committed
- ★ Objective
- ★ Diplomatic

browse this website

www.gner.co.uk

Appropriate dress

What you wear at work says a lot about you and the organisation that employs you. Wearing 'appropriate dress' does not necessarily mean wearing the smartest clothes that money can buy! 'Appropriate' is the key word. If you were a sales representative for a major holiday company regularly visiting travel agencies, smart formal clothes such as a suit may well be the most appropriate. On the other hand, staff working in the health and fitness suite of a large city centre hotel would be more appropriately dressed in casual sportswear. Many people working in travel and tourism wear uniforms in order to present a consistent image to the public and help to build customer loyalty, for example customer service staff working for train companies, travel agency personnel, air cabin crew and overseas tour representatives (see Figure 5.5).

Uniforms help to create a positive first impression with customers and make staff easily identifiable if customers need help or advice.

In summary, clothes worn by staff working in travel and tourism should be:

- ✪ **Functional – suited to the demands of the job**
- ✪ **Appropriate – given the nature and location of the job**
- ✪ **Smart – creases and stains on clothes look unprofessional**
- ✪ **Discreet – short skirts and body-hugging garments may be neither appropriate nor comfortable in a work situation!**

Figure 5.5 *Overseas representatives in uniform*
Supplied by Unijet Travel Ltd

Staff should be informed at interview about the dress code for the job and whether or not a uniform is supplied.

browse this website

www.hertz.co.uk

Personal hygiene

This can be a sensitive area, particularly when supervisors and managers have to remind staff about the importance of arriving at work in a clean, hygienic and presentable fashion. All staff working in travel and tourism, but especially those whose work brings them into close contact with customers, must:

- **Be generally clean**
- **Have hair that is clean and combed**
- **Have fresh breath**

Customers will not tolerate staff with poor body odour or bad breath and may well take their custom elsewhere. It is important to remember that the staff are the outward image of an organisation. For example, if you are greeted at a hotel by a doorman who smells of stale cigarettes or whose hair is unkempt, your first impressions of the hotel and of your stay are likely to be negative. If, on the other hand, the doorman is smartly presented, with a pleasant smile and tidy hair, you are much more likely to be impressed with the hotel from the outset.

Personality

There is a saying in travel and tourism that to get on in the industry you must like people. While this may seem an obvious statement, it cannot be emphasised enough; if you don't like dealing with people, don't work in travel and tourism!

It is often said that people with the 'right' personality will do very well in the travel and tourism industry. Employers are always keen to employ staff who are:

- **Good communicators**
- **Outgoing and confident when dealing with the public**

- ✪ **Good at relating to customers**
- ✪ **Able to work under pressure**
- ✪ **Reliable and trustworthy**

Many of the job opportunities in travel and tourism involve dealing with the public, so a pleasant personality and helpful manner are essential. People are on holiday to have fun and relax, and staff play an important part in providing a pleasant experience for customers.

Attitude

We mentioned earlier in this unit that the 'take it or leave it' attitude can still be a problem with a minority of staff working in the travel and tourism industry. It is important to remember that every member of staff is a representative of the organisation and should always have a positive attitude to customers, acting in a professional manner at all times. There are certain ground rules that you must respect when working in travel and tourism. For example, you should **always**:

- ✪ **Be loyal to the organisation**
- ✪ **Follow organisational procedures**
- ✪ **Respect the buildings and equipment where you work**
- ✪ **Be friendly and courteous with both colleagues and customers**
- ✪ **Separate your private and professional life as far as possible**
- ✪ **Respect the views of others**
- ✪ **Treat both colleagues and customers as you would want to be treated yourself**
- ✪ **Be honest and constructive**
- ✪ **Ask if there is anything you are unsure about**

To make sure that you project a professional attitude at work, you should **never**:

- ✪ **Criticise the organisation to, or in front of, customers**
- ✪ **Discuss confidential information outside work**
- ✪ **Argue or swear in front of customers**
- ✪ **Lose your temper at work**
- ✪ **Drink alcohol at work**
- ✪ **Act in a way that could put anybody at risk**

By following these common sense guidelines you will provide customers with a pleasant and courteous service.

Exercise 5.3

Imagine that you have been asked to help write a job description for a new job of Customer Service Assistant in a busy tourist information centre. List the key points about appropriate dress, personal hygiene, personality and attitude that you think should be included in the job description.

browse this website

www.haven
holidays.co.uk

Industry example

Haven Holidays, part of the The Rank Organisation, is the UK market leader in self-catering caravan holidays, operating 56 holiday parks in England, Scotland and Wales. Its staff are fully trained in customer service, in particular the importance of having the right attitude towards customers. The company's customer care programme stresses that employees with the right attitude are:

★ Able to create a great first impression

★ Positive in outlook

★ Clean, neat and well groomed

★ Welcoming to customers – using their names if they can and remembering that a smile costs nothing

★ Proud of doing their jobs as well as they can

★ Ready to take the initiative

★ Friendly and sincere

★ Willing to act promptly and effectively

★ Ready to take extra trouble and make extra effort to give the customer what they need

Types of customers

Key topics in this section:

- **What is a customer?**
- **Meeting the needs of individuals**
- **Meeting the needs of groups**
- **People of different ages**
- **People from different cultures**
- **Non-English speakers**
- **People with specific needs**

What is a customer?

Travel and tourism products and services are used by people of all ages, types and nationalities, including those with specific needs, such as people with disabilities or with young children. Staff working in travel and tourism must be trained in identifying and meeting the differing needs of a wide variety of customers.

Before we can begin to consider the different types of customers found in the travel and tourism industry, it is important to spend a little time defining exactly what is meant by the term 'customer'. Many organisations that are striving to improve their customer service use statements similar to the following to answer this question.

Customers:

- **Are the most important people to our organisation**
- **Are not dependent on us – we are dependent on them**
- **Are not an interruption of our work – they are the purpose of it**
- **Are not people to argue with or match wits against**
- **Are not statistics but human beings with feelings and emotions**
- **Are the people who bring us their needs – it is our job to handle these profitably for them and for ourselves**
- **Are always right!**

Everybody working in a travel and tourism organisation has 'customers', whether or not they deal face to face with the general public. 'Internal' customers are people working in the same organisation as you, for example clerical staff, maintenance staff, receptionists, etc., who you come across in the normal daily course of events and who provide you with services and support. Good customer service requires a team approach and a recognition that it is not just the customers 'on the other side of the counter' who need respect and consideration, but that colleagues within the organisation need to be dealt with in the same supportive manner.

browse this website

www.towerbridge.
org.uk

Industry example

Managers at The Tower Bridge Experience, one of London's best-known tourist attractions, believe that each section of the attraction plays a unique part in ensuring customer satisfaction. The exhibition, ticketing, retail and guiding staff who, together with security, are in daily face-to-face contact with the public, as well as the technical, finance, marketing, education and office staff, are all part of the same team behind the 'Experience', dedicated to providing the highest standards of service to customers.

The sort of people we normally think of as customers are sometimes referred to as 'external' customers, to distinguish them from work colleagues. If we begin from the point of view that everybody is unique, then the number of 'external' customers for any travel and tourism enterprise is likely to be immense, each with different needs and expectations. At a popular tourist attraction in a large urban area, for example, the range of customers is likely to include:

- **Individuals**
- **Groups**
- **People of different ages**
- **People from different cultures**
- **Non-English speakers**
- **People with specific needs, for example those needing wheelchair access, people with sensory disabilities and those with young children**

Achieving high standards of customer service to such a wide range of people with very different needs requires commitment and enthusiasm on the part of the staff involved and the correct training provided by a supportive management team.

Exercise 5.4

Choose two contrasting travel and tourism enterprises with which you are familiar and list the different types of customers each serves. For each type of customer, write down statements about their particular needs.

browse this website

www.air2000.co.uk

Industry example

Air 2000 gives its customers the opportunity to order special meals (vegan, diabetic, low fat or gluten-free) in advance at no extra cost. Kosher meals are also available on payment of a small supplement. All of the airline's vegetarian meals are prepared to vegan standard.

Meeting the needs of individuals

As you know, people come in all shapes and sizes! We all have different leisure needs and, in the context of travel and tourism, are looking to friendly and efficient staff to meet these needs. Meeting the needs of individuals is all about building a one-to-one relationship. Customers like to feel that they are special and, in a one-to-one situation, want to be put at ease and have the full attention of the member of staff serving them. Staff should not become distracted when dealing with individuals and should be trained in prioritising requests for their time and attention.

Meeting the needs of groups

Dealing with groups can be an altogether more skilled task than meeting the needs of individuals. There are many occasions in travel and tourism when customer service staff are called upon to deal with group situations, for example an overseas tour representative hosting a welcome meeting for new holidaymakers, a courier dealing with a coachful of schoolchildren or a guide leading a group on a tour of historic sites. Dealing with groups calls for good organisational and communication skills, so that every member of the group turns up in the right place at the right time! Although the group you are dealing with may be very large, it is important to make every effort to treat the members of the group as individuals by, for example, addressing people by name and taking time to talk to them on a one-to-one basis, particularly those that you feel may need a little more attention or support.

There are certain ground rules that you need to adopt when communicating information to a group of customers, including:

- ✪ **Make sure that members of the group can see, hear and understand you**
- ✪ **Communicate effectively using simple language and a clear, confident tone of voice**
- ✪ **Make sure that everybody has understood what you have said by allowing time for questions**
- ✪ **Make yourself available afterwards if people want further clarification on a one-to-one basis**

Activity 5.3

Take turns at playing the role of a tour guide by taking the rest of your group on a tour of your school/college or the local area. When the tour has finished, the 'customers' should discuss the strengths and weaknesses of each guide, concentrating on communication with the group as a whole as well as with individual group members.

People of different ages

Customers in travel and tourism span right across the age range. At one end, a member of staff may be dealing with very young children in a crèche at an overseas campsite. At the other end of the range, you may find yourself attending to the needs of senior citizens on a Mediterranean cruise or perhaps a coach holiday in the Lake District. Research shows that we have an ageing population, with people generally living longer and taking holidays well into their 80s and 90s. In between these two extremes are a wide variety of different age groups, all with very different needs, for example.

- ✪ **Schoolchildren – looking for education mixed with some fun!**
- ✪ **Young adults – perhaps experiencing an overseas holiday for the first time (see Figure 5.6)**
- ✪ **Young couples – looking for a mixture of relaxation and nightlife**

Figure 5.6 *Young people enjoying their holiday*
Courtesy of Airtours

- ✪ **Middle-aged people – perhaps more interested in food, drink and culture than all-night clubbing!**
- ✪ **Early retired people – a growing market, with plenty of time on their hands and sometimes enough spare cash to take more than one trip**

Clearly, all the above have very different needs and it is the job of customer service staff in travel and tourism to be able to identify and meet these needs.

Industry example

In its National Tourism Strategy document *Tomorrow's Tourism* (Department for Culture, Media and Sport, 1999) the UK government has stressed that it will:

> ... *encourage the adoption of more family friendly policies, for example, the provision of baby changing equipment in hotel rooms, multiple entry tickets to attractions and activity clubs for teenagers at holiday parks.*

browse this website

www.culture.gov.uk

People from different cultures

Britain attracts overseas visitors from all corners of the globe and from a wide variety of cultural backgrounds. Their needs may be very different in a number of respects, for example:

- ✪ **Language spoken**
- ✪ **Religious codes**
- ✪ **Cultural traditions**
- ✪ **Food and drink**

Front-line customer service staff whose work brings them into contact with customers from a variety of different cultures must be trained to recognise and respect these different needs, and to respond positively and sensitively to customers' requests. The Welcome Host International training course (see below) provides an introduction to dealing with overseas visitors and is a good first step in meeting the needs of visitors from different cultures.

Non-English speakers

We saw in Unit 1: Investigating Travel and Tourism that Britain is very successful at attracting overseas visitors. Where we are not quite so good is in training customer service staff to meet and greet foreign visitors in their own language and to develop an understanding of their particular needs. Knowing just a few words of a foreign language makes an immediate impression on overseas visitors, helping to put them at ease and creating an excellent first impression of your organisation.

Activity 5.4

Working with another member of your group, do some research to find out how to say 'good morning/good afternoon, welcome to Britain' in six different languages. Try to memorise each of the phrases and practise them with other people in your group.

Industry example

Welcome Host International is a one-day customer service training course developed by the English Tourist Board (now the English Tourism Council). It addresses the need for travel and tourism staff to improve their foreign language skills and understand better the needs and expectations of overseas visitors to Britain. The course comprises:

★ A basic introduction to the languages of up to six different countries, enabling staff to meet, greet and assist non-English speaking visitors

★ Accompanying cultural awareness and understanding of the expectations of visitors from different countries

Staff who complete the course successfully are presented with a certificate and badge.

People with specific needs

Travel and tourism organisations should strive to provide excellent standards of service to **all** their customers, regardless of their circumstances, age, abilities or disabilities. Some customers have specific needs which may require a particular type of customer service. This may be because of:

✪ **The need for wheelchair access**
✪ **Sensory disabilities**
✪ **Mobility problems**
✪ **Being accompanied by young children**

Research has shown that around 14 per cent of all people living in Europe have some form of disability. Added to this are the many millions who, through age or circumstances, have a particular special need. The ageing population means that there are increasing numbers of people with deteriorating eyesight and hearing, and an inability to move around with ease.

The important point for customer service staff to remember is that visitors with specific needs do not want to be made to feel different from other customers or a nuisance, but do welcome a little extra appreciation of, and respect for, their particular needs. Remember too that disabled people's ability to carry out their normal day-to-day activities is very often constrained by the environment in which they find themselves, rather than the disability they live with, for example problems getting on and off buses, coaches, trains and aircraft, and narrow doorways that do not allow wheelchair access.

Activity 5.5

Ask your tutor to arrange a visit to a local travel and tourism facility, perhaps a hotel, tourist attraction or tourist information centre. Make a list of any special facilities provided for customers with specific needs. After the visit, discuss with the rest of your group whether the facility fully meets the needs of these customers. Suggest any improvements that could be made to accommodate visitors with specific needs.

Industry example

browse this website

www.english-heritage.org.uk

English Heritage, the body that advises government on the conservation of the historic environment, has made great strides in meeting the needs of visitors with specific needs. It provides audio tours at many of its sites and a number have tape tours for visually impaired visitors. A number of publications, including wheelchair routes, Braille guides and large-print visitor guides, have been produced. In terms of facilities, English Heritage provides wheelchairs and special lavatories at many of its sites, and there is an ongoing programme of introducing wider entrances, special routes, ramps and handrails. Guide dogs and hearing dogs for the deaf are welcome at all of its properties and free admission is offered to the companion of a wheelchair user or visually impaired visitor.

Disability Discrimination Act

The Disability Discrimination Act 1995 (DDA) was designed to protect disabled people from discrimination in employment and to increase access to goods, facilities and services. The Act defines 'disability' as:

browse this website

www.disability.
gov.uk

A physical or mental impairment which has a substantial and long term adverse effect on a person's ability to carry out normal day-to-day activities.

The DDA employment provisions and the duty on service providers not to treat disabled people less favourably have been in force since December 1996. From October 1999, service providers have had to make 'reasonable adjustments' for disabled people. From 2004, they will have to consider making alterations to the built environment, for example access to buildings and the ability to move freely inside buildings.

Industry example

In its National Tourism Strategy document *Tomorrow's Tourism* (Department for Culture, Media and Sport, 1999) the UK government has stressed that it will:

... work with trade associations, major tourism and leisure groups, local authorities and tourist boards to develop a national campaign which aims to change public attitudes to disability.

... encourage organisations to incorporate disability awareness and training as an integral part of all hospitality and tourism courses.

... encourage architectural colleges to ensure that course curricula include an emphasis on making provision for disabled access within building design.

Dealing with customers

Key topics in this section:

- **Introduction**
- **Dealing with customers face to face**
- **Using the telephone**
- **Communicating in writing**
- **Verbal communication**
- **Non-verbal communication**

Introduction

There is a saying that dealing with customers is easy, but dealing with customers successfully is the difficult bit! The key to effective customer service is good communication, i.e. meeting customers' needs through positive interaction between customer and member of staff. Employees in travel and tourism must know how to deal with customers in a variety of different situations, for example:

- ✪ **In face-to-face situations**
- ✪ **On the telephone**
- ✪ **In writing**

We will now investigate each of these in more detail.

Activity 5.6

Under the direction of your tutor, brainstorm all of the ways in which staff in travel and tourism come into direct and indirect contact with customers. Identify the customer needs for each situation you have listed.

Dealing with customers face to face

There are many situations in travel and tourism where customer service staff deal directly with customers face to face, either on an individual basis or in a group

Figure 5.7 *Dealing with customers face to face in a travel agency*

situation, for example tourist information centre staff directing a party of overseas visitors to nearby attractions, a hotel receptionist welcoming a guest or a travel agent advising a client on the benefits of a particular holiday (see Figure 5.7).

Important ground rules when dealing with customers face to face include the following:

- ✪ **Smile when you greet the customer**
- ✪ **Listen to what the customer is saying**
- ✪ **Make eye contact but don't stare**
- ✪ **Make sure you look interested (even if you're not!)**
- ✪ **Address the customer by name**
- ✪ **Don't interrupt the customer**
- ✪ **Keep a reasonable distance from the customer, not too close and not too far away**
- ✪ **Always thank the customer when appropriate**

Face-to-face communication has distinct advantages when compared to other situations when you cannot see the customer. It is the best way of creating a positive impression with the customer through a welcoming smile, professional manner and smart appearance. Face-to-face communication allows you to see customers' responses to what you are saying. You can also reinforce your message using facial expressions and gestures, a subject which we cover in more detail when we investigate non-verbal communication (see page 338).

Using the telephone

The telephone is an increasingly important part of daily life, not least in the travel and tourism industry. Staff use telephones to keep in touch with each other, while many customers' requests for information, advice or to make a booking are now handled over the phone. From the customers' point of view, using the telephone is fast, convenient and relatively cheap, as well as enabling instant feedback. Disadvantages include the fact that the callers cannot see each other (non-verbal communication is not possible) and there is no written record of what was said, although it is now common for many organisations to record telephone calls for security and as a staff training aid.

There are a number of important points to bear in mind when dealing with customers' incoming telephone calls, for example:

- **Answer all calls quickly – leaving a call for more than five rings is considered inefficient**
- **Greet the caller with your name and/or your organisation and ask how you can help**
- **Smile while you are talking – this may sound crazy, but it really does help you to project a welcoming tone to the customer**
- **Listen carefully to what the caller is saying**
- **Always speak clearly and use language appropriate to the caller**
- **Take notes if there is a message for another member of staff**
- **Transfer calls to another appropriate member of staff if you cannot deal with the customer yourself**
- **If you promise to call a customer later, make sure you do it!**

Similar rules apply if you are telephoning a customer, except that you will be paying for the call!

browse this website

www.thomascook.
co.uk

Industry example

Like many UK-based tour operators, Thomas Cook now offers its customers a number of ways of making a booking or getting advice on holiday choices. They can choose any of the following:

★ Call in to any of the company's 750 shops throughout the UK and talk face to face with a

continued

continued

trained consultant. This is particularly useful for customers who need extra advice on holiday or destination choices.

★ Call Thomas Cook Direct, the company's call centre operation, with telephone lines open later than the holiday shops (see Figure 5.8). This method offers convenience and flexibility, allowing customers to book a holiday at a time and in a place that suits them. Using the call centre is particularly suited to customers who have a good idea of where they want to go and when they want to travel.

★ Log on to the Thomas Cook website at www.thomascook.co.uk, the company's on-line travel shop containing details of all JMC (Thomas Cook's holiday company) resorts and properties. Like all websites this has the advantage of being available 24 hours a day, every day of the year.

Figure 5.8 *Thomas Cook Direct's call centre*
Courtesy of Thomas Cook

Communicating in writing

With the many developments in telephone and Internet systems, it would be easy to think that customer service staff no longer need to communicate in writing, but it does still happen! In fact, there are many types of written communication used in travel and tourism, for example:

- **Letters, faxes and e-mail**
- **Memos**
- **Brochures and leaflets**
- **Reports**
- **Documents for meetings**
- **Notice boards**
- **Posters and advertisements**
- **Press releases and articles**
- **Annual reports**
- **Timetables**

Written communication may be **formal**, for example a reply from a hotel manager to a customer's letter of complaint, or **informal**, such as a hand-written telephone message from one member of staff to another. Remember too that written communication may be targeted at **external** customers, for example a poster or advertisement, or circulated to **internal** customers in an organisation, for example a staff newsletter.

Whatever type of written communication is used, there are certain important rules that should be followed, including:

- **There should be no mistakes in spelling, grammar and punctuation**
- **The intended message should be conveyed effectively and accurately**
- **In the case of messages, it should be made clear who it is to, who it is from, when it was sent and if any action has been taken or needs to be taken**
- **The written communication should be clearly legible and pleasing to the eye, whether it is a professional business letter, a company report or a memo**
- **The language used should be appropriate for the intended audience**

Exercise 5.5

Design and write a memo to be sent by the Marketing Director of a specialist ski tour operator to all members of staff in the organisation, inviting them to the launch party of the new winter season brochure in two weeks' time at a nearby venue of your choice.

Verbal communication

Verbal communication is an integral part of working in customer service in the travel and tourism industry. Verbal communication can be both formal and informal; an example of informal communication would be work colleagues meeting in the staff restaurant to discuss work and non-work issues. Attending a job interview or taking part in a meeting are examples of formal verbal communication. It is important for customer service staff to remember that listening skills are often just as important as speaking skills when dealing with customers in many situations in travel and tourism, for example selling, handling complaints and dealing with emergencies.

Non-verbal communication

Non-verbal communication (NVC) is the process by which we send and receive messages without the use of spoken or written words. For example, we all use our eyes, hands and facial expressions to emphasise points and to confirm information we have received. These are all examples of body language, the most common type of non-verbal communication. Body language is sometimes classified as:

- **Bodily contact – shaking somebody's hand is an example**
- **Physical proximity – the distance we feel we need to keep between ourselves and other people, for example when queuing at a tourist attraction**
- **Orientation – where we place ourselves in relation to others, e.g. by tradition, a manager or supervisor running a team meeting will sit at the head of the table**
- **Posture – whether standing, sitting, lying down, walking or running, there is often something about our body posture that relays a message to those around us (make sure you're not slumped in a seat at the moment!)**

- ✪ **Gestures – we all make gestures from time to time to signal approval or disapproval, for example a 'thumbs up' to show that all is well or banging on a desk to show that you are not happy with a decision!**
- ✪ **Facial expressions – the face can transmit an enormous variety of messages and emotions, either consciously or subconsciously**
- ✪ **Eye contact – whether we are aware of it or not, we pay a great deal of attention to a person's eyes when they are communicating with us**

Customer service staff should be trained in recognising non-verbal communication signals and acting in an appropriate fashion.

Selling skills

Key topics in this section:

- **Introduction**
- **Sales objectives**
- **Selling skills and techniques**
- **AIDA** technique

Introduction

Selling products and services is vital to the success of a wide range of travel and tourism organisations. In some senses, we are all involved in a subtle type of selling every day of our lives, trying to get other people to take on board our ideas or suggestions. It might be a daughter trying to persuade her father to take her to the shops, a schoolboy persuading his friend to lend him his bike or your boss trying to get you to work late! However, to many people in the UK, selling is a dirty word! There is no doubt that selling has an image problem and that, as a nation, we tend to look down on people who sell goods and services for a living, whether it is electrical goods in a shop, a telesales operator for a local newspaper or a sales representative for an engineering firm. This is rather surprising when we consider the continuing shift away from a manufacturing towards a service economy in this country and the fact that so many people work in sales jobs. In the travel and tourism industry, it is easy to think of many situations in which selling takes place, for example:

- ✪ **A travel agent selling a holiday to a client (see Figure 5.9)**
- ✪ **A conference organiser selling the benefits of a particular hotel to a company**
- ✪ **A receptionist at a holiday centre selling a course of golf lessons to a couple**
- ✪ **A ticket agency employee selling a pair of tickets to see _Grease_ over the telephone**
- ✪ **An overseas representative selling tickets for an evening excursion**
- ✪ **A fast-food outlet selling a family meal for four**
- ✪ **Airline staff selling drinks and perfumes during a flight**

Even staff who are not employed as salespeople come into contact with selling when they themselves are customers, expecting the highest levels of customer service, courtesy and attention.

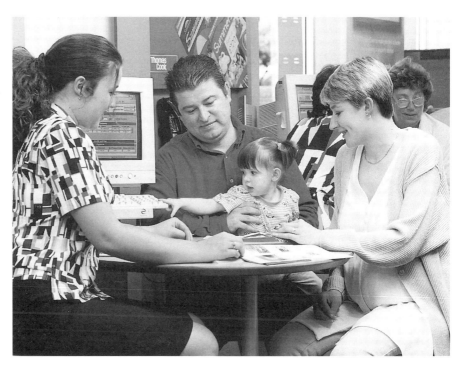

Figure 5.9 *Selling skills are important in the travel and tourism industry*
Courtesy of Thomas Cook

Sales objectives

We saw in Unit 4: Marketing Travel and Tourism that personal selling is an essential component of the marketing process in travel and tourism organisations. Selling is, however, much more than just a part of wider marketing activity; it should be seen as a continuous process that can help cement customer relationships, build customer loyalty and provide lasting benefits for an organisation.

Selling involves communication between a buyer and a seller, which is designed to persuade the customer to purchase the products or services on offer. It can be thought of as the culmination of all the marketing activities that have taken place beforehand in the organisation. It involves matching a customer's needs with the goods and services on offer; the better the match, the more lasting the relationship between the seller and the buyer.

All staff employed in travel and tourism are likely to be employed in some form of 'selling' during the course of their work, although the importance of selling will vary between different organisations. The majority of organisations in the travel and tourism industry operate in the private sector, so that selling will be geared towards meeting **commercial** objectives. Public and voluntary sector organisations, such as a local authority tourism department or the National Trust, will still be involved in selling products and services, but will be using selling to achieve **non-commercial** objectives, perhaps providing information to holidaymakers, arranging school visits to tourist attractions or preserving historic houses.

Not surprisingly, the prime objective of selling is to make a sale! This may seem a glaringly obvious statement, but there are likely to be other related aims to the selling process, including:

- **Generating repeat business – hanging on to your existing customers**
- **Meeting planned increases in sales volume – common in package holiday companies**
- **Increasing customer satisfaction levels – selling and providing excellent customer service are very closely linked**
- **Increasing profitability – more sales should lead to more profits**
- **Securing competitive advantage – keeping one step ahead of the competition**
- **Targeting specific sectors of the market – perhaps as part of a campaign aimed at increasing sales from particular overseas countries**
- **Raising awareness of a new facility – selling can complement other publicity campaigns to spread the word about new facilities, products or services**

Simply saying that the principal objective of selling is to make a sale also masks the very complex nature of the sales process in travel and tourism, involving the use of a whole set of skills and techniques linked to communication and interpersonal skills. The next section of this unit looks in detail at sales techniques used in travel and tourism organisations.

Selling skills and techniques

Successful selling is a structured activity, not just 'something that happens'. Figure 5.10 shows the six key stages of the sales process in travel and tourism.

The following sections look in detail at each of these key stages.

Raising customer awareness

Although not strictly speaking a sales technique, raising awareness of a travel and tourism product or service is an essential prerequisite to any selling activity; put simply, if a customer is not aware of a product's existence, it will be extremely hard to sell it to them! Unit 4: Marketing Travel and Tourism showed us that travel and tourism organisations use a wide range of promotional tools to raise awareness of their facilities and products. Sometimes referred to as the 'promotional mix', these include:

Stage one
Raising customer awareness

Stage two
Establishing rapport with the customer

Stage three
Investigating customer needs

Stage four
Presenting the product

Stage five
Closing the sale

Stage six
After-sales service

Figure 5.10 *The sales process in travel and tourism*

- ✪ **Advertising**
- ✪ **Public relations**
- ✪ **Sales promotion**
- ✪ **Direct marketing**

If we take the example of a high street travel agency and how it makes potential clients aware of its products, it is likely to use a number of techniques, including:

- ✪ **Its own advertising in local and regional media (newspapers, local radio and television)**
- ✪ **Advertising carried out by the companies whose products it sells**
- ✪ **Window displays and point-of-sale materials (see Figure 5.11)**
- ✪ **Brochure displays in the agency**
- ✪ **Late availability cards**
- ✪ **Newsletters mailed to existing clients**
- ✪ **Attendance at holiday shows and exhibitions**
- ✪ **Presentation evenings arranged in conjunction with tour operators and airlines**
- ✪ **Press releases to the local media resulting in 'free publicity'**

Figure 5.11 *Travel agents use window displays to raise awareness of their products*

Travel and tourism organisations operating in the public and voluntary sectors will use a similar array of techniques to attract their customers.

Activity 5.7

Carry out a small-scale survey of friends to find out how they were made aware of a recent travel and tourism product that they purchased (holiday, short break, etc.) or facility they visited (museum, theme park, etc.). Present your findings as a bar chart, indicating the least and most popular techniques mentioned.

Establishing rapport with the customer

Once a customer has been made aware of a product or service, the true art of selling can begin. The broad nature of the travel and tourism industry means that there will be a wide range of customers, of all ages and social backgrounds, with varying budgets. It is important that sales staff are sympathetic to the specific needs of different customers and respectful of their wishes. Being a very wide-ranging industry means also that the actual setting where the selling takes place will differ from sector to sector. Selling may, for example, take place:

- ❂ *In a shop*, e.g. when buying travel goods before a holiday or short break
- ❂ *In a hotel*, e.g. when purchasing a ticket for an excursion or using the fitness suite
- ❂ *In a restaurant*, e.g. when buying a bottle of champagne
- ❂ *At home*, e.g. when ordering tickets for the theatre over the telephone or via the Internet
- ❂ *In an agency*, e.g. when buying a holiday or travel ticket
- ❂ *In an office*, e.g. when finalising the venue for a business conference

Whatever the location for the sales activity, the principle of engaging the customer in conversation, or establishing rapport, still applies. In order to meet the objective of making a sale, this initial task of engaging the customer in conversation is very important, since it gives the salesperson the opportunity to gain the trust of the customer and to discover his or her needs. Some customers are suspicious of any attempts to sell them products, often preferring to make their own decisions on product selection and purchase. They may consider sales staff to be 'pushy' or arrogant, but even such reluctant customers can be put in the right frame of mind to buy a particular product or service if they receive a friendly and attentive level of service.

First impressions count!

In service industries such as travel and tourism first impressions are always important. This is particularly the case in a selling situation, when customers sometimes have to make an instant decision as to whether they can trust the person who is trying to sell them a product or service. There are a number of factors that influence customers and that may ultimately make them decide to buy or go elsewhere, including:

- ❂ *The sales environment* – is the facility clean, tidy, well maintained, well designed, the right temperature, with good air quality?
- ❂ *The appearance of the sales staff* – are they well dressed, of pleasant appearance, knowledgeable, business-like?
- ❂ *Attitude towards the customer* – are they welcoming, interested, attentive, willing to listen, good at answering questions, confident, professional?

It is advisable for sales staff to avoid using the phrase 'can I help you?' as a way of striking up a sales conversation. This sort of 'closed' question simply invites the reply 'no thank you, I'm just looking'. It is far better to ask more 'open' questions, such as:

- ❂ **How many times have you used the facility before?**

- **Which particular National Park are you visiting?**
- **Which country are you thinking of visiting?**
- **Which company have you travelled with in the past?**

The secret of developing 'open' questions is to begin with the words 'where', 'why', 'who', 'when', 'which', 'what' and 'how'.

Sales staff must be conscious of the signals, sometimes hidden, that customers give when in a selling situation. A customer who is obviously in a hurry will not thank a sales assistant who asks complicated questions and insists on engaging in a lengthy conversation.

Having established a rapport with the customer and gained a degree of trust, the salesperson's next task is to investigate the customer's needs.

Exercise 5.6

Working with another member of your group, change the following 'closed' questions into 'open' questions.

1 Are you travelling to Greece?
2 Do you want to use the fitness suite?
3 Do you want a window seat in the coach?
4 Do you want a morning flight?
5 Do you want that computer game?

Investigating customer needs

The aim of this stage of the selling process is to help the customer to state his or her needs clearly, so that the salesperson has the best chance of presenting a product or service that the customer will want to buy. Again, it is helpful to ask 'open' questions, rather than those that call for yes/no replies, to give the customer more opportunity to express a preference and to help the conversation to continue. It is important, also, not to assume that you know a customer's needs and to understand that the process of investigating customer requirements is a two-way affair, with the salesperson acting in a supportive role.

In the case of a travel agency, the following are the types of questions that will help the salesperson build up a picture of the client's needs:

- **What is the size of the party travelling?**
- **Are there any children and, if so, what ages are they?**
- **When do you want to travel and for how long?**
- **Where do you want to go?**

- ✪ **Is there a particular company you prefer to travel with?**
- ✪ **How do you want to travel?**
- ✪ **How much do you expect to pay?**
- ✪ **Does anybody in the party have any special requirements?**

Customers will not necessarily know the answers to all the questions a salesperson may be asking them, so it is important to start with easy questions to which they can give an immediate answer and go into more depth as the sales conversation continues.

Presenting the product

Having determined the customer's needs, the next stage of the sales process is to present the product to the customer. Presenting a travel and tourism product to a customer is rather more difficult than, say, showing him or her an electric iron or toaster in a shop! The intangible nature of travel and tourism products (the fact that you cannot see or touch them) means that sales staff are often showing the customer brochures and other publicity material to help them make a decision. This indicates the crucial importance of well-designed promotional items to achieve sales in travel and tourism.

The key to success in this stage of the sales process is to concentrate on three types of statements during the product presentation, namely:

- ✪ **Features statement:** This involves highlighting the features of a particular product or service to the customer, for example the number of rooms in a hotel or the facilities on offer in a holiday centre. Often the customer's reaction is one of indifference at this stage.
- ✪ **Advantages statement:** This indicates what the product or service can do in general for the customer. For example, the fact that a departure time of 15.30hrs for a flight means that the client will not have to get up early to get to the airport. Again the reaction may be that the customer needs a little more specific information and persuasion.
- ✪ **Benefits statement:** This expresses specifically what the product can do for the individual customer. The information is selected on the basis of the customer's needs and is seen to be entirely relevant and easier to absorb.

Product knowledge is crucial to the success or otherwise of this part of the selling process. Staff must familiarise themselves with the features of particular products and take every opportunity to experience the products and facilities for themselves, in order to be able to speak with authority and confidence.

Industry example

Customer service staff at Superbreak Mini-Holidays, one of the UK's leading short break operators, use the following top ten sales tips to generate extra business:

UK SHORT BREAK SALES – TOP 10 SALES TIPS

1 TARGET YOUR EXISTING CUSTOMERS

★ 40% of your customers will take a UK break ... 50% will take more than one per year

★ 40–60 age group – high spenders, faraway, cruise customers

★ Ask them the question ... 'Have you thought of a UK short break this year?'

★ Welcome home letters, direct mailings, quote a short break offer

2 THE ALTERNATIVE WINDOW CARD

★ Offers from Viewdata. Place alongside late availability offers. A customer looking for a holiday in Corfu or the States may also be interested in a theatre break!

3 KEY SELLING OPPORTUNITIES

★ Father's Day/Mother's Day, Valentine's Day, Bank Holidays, sporting events (London Marathon, soccer matches) ... we all have birthdays and anniversaries. Look to promote 3 to 4 weeks prior to the event

4 CHILD REDUCTIONS

★ Free or 50% – all year round including Bank and school holidays plus free or reduced rail travel

5 GROUP BOOKINGS

★ Contact local amateur dramatic societies, place theatre break offers in rehearsal rooms

★ Sports clubs, special interest groups

continued

continued

★ Contact our groups department for a quote on any group idea or activity

6 PEOPLE COMING TO STAY IN YOUR AREA

★ Family and friends attending a wedding often need hotel accommodation. Don't let them book direct, check out our availability and prices. Earn money on your own doorstep!

7 AIRPORT HOTEL ADD-ONS

★ Offer your customer the comfort of a night's stay before flying off on their two weeks in the sun (or when flying back!). Sell in the free car parking facilities too.

8 VIEWDATA

★ Use as a sales tool. Sit the customer down and check out the availability search. Close the sale.

9 THEATRE/EVENT BREAKS

★ Best seats, theatre dinners, London and provincial shows – check out our separate brochure.

★ Concerts, shows, sports from the British Grand Prix to the Chelsea Flower Show, including accommodation, breakfast, coach transfers between hotel/venue and most importantly the ticket to the event.

10 RACKING

★ Vital to tempt the sale.

★ Similar to buying a chocolate bar at the supermarket (they are always placed to tempt you near the checkout!). A UK short break is an impulse purchase, so try racking our programmes near your door.

Handling objections

One aspect of the sales process that often occurs at this stage is the need to handle objections from the customer. These may be genuine, perhaps based on price or availability of services, or they may be the result of a customer being offered insufficient choice by the salesperson. Alternatively, there may be an additional need not already identified to the member of sales staff. Whatever the reason, it is important to respect the wishes of the customer and perhaps investigate further in order to fully match the product to their particular requirements.

Closing the sale

With all objections having been successfully overcome, we are now at the stage of getting the customer to make a commitment, sometimes referred to as 'closing the sale'. Throughout all the sequences of the sales process, sales staff use their product knowledge and communication skills to match customer needs with identified products and services. Rapport is established and the benefits of a selection of products are highlighted. However, none of these actions commits the customer to buy the product or service, or do anything at all. Helping the customer to move from 'I'd like' to 'I'll buy' is what this part of the sales process is all about.

Staff should be continually looking for buying signals from the customer to trigger the process of closing the sale. Statements such as 'that sounds fine' or 'yes, I like that' clearly indicate a desire on the part of the customer to buy. When such signals are evident, the member of staff should begin to finalise the deal, remembering that clients should never be forced into making a decision that they may later regret.

Not every sales conversation will necessarily end in a sale; what is important from the organisation's point of view is to end up with the best possible outcome to the process. For large purchases, customers may wish to consider the benefits in greater detail or discuss the sale with other people, before making a commitment to buy. In this situation, all sales staff can do is to ensure that the customer has been given excellent customer service throughout, thus increasing the chances of an eventual positive sales outcome.

After-sales service

It is important for all organisations and staff involved in selling to remember that the process does not end when the customer has parted with his or her money. Just as we expect an after-sales service for consumer and household items we buy, the sellers of travel and tourism products too must offer this service to their customers. Adding a new customer's details to an existing database should be the first step in developing a long-term relationship that will hopefully benefit both the organisation and the customer.

Activity 5.8

Working with a partner, role play the situation of a member of the public being sold a package holiday to the Algarve. Ask another member of your group to evaluate how the 'seller' performed in relation to each of the key stages of the sales process.

AIDA technique

We saw in Unit 4: Marketing Travel and Tourism that when designing advertisements and other promotional items, organisations should follow the technique known as AIDA, which stands for:

✪ **A**ttention

✪ **I**nterest

✪ **D**esire

✪ **A**ction

In the case of a newspaper advertisement for a newly opened theme park, for example, the person responsible for writing it may choose to:

✪ Attract **attention** to the advertisement by using colour, bold headlines, a picture of a famous personality or striking graphics

✪ Maintain the readers' **interest** by keeping the wording of the advertisement as brief as possible, including language and images that the reader can easily relate to

✪ Create a **desire** to visit the theme park by perhaps offering a discount voucher or other incentive as part of the advertisement

✪ Trigger **action** on the part of the reader by clearly letting him or her know what to do next, e.g. by including a simple map or directions to the park, printing the address and telephone number clearly, or displaying the opening times

The AIDA technique is equally applicable to sales situations in travel and tourism, for example:

✪ Attract **attention** by using imaginative window displays and having attentive, well-trained customer service staff

✪ Maintain the customers' **interest** by asking 'open' questions and showing details of the product in a brochure, on a video or on a computer screen

✪ Create a **desire** to buy, perhaps offering a discount or including extras in the price at no extra cost to the customer, e.g. free insurance or an upgrade on a flight

✪ Trigger **action** by moving the customer from 'I'd like that' to 'I'll buy' using the sales closing techniques described on page 350.

Customer service situations

Key topics in this section:

- **Introduction**
- **Providing information**
- **Giving advice**
- **Taking and relaying messages**
- **Keeping records**
- **Providing assistance**
- **Dealing with problems**
- **Handling complaints**
- **Customer service in action – Center Parcs**

Introduction

The previous section of this unit has highlighted the importance of selling in customer service, but it is important to remember that dealing with customers is not always about selling them something. Staff may also be called upon to:

- **Provide information:** This is an important aspect of working in the travel and tourism industry. Whether it is the time of the next train to Edinburgh, the cost of a return flight to Geneva, the price of a holiday for a family of four in October or the admission price for a tourist attraction, customers need reliable information that is readily available and delivered by well-trained staff in a professional and competent fashion (see Figure 5.12). Staff are not expected to know the answer to every question asked, but they should, at least, know where to get hold of the information.

- **Give advice:** This may be before customers have made a booking, while they are travelling to their destination, while they are at their destination or on the return journey home. Again, customers are looking for reliable, unbiased advice that will answer their particular queries.

- **Take and relay messages:** This is an important part of effective communication.

- **Keep records:** These may be needed for internal management purposes, e.g. admission numbers at a tourist attraction or sales of holidays

Figure 5.12 *Providing information is an important part of customer service*
Courtesy of Unijet Travel Ltd

in a particular week, or for external bodies, such the Inland Revenue, Health and Safety Executive or Customs and Excise.

- ✪ **Provide assistance:** This may be in face-to-face situations with customers, on the telephone or in response to a written enquiry. Some customers have specific requirements that may call for extra assistance in certain circumstances (see page 330).

- ✪ **Deal with problems:** Being able to react quickly and decisively to problems is a useful skill for staff working in travel and tourism. Key staff are trained in first aid and emergency procedures.

- ✪ **Handle complaints:** Thankfully, this is not as common as you might think! The next section of this unit gives you ideas on how to handle complaints successfully.

In all dealings with customers, you must appreciate the importance of listening to what they have to say and keeping calm. Also, you need to know when to refer a customer to a more senior member of staff if you are not able to deal with their enquiry or complaint.

Case Study
Customer service in action – Center Parcs

Center Parcs originated in Holland 25 years ago when Dutchman Piet Derksen hit on the deceptively simple idea of 'a villa in a forest', where city dwellers could escape from the stresses of everyday life and find real relaxation. The idea was so successful with the Dutch that Center Parcs expanded rapidly and now has 13 villages across Europe: five in Holland, two in Belgium, two in France, one in Germany and three in the UK.

Center Parcs opened its first UK village in Sherwood Forest in 1987, followed closely by a second at Elveden Forest near Newmarket, Suffolk. A third village opened at Longleat Forest in Wiltshire in the summer of 1994. The Center Parcs' concept is based on a high quality holiday or short break that cannot be spoiled by the weather; all UK sites have covered leisure pools with controlled temperature

Figure 5.13 *Center Parcs' subtropical swimming paradise*
With kind permission of Center Parcs Ltd

continued

continued

and atmosphere (see Figure 5.13). The recipe certainly seems to work, with all villages enjoying over 95 per cent occupancy and 365 days a year opening.

The company's customer care strategy is centred on its mission statement, which is:

Every day, the perfect break, naturally.

In order to achieve its mission, the company has established a number of primary goals, which focus on:

★ A visionary approach to creative management

★ Continually striving for the highest standards of product available

★ Having an approach to guest service which is second to none

★ A genuine recognition of its own employees

★ Investing in the business and the personal development of all staff

★ Stimulating repeat business

★ Optimising profitability

★ Maintaining its position as market leader

The company gives staff training a high priority, with all staff attending a three-day 'caring for people' course, which aims to enable participants to take personal responsibility for the delivery of excellent guest care. By the end of the course, all staff should be able to:

★ Understand their contribution to the reputation and success of their department and Center Parcs as a company

★ Identify and utilise the skills necessary to create good guest relations

★ Communicate a professional, approachable image

★ Increase their personal confidence and self-esteem

★ Utilise the skills of promoting/selling the product and service

continued

continued

★ Identify and utilise the skills necessary to effectively handle guest complaints

Further customer service training deals with issues such as:

★ Interpersonal skills

★ Written and oral communication

★ Problem solving

★ Team building

★ Managing people

★ Target setting

It is clear from the above initiatives that Center Parcs takes customer care training very seriously and is committed to the growth of a culture that stresses excellence in customer relations through individual personal development.

Case study discussion questions

browse this website

www.centerparcs. com

1 How does Center Parcs ensure the highest standards of customer service?

2 Why does the company invest so much in training its staff in providing excellent customer service?

3 What part does customer service play in helping the company to achieve its mission and objectives?

4 Why has the Center Parcs concept been so successful in the UK?

Handling complaints

Key topics in this section:

- **Introduction**
- **Why do people complain?**
- **Handling complaints successfully**

Introduction

Most of the time, dealing with customers in travel and tourism is rewarding and interesting. From time to time, however, you may have to deal with customer complaints. In general, British people are rather reluctant to complain. When they do, staff in travel and tourism organisations must know how to handle the situation and even turn the complaint to positive advantage. Handled correctly, complaints can be thought of as another type of market research that gives the organisation a second chance to put things right and satisfy the customer.

browse these websites

www.bestwestern.
co.uk

www.bestwestern.
com

Industry example

The Best Western Hotel Consortium, with more than 200 affiliated hotels in the UK, stresses to its customer service staff the importance of dealing with complaints successfully. People who complain can become a hotel's best friend!

It is the goal of the customer service department to turn every complainant into an ambassador for Best Western by providing an effective and professional service to customer complaints and enquiries.

Why do people complain?

All people are individuals and so the reasons why they complain are many and varied. Some of the most common reasons include:

- ✪ **Bad products or service:** To the customer, there is a strong link between quality of products and quality of service. If a customer has poor service in getting advice on choosing, for example, a European city break, the quality of the product itself tends to be put in doubt. Poor service, whether it be in person, on the telephone or in writing, is one of the main reasons why people complain.

✪ **Waiting:** People hate waiting around for attention and wasting their valuable time. The longer the wait the more likely customers are to complain. Mechanisms can be put in place to reduce conflict when a certain amount of waiting or queuing is unavoidable; entertainers are sometimes employed to keep the crowds happy outside London theatres, and TV/video screens or the use of music can sometimes have a positive effect at tourist attractions.

✪ **Being patronised:** Nothing is guaranteed to turn frustration into fury quicker than a patronising tone of voice on the part of the member of staff dealing with a customer. It is wise to assume that the customer has some knowledge of the product or service being bought and staff should be trained not to take a 'we know best' attitude.

Specific examples of situations in travel and tourism when customers are prone to complain include:

✪ **Having the time of the flight changed on their package holiday at the last minute**

✪ **Not being able to get through to the information department of a tourist board as the line is constantly engaged**

✪ **Finding that a hotel room has not been properly prepared for new guests**

✪ **Not being able to find a parking space in a holiday centre car park**

✪ **Being served a meal which has gone cold by the time it reaches the table**

✪ **Being served cloudy beer in a nightclub or pub**

✪ **Booking a window seat on a coach tour only to find that all the window seats are taken when you get on the coach**

Activity 5.9

Working as a member of a small group, list examples of when you or other members of your family recently had cause to complain when buying goods or services. Consider how well your complaint was dealt with and whether you, if put in the position of the member of staff dealing with the complaint, would have handled matters differently.

Handling complaints successfully

The key actions to take when handling complaints are:

1 **Listen attentively so that you get the whole story first time**
2 **Thank the customer for bringing the problem to your attention**
3 **Apologise in general terms for the inconvenience but do not grovel**
4 **Provide support for the customer by saying that the complaint will be fully investigated and matters put right immediately**
5 **Sympathise with the customer and try to see the situation from his or her point of view**
6 **Don't justify the circumstances that led up to the complaint and go on the defensive**
7 **Ask questions if you are not clear on any points of the customer's complaint**
8 **Find a solution to the problem**
9 **Agree the solution with the customer**
10 **Follow through to make sure that what you promised has been done**
11 **In future, try to anticipate complaints before they happen!**

One step on from somebody who has a justifiable complaint is the customer who is intent on 'causing a scene'. Just like handling complaints, there are tried and tested ways of dealing with these 'awkward' individuals:

1 **Try not to let them get you down or get under your skin; the fact that they wish to cause a fuss may be a sign of their own insecurity**
2 **Never argue with them – it can often get the member of staff into deeper trouble**
3 **Never be rude to customers, however rude they are being to you!**
4 **Try not to take any remarks personally – you may have had nothing to do with the alleged incident but are simply the nearest member of staff**
5 **Let customers do the talking and listen to what they have to say**
6 **If in any doubt, seek help from another member of staff or senior management**

Assessing the quality and effectiveness of customer service

Key topics in this section:

- **Introduction**
- **Benchmarking**
- **Key quality criteria**
- **Analysing the quality of customer service**

Introduction

Many travel and tourism organisations continually assess and monitor the quality of customer service they provide. They do this to make sure that their service is meeting the needs of customers and, if not, then necessary changes can be made. Customers' needs and expectations are constantly changing, so any customer service programme in travel and tourism must be flexible enough to meet the requirements of an increasingly demanding public.

Benchmarking

browse this website

www.english
tourism.org.uk/
quality

Some travel and tourism organisations use a system known as 'benchmarking' to assess their customer service, where they measure their own standards against the best in the industry. The English Tourism Council encourages the use of the benchmarking technique to enable visitor destinations such as towns, cities and seaside resorts to improve their standards of customer service.

The Xerox Corporation defines benchmarking as:

> . . . the continuing process of measuring products, services and practices against the toughest competition of those recognised as leaders.

Benchmarking performance against competitors enables organisations to identify aspects of their own products, service or processes which are under-performing and where shared best practice can help to improve quality standards. It can also highlight strengths that can be capitalised upon. Benchmarking has only recently been applied to the travel and tourism industry, although it certainly has the potential to help improve customer service standards.

Key quality criteria

The precise criteria that a travel and tourism organisation selects as its measure of customer service quality will differ between enterprises, but could include any of the following:

- ✪ **Price/value for money – e.g. as perceived by customers, when compared to competitor organisations, in relation to profitability, etc.**
- ✪ **Consistency/accuracy – e.g. published timetables, information given in brochures, etc.**
- ✪ **Reliability – e.g. rides at theme parks, scheduled transport services, etc.**
- ✪ **Staffing levels and qualities – e.g. can they cope at peak periods, do customers experience high quality customer service?**
- ✪ **Enjoyment of experience – from the customers' perspective**
- ✪ **Health and safety – e.g. in relation to codes of practice and company safety standards**
- ✪ **Cleanliness and hygiene – are customers happy with the standards?**
- ✪ **Accessibility and availability – e.g. in terms of customers with specific needs, such as wheelchair access**
- ✪ **Provision for individual needs – e.g. are staff trained to appreciate and respond positively to particular needs?**

Organisations will select their key quality criteria against which their customer service quality will be assessed.

Analysing the quality of customer service

There are three main elements to the analysis of an organisation's customer service quality, namely:

1   **Setting performance standards/criteria**
2   **Measuring to see if the standards are being met**
3   **Putting in place measures to rectify any shortcomings**

We will now look at each of these in detail.

Setting performance standards/criteria

When travel and tourism organisations strive for excellence in customer service, it soon becomes clear that it is not enough simply to encourage staff to 'treat the customers well'. There comes a point when the management has to define just what 'well' means. Employees need to know the standards against which their performance will be measured. Staff will need both a clear job description and a set of performance standards or performance criteria for each of the tasks they carry out. Many organisations talk at great length about their excellent customer service, but few are prepared to put in place the necessary performance standards to measure objectively just how good their service really is.

Devising and implementing performance standards is a very time-consuming task and one which, if done properly, will call for an investment of financial resources from the organisation. Large travel and tourism organisations, with extensive personnel and training departments, may well carry out the task themselves. Smaller organisations are likely to appoint a consultant to devise the standards on their behalf or use criteria already available through professional bodies and other industry organisations. In travel and tourism, much work is currently in progress to establish occupational standards in particular sectors to act as a starting point for performance appraisal and identification of training needs.

The following example of typical performance standards that could be used in a restaurant, hotel or any catering outlet shows the detail needed for the exercise to be a success.

Industry example
Typical performance standards in customer service

Staff role: Waiter/waitress

Task: Serving a light meal or snack to a customer

Step One: Greeting the customer

Standards:

1   Smile pleasantly while you wish the customer a pleasant good morning/afternoon/evening

continued

continued

2   Ask for the customer's order courteously

3   Use the customer's name if you know it to add a touch of warmth

4   Offer the customer a menu if he or she doesn't have one

Step Two: Taking the customer's order

Standards:

1   Be familiar with all items on the menu

2   Ask the customer for his/her order

3   Answer any questions the customer may have precisely and courteously

4   If something is requested which is not on the menu, suggest an alternative

5   Accept any special orders graciously

6   Thank the customer for the order and let him or her know how long the meal will take to prepare

7   Pass the order to the relevant member of staff for preparation

(*Note:* This is only a small section of a typical performance standards system.)

Measuring to see if the standards are being met

One of the most important aspects of service industries such as travel and tourism is for operators to provide facilities and services that the customers are happy with. The level of customer satisfaction can also be a very potent weapon when it comes to evaluating performance of an organisation; get it wrong, and you won't have any customers to ask if they are happy with the service! There is a general acceptance by owners and managers that customers have increasing expectations from the travel and tourism organisations they use, and that they are becoming more assertive in demanding higher standards of customer service.

Travel and tourism organisations that are truly customer-centred will gear all their activities and operations to the needs of their customers. Customers will form the focus of a total management system that acknowledges they are the reason for the organisation's very existence; without them there would be no organisation. These enlightened and 'open' operators will welcome **feedback** from customers, both positive and negative, and will use it as a way of improving organisational performance. Feedback is seen as vital to effective management and is built in to evaluation procedures and practices from the outset, rather than being considered as an additional and onerous duty.

The fact that travel and tourism is a service industry makes standards measurement a complex process. Whereas a company in the manufacturing sector can reasonably easily set standards for the quality of its products, and measure to see if the standards are being met, this process is much more difficult in industries so heavily dependent on customer service. However, although a difficult task, it is essential that any travel and tourism organisation that is committed to improving the quality of its customer service develops systems and procedures to measure the effectiveness of its activities.

Some of the most common techniques for measuring to see if customer service standards are being met include:

- ✪ **Informal feedback**
- ✪ **Surveys**
- ✪ **Suggestion boxes**
- ✪ **Focus groups**
- ✪ **Mystery shoppers**
- ✪ **Observation**

Informal feedback

Information from customers on their attitudes to a particular travel and tourism organisation can be gathered either informally or formally. Informal feedback is often spontaneous, making it just as valuable as information that is given in a more formal manner. Indeed, many would say that a customer is more likely to reveal his or her true feelings and attitudes in an unprompted chat with a member of staff, than when that same member of staff is carrying out a questionnaire survey of users. Informal feedback can take many forms, including:

- ✪ **A remark to a holiday representative about the poor standard of the food in a resort hotel**
- ✪ **A member of staff overhearing customers praising the standard of service received at a holiday centre**
- ✪ **A child heard complaining to a parent about the length of time they are having to queue for a ride at a theme park**

It is important that management establish a mechanism by which this informal feedback is collected and monitored. We are all well aware of the influence that unhappy customers can have on the image of an organisation and thereby its success. We all like to talk about our travel and tourism experiences, which, if negative, can spread very quickly by 'word of mouth'. This powerful mechanism can also be beneficial for those organisations that have provided an excellent standard of service.

Many travel and tourism operators now have regular staff meetings at which employees are invited to share any informal feedback that they have picked up. They are also encouraged to record comments from customers on specially designed feedback forms, so that management can monitor the situation to see if corrective action is needed in any areas. The management at Disneyland Paris follows the legendary Disney management philosophy of putting the customer at the heart of the operation. All staff are trained in customer service skills and have regular training sessions at which they discuss the importance of informal feedback and share their experiences with other employees.

Surveys

Surveys are the most common method of monitoring levels of performance in customer service programmes. An organisation will carry out a survey to see if the targets it set itself are being achieved in reality. A survey provides a 'snapshot' of an organisation's health at a particular time. Surveys are important to management since they measure the satisfaction levels within the organisation and provide crucial information on which decisions can be made.

Surveys as part of a customer service programme can be directed at:

- ✪ **Customers:** A survey of visitors at a tourist attraction or a customer satisfaction survey at a resort complex will provide valuable information about how customers perceive their experience; how they feel about the standard of service, the attitude of the staff, how any queries have been dealt with, etc.

- ✪ **Staff:** It is important to continually seek and act on the views of staff at the 'sharp end' of dealing with customers. Without their continuing support, excellent customer service cannot be guaranteed. An employee attitude survey will give them the chance to have their ideas and concerns formally noted. Management will be able to see if particular concerns are being expressed by more than one individual and act accordingly.

- ✪ **'Internal customers':** We have seen that all staff in travel and tourism organisations have 'customers', whether or not they deal with the public face to face. Internal customers are colleagues in the same organisation, who may be in a different department, but whose co-operation and support is vital if the move towards excellence in customer service is to be successful. Surveys can be a useful way of establishing whether all departments are happy with the standards of customer service.

- ✪ **Management:** The managers in the organisation should be surveyed routinely to see if they are clear on their role in achieving total customer satisfaction. If the management is unclear or unhappy about the culture of the organisation, these fears may be transmitted to other staff and even customers.

- ⊗ **Non-users:** It may be useful to find out why people are not using your facilities but are choosing to spend their money on competitor products and services. Such a survey, which is normally carried out in the street or door to door, may highlight aspects of poor customer service that could be put right.

Activity 5.10

Working as a member of a group, prepare a draft non-user survey that could be used by a local tourist attraction that is keen to find out why customers are not using its facilities.

Managers will also use sales and profitability figures as another important measure of customer satisfaction, as well as analysing data on customers, such as the volume of repeat business, frequency of bookings, satisfaction levels, customer spend, etc. Monitoring such information, either manually or with the help of a computer-based system, will allow managers to see if performance standards and specific objectives of the customer service programme are being met.

browse this website

www.thomson-holidays.com

Industry example

Thomson Holidays, the UK's largest tour operator, introduced a customer satisfaction questionnaire (CSQ) in 1975 and it is now one of the biggest consumer surveys in the world. Distributed on board its Britannia aircraft or in resorts, the CSQ gives holidaymakers the opportunity to rate their overall holiday as excellent, good, fair or poor. Approximately 40 per cent of adult customers complete and return a CSQ. The company distributed 4 million questionnaires during the 1999 summer season, with results showing that 94 per cent of customers rated their holiday good or excellent.

OUR HOTEL

How well did we meet your expectations?
(Please tick the appropriate box)

	Excellent	Good	Fair	Poor
Finding the hotel from our literature (if applicable)	☐	☐	☐	☐
Your welcome on arrival	☐	☐	☐	☐
In Reception: Check in procedure	☐	☐	☐	☐

In the Bedroom:
Cleanliness of room	☐	☐	☐	☐
Overall comfort of room	☐	☐	☐	☐
Standard of decor	☐	☐	☐	☐

In the Restaurant:
Quality of food - Breakfast	☐	☐	☐	☐
Quality of food - Dinner	☐	☐	☐	☐
Standard of ambiance	☐	☐	☐	☐

In the telephone service:
Staff telephone manner	☐	☐	☐	☐
Speed of response	☐	☐	☐	☐

Leisure facilities if used: ☐ ☐ ☐ ☐

When in the area again, what is the likelihood that you would stay with us?
- Definitely ☐
- Very Likely ☐
- Not Very Likely ☐
- Not At All Likely ☐

Any other comments: ....
....
....
....
....

OUR TEAM

How would you rate our team overall in terms of:
(please tick the appropriate box)

	Excellent	Good	Fair	Poor
Friendliness	☐	☐	☐	☐
Efficiency	☐	☐	☐	☐
Reliability	☐	☐	☐	☐
Anticipating your needs	☐	☐	☐	☐
Ability to resolve problems	☐	☐	☐	☐

We operate a bonus scheme for staff who go out of their way to make your stay enjoyable. If there is someone you would like to mention, please do so below:

Name: ....

Any other comments: ....
....

OUR SERVICE

How would you rate the service given.
(Please tick the appropriate box)

	Excellent	Good	Fair	Poor
Reception	☐	☐	☐	☐
Porterage	☐	☐	☐	☐
Lounge & Bar	☐	☐	☐	☐
Restaurant	☐	☐	☐	☐
Housekeeping	☐	☐	☐	☐
Leisure Club	☐	☐	☐	☐
How do you rate the hotel in terms of value for money	☐	☐	☐	☐

Some general points:
What did you most enjoy about your stay:
....

What did you least enjoy about your stay?
....

Any other comments: ....
....

Was this your first visit to the area? Yes ☐ No ☐

What was the primary purpose of your visit?
- Business ☐
- Pleasure ☐
- Conference ☐
- Weekend Break ☐

Finally, please, a few details about yourself.

Your age:
- Under 25 ☐
- 25 - 35 ☐
- 36 - 45 ☐
- 46 - 55 ☐
- Over 55 ☐

Are you Male? ☐
Female? ☐

Number of nights stay ....

Your Room Number ....

What other hotels have you stayed at in this area?
....

Was the service they gave you:
- Much better ☐
- Better ☐
- The same ☐
- Worse ☐

than the service you received with us.

Name: ....

Address: ....
....

Please place this questionnaire in the box at reception. Thank-you once again for your time.

Figure 5.14 *An example of a customer comment form*
Courtesy of The Low Wood Hotel

Suggestion boxes and customer comment forms

Suggestion boxes are a novel way of inviting customer feedback. A simple form can be provided, which, when completed, is put into the box to be looked at by staff and management. Suggestion boxes often highlight ways in which travel and tourism organisations can make simple alterations to facilities that will improve the customer experience. They can help in the process of monitoring customer complaints; management should aim to keep these to a minimum by setting targets for the number of complaints received, which should be reduced over time.

Customer comment forms give visitors an immediate opportunity to tell the management what they think of the service and facilities they have used. Figure 5.14 shows an example of a customer comment form used at the Low Wood Hotel in the Lake District.

This example asks guests to comment on the facilities in the hotel itself, the quality of the staff and the standard of service received. The form finishes with some questions relating to the purpose of the visit and the profile of the customer. Completed forms are monitored by the general manager and discussed at regular staff meetings. Customer comment forms are in widespread use throughout all sectors of the travel and tourism industry, including tour operators, travel agencies, leisure centres, hotels, transport operators, destinations and tourist information centres.

Focus groups

Market research organisations are sometimes asked to assemble focus groups to look in detail at what influences people when they are deciding which product or service to buy. A small number of customers who already use a particular product, or those with specific social and economic characteristics, are invited to spend a couple of hours with a trained interviewer, employed by a company or group of companies to help them increase their market share. Although not widely used in the travel and tourism industry, there are examples of airlines holding focus group sessions with business travellers, and some conference and business organisers are known to use the technique.

Mystery shoppers

A 'mystery shopper' is somebody who is employed by an organisation to anonymously visit a facility or use a product or service, and report back to management on his or her experiences. It can be used to gain information on the performance of staff, for example in the management's own organisation, or to look into the service offered by competitors. The technique is widely used in the commercial sectors of travel and tourism, most notably in airlines, hotels and travel agencies.

Activity 5.11

With the prior approval of your tutor or teacher, visit a selection of local travel and tourism facilities and assess the levels of customer service you received at each. Compare your findings with those of other members of your group.

Observation

Observing what people do and say, whether they are customers, managers or staff, can provide useful feedback on the effectiveness of customer service. It is common for an employee, who has been given clear performance standards to achieve, to be observed in the workplace by his or her line manager or supervisor. Indeed part of the evaluation process of a customer service programme may be a manager observing staff and recording their progress over a period of time. Staff in certain travel and tourism organisations may also be tested from time to time by management on such matters as pricing and product knowledge.

Customers may be observed as well as surveyed in order to get a fuller picture of their satisfaction levels. Staff may be given the task of 'mingling' with customers to listen to their views; people are often more open with their comments if they know their answers or reactions are not going to be recorded on a questionnaire. The sectors of the industry where observation of customers is a particularly useful technique include visitor attractions, restaurants, cafés, museums and art galleries.

Putting in place measures to rectify any shortcomings

If the process of measuring actual performance against the performance standards shows that targets are not being met, measures to rectify the situation will need to be implemented as soon as possible to maintain excellent standards of customer service. Feedback from customers may highlight the need for more training for staff or management, or perhaps alterations to systems in order to improve matters. Once the measures have been put in place, the process of monitoring and evaluation will continue using a mixture of the techniques described above.

Maintaining the momentum

We have seen that working towards excellent customer service in travel and tourism is a very complex and time-consuming process. Any faltering on the part of management or staff could lead to the whole exercise failing to meet its objectives. One of the most important tasks for management is to make sure that staff remain committed to serving customers well. Some managers adopt a 'campaign' approach to this by involving staff in devising slogans, having T-shirts, posters and pens printed with the slogans, and arranging extra social and sporting activities within the organisation.

Managers and staff should not be afraid of publicising achievements within the organisation; perhaps a performance standard has not only been met but exceeded. Newsletters and notice-boards should be used to communicate such examples to all staff to help maintain the momentum. Above all, managers should appreciate what their staff are doing to achieve excellence in customer service and reward them accordingly.

Travel and tourism in action

6

This is a very practical unit that builds on the work you have completed in other units on your Vocational A-Level course, putting theory into practice. The unit gives you the opportunity to plan, carry out and evaluate a real travel and tourism project that is of interest to you. You will produce a business plan for your chosen project before it takes place, looking at matters such as aims and objectives, how the project will be marketed, finance and staffing the project. You will also keep a log of your involvement in the project, as well as contributing to an evaluation to discover what went well and what could have worked better. Throughout the unit, you will be working as part of a team and advice is offered on how to do this effectively. This unit provides the opportunity for the practical application of much of your knowledge and experience of travel and tourism, giving you the chance to develop essential business skills.

This unit is divided into four main areas:

- **Feasibility of the project**
- **Teamwork**
- **Carrying out the project**
- **Evaluating the project**

We guide you through each of these areas using examples and case studies from the travel and tourism industry. At the beginning of each section you will see a list of key topics to help you fully understand what you need to learn. Look out for the links to websites so that you can learn more about a particular travel and tourism company or topic.

Feasibility of the project

Key topics in this section:

- **Introduction – choosing a project**
- **Writing a business plan**
- **Details of your project**

Introduction – choosing a project

This is likely to be one of the most demanding and challenging units on your Vocational A-Level course. Equally, it should be one of the most rewarding, enjoyable and memorable, as long as you plan well ahead and work as part of a team. In completing this unit you will be developing and applying many of the skills that employers in travel and tourism say they are seeking in new recruits, for example communication skills, problem solving, team working and project management.

Thinking of the type of project you will carry out is known as the 'ideas' or pre-feasibility stage of project management. The aim is to consider a variety of possible ideas and sift out the one that you, and the rest of your team, feel most comfortable with. In choosing your project, you should think carefully about the following important points:

- ✪ **Likes and dislikes of the project team members:** Find out the sort of project that people would be happy to complete. Taking a little time at this stage could minimise problems in the future, such as lack of interest or commitment.

- ✪ **The size of your team:** You may be working with just one other colleague or be part of a group of 30 or more. Make sure you choose a project that is manageable in terms of the size of your team.

- ✪ **Your location:** Where you are located could influence your choice of project. If you are in a busy tourist area, there may be the chance to carry out a project that directly involves tourists. There may be opportunities to run a project that supports your local community.

- ✪ **Time constraints:** Your tutor will tell you how much time you have available for your project. You should be realistic in choosing a project that can be successfully completed within the time you have available (always allowing a margin of error for unforeseen events).

- ✪ **Available resources:** You will need to choose a project that will not stretch the resources you have at your disposal, e.g. people in the project team, buildings, finance, equipment, materials, etc.

✪ **Local support:** Local businesses, the council or voluntary groups may wish to join forces with you in running your project or loaning materials and equipment.

Having considered these points, you should be in a position to finalise your project topic, in conjunction with the other members of your team. There are many possible projects that you could choose. Your team could, for example:

✪ **Organise an outing to the seaside for a group of senior citizens**
✪ **Plan and run a guided walk for visitors to your local area**
✪ **Sell souvenirs to tourists**
✪ **Arrange an overseas visit for students**
✪ **Plan a small business venture in travel and tourism**
✪ **Operate a travel and tourism information and advice centre**
✪ **Run a coach trip for a group of local people**
✪ **Operate a cycle hire scheme for tourists**

Remember that whatever you choose must be related to travel and tourism. Your tutor will give you advice and ideas about what your team could do. It may be possible to run the project in conjunction with a local organisation, perhaps a charity, with any profits being donated once the project is completed. Alternatively, there may be a local travel and tourism organisation that would welcome the chance to become involved with the project, adding realism to your work.

Activity 6.1

If you are having difficulty thinking of a suitable idea for your project, have a brainstorming session with others in your group, listing as many projects as you can. When you have finished your list, take each idea in turn and discuss its feasibility with the rest of your project team. If all goes according to plan, you should be able to reach a consensus on which project to tackle.

Writing a business plan

Having agreed your project topic with your tutor, your team is now in a position to begin writing the business plan. You should divide the work equally among the team members, each researching and writing their own part of the plan. A business plan is a document that sets out the details of a proposed project or venture. It has both **internal** and **external** uses. Internally, the business plan acts as a focus for all concerned with the project, since it provides a purpose, direction and a set of targets to achieve. It also allows a project team to check progress from time to time to see that the project is on target. Externally, a business plan may be needed to convince others, such as banks, other investors, development agencies or local authorities, that a project is viable. A business plan sets out to answer a number of questions about a project, for example:

- ✪ **What is the project trying to achieve?**
- ✪ **What is the timescale for the project?**
- ✪ **Who are the customers?**
- ✪ **Which staff are involved with the project?**
- ✪ **Is the project financially sound?**
- ✪ **How will the project be marketed?**
- ✪ **Does the project team have sufficient physical resources to complete the project?**
- ✪ **Have any legal aspects been satisfied?**

Although you are unlikely to be looking for outside financial support for your project, it is important that you know how to write a business plan for your future career development.

The precise content of a business plan will vary, depending on the type of project being undertaken. There are, however, certain key features that any plan should contain, as shown in Figure 6.1.

Your business plan should be laid out in a professional fashion with a table of contents, an introduction and a bibliography/list of sources consulted.

1 The aims and objectives of the project
2 Your customers, their needs and how these will be met
3 How the project will be marketed
4 Physical resource needs (e.g. equipment, venue/premises, materials)
5 Financial aspects of the project (e.g. budgeting, start-up costs, income, handling payments)
6 Staffing for the project
7 Administration systems (e.g. bookings, record-keeping, paper-based/computer-based)
8 Project timescales
9 Legal aspects of the project (e.g. health and safety, security, insurance)
10 Contingency plans
11 How the project will be reviewed and evaluated

Figure 6.1 *Key features of a business plan*

> **Industry example**
> All the major high street banks, as well as small business
> advisory services and development agencies, supply
> information for people wanting to start their own
> businesses. This often includes details of how to develop a
> project and write a business plan.

Details of your project

Your team now needs to write its business plan using the information in Figure 6.1 as a guide. Remember that the business plan needs to be finished **before** you carry out the project. The following sections of this unit will take you through the key points to be included in your business plan, providing guidance on what to consider and how best to proceed.

Aims and objectives of the project

You, and the rest of your team, must be clear from the outset what exactly your project is trying to achieve. In other words, you must have a clear aim and objectives. An **aim** is a general statement about the overall target of a project. For example, the aim of your project could be 'to run a successful guided walk for tourists'. Anybody reading this aim will be clear as to what the project involves. **Objectives** are more specific and give greater detail about the project. In this example, the objectives could include 'to attract 20 people to the guided walk' or 'to break even financially, after making a donation of £15 to charity out of the proceeds'.

You will need to work with the other members of your team to agree your project objectives. Whatever objectives you decide upon, remember that they must be SMART, in other words:

Specific: It is no use having 'woolly' ideas that are not well thought through or clearly defined

Measurable: Objectives must be capable of being measured so that you know if you have achieved your targets

Achievable: Setting objectives that are wildly optimistic wastes everybody's time

Realistic: Objectives must fit in with the organisation's overall business aims

Timed: It is important to set time deadlines to review progress

Remember also that setting objectives is not a 'one off' activity; they must be constantly monitored and, if necessary, updated during the life of your project in the light of changing circumstances. The evaluation of your project will be based on the objectives you agree at this stage, so take your time and work as a team to get them right!

Activity 6.2

> Write down the aim and objectives of your project in collaboration with the other members of your team. Remember that the objectives must be SMART!

The following case study looks in detail at a successful project initiative that has clearly defined aims.

Case Study
Mid Wales Festival of the Countryside

The Festival of the Countryside promotes sustainable tourism in Wales by encouraging awareness and enjoyment of the countryside in ways which do it no harm. Launched in 1985 as a contribution to the World Conservation Strategy, the Festival has grown into a pioneering model of responsible rural tourism. It seeks to show that informed concern and respect for the environment can go hand in hand with economic development, in an area of Britain that is working hard to attract inward investment, create new jobs and improve the social fabric for the local people. An avid supporter of the Festival of the Countryside is the leading environmentalist David Bellamy, who visits Mid Wales every year to take part in events. He said of the Festival recently:

> *It's the only place I know where the people who have gold chains round their necks and who sit in committees are actively working with conservation to make their landscape wonderful for ever and ever.*

continued

continued

The Festival, based at Newtown in the heart of Mid Wales, acts as an 'umbrella' organisation for marketing purposes and as a catalyst for the development of events, linking with individuals, voluntary groups and the private sector.

▶ FESTIVAL AIMS

The aims of the Festival of the Countryside are:

- ★ Environmental education – to convey, in an interesting and coherent way, the messages of the countryside and conservation
- ★ Enjoyment of the countryside – to help satisfy the varied recreational demands of residents and tourists
- ★ Socio-economic development – to stimulate the rural economy, to support providers of rural attractions and to involve the local community in culturally acceptable ways

▶ OPERATIONS

The Festival promotes a series of events (some of which have existed for some time, some new) which take place in the countryside, towns and villages of Mid Wales. It publishes two magazines every year, one for the summer season and one listing winter events (see Figure 6.2). The combined print run of the two magazines for 1998 was 130,000. The magazines are distributed through more than 280 outlets, including tourist information centres throughout Wales and the border counties, all libraries in the area covered by the magazines, tourist accommodation and visitor attractions. With the rapid growth of the Internet, the Festival is investigating how the development of information technology can be used to further its aims and to promote its programmes to a wider market.

The Festival also supports events and attractions during the year through a small grants scheme and by adding value to events (see Figure 6.3). To enable tourism businesses to

continued

continued

clearly demonstrate their growing commitment to sustainability, the Festival is also considering a badging/branding scheme. Linked to this, it is promoting a flagship scheme to assess and promote examples of good practice in sustainable tourism.

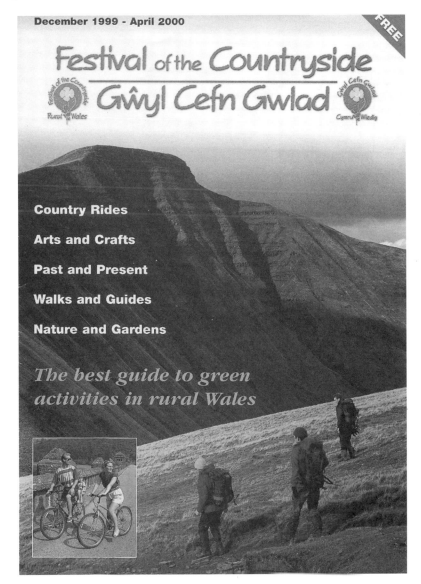

Figure 6.2 *The winter 1999–2000 Festival of the Countryside magazine*
Courtesy of Mid Wales Festival of the Countryside

continued

continued

Figure 6.3 *Activities are an important part of the Festival*
Courtesy of Michael D. Smith

STAFFING, FUNDING AND PARTNERSHIPS

The Festival is constituted as a company limited by guarantee, with a board of directors, an executive committee, four full-time members of staff and a part-time project consultant. In the 1998–99 financial year, the following organisations contributed financially to the work of the Festival:

★ European Regional Development Fund (ERDF)

★ Wales Tourist Board

★ Countryside Council for Wales

★ Gwynedd County Council

★ Powys County Council

★ Brecon Beacons National Park Authority

★ Snowdonia National Park Authority

★ Menter Powys

continued

continued

★ Severn–Trent Water Limited

★ Ordnance Survey

Each year, the Festival works in partnership with a variety of organisations. Recent collaborative ventures have included:

★ Kite Country Tourism Project

★ Festivals of Wales Initiative

★ Eco-labelling Project to establish good practice in sustainable tourism

★ Lake Vyrnwy Sculpture Trail

For the future, the Festival will continue to widen its work beyond the two event programmes, contributing to the viability of rural communities in a sustainable way.

(Information courtesy of Mid Wales Festival of the Countryside)

Case study discussion questions

1 Explain in your own words the aims of the Festival of the Countryside.

2 What benefits does the Festival gain from working in partnership with other organisations?

3 How does the Festival help small tourism businesses in Mid Wales?

4 How could the Festival widen its appeal and attract even more visitors to the events it publicises?

Your customers, their needs and how these will be met

Unit 5: Customer Service in Travel and Tourism has highlighted the importance of providing excellent standards of service to customers. Nowadays in the highly competitive travel and tourism industry, customer service is not just about **meeting** customers' needs, but **exceeding** them. You should aim to apply the same high standards of customer service in this project as if you were working in the industry.

In this section of your business plan you will need to include two components:

1   A profile of your customers

2   A statement of their needs and how these will be met

The customer profile will provide your team with detailed information on the people you are going to serve. These could include:

✪   **Individuals**

✪   **Groups**

✪   **People of different ages**

✪   **People from different cultures**

✪   **Non-English speakers**

✪   **People with specific needs, for example those needing wheelchair access, people with sensory disabilities and those with young children**

▼ ▼ ▼ ▼ ▼ ▼ ▼ ▼ ▼

Unit link
Look at Unit 5: Customer Service in Travel and Tourism for more on meeting customers' needs and personal presentation.

▲ ▲ ▲ ▲ ▲ ▲ ▲ ▲ ▲

Having established the profile of your customers, you need to identify their needs as clearly as possible and describe how these will be met. It may be difficult to meet the needs of everybody and you may need to prioritise customer needs, identifying those that are essential and those that are desirable. Your project timescales and budget may mean adopting a flexible approach to meeting customer needs. Unit 5: Customer Service in Travel and Tourism has some good advice on meeting different customers' needs (see page 324).

Personal presentation is an important aspect of customer service and you should include information in your business plan on dress to be worn, as well as the importance of the right personality and attitude when dealing with the public.

**Activity
6.3**

Finalise the 'customer' section of your business plan, to include a customer profile, details of their needs and how these will be met. Discuss among the team members whether you should also include a customer service mission statement and/or a customer service charter.

How the project will be marketed

Deciding how to market your project will be crucial to its success. You could think of a really original idea, but if nobody knows about it you are in trouble! You will need to devise a promotional campaign that will raise awareness of your project – whether it happens to be an event or business enterprise – and make people want to part with their money by taking part. You will already have established who your customers will be, which, for the purposes of marketing, now become your target market. The promotional campaign that is included in your business plan should specify:

▼ ▼ ▼ ▼ ▼ ▼ ▼ ▼ ▼

Unit link
Look at Unit 4: Marketing Travel and Tourism for more details on sponsorship and promotional techniques used in travel and tourism.

▲ ▲ ▲ ▲ ▲ ▲ ▲ ▲ ▲

✪ **Details of your target market**

✪ **Any budget that you have at your disposal for promotion**

✪ **The 'message' that you want to convey about your project**

✪ **The media you will use to convey the message (e.g. advertising, direct mail, press releases, posters)**

✪ **Examples of the promotional items (e.g. press release, poster, direct mail letter, advertisement)**

✪ **Details of how your team will monitor the promotional campaign**

You may also like to consider whether sponsorship by a local organisation may be appropriate for your project.

Activity 6.4

Devise a promotional campaign for your project to be included in your business plan.

Physical resource needs

The physical resources that you may need could include premises, equipment and materials. Depending on the type of project you are carrying out, these may have to be bought, hired or even borrowed! Your centre may be able to meet most of your resource needs, or you may be considering a joint project with a local organisation or voluntary group that would be able to help out. Use of a computer is likely to be high up on your list of resource needs, perhaps even a laptop if your project involves a lot of working away from your centre. A base room where you can hold team meetings and work on your business plan would be very useful.

Activity 6.5

Include in your business plan a list of the physical resource needs, how they will be provided and any costs that will be incurred.

Financial aspects of the project

The section covering finance is often the most important part of a business plan, particularly if the prime purpose of the plan is to raise finance for setting up a new project. In the real world of travel and tourism, potential investors will want to be assured that the individuals seeking the funding have been objective and realistic in their assessments of future financial performance. Since a business plan is essentially concerned with looking to the future, the financial information must include projections of likely costs and revenue. A fully costed, professional business plan will include:

- ✪ **Cash flow budgets and projections**
- ✪ **Anticipated profit and loss figures**
- ✪ **Balance sheet projections**

For the purposes of this project, you should concentrate on working out a cash flow budget and profit/loss figures to be included in your business plan.

Cash flow budget

The cash flow budget will show the expected flows of cash into and out of your project during its life. Detailed cash flow management is critical to any travel and tourism organisation, so that it can:

- ✪ **Be in a position to meet cash demands**
- ✪ **Ensure that maximum credit is being obtained**
- ✪ **Make sure that debtors are kept under tight control**
- ✪ **Determine when extra borrowing is needed**

Figure 6.4 gives an example of a cash flow budget for a travel agency over a three-month trading period.

	Jan	Feb	Mar
Cash at start	32	57	59
Total cash inflows	135	120	116
Total cash outflows	110	118	121
Net cash flow	+25	+2	−5
Cumulative cash	57	59	54

Figure 6.4   *Cash flow budget (£000) for a three-month trading period*

Activity 6.6

Draw up a cash flow budget for your project, using the example in Figure 6.4 as a guide.

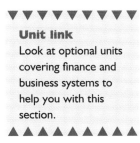

Unit link

Look at optional units covering finance and business systems to help you with this section.

Lakeview Country House Hotel	
Profit and Loss Account for the year ending 31.3.2000	
	£000
Sales	
Rooms	120
Food and beverage	160
Other	24
Total	304
Cost of sales	65
Gross profit	239
Expenses	178
Operating profit	61
Interest	38
Net profit	23

Figure 6.5 *Profit and loss account for a small country house hotel*

The profit and loss account

The information contained in the profit and loss account is probably the most important in managing and controlling a travel and tourism organisation. The profit and loss account for your project will provide a summary of all the estimated income and expenditure during the life of the project. Figure 6.5 shows the profit and loss account for a small country house hotel.

Activity 6.7

Draw up a profit and loss account for your project, using the example in Figure 6.5 as a guide.

As well as including a cash flow budget and profit and loss account, your business plan should also detail any start-up costs you may incur and a statement of how any payments will be handled (see section on administration systems on page 387). Strict financial procedures must be set and adhered to by all members of the team.

Staffing for the project

Your team needs to be assembled so that all project tasks can be completed successfully, with work divided equally among team members. Depending on the size of your group, you may not have a great deal of choice when selecting team members. You will need a team leader (and a deputy to cover when he or she is unavailable), plus team members who are selected on the basis of their skills, preferences and enthusiasm. Team members will need to take responsibility for completing a number of tasks concerning:

- ✪ **Marketing**
- ✪ **Finance**
- ✪ **Personnel/human resources**
- ✪ **Health, safety and security**
- ✪ **Physical resources**
- ✪ **Administration**
- ✪ **Legal aspects**
- ✪ **Project review and evaluation**

You will need to think carefully about what needs to be done under each of these headings by preparing a job analysis, and write a job description for each. For example, one person in your team could take responsibility for all marketing activity to do with the project. He or she could be named the marketing co-ordinator, with a detailed job description that explains what the job entails. A typical job description is likely to include:

Job description	
Job title:	Seasonal Shop Supervisor
Responsible to:	Merchandise Senior Supervisor Assistant Merchandise Manager Merchandise Manager
Responsible for:	(a) Maintaining stock levels. (b) Stock ordering. (c) Ensuring unit is kept in a clean and tidy state at all times. (d) Ensuring staff in their unit are suitably dressed. (e) Cashing up.
Position in company:	General Manager Business Retail Manager Merchandise Manager Assistant Merchandise Manager Merchandise Senior Supervisor Shop Senior Supervisor Seasonal Shop Supervisor
Job purpose:	To ensure smooth running of unit.
Job description:	(a) Stock ordering. (b) Maintaining a clean and tidy unit. (c) Organising breaks. (d) General organisation of unit of responsibility. (e) Cashing up.
Authority:	(a) To authorise customer refunds and voids.
Hours of work:	40 hrs, as and when required, i.e. Bank Holidays.

Figure 6.6 *Job description for a post at a theme park*

- ✪ **Basic details** – title of post, grade, post number, department/section, location, etc.
- ✪ **Summary of the job** – outlining the key objectives of the post
- ✪ **Responsibilities** – clarifying the position in the organisational structure, detailing to whom responsible and for whom responsible
- ✪ **Detailed duties** – a list of all the relevant duties attached to the post
- ✪ **Conditions of employment** – general information on salary/wage, holiday entitlement, hours of work, pension arrangements, welfare and social facilities, trade union membership arrangements, training, etc.

Figure 6.6 shows an example of a job description for a seasonal shop supervisor at a theme park which you should use as a guide when completing Activity 6.8.

Activity 6.8

Working with the other members of your team, write a job analysis and a job description for each of the project tasks, i.e. marketing, finance, personnel/human resources, health, safety and security, physical resources, administration, legal aspects, project review and evaluation.

Unit link
Look at the optional unit on human resources for more information on staffing aspects of your project.

There are a number of ways of finally deciding which member of your team is going to take responsibility for which task or tasks. It may be that each student chooses the job that appeals most to him or her. Alternatively, your tutor may suggest holding a series of interviews, with students applying for particular jobs. In certain circumstances, your tutor may allocate tasks to team members. Whichever way the tasks are allocated, you must make sure that you maximise the strengths of the group and minimise the weaknesses. Each member of the group could make a list of what they consider to be their own strengths and weaknesses, matching the criteria chosen to the job descriptions your team has written.

Administration systems

All projects have a certain amount of administrative work associated with them. The administration system that you set up for this project must be:

- ✪ **Accurate**
- ✪ **Accessible**
- ✪ **Up to date**

- ✪ **Reliable**
- ✪ **Easy to use**

Depending on the type of project you carry out, your administration system may need to cover:

- ✪ **Bookings from customers**
- ✪ **Record keeping**
- ✪ **Stock control**
- ✪ **Handling cash payments**

You will need to decide whether to use a paper-based or computer-based system to handle your administration. This will depend on:

- ✪ **The size of your team**
- ✪ **The complexity of the administration system**
- ✪ **Access to computers**
- ✪ **The levels of computer literacy of the team members**

The main advantage of using a computer-based system is that it is quick and easy to update, although it is more expensive than a paper-based system. You will need to discuss among the team members which system to operate.

Where cash is concerned, you will need to devise systems to keep very strict control over its movement and storage. It is essential that every member of

W/E	Monday	Tuesday	Wednesday	Thursday	Friday	Saturday	Sunday	Total
Accom./Room hire								
Restaurant								
Lounge bar								
Wines								
Bar Meals								
Functions Food								
Functions Wines								
Functions Bar								
Telephone								
Miscellaneous								
Deposits								
Total								

Maesmawr Hall Hotel
Daily receipts summary

Figure 6.7   *Daily receipts summary as used in a hotel*
Courtesy of Maesmawr Hall Hotel

your team is aware of the importance of handling cash securely, and that any money, in its various forms, is credited to a bank account in a safe way and without any undue delay. A daily receipts summary, similar to that shown in Figure 6.7, will help keep track of cash takings.

Although you are likely to be working with cash and possibly cheques in this project, it is important that you are aware of the full range of payment methods used in the travel and tourism industry, which include:

✪ **Bank notes and coins**

✪ **Cheques and postal orders**

✪ **Credit cards, debit cards and charge cards**

✪ **Banker's drafts and certified cheques**

✪ **Travellers' cheques**

Although it is becoming a little unfashionable to carry coins and notes, there are still a lot of people who would not think of using anything else. Cash is the main payment method in many travel and tourism facilities, such as leisure centres, museums, catering outlets and sports venues. It is usual practice to issue a receipt immediately for cash transactions, which acts as proof of purchase (see Figure 6.8). Cash paid into a bank account does not need 'clearing' and is immediately credited to the organisation's account.

Accepting cheques is a very common method of payment in many travel and tourism organisations, and you may have to deal with them during this project. Once paid into a bank account, it will take a minimum of three working days for the cheque to be processed, during which time it remains 'uncleared'; clearing is the process of passing the cheque to the customer's bank, debiting their account and crediting your own. Staff should always ask for a cheque guarantee card to be presented; most will honour cheques up to the value of £50, although it is becoming increasingly common to see £100 cheque

Viewside Arts Centre

Tel: (0123) 45613
VAT Reg. No. 263 7633 25

Date:

Received from:

For:

Amount:

Signed on behalf of Viewside Arts Centre

Receipt no:

Figure 6.8 *An example of a receipt used in an arts centre*

guarantee cards in use. Cheques for values in excess of that quoted on the card should not normally be accepted; it is safer to ask the customer to provide another form of payment.

Whichever methods of payment you are accepting, the stages that the payment will go through are as follows:

1   **Payment received**
2   **Receipt issued to customer (see Figure 6.8)**
3   **Entry made on daily cash summary sheet (see Figure 6.7)**
4   **Receipts and summary sheets reconciled**
5   **Bank paying-in slips completed**
6   **Monies paid into the bank account**
7   **Paying-in slips stamped by bank**

▼ ▼ ▼ ▼ ▼ ▼ ▼ ▼ ▼
Unit link
Look at the optional unit covering business systems to help you with this section.

▲ ▲ ▲ ▲ ▲ ▲ ▲ ▲ ▲

Activity 6.9

Working with the other members of your team, write a description of the administration systems associated with your project. Include this information in your business plan.

Project timescales

We all have deadlines to meet in our daily lives and this project is no different! Your team will need to demonstrate excellent time management skills if the project is to achieve its objectives. There should be an overall project timetable that details the main deadlines. In addition to this, team members will need to devise their own deadlines for their area of responsibility. The marketing co-ordinator, for example, will need to work back from the date of the event or business enterprise you are planning, setting dates for the completion of key tasks, such as writing a press release, submitting an advertisement, etc.

It is essential that all key project dates are agreed by all team members. Everybody in the team must be committed to meeting project deadlines and must understand the consequences of failing to meet them.

Activity 6.10

Include in your business plan the overall project timetable and deadlines for the major areas of responsibility.

Legal aspects of the project

Hopefully, you will not get too closely involved with the law on this project, but you should be aware of the range of legislation that can affect the planning and carrying out of a project. Depending on the nature of your project, you will need to consider any, or all, of the following:

- ✪ **Health and Safety at Work Act**
- ✪ **Trades Description Act**
- ✪ **Food Safety Act and Food Hygiene Regulations**
- ✪ **Public Order Act**
- ✪ **Licensing Acts**

There may be other regulations that your particular project must comply with, if, for example, you are working with children or offering outdoor activities. Check with your tutor if you are unsure about this. In general terms, you should be aware that we are all bound by a common law duty of care, under which each citizen owes a duty to all others who may be affected by his or her activities.

Activity 6.11

Include in your business plan details of the relevant legal aspects of your project and how you will meet the requirements of specific regulations.

Contingency plans

Murphy's Law applies just as much to managing projects in travel and tourism as it does to any other aspect of everyday life, so 'if anything can go wrong it will!' Some things that happen to test the nerve of even the best-prepared project team can truly be said to be unforeseen, but many can be anticipated, with contingencies or alternatives ready to hand. If your project involves planning an event, the weather will be one of the least predictable factors, be it in summer or winter. You can reassure the public that an outdoor event will go ahead 'whatever the weather' by publicising this fact from the outset and giving an alternative venue should the worst happen. A cold spell or sudden downpour can also affect attendances at indoor events, with people choosing to stay in the comfort of their own homes rather than venturing out.

In the case of an event, other considerations that may need contingency plans include:

- ✪ **Failure of power supplies (is a back-up alternative source of supply needed?)**
- ✪ **Non-arrival of key staff or personalities (have 'extras' on hand)**
- ✪ **Heavy traffic (consider an alternative point of entry for key personnel)**
- ✪ **A major accident (make sure that all emergency services have been told of the event and means of entry and exit worked out)**
- ✪ **For an outdoor event, parts of the site may be waterlogged (have alternative areas available to move into)**

There are occasions when an event will have to be called off altogether, often for reasons outside the control of the organisers. Although very disappointing for both organising staff and the visitors, the same degree of professionalism that was in evidence for the planning of the event must be maintained to deal with this situation. Your team will need to make the decision to either cancel or postpone until a future date. Whatever is decided, it must be communicated as quickly as possible to your customers; for large events, an excellent way of doing this is by contacting the local radio station, which will gladly broadcast regular information so as to let as many people as possible know. There must be a method by which any advance payments can be returned in the event of cancellation, or tickets can be reused if the event is only postponed. Your team member(s) responsible for press and public relations will need to handle the situation sensitively and have their own contingency plans for dealing with any adverse publicity.

Some of the problems associated with events will apply equally if your project is a business venture, such as a cycle hire scheme for tourists or selling souvenirs to visitors. In these situations, you will also need contingency plans for such matters as equipment failures and handling customer complaints.

Activity 6.12

Include a section in your business plan that identifies possible problems with your project and explains the contingency plans you have in place to deal with them.

How the project will be reviewed and evaluated

You need to include in your business plan information on how you will review and evaluate your project. Your evaluation will be based on your project objectives and you need to discuss the various evaluation criteria and techniques that you will use. These could include a team de-brief, individual appraisal, peer appraisal, tutor feedback, customer feedback and feedback from suppliers. As part of your project timescales you will need to identify dates and times when you will review progress. This is likely to be achieved best by holding regular team meetings. The last section of this unit (see page 421) gives more details on the criteria and techniques used for project evaluation.

Write a project review and evaluation plan for inclusion in your business plan.

Teamwork

Key topics in this section:

- **Introduction – teamwork in travel and tourism**
- **The purpose of your team**
- **Team structure**
- **Roles and responsibilities of team members**
- **Team building and interaction**
- **Factors influencing how well the team works**

Introduction – teamwork in travel and tourism

The success, or otherwise, of your project will be linked closely to your ability to work effectively as a member of a team. Developing teamwork skills is important for anybody wanting to work in the travel and tourism industry, whether at home or abroad, and working on your project will help you to achieve this. All sectors of the travel and tourism industry, from hotels and tourist attractions to airlines and tour operators, rely on teams of people to get things done. There are countless examples of team situations in travel and tourism, including:

- ✪ **A team of three students carrying out a visitor survey for a local tourist attraction**
- ✪ **A conference organiser and her team of two who organise business conferences and meetings at a country house hotel**
- ✪ **The crew of a Britannia Airways jet flying from Manchester to Palma in Majorca with 190 holidaymakers on board**
- ✪ **A small independent tour operator with a team of four sales and reservations staff**
- ✪ **A team responsible for organising a charity event such as a fun-run**
- ✪ **The cast of a major West End musical such as Grease**
- ✪ **An English couple who own and run a wine bar in Benidorm**
- ✪ **A team of representatives working overseas for a tour operator (see Figure 6.9)**

It is a fact of life in travel and tourism that most tasks are carried out by teams rather than by individuals. Good products, services and facilities do not just

Figure 6.9 *Overseas representatives work as part of a team*
Courtesy of Unijet Travel Limited

happen, but are the result of concerted effort by groups of people seeking to achieve a common goal. By the same token, the skills of teamwork are not always built into an individual's character, but frequently have to be learned through training and experience. It is important to remember that teamwork is both a philosophy and a skill; it is one of the roles of the travel and tourism manager to create the organisational culture within which teamwork is encouraged and supported, and to allow staff to develop the skills needed to operate as effective team members.

The purpose of your team

The members of your team will have been chosen to achieve the aims and objectives of your project. It is hoped that by adopting a team approach to your task you will achieve your objectives more effectively than if you worked in isolation. Many of the tasks carried out in travel and tourism organisations can only be accomplished through the efforts of a team of people. Tasks such as staging a banquet for 150 guests or operating a major tourist attraction are too large and complex to be left to a single individual or workers who neither communicate with each other nor work as part of a team; in many cases, a team approach is the only solution.

Effective teamwork brings benefits both to the organisation that sets up the team and to the individual team members. Benefits to the organisation will vary depending on its size, structure and culture, but are likely to include:

- ✪ *Increased efficiency:* **An example of this could be that an effective team working in the information department of a national tourist office will be able to handle more enquiries from customers**
- ✪ *Increased sales:* **A teamwork approach to selling holiday insurance by telephone is likely to yield increased sales when compared with the same activity carried out individually**
- ✪ *Less staff conflict:* **A team that is trained to take responsibility for its own work and decision making is likely to be better at resolving its own internal problems, thus saving valuable management time**
- ✪ *Reduced absenteeism:* **Staff who see themselves as valued members of a team are likely to be more content and take less time off work**
- ✪ *Increased loyalty:* **Teamwork instils a sense of loyalty and commitment into members of staff**
- ✪ *A more creative workforce:* **Team members are more likely to come forward with ideas for improving work practices, reducing costs or increasing efficiency**
- ✪ *A happier workforce:* **Teamwork allows individuals to work to their full potential and feel good about themselves and their work**

Above all, management is keen to see that by establishing a team to carry out a task, they are getting more than just the 'the sum of the parts'. For example, three waiters who previously worked individually in a restaurant, and were able to service four tables each per shift, would be expected to service more than 3 x 4 tables per shift when working as a team.

Benefits to individual team members may include:

- ✪ **An enhanced sense of their worth within the organisation**
- ✪ **The ability to use their talents to the full**
- ✪ **Increased status within the organisation**
- ✪ **The chance to be innovative and creative**
- ✪ **Increased rewards for their work made possible as a result of greater efficiency, e.g. a productivity bonus or extra 'perks'**
- ✪ **The support of other team members**
- ✪ **More job satisfaction**

Thinking of your involvement in this project, list the purpose of your team as well as the benefits that you hope to gain and the skills you hope to develop from being a member of a team.

Team structure

An effective team would consist of a group of people who:

- ✪ **Are working towards a clearly defined goal or objective**
- ✪ **Are individuals committed to the task**
- ✪ **Are given the necessary authority to carry out the task**
- ✪ **Are allocated the necessary resources to do the job properly**
- ✪ **Operate in an 'open' fashion, sharing ideas and concerns**

A team may develop formally or informally. An example of a formal team is given in Figure 6.10, where the team leader reports to an organising committee and leads a team of individuals who take on the responsibility for a range of activities.

As well as having a team leader, formal teams also:

- ✪ **Are established to carry out specific tasks and to help achieve project objectives**
- ✪ **Assign specific roles to each team member**
- ✪ **Have clearly identified channels of communication**

Figure 6.10   *A typical formal team structure*

✪ Have clear lines of authority and responsibility

Informal teams also exist in travel and tourism organisations. They tend to develop organically rather than through an organisational structure. They may form for social or work-related reasons. In the work situation, colleagues often find it easier to make decisions through talking informally rather than in a formal setting, such as at a meeting or group presentation. The importance of informal teams should not be underestimated, but there should be mechanisms in place to channel the outcome of informal gatherings into the more formal team setting.

Activity 6.14

Draw up your team structure, which may be either formal or informal, and include this in your business plan.

Roles and responsibilities of team members

We saw earlier in this unit when we investigated staffing that the tasks associated with your project need to be divided equally among team members, so as not to overburden individuals. It is usual in project management to appoint a team leader, who oversees the smooth running of the project, and a team of individuals who take on the responsibility for a task or series of tasks, on the basis of their skills, preferences and enthusiasm. You should also appoint a deputy team leader to take on the role of team leader in his or her absence. For this project, team members will need to complete a number of tasks concerning:

- ✪ **Marketing**
- ✪ **Finance**
- ✪ **Personnel/human resources**
- ✪ **Health, safety and security**
- ✪ **Physical resources**
- ✪ **Administration**
- ✪ **Legal aspects**
- ✪ **Project review and evaluation**

Figure 6.11 shows an example of areas of responsibility and tasks for a farm open day.

Unit area 1:	Site preparation and management
Tasks:	1 Public and vehicle access
	2 Car parking
	3 Signposting
	4 Interpretive materials
	5 Equipment
	6 Admission

Unit area 2:	Event promotion
Tasks:	1 Production of promotional literature
	2 Advertising
	3 Media liaison
	4 VIP guests
	5 Ticket sales

Unit area 3:	Staffing
Tasks:	1 Recruitment
	2 Training
	3 Payment
	4 Facilities for staff

Unit area 4:	Finance and legal
Tasks:	1 Budgetary control
	2 Fund-raising and sponsorhip
	3 Banking
	4 Production of accounts
	5 Legal permissions
	6 Health, safety and security

Unit area 5:	Support services
Tasks:	1 Catering
	2 First aid
	3 Toilets
	4 Lighting and public address (PA) system
	5 Staff communication system
	6 Cloakroom
	7 Facilities for disabled visitors
	8 Entertainment

Figure 6.11   *Areas of responsibility and tasks for a typical farm open day*

All team members should take a responsible attitude towards completing the tasks they have been allocated. Teamwork is all about pulling together, in good times and bad. Figure 6.12 has some golden rules of working together. Make sure you apply them!

The team leader

It is likely that you will appoint a team leader for your project. In project management the team leader must be not just a figurehead but an effective manager as well. Good team leaders do not wallow in the glory and prestige of their position, but get involved with guiding their team to eventual success in its task. Once the decision has been taken to form a team to carry out a

- Give and accept constructive criticism
- Don't bear grudges
- Be punctual
- Complete the tasks you have been allocated
- Listen to what other team members have to say
- Be honest with each other
- Tackle problems as they arise
- Be accurate and precise in your work
- Tolerate each other's weaknesses
- Support each other
- Focus on the task and not the person
- Leave your emotions at home
- Enjoy working with each other and have fun!

Figure 6.12   *Golden rules of teamwork*

specific task or tasks, the choice of leader must be the first consideration. He or she must be involved in all stages of team development (see Figure 6.13).

In the real world of travel and tourism, a team leader may not have the luxury of selecting a complete team from scratch. He or she will often be in the position of taking over an existing team of people who may have been together for a long period of time. Whenever feasible, however, the leader must be involved at the team building stage in selecting team members for a new team or one that is being reorganised. An organisation that arbitrarily selects team members over the head of the team leader is immediately undermining the leader's position.

The leader will act as a facilitator during the team management stage when the real work of the team is underway. The leader should not try to dominate proceedings but rather create the right atmosphere to give team members the best chance of success.

The leader will need to constantly monitor how the team is functioning and will need to reflect on how well it performed at the end of the project. Evaluation is all about measuring team effectiveness, i.e. how well did the team perform? If clear objectives have been set for the team, it will be easier to answer this question.

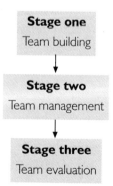

Figure 6.13   *The key stages in team development*

The perfect team leader

Finding the 'perfect' team leader, and being able to give him or her all the 'tools' needed to carry out an effective job, is not an easy task. When looking for a team leader, however, it is important to appoint the best person for the job within the resource constraints, whether it is somebody already working for the organisation or a candidate from outside. When looking for the 'perfect' team leader, an organisation needs to find an individual who will:

1 **Accept the challenge and responsibility of leading the team from day one**

2 **Be enthusiastic about the task and spread this enthusiasm to all members of the team**

3 **Communicate effectively with other team members and those outside the team who need to be kept abreast of developments**

4 **Plan and co-ordinate, with all team members, the strategy that the team will adopt, while keeping the objectives of the team constantly in mind**

5 **Develop skills and qualities in other team members so that they may achieve their full potential**

6 **Promote an 'open' style of management by discussing all matters of concern to the group and by listening to the views and concerns of all team members**

7 **Adopt an action-orientated approach to making things happen, by firstly identifying what needs to be done in a certain situation, then confirming the action that needs to be carried out, who is responsible for carrying it out and a date or time by which it must be completed**

8 **Constantly promote a positive approach to solving problems and pushing the work of the team forward in a positive manner**

9 **Manage the evaluation process to identify any ways in which the team could have worked more effectively or how particular problems could have been resolved**

10 **Acknowledge the achievements of team members and publicise successes both internally and externally**

11 **Not be afraid of admitting mistakes, but will build on them and actively work towards quality in all aspects of team operation**

12 **Involve all team members in the decision-making process**

Activity 6.15

Appoint your project team leader (and deputy) using the 12 points above to guide your selection. If more than one team member wants to take on the role of team leader, you will need to carry out a selection procedure.

Team building and interaction

Today's most effective and efficient travel and tourism organisations, in the private, public and voluntary sectors, have recognised that time, money and effort spent on team building pays dividends. Using techniques and practices developed in the USA, Europe and the Far East, many UK travel and tourism organisations have changed their structures, increased their staff training and developed a culture that is based on decision making by teams of people rather than individuals. These organisations have become more successful in achieving their objectives and individual employees have benefited from a more 'open' management style and a more cohesive approach to work.

There are six main stages in building an effective team:

1 **Team rationale and objectives – these will be closely allied to your project aims and objectives**

2 **Selection of staff – you will have in place a team leader and team members who have agreed to take on certain responsibilities**

3 **Resource provision – your project team will need access to the necessary 'tools' to do the job properly, e.g. computers, equipment, materials, premises, etc.**

4 **Developing a team approach – the team leader will be responsible for driving the work of the team, instilling motivation, enthusiasm and commitment in all team members**

5 **Encouraging team development – see the example of Tuckman's stages of team development below**

6 **Evaluating team performance – as well as evaluating the performance of the team as a whole, all team members should be encouraged to constantly monitor their individual activities during the project**

Encouraging team development

B W Tuckman wrote an article in the mid-1960s which looked at the different stages of team development and the relationships that develop between team members. Tuckman's work, which is still often quoted today by researchers and academics who specialise in team building, identified four stages of team development: forming, storming, norming and performing.

Forming

This describes the initial stages in the formation of the group, when the objectives and team roles are being clarified. Team members are likely to feel anxious at this stage and will be trying to establish their credentials and create an impression on both the team leader and the other members of the team. The leader too may feel unclear about the capabilities of team members and be unsure about his or her own performance.

Storming

Once individual team members get to know each other, they will be more willing to enter into debate and challenge colleagues on issues that they are concerned about. This should be encouraged by the team leader, since, if handled constructively, it will often lead to the team as a whole clarifying its rationale and the way in which it operates. Having a clear purpose will also help to mould the team into an effective force.

Norming

Norming is all about setting the guidelines, standards and levels of acceptable behaviour under which the team will function. The storming stage should have united the team members and identified where each person stands on the sorts of issues to be dealt with at the norming stage. In other words, the norming stage sets the ground rules for all team members. At this stage, the team leader may feel the need to intervene when decisions made by the team could be seen as controversial or contrary to the project's objectives.

Performing

Having progressed through the first three development stages, the team will now be in a position to perform the role or roles for which it was established, with a cohesive team framework allowing all team members to contribute to the achievement of the project's objectives.

Factors influencing how well the team works

Selecting individuals to be part of a team is not an easy task. Travel and tourism managers who think that building a team involves nothing more than selecting the brightest staff and locking them away in a room are in for a nasty shock! It is essential to be aware of group dynamics, i.e. how individuals relate to and interact with each other, when choosing staff for a team. A lack of awareness of **group interaction** is one of the main factors that influences how well a team works.

Another reason why teams fail is that they are not given, or do not develop, **clear aims and objectives** from the outset. If members of a team are unclear as to what it is they are supposed to be achieving, then their performance will suffer and their work will lack direction and purpose.

Vested interests can sometimes lead to the downfall of a team. For example, a group of local council tourism development officers who have come together to mount a major county-wide tourism promotion event may be hampered in their efforts by one of their number who insists that his district must always have the last word when any decisions are made. Individuals who put their own vested interests before the good of the team as a whole are of little use to a team that is trying to be as effective as possible.

The remainder of this section considers some other common factors that affect team performance, starting with communication.

Communication

Of all the reasons why teams fail to fulfil their objectives, poor communication is probably the most common. A team that is unable to develop an 'open' culture, with effective communication channels both within the team and outside, will not achieve its full potential. The team leader will have a crucial role to play in ensuring that effective communication takes place, and, just as importantly, takes place in a way that encourages team members to perform to their maximum; handled badly, communication can be a distinct disincentive to good team performance.

Communication within a team means more than just the occasions when the team members are talking to each other in a meeting. This verbal communication is obviously very important, but is only a small part of the total communication process. Communication by team members can also be in written form, for example minutes of meetings, fax/telex messages, e-mail or a report on a particular subject. Often as important as written and verbal communication is the way in which information is sent, received and understood by others, commonly known as non-verbal communication (NVC). The most talked-about type of NVC is body language, the process by which we send and receive messages without using words. A team leader who is making an important point during a meeting may well bang the table or wave his or her arms about to stress the importance of what is being said. Body language is sometimes classified as:

✪ *Bodily contact* – **shaking hands, for example**
✪ *Physical proximity* – **the distance we feel we need to keep**

between ourselves and other people, for example as a spectator at a football match

- ✪ *Orientation* – where we place ourselves in relation to others; by tradition, a leader running a team meeting will sit at the head of the table
- ✪ *Posture* – whether standing, sitting, lying down, walking or running, there is often something about our body posture which relays a message to those around us, either consciously or unconsciously
- ✪ *Gestures* – we all make gestures from time to time to signal approval or disapproval, for example a 'thumbs up' to show you agree with what is being suggested
- ✪ *Facial expression* – the face can transmit an enormous range of messages and emotions, either consciously or subconsciously; like much non-verbal communication, facial expressions can sometimes be misinterpreted
- ✪ *Eye contact* – whether we are aware of it or not, we pay a great deal of attention to a person's eyes when they are communicating with us

The team leader must lead by example by developing clear lines of communication between all team members.

Leadership

We have already discussed the pivotal role that the team leader plays in managing the work of a project team. He or she should not try to dominate proceedings within the group but rather act as a 'catalyst' who creates the right environment and conditions in which the team can operate effectively. While the leader of the team may have a very 'open' management style, he or she may be constrained by the decisions of senior management, who may appear distant and bureaucratic. For a team to be completely effective, the senior management of the organisation must also adopt an 'open' style of management and give the leader and team members the freedom to take risks in seeking to achieve their objectives. A good example of this enlightened style of management is Richard Branson, Chairman of the Virgin Group, an organisation that is willing to take risks to achieve its objectives, and, in so doing, is committed to an 'open' style of management with team decision making in evidence throughout the organisation, from Virgin Atlantic Airways and Virgin Megastores to Virgin Trains and Virgin Cinemas.

Group motivation

The more successful the team, the more motivated its members are likely to be, and vice versa. The project team leader should aim to maintain this cycle of motivation and success, which will lead to effective team performance, by praising individuals and the team as a whole when successes have been achieved. There may be times when the team deserves more than just praise from the team leader or senior management, but has earned a reward for its efforts. Rewards can act as positive motivators if handled carefully and in such a way that does not build resentment between those in the organisation but outside the team, who do not receive the reward. Typical rewards for teams working in travel and tourism include bonus payments, social events, free holidays or short breaks. While you may not be able to match these 'perks' during your project, praise and rewards of a verbal nature are to be encouraged.

Personality clashes

The mix of personal characteristics in members of a team is a major determinant of its success. Simply bringing together the individuals with the greatest technical expertise, best qualifications or most experience does not guarantee success in a team. These qualities are obviously important, but just as important is the way in which the team members interact. All human beings have a unique personality and will react in different ways when in a team situation. Some will be quiet and reflective while others will be loud and try to dominate the group. It is the team leader's role to give all team members the opportunity to state their views, while building on the positive characteristics of individuals. The leader must anticipate potential conflict and have measures ready to resolve any problems caused by differing personalities.

Conflict in teams

All organisations in travel and tourism will, from time to time, have to deal with conflict in their staff. Teams, which by their very nature are made up of people working closely together, are perhaps more prone to conflict situations, particularly if the same team members are together over an extended period of time or are sharing the same workspace. A degree of healthy debate and criticism within a team is not of itself necessarily a bad thing; it is only through open discussion of issues that good decision making and problem solving can take place. Conflict, however, is a stage removed from healthy debate and discussion, and, if not managed well, can have serious implications for the organisation in which the team is working. Conflict in teams can lead to:

- ✪ **Poor levels of customer service**
- ✪ **Reduced profitability**
- ✪ **Increased staff absenteeism**
- ✪ **Reduced staff morale and commitment**
- ✪ **Increased disciplinary problems**

- ✪ **More management time being devoted to dealing with the problem**
- ✪ **High staff turnover**

There are two types of conflict situations that may arise in travel and tourism organisations: that which develops within the team (intra-team) and that which may exist between teams (inter-team). Intra-team conflict usually arises from a clash of personalities between one or more members of the team. An individual's personality is often very complex, but there are some clashes which appear frequently in team situations; for example, there may be a member of the team who is:

- ✪ *Aggressive* – **often contributing unnecessarily hostile comments**
- ✪ *Cynical* – **seeing no point in going on**
- ✪ *Critical* – **unable to think positively about the team and its work**
- ✪ **A** *perfectionist* – **constantly revising decisions and ideas**
- ✪ **A** *liar* – **out to dismantle the team at all costs**
- ✪ **A** *gossip* – **constantly spreading rumours**
- ✪ **A** *time waster* – **continually interrupting with insignificant remarks**

Conflict may develop between the team leader and a member or members of the team. In this situation, senior management may well need to intervene to sort things out. When we consider inter-team conflict, that is conflict existing between one or more groups in the same organisation, there is often more to the problem than personality clashes alone. Inter-team conflict can result in one group becoming hostile to another, and can lead to a breakdown in communication or a mistrust of one group by another. If we take as an example a large theme park such as EuroDisney, with many different teams controlling the rides, the car parking, catering, maintenance, litter and a host of other duties, a little rivalry between teams is to be encouraged in order to increase job satisfaction and team performance. However, conflict could arise when one team is regarded by some of the others as being of a lower status; the staff responsible for litter collection, for example, may be considered of less value than those operating the rides. This could be overcome by rotating jobs on a regular basis, so that the rides operator in week one takes on the role of the litter collector in week two, and so on. Management must also continually stress that every member of staff is crucial to the success of the team.

Inter-team conflict can also arise when one team considers that it is not getting the same treatment as another team. Management must strive to treat all teams on an equal basis and, if there are reasons why one team is better rewarded than another, then an explanation is given.

Activity 6.16

In your project team, try to anticipate any potential conflicts that may arise and decide how you will handle these situations.

Access to resources

Access to the necessary resources will be vital to the team if it is to stand any chance of meeting its project objectives. Depending on the nature of your project, your team may need to have access to:

- **Technical equipment, e.g. computers, audio-visual aids, catering equipment, etc.**
- **Communications equipment, e.g. fax machine, telephone, etc.**
- **Premises and/or land**
- **Finance**
- **The use of vehicles for transporting people and equipment**
- **Materials**
- **A base room**

Given the right level of equipment, the team will feel comfortable about having sufficient resources to do the job it has been set.

There may be times when the team will need the support of other people in order to function effectively. These people may be from inside your centre, so it is important that key people are aware of your project and what it involves. The team may sometimes feel that it would be helpful to ask somebody from outside the centre to join the team, perhaps for a short period of time or for a particular task that cannot be carried out by the current team members. This could be somebody from a local travel and tourism organisation or voluntary group.

The working environment

A team often functions best if its members all work in the same location or at least in close proximity to each other. Team members who share the same office, for example, are likely to form into a cohesive group. Where it is not possible for all the members of a team to be housed together, perhaps because the group is simply too large, there must be effective means of communication so that ideas and decisions can be swiftly conveyed to all staff. The nature of many travel and tourism organisations will mean that the work environment for the team will be the facility itself, e.g. a leisure centre, hotel, museum, aircraft or outdoor activity centre. Working in close proximity to colleagues in these situations with few physical barriers can mean that teams perform particularly well and that a tremendous team spirit is built up. The team leader needs to be aware, however, of the potential pressures and conflicts that can arise in such circumstances and be prepared to take whatever action is necessary to manage the situation.

Case Study
Project teamwork in action – The British Travel Trade Fair

The British Travel Trade Fair (BTTF) is an annual exhibition that gives suppliers of British tourism 'products' the chance to introduce themselves and their organisations to potential buyers, who may be coach operators, conference organisers, tour operators, excursion organisers, the travel press, overseas buyers or travel agents. The buyers need up-to-date information on new products on offer from British suppliers and the BTTF is a cost-effective way of doing business 'under one roof'. The exhibition is held at the National Exhibition Centre (NEC) in Birmingham, chosen for its central location and excellent road, rail and air links. BTTF attracts more than 300 exhibitors, which include:

★ Hotels and other accommodation providers – e.g. Best Western Hotels, YHA, Consort Hotels, Forte Hotels

★ Visitor attractions – e.g. Alton Towers, English Heritage, London Zoo, Wembley Stadium Tours, the World of Robin Hood

★ Destinations – e.g. City of Bath, Black Country, Cheshire, Llangollen, City of Gloucester, Portsmouth Tourism, York Visitor and Conference Bureau

★ Tourist boards – e.g. London Tourist Board, West Country Tourist Board, Wales Tourist Board, British Tourist Authority

continued

continued

★ Operators and transport providers – e.g. Channel Island Ferries, Butlin's Holiday Worlds, Jersey European, Rainbow Holidays, Le Shuttle (Eurotunnel)

★ Suppliers, services and publications – e.g. Bus and Coach Council, Travel GBI newspaper, Conference Blue & Green Books, 'In Britain' Magazine

The organisation of the BTTF is very much a team affair. It is organised by Group Travel Trade and Events, a subgroup of the English Tourism Council (ETC) Marketing Department, in co-operation with the Scottish (STB), Wales (WTB) and Northern Ireland (NITB) Tourist Boards. The BTTF organising team is made up of:

★ Exhibition Manager
★ Exhibition Operations Manager
★ Exhibition Executive
★ Events Co-ordinator
★ Press Office Manager
★ ETC Marketing Department Staff
★ STB Marketing Department Representative
★ WTB Marketing Department Representative
★ NITB Marketing Department Representative

This team is given the overall responsibility for planning, staging and evaluating the event. For the duration of the BTTF, which generally runs over two days, the organising team is joined by extra ETC marketing staff to cope with day-to-day management.

As well as attending training and briefing sessions about the event, all team members are issued with BTTF briefing notes, compiled by the organising group to give details of the roles and functions of the team members. The briefing notes cover:

★ Names of the organising team
★ Categories of exhibitors (distinguished by

continued

continued

colour-coded badges)

★ Types of buyers (again given different colour badges)

★ The location

★ Registration information

★ Organisers' office

★ Press office

★ 'Privilege' club (for VIP guests and buyers)

★ Students' room

★ The official BTTF guidebook

★ Storage facilities

★ Catering facilities

★ Canvassing (only exhibitors are allowed to distribute printed material)

★ Telephones/radios (for the team to keep in touch)

★ Accommodation for the team

★ Dress (which staff wear which 'uniform')

TEAM OPERATION

A typical rota for day one of the BTTF is given in Figure 6.14, together with an explanation of the codes used in the rota.

The chart in Figure 6.14 clearly identifies the role that each team member should take up at the relevant time. We can see how the rota works by looking at one of the team members, John, in more detail. Between 0830 and 1130 John is covering role 'H', which according to the code explanation means that he is generally helping wherever needed; a roving troubleshooter! Between 1130 and 1330 John is assigned role 'O', working in the organisers' office. For the rest of the day, between 1330 and 2030, he goes back to role 'H', helping wherever needed. A glance at the rest of the team members along the top of the rota will show their respective roles and duties.

continued

continued

<table>
<thead>
<tr><th></th><th colspan="10">Tuesday</th></tr>
<tr><th></th><th>John</th><th>Kirsty</th><th>Emma</th><th>Dave</th><th>Josie</th><th>Diana</th><th>Helen</th><th>Dolores</th><th>Kerstin</th><th>Jo</th></tr>
</thead>
<tbody>
<tr><td>0830</td><td>H</td><td>F</td><td>F</td><td>F</td><td>*</td><td>*</td><td>*</td><td>*</td><td>F</td><td>F</td></tr>
<tr><td>0900</td><td>H</td><td>F</td><td>F</td><td>F</td><td>*</td><td>*</td><td>*</td><td>*</td><td>F</td><td>F</td></tr>
<tr><td>0930</td><td>H</td><td>F</td><td>F</td><td>F</td><td>*</td><td>*</td><td>*</td><td>*</td><td>F</td><td>F</td></tr>
<tr><td>1000</td><td>H</td><td>H</td><td>H</td><td>H</td><td>*</td><td>*</td><td>*</td><td>*</td><td>H</td><td>H</td></tr>
<tr><td>1030</td><td>H</td><td>H</td><td>H</td><td>H</td><td>*</td><td>*</td><td>*</td><td>*</td><td>H</td><td>H</td></tr>
<tr><td>1100</td><td>H</td><td>H</td><td>H</td><td>H</td><td>*</td><td>*</td><td>*</td><td>*</td><td>H</td><td>H</td></tr>
<tr><td>1130</td><td>O</td><td>O</td><td>H</td><td>O</td><td>*</td><td>*</td><td>*</td><td>*</td><td>H</td><td>H</td></tr>
<tr><td>1200</td><td>O</td><td>O</td><td>H</td><td>O</td><td>F</td><td>F</td><td>F</td><td>F</td><td>H</td><td>H</td></tr>
<tr><td>1230</td><td>O</td><td>O</td><td>H</td><td>O</td><td>F</td><td>F</td><td>F</td><td>F</td><td>H</td><td>H</td></tr>
<tr><td>1300</td><td>O</td><td>O</td><td>H</td><td>O</td><td>F</td><td>F</td><td>F</td><td>F</td><td>H</td><td>H</td></tr>
<tr><td>1330</td><td>H</td><td>O</td><td>H</td><td>H</td><td>H</td><td>H</td><td>H</td><td>H</td><td>H</td><td>H</td></tr>
<tr><td>1400</td><td>H</td><td>O</td><td>H</td><td>H</td><td>H</td><td>H</td><td>H</td><td>H</td><td>H</td><td>H</td></tr>
<tr><td>1430</td><td>H</td><td>C</td><td>H</td><td>H</td><td>C</td><td>H</td><td>H</td><td>H</td><td>H</td><td>H</td></tr>
<tr><td>1500</td><td>H</td><td>C</td><td>H</td><td>H</td><td>C</td><td>H</td><td>H</td><td>H</td><td>H</td><td>H</td></tr>
<tr><td>1530</td><td>H</td><td>C</td><td>H</td><td>H</td><td>C</td><td>H</td><td>H</td><td>H</td><td>H</td><td>H</td></tr>
<tr><td>1600</td><td>H</td><td>C</td><td>H</td><td>H</td><td>C</td><td>H</td><td>H</td><td>H</td><td>H</td><td>H</td></tr>
<tr><td>1630</td><td>H</td><td>C</td><td>H</td><td>H</td><td>C</td><td>H</td><td>H</td><td>H</td><td>H</td><td>H</td></tr>
<tr><td>1700</td><td>H</td><td>C</td><td>H</td><td>H</td><td>C</td><td>H</td><td>H</td><td>H</td><td>H</td><td>H</td></tr>
<tr><td>1730</td><td>H</td><td>H</td><td>H</td><td>H</td><td>H</td><td>H</td><td>H</td><td>H</td><td>H</td><td>H</td></tr>
<tr><td>1800</td><td>H</td><td>H</td><td>H</td><td>H</td><td>H</td><td>H</td><td>H</td><td>H</td><td>H</td><td>H</td></tr>
<tr><td>1830</td><td>H</td><td>H</td><td>H</td><td>H</td><td>H</td><td>H</td><td>H</td><td>H</td><td>H</td><td>H</td></tr>
<tr><td>1900</td><td>H</td><td>H</td><td>H</td><td>H</td><td>H</td><td>H</td><td>H</td><td>H</td><td>H</td><td>H</td></tr>
<tr><td>1930</td><td>H</td><td>H</td><td>H</td><td>H</td><td>H</td><td>H</td><td>H</td><td>H</td><td>H</td><td>H</td></tr>
<tr><td>2000</td><td>H</td><td>H</td><td>H</td><td>H</td><td>H</td><td>H</td><td>H</td><td>H</td><td>H</td><td>H</td></tr>
</tbody>
</table>

Stand rota code explanation

C Conferences... and Forums and Seminars and Meetings
- Generally looking after people;
- Before: showing them where coffee is, directing them into Seminar Suites;
- During: operating roving mikes;
- After: directing them to hall 6 (or to Coach and Bus Week Reception).

E Exhibitor Registration Desk
- Inserting Exhibitor badges into red badge holders; answering questions.

F Familiarisation
- Familiarising yourself with the British Travel Trade Fair!

H Helping wherever needed
- Setting up (stands; Press Office; Privilege Club; Students' Room);
- Doing stand drops;
- Being welcoming at the Welcome Reception;
- Being sociable at the Coach and Bus Week Reception/CTC Ball;
- Helping on Registration, including Exhibitor and Information desks; acting as a runner;
- Stage managing (John); poster mounting signing and prop moving including signs upstairs and downstairs (John and Dave);
- Looking round the show; talking to exhibitors and buyers.

I Information Desk
- Giving directions; answering questions; solving problems.

O Organisers' Office
- All the time: answering telephone/fax messages; dealing with problems; ordering food and drink; keeping office tidy;
- During Build Up: registering buyers; inserting Exhibitor badges into Red badge holders; exchanging guides for vouchers; allocating welcome reception welcome drink vouchers;
- During Business Hours: giving callers for exhibitors the Heart of England stand Tel. 021–780 2266; sorting/counting registration cards.

P Privilege Club
- Being the VIP public face of BTTF (and ETB); keeping room tidy.

R Registration Area
- Directing visitors to the right registration points, i.e.
  - Exhibitors
  - Buyers With Badges
  - Buyers Without Badges
  - Overseas Buyers
  - Press Office
  - Students' Room
- Assisting CES Team in selecting correct-colour badge holder; handing out carrier bags; keeping area tidy and people flowing through.

* Staff rest period

Figure 6.14 _Team rota for day one of the British Travel Trade Fair_

After the event, the organising team holds a debriefing session where good and bad experiences are shared, with a view to making the subsequent events even better.

(Information courtesy of ETB/ETC)

Case study discussion questions

1   What is the overall aim of the
    British Travel Trade Fair?

2   Why is it important to have a
    duty rota for an event such as
    this?

3   Who is responsible for
    organising the event?

4   What are the specific duties that
    are carried out by staff working
    in the organisers' office?

Carrying out the project

Key topics in this section:

● **Introduction**

● **Running a major project – the London Marathon**

Introduction

Having investigated the feasibility of your project by completing your business plan and having assembled your team, you are now in a position to carry out your project. This is where you put travel and tourism into action! You will be expected to take on your agreed role(s) positively and to work with the whole team in a constructive fashion. In particular, you will need to be aware of:

✪ **Completing the task(s) you have been allocated**

✪ **Dealing politely with customers, other members of your team, your tutors and any other people involved with the project**

✪ **Supporting other team members while the project is being carried out**

✪ **Reacting quickly and confidently to any problems that may arise**

✪ **Keeping to any agreed time deadlines**

✪ **Knowing when to get help and advice from others**

Whether your project is an event or a business enterprise, you would be well advised to hold a team briefing meeting the day before, or on the morning of, the start of the project. At this meeting, the team leader will cover a number of items, including:

✪ **Final timings, roles and responsibilities**

✪ **Contingency plans**

✪ **The importance of looking after customers well**

Activity 6.17

Remember to keep a logbook throughout the project, detailing your involvement in the completion of key tasks. This will be needed for your assessment and for when you carry out your project evaluation.

The following case study looks in depth at an annual event that involves a large number of team members, each with a clearly defined role.

Case Study
Running a major project – the London Marathon

The first London Marathon was held in 1981 and was the brainchild of former British athlete Chris Brasher, now the Chairman of the London Marathon Company which organises the annual event. The idea came out of seeing other city marathons operating around the world, most notably the New York Marathon. London has hosted a marathon every year since 1981 and staged its twentieth event on 16 April 2000. In 1981, some 20,000 people applied to run, 7,747 were accepted and 6,255 finished. In 1999 there were a record 30,809 finishers in the London Marathon, made up of club runners, individuals and a field of 'elite' competitors.

▶ **AIMS OF THE EVENT**

Chris Brasher devised the following six aims for the London Marathon:

1   *To improve the overall standard and status of British marathon running by providing a fast course and strong international competition*

2   *To show to mankind that, on occasions, the Family of Man can be united*

3   *To raise money for the provision of recreational facilities in London*

4   *To help London tourism*

5   *To prove that when it comes to organising major events, 'Britain is best'*

6   *To have fun and provide some happiness and sense of achievement in a troubled world*

It is estimated that over £80 million has been raised for a variety of charities since the first London Marathon. The amount raised by runners has grown significantly each year

continued

continued

and positions the race as one of Britain's most successful annual charity fundraising events. Projects that help those with special needs are particularly supported; for example, one of the recent projects involved installing a hoist for disabled people in a swimming bath. The London Marathon also aims to help British marathon running and to give competitors the opportunity to enjoy themselves. Because the London Marathon is organised by a limited company, it has short-term aims that are similar to any other commercial sector leisure or tourism organisation, namely to ensure that the company continues to exist and continues to generate a working surplus.

▶ FUNDING

The London Marathon Company has an annual turnover of approximately £2 million. Sponsorship is vital to the existence of the company and, therefore, the event. Without sponsorship, there would be no London Marathon. Total funds from sponsors amount to around £1 million. The event has attracted a number of major sponsors since it began back in 1981; the first was Gillette, followed by Mars, then ADT, next NutraSweet and finally Flora. In addition to the main sponsor, there are many 'suppliers' who contribute to the funding of the event in return for publicity. In recent years, these have included the sports clothing and footwear company ASICS, Citizen Timing and a host of other companies supplying everything from drinks to cars. The London Marathon Company aims to maximise revenue from sponsors and suppliers in order to make the surplus available for distribution to charities and worthy causes as large as possible.

▶ MANAGEMENT STRUCTURE

Ultimate responsibility for the organisation of the London Marathon lies with the General Manager, who is supported by a number of full- and part-time staff, including:

★ A Marketing Consultant

continued

continued

- ★ A Press Officer
- ★ An Administrator
- ★ An Entry Co-ordinator
- ★ A Course Director
- ★ An Accountant
- ★ The Start Co-ordinator
- ★ The Finish Director

There are three committees overseeing different elements of the organisation:

- ★ The Organising Committee which meets once a month for most of the year
- ★ The Executive Committee
- ★ The General Purposes Committee which meets three times a year and includes representatives of the police, fire authority, local boroughs, etc.

On the day of the Marathon itself, nearly 5,000 voluntary helpers recruited from clubs and societies help with all the tasks needed to ensure the success of the event. Team leaders are identified and are asked to attend a two-day briefing session where their roles are clarified. Because of the scale of the event and the logistics involved in making it happen, the organisers use volunteers who have worked with the Marathon before, in order to give continuity and help develop the essential teamwork skills as quickly as possible. There is no dress rehearsal of the event; it has to be right first time!

THE PLANNING CYCLE

The first stage in the planning cycle is fixing the date for the Marathon, which is finalised some 18–20 months in advance. In deciding on a date, the organisers have to consult widely so as not to clash with other events of equal significance. This involves consultation with:

continued

continued

Figure 6.15 *The view from Tower Bridge of the London Marathon*
Courtesy of London Marathon Company

★ The Royal Diary (since 1994 the finish of the London Marathon has been in the Mall, close to Buckingham Palace)

★ Television companies

★ The athletics calendar

★ The British sporting calendar

★ The police and security forces

Once the date has been fixed, detailed planning for the event can begin in earnest.

▶ COMMUNITY LIAISON

The organisers of the Marathon keep local communities up to date with the planning and staging of the event. A representative of the London Marathon sits on committees of all London Boroughs through which the route passes. Every house and car on the route is given a leaflet twice before the day of the event to let people know that it is

continued

continued

taking place. Local newspapers and radio are kept informed of road closures and other relevant information about the Marathon. Local people are encouraged to join in with the spirit of the event, perhaps by organising a street party or other celebration.

► HEALTH AND SAFETY

There are 30 St John Ambulance stations on the course with trained first aiders and support staff. The emergency services are on hand in case of serious illness or injury. All competitors are sent a detailed training schedule four to five months before the event itself in order to be as fit as possible on the day. Those who fall ill just before the Marathon are encouraged to defer their entry until the following year.

► MARKETING

Much of the marketing effort surrounding the Marathon is concerned with attracting potential sponsors and suppliers. In order to attract sponsorship, organisations are offered advertising space in official programmes and magazines, on vehicles and along the route. There are also VIP hospitality facilities on race day which the sponsors can use. Television coverage is a major incentive when it comes to attracting sponsors; the event is shown live in the UK and Japan, and is distributed to another 50 countries worldwide. In addition to the work on sponsorship, the organisers have to spend time and money to attract the 'ordinary' members of the public who do not read running magazines and are not members of a running or athletics club. As this group accounts for 50 per cent of all applications to run, the task is by no means an easy one. Local and regional newspapers and local radio stations are used to alert the general public when applications for the Marathon are being accepted.

(Information courtesy of the General Manager of the London Marathon)

Case study discussion questions

1 Why do you think the London Marathon has been such a successful event?

2 What marketing activities do the event staff carry out?

3 How do you think the organisers could measure the success of the event?

4 Why is sponsorship so important to the London Marathon?

Evaluating the project

Key topics in this section:

- **Introduction**
- **Evaluation criteria**
- **The project evaluation process**
- **Team evaluation**

Introduction

It is true to say that we all learn from our mistakes and experiences; there is invariably something that we would have done in a different way if we had the chance again. Once your project is finished, it is important to evaluate what happened to decide whether the objectives set by your team at the outset have been achieved. You should regard the evaluation process as an essential way of improving both individual and team performance. When evaluating your project, all team members should try to answer the following questions:

- ✪ **Did the project meet its aim and objectives?**
- ✪ **Did individual team members meet their particular objectives?**
- ✪ **Were key deadlines met?**
- ✪ **Did the team's planning promote effective performance?**
- ✪ **Was the project effective/successful?**
- ✪ **What went well and what went badly for individual team members?**
- ✪ **How well did the team work as a whole?**
- ✪ **How did working as part of a team help or hinder you?**
- ✪ **Were your customers satisfied?**
- ✪ **What changes would you make if the project was carried out again?**

The team leader should hold a debriefing meeting as soon as possible after the project has been completed, at which the above points should be addressed while still fresh in the mind. The outcome of this meeting should be an evaluation report, with contributions from all team members.

Although it may be outside the scope of your particular project, travel and tourism organisations often need to measure the impact that their projects have outside their immediate environment. This could be in relation to economic, environmental and social/cultural factors. A large annual event, for example, will certainly have an impact on the economy of the local area by creating jobs and attracting visitors who will spend money on local goods and services. At the same time, it may have an adverse effect on the local environment and its operations will need to be constantly monitored and evaluated. If not planned carefully, the event may, for example, generate traffic congestion and noise in its vicinity, thereby causing problems for local people.

Evaluation criteria

In order to decide whether or not your project was a success, it must be judged against the original objectives that the team agreed. Assuming that these objectives were SMART, i.e. specific, measurable, achievable, realistic and timed, this process should not cause much of a problem. For example, you may have set yourself the objective of selling £100 worth of souvenirs to tourists. Your financial records will soon tell you if this objective was achieved.

The precise criteria you choose will depend on the nature of your project, but are likely to include:

- ✪ **Financial performance: Did the project meet its income and expenditure targets?**
- ✪ **Operational performance: Did the project run smoothly, with minimal problems?**
- ✪ **Customer satisfaction: Were the visitors to the event satisfied with their experience?**
- ✪ **Compliance with health and safety and other legal requirements: Were measures adequate to cover any eventualities?**
- ✪ **Environmental impact: Was damage to the immediate environment kept to a minimum?**
- ✪ **Economic, social and cultural impacts: Did the project meet its social, cultural and economic aims?**

The project evaluation process

Depending on the type of project you completed, information that may be helpful during the evaluation process can come from a number of different sources, including:

- ✪ **Records:** Any information or data about the project which has been recorded will help in the evaluation. Items such as financial accounts, attendance figures, ticket sales, receipts, photographs, video clips and media coverage can be used to reflect on the event and draw conclusions.

- ✪ **Customer feedback:** This can be both formal and informal. Formal feedback can be from surveys carried out during the project, and sometimes immediately after its completion. As well as information on the profile of your customers, your team can use visitor surveys to discover attitudes and opinions. All staff should be trained to register informal feedback in the form of comments, complaints and suggestions from customers, since this is often as valuable as the formal data.

- ✪ **Comments from observers**: It is useful to have the views of respected individuals who lie outside your team framework, but whose comments are nonetheless valuable and can help the evaluation process.

- ✪ **Comments from team members:** All team members are likely to have useful ideas as to how their particular role could have been improved. The team leader should note their comments at the debriefing meeting and feed these into the evaluation process.

Probably the best question to ask at the evaluation stage is, 'was the event worth all the hard work, money, time and effort that went into its planning and staging?' If all concerned can answer *yes* to this, then the event can truly be said to have been a success.

Team evaluation

As well as evaluating the overall success of your project, you will also need to carry out a team evaluation, investigating how the team as a whole and individual team members performed. This could take a number of forms, for example:

- ✪ **Whole team debrief:** This should take place soon after your project debriefing meeting, drawing on both formal and informal feedback. Your completed logs will play an important part in this process. Informal feedback from the team members will include their personal views and comments on their own performance and the effectiveness of the whole team, including the team leader. While informal feedback is a very useful tool for identifying broad areas of success and failure, a more formal reporting mechanism will be needed to measure team effectiveness, based on the original project objectives.

- ✪ **Tutor interview:** Your tutor may wish to interview members of the team individually as part of the team evaluation process. This interview will include an exchange of views about your performance at different stages of the project.

- ✪ **Self-appraisal:** Team members may be asked to formally evaluate their own performance against objectives and performance criteria by carrying out a self-appraisal, which, if undertaken in as objective a way as possible, can produce useful feedback for both the individual and his or her tutor.

✪ **Peer appraisal:** This involves the evaluation of a member of the team by his or her peers, i.e. the other members of the team. Formal rather than informal peer appraisal is more useful, since it can prevent the exercise becoming too personal. If managed effectively by the team leader, however, it can be very enlightening and can help to identify strengths and weaknesses in individual team members, who can use the outcomes to identify any remedial measures that may be necessary.

Whichever team evaluation method(s) you use, it is important to remember that by planning and carrying out the project, you will have gained valuable team-building skills that will set you in good stead for your future career development.

Glossary

'above the line' refers to marketing and promotional activity for which a commission is normally paid by the chosen media to an advertising agency, for example advertising by a tourism organisation on television, at the cinema, in newspapers and magazines, or on commercial radio.

ABTA Association of British Travel Agents, the trade body that represents over 90 per cent of all travel agents and tour operators in the UK. The Association is a self-regulatory body run by its membership, via a network of councils and committees, with members appointed by member travel agents and tour operators.

Agenda 21 a set of principles for future sustainable development agreed at the Earth Summit in Rio in 1992. Agenda 21 has since been interpreted and expanded at national, regional and local level in many of the world's countries. Many communities in the UK have developed their own action plans, referred to as Local Agenda 21.

'below the line' refers to marketing activity for which a commission is not normally paid to an advertising agency, but the work is carried out on a fee basis instead. For example, an agency may charge a fee of £2,000 to carry out a small direct mail campaign for a travel company. As well as direct mail, other below-the-line activities include public relations, sales promotions and merchandising.

branding the practice of giving a product or service a distinctive name or logo, in the hope that it will become easily identifiable from its competitors and take on a certain identity. Common brand names used in the tourism industry include Holiday Inn, Hertz and Lunn Poly. Organisations hope that customers will show brand loyalty, by buying their particular products above all others.

break-even load factor a measure of the number of seats that need to be sold on an airline flight, as a proportion of total seats available, before all operating, marketing and administrative costs are covered. It is only when the break-even load figure has been reached that the airline will begin to make a profit on the flight.

business tourism the category of the tourism industry concerned with travel for business purposes, rather than travel for leisure purposes. Business tourism includes travel for meetings, exhibitions, trade fairs, conferences, conventions and incentive travel.

carrying capacity the maximum number of people that a resort, site or other area can sustain, before there is a reduction in the quality of the visitor experience or adverse effects on either the physical environment or the host community.

catchment area the geographical limit from within which a tourism facility draws its customers. The size of the catchment area will depend on a number of factors, such as the availability and quality of transport links, the uniqueness of the facility and the population density of the area.

chartered air services when aircraft are commissioned for a set period of time, flying to a particular destination and able to offer reduced fares by setting high load factors. Most package holidays that include air travel will use charter flights (known as inclusive tours by charter).

commission a payment made to an agent for selling the products and services of a principal, for example a travel agent is paid a commission for selling a tour operator's package holidays. The commission is usually an agreed percentage of the selling price, which may be increased for higher sales levels.

day visitor a term which describes a tourist who makes a visit which does not involve an overnight stay away from their normal place of residence.

demarketing the technique of withdrawing marketing activity from a product or service so as to dissuade customers and thereby reduce demand. In tourism, it can be applied to a destination that has become too popular and is giving rise to complaints of overcrowding and damage to the environment.

demographic factors concern the characteristics of the population of a country or region, for example age structure, proportion of males and females, social class, level of income and employment status.

demonstration effect seen most often in developing countries, when members of the host communities begin to imitate the patterns of behaviour of their (often) wealthier Western visitors. Some residents are curious about and may yearn for the consumer goods belonging to the tourists, such as cameras, personal stereos and radios.

deregulation the withdrawal of local or central government control over industries to encourage greater competition between companies, for example the airline industry in the USA and the coach industry in the UK.

direct marketing the term used to describe the various techniques that an organisation can use to sell its products and services on a personalised basis direct to the consumer, without the need for an intermediary. These include direct mail, telemarketing, door-to-door distribution and direct response advertising.

direct sell when a tourism organisation sells its products and services direct to the consumer, rather than through an intermediary, sometimes called a 'middle man'. In the package holiday industry, direct sell operators, such as Portland Direct, suggest that they can sell holidays more cheaply since they do not have to pay any commission to travel agents.

domestic tourism the type of tourism where people take holidays, short breaks and business trips in their own country.

economic impacts refers to the positive and negative effects of tourism on national and local communities, for example wealth generation, employment creation, urban regeneration and contributions to gross national product (GNP).

ecotourism defined by the Ecotourism Society as 'purposeful travel to natural areas to understand the cultural and natural history of the environment, taking care not to alter the integrity of the ecosystem, whilst producing economic opportunities that make the conservation of natural resources financially beneficial to local citizens'.

'empty nesters' a term used by tourism marketers to denote couples whose children have moved away from the household, thereby increasing their available disposable income.

entrepreneur an individual who is prepared to take a risk and accept a challenge or undertake a venture that has no guarantee of success. Richard Branson, chairman of the Virgin Group, is often cited as a good example of an entrepreneur working in the tourism industry.

environmental impacts refers to positive and negative impacts of tourism, for example initiatives such as the Britain in Bloom competition and the Seaside Award helping to improve environments for both locals and visitors. Problems associated with the environmental impacts of tourism include litter, pollution, physical erosion and loss of habitats.

European Blue Flag Campaign a scheme that provides a comparison between standards of cleanliness and management at European resort beaches. Launched in 1987, the European Year of the Environment, a Blue Flag is awarded to resort beaches which have achieved the guideline standard of the EU Bathing Water Directive.

familiarisation visit an educational trip which gives travel agents, tour operators and other members of the travel trade the opportunity of trying tourism facilities and services at first hand, so that they are in the best position to advise clients on their holiday choices.

globalisation the process whereby large companies and markets become increasingly multinational through company takeovers, strategic alliances, vertical and horizontal integration, allowing businesses to switch operations around the world with ease.

green tourism a general term used to describe a type of tourist activity that aims to be respectful of the environment in which it takes place and the communities that live there. Variously described as alternative tourism, appropriate tourism, intelligent tourism, 'soft' tourism, responsible tourism and ecotourism, 'green' tourism is characterised as small-scale activities which make use of local products and labour to produce a holiday experience that is an alternative to mass tourism.

'honey pot' the term used to describe the convergence of visitors in popular tourist destinations.

horizontal integration the process whereby companies at the same level in the distribution chain merge to gain competitive advantage, for example a large hotel chain taking over a small independent hotel.

host community a term used in the debate on sustainable tourism to denote a place where people go for holidays and the people who live there. There is a growing acceptance that the wishes of host communities in relation to tourist development need to be given a higher priority to ensure minimum disruption to their lives, while at the same time providing economic benefits.

IATA International Air Transport Association, a voluntary international trade body representing the interests of more than 80 per cent of the world's major airlines. IATA's principal aim is to promote safe, regular and economic air travel.

impacts of tourism these are generally characterised as economic, environmental, socio-cultural and political. Tourism impacts may be either positive or negative.

inbound (incoming) tourism a form of international tourism which deals with people entering another country from their own country of origin or another country which is not their home.

incentive travel a type of business tourism concerned with offering holidays and leisure products as incentives for staff.

inclusive tour (IT) another term used for package holiday.

inclusive tour by charter (ITC) the term used for a package holiday where the travel component is made up of a charter flight, as opposed to a scheduled flight. The vast majority of mass market package holidays use this arrangement.

inclusive tour by excursion (ITX) a package holiday where the travel component consists of a scheduled flight, rather than a charter flight. In the UK this arrangement is less common and more expensive than an inclusive tour by charter.

infrastructure refers to facilities such as airports, communications, roads, railways, water supply and sewage services, i.e. all those services that need to be in place before tourism development of any kind can go ahead. A country's infrastructure is generally financed and built by the public sector, or is part of a public/private partnership arrangement, with private sector operators developing the tourism superstructure.

integration refers to tourism organisations merging their operations for commercial advantage. The most common types in tourism are horizontal and vertical integration.

international tourism refers to inbound and outbound tourism.

invisibles these are services whose value is shown on a country's balance of payments, i.e. those items that cannot be seen or touched, for example banking, financial services, shipping and tourism.

leakage the loss of revenue from a local or national economy as a result of, for example, fluctuations in exchange rates, payments to shareholders, taxation and purchases of goods and services from external distributors.

leisure tourism the category of tourism concerned with travel for leisure purposes, rather than travel for business purposes. Leisure tourism includes taking holidays at home and abroad, visiting friends and relatives (VFR) and travel for a variety of reasons, such as for health and fitness, sport, education, culture, religious and spiritual.

market orientation a philosophy concerned with researching the needs of the market and providing tourism products and services that customers will want to buy. It is more concerned with giving customers complete satisfaction than purely concentrating on the details of the products and services that are supplied.

market research the process of gathering information on existing and potential customers and its use for management purposes.

market segmentation the technique of subdividing the total market for a tourism product or service into different groups, each consisting of people with similar characteristics. Market segmentation enables an organisation to target a particular group, whose members become the focus of all its marketing efforts.

market share the proportion of a total market that is held by an organisation, in relation to its main competitors. In tourism, market share is usually measured either by volume, for example the number of holidays sold to a particular destination, or by value, for example the revenue generated by sales to a particular country.

marketing the process concerned with identifying customers' needs and supplying products and services in the right place, at the right time and at the right price. It is defined by the Chartered Institute of Marketing as 'the management process for identifying and satisfying customer needs profitably'.

marketing consortium a grouping of independent tourism businesses or other organisations working together for a common purpose or benefit.

marketing mix commonly referred to as the 4 Ps, the marketing mix refers to product, price, place and promotion, and the emphasis placed on each component in seeking to achieve marketing objectives.

marketing objectives the specific aims or goals that an organisation has in mind when planning and implementing its marketing activity.

marketing strategy refers to the overall means by which an organisation hopes to meet its marketing objectives.

mass tourism the term used to describe the movement of people in large numbers for leisure tourism purposes, a characteristic of the tourism industry since the 1960s in Western, developed countries.

merchandising a range of methods adopted by travel and tourism retailers to stimulate customers to purchase at the point of sale (POS). This may include brochure racks, posters, hanging cards, displays and signs.

mission statement a brief explanation of an organisation's fundamental purpose. Its aim is to convey to all those with an interest in the organisation, be they staff, shareholders or the public in general, what business it is in, where it sees itself going and how it will relate to its environment and other organisations.

multinational corporation a company that operates across international frontiers, with its headquarters in one country and operating interests in a number of others.

multiplier effect an economic concept which, when applied to tourism, shows that the money spent by visitors to an area is respent in the local economy and is actually worth more than its face value.

national tourism refers to domestic and outbound tourism.

'niche' marketing the process of targeting small, readily identifiable sections of a tourism market, each with clearly defined characteristics, rather than trying to cover it all.

outbound tourism the form of international tourism which concerns people travelling away from their main country of residence for leisure or business purposes.

Package Travel Directive a European Union Directive that seeks to give people buying package holidays greater protection in law and access to compensation when things go wrong.

passenger load the number of people travelling on a particular journey.

primary data refers to data that is collected for the first time, usually as part of a market research study.

principal the name given to a company that a travel agent does business with and whose products and services it sells.

private sector tourism the sector of the tourism industry that is concerned principally with commercial activities and maximising profits. The majority of tourism organisations are private sector enterprises, for example hotels, airlines, travel agencies, tour operators, car hire firms, tourist attractions and transport operators.

product development the techniques and processes that an organisation will use to make its product portfolio as appealing as possible to existing and potential customers.

product orientation a business philosophy and management style that focuses on the details of products and services supplied rather than the needs of customers.

product portfolio the mix of products or services offered by a tourism organisation to its customers.

promotional mix the different promotional techniques that a tourism organisation will use to raise awareness of its products and services, and to stimulate sales. These could include advertising, direct marketing, sales promotion and public relations activities.

public sector tourism the sector of the tourism industry concerned with providing a service to a local community or society in general, rather than having profit maximisation as a prime objective.

qualitative data refers to information, often gathered as part of a market research process, that is concerned with an organisation's standing in the marketplace, rather than an exact measurement of its performance. An example of qualitative data would be tourists' opinions of an attraction.

quantitative data factual information that can be measured, often gathered as part of a market research process, for example the number of visitors to a theme park, the stock of accommodation in a holiday resort or the country of origin of visitors to Britain.

racking policy refers to the tour operators' brochures that a travel agent will have on display in the agency.

scheduled air services flights that operate to a published timetable on specific routes. Unlike charter flights, scheduled services are committed to operate even if the load factor is very low.

seasonality refers to variations in the demand for tourism products and services at different times of the year.

seat-only sales the name given to purchases of flight tickets without any accommodation or other services provided.

secondary data information available from existing sources, usually in written form, but increasingly now available from electronic media such as CD-ROMS and the Internet.

Section 4 grants funds that were made available to tourism businesses under the 1969 Development of Tourism Act to encourage new tourism projects. Although initially available in England, Scotland and Wales, the English Tourism Council no longer has powers to distribute 'Section 4' grants.

self-catering accommodation regarded as any type of accommodation where guests take care of themselves and where, unlike serviced accommodation, there are no, or very few, services provided for them during their stay.

serviced accommodation refers to hotels, guesthouses and any other type of accommodation where guests are offered a range of different services during their stay, such as food, portering, valet services and possibly entertainment.

shoulder periods times of the year either side of tourism's peak season.

socio-cultural impacts positive and negative effects of tourism on societies and communities, and their cultural traditions.

strategic alliance when two or more enterprises work collaboratively for mutual benefit or self-interest.

strategic marketing the medium- to long-term process of determining how best a tourism organisation can achieve its marketing objectives.

superstructure any construction that takes place above ground and which uses a pre-existing infrastructure. In the case of travel and tourism, superstructure projects would include hotels, attractions and transportation.

sustainable tourism a concept that seeks to address the long-term environmental and socio-cultural issues surrounding uncontrolled tourist development worldwide. An extension of 'green' tourism, it is part of a much wider global debate on sustainable development, highlighted by the Brundtland Report in 1987 and the Earth Summit in Rio in 1992.

SWOT analysis one of the most common techniques that an organisation can use to try to establish where it stands in the marketplace and what it needs to do to maintain or improve its competitive position. SWOT stands for strengths, weaknesses, opportunities and threats.

tactical marketing short-term marketing activity carried out in response to unforeseen or unplanned occurrences in the marketplace.

target audience the individuals that a tourism organisation seeks to attract and influence via its marketing activity.

target marketing the practice of selecting particular groups or individuals (known as the target market), and using the different components of the marketing mix to encourage them to buy or use products or services.

tourism balance the difference between the value of a country's earnings from inbound tourism and the expenditure by its residents on overseas tourism.

tourist enclave a clearly defined enclosed area within which tourists are isolated from the residents of a destination (the host community), sometimes for security and safety reasons.

tourist generating country refers to the country of origin of travellers, as opposed to the tourist receiving country, which is their destination country.

tourist receiving country the destination country that travellers arrive at, as opposed to the tourist generating country, which is the origin of their journey.

travel trade the term used to describe all the commercial sectors within the tourism industry, including travel agents, tour operators, coach operators, car hire firms, airlines, ferry companies and providers of specialist support services.

unique selling proposition (USP) denotes the particular benefit that one product or service is said by its promoters to have over another product or service, i.e. the reason why customers will choose that item instead of an item from a competitor.

vertical integration the process whereby companies at different levels of the distribution chain are linked in some way in order to gain competitive advantage.

VFR visiting friends and relatives, an important revenue source for most nations involved in tourist activity.

viewdata a computer-based interactive system used by travel agents to display information on VDUs and to access the computerised reservation systems of principals, mainly airlines and tour operators, via a telephone line.

World Tourism Organisation the established inter-governmental agency for tourism policies worldwide, representing public sector tourism bodies from the majority of countries in the world.

Sources of further information

England's regional tourist boards

Cumbria Tourist Board
Ashleigh
Holly Road
Windermere
Cumbria LA23 2AQ
(covers the county of Cumbria)

East of England Tourist Board
Toppesfield Hall
Hadleigh
Suffolk IP7 5DN
*(covers the counties of Cambridgeshire, Essex, Hertfordshire, Bedfordshire,
Norfolk, Suffolk and Lincolnshire)*

Heart of England Tourist Board
Woodside
Larkhill Road
Worcester WR5 2EF
*(covers the counties of Derbyshire, Gloucestershire, Herefordshire, Leicestershire,
Northamptonshire, Nottinghamshire, Rutland, Shropshire, Staffordshire,
Warwickshire, Worcestershire, the West Midlands and represents the districts of
Cherwell and West Oxfordshire)*

London Tourist Board
Glen House
Stag Place
London SW1E 5LT
(covers the Greater London area)

Northumbria Tourist Board
Aykley Heads
County Durham
DH1 5UX
(covers the counties of Durham, Northumberland, Tees Valley and Tyne & Wear)

North West Tourist Board
Swan House
Swan Meadow Road
Wigan Pier
Wigan
Lancashire WN3 5BB
*(covers the counties of Cheshire, Greater Manchester, Lancashire, Merseyside and
the High Peak District of Derbyshire)*

South East England Tourist Board
The Old Brewhouse
1 Warwick Park
Tunbridge Wells
Kent TN2 5TU
(covers the counties of East and West Sussex, Kent and Surrey)

Southern Tourist Board
40 Chamberlayne Road
Eastleigh
Hampshire SO50 5JH
(covers the counties of Berkshire, Buckinghamshire, East and North Dorset, Hampshire, Isle of Wight and Oxfordshire)

West Country Tourist Board
60 St Davids Hill
Exeter
Devon EX4 4SY
(covers Bath, Bristol, Cornwall & Isles of Scilly, Devon, West Dorset, Somerset and Wiltshire)

Yorkshire Tourist Board
312 Tadcaster Road
York
North Yorkshire YO24 1GS
(covers the counties of Yorkshire and North East Lincolnshire)

National tourist organisations

British Tourist Authority
Thames Tower
Black's Road
Hammersmith
London W6 9EL
(promotes tourism to Great Britain from overseas)

English Tourism Council
Thames Tower
Black's Road
Hammersmith
London W6 9EL

Northern Ireland Tourist Board
St Anne's Court
59 North Street
Belfast BT1 1NB

Scottish Tourist Board
23 Ravelston Terrace
Edinburgh EH4 3EU

Wales Tourist Board
Brunel House
2 Fitzalan Road
Cardiff CF2 1UY

Isle of Man Department of Tourism and Leisure
Sea Terminal Buildings
Douglas
Isle of Man
IM1 2RG

Jersey Tourism
Liberation Square
St Helier
Jersey
JE1 1BB

States of Guernsey Tourist Board
PO Box 23
St Peter Port
Guernsey
GY1 3AN

Other organisations with interests in travel and tourism

Arts Council of England
14 Great Peter Street
London
SW1P 3NQ

Association of Independent Tour Operators (AITO)
St Margarets Road
Twickenham
Middlesex TW1 1RG

Association of Independent Travel Agents
Herlington
Orton Malbourne
Peterborough PE2 5PR

Association of Leading Visitor Attractions
4 Westminster Palace Gardens
Victoria
London SW1P 1RL

Association of Scottish Visitor Attractions
Suite 6
Admiral House
Maritime Street
Edinburgh EH6 6SG

British Activity Holiday Association
Green Lane
Hersham
Walton-on-Thames
Surrey KT12 5HD

British Association of Leisure Parks, Piers and Attractions
25 Kings Terrace
London NWI 0JP

British Association of Tourism Officers
PO Box 547
Brighton BNI 6WW

British Hospitality Association
Queen's House
55/56 Lincoln's Inn Fields
London WC2 3BN

British Institute of Innkeeping
Wessex House
80 Park Street
Camberley
Surrey GU15 3PT

British Resorts Association
8 Post Office Avenue
Southport
Lancashire PR9 0US

British Waterways
Church Road
Watford WD1 3QA

City & Guilds of London Institute
Giltspur Street
London EC1A 9DD

Countryside Agency
John Dower House
Crescent Place
Cheltenham
Gloucestershire GL50 3RA

Department for Culture, Media and Sport
4 Cockspur Street
London SW1Y 5DH

Edexcel Foundation (formerly BTEC)
Stewart House
Russell Square
London WC1B 5DN

English Heritage
23 Savile Row
London W1X 1AB

Farm Holiday Bureau (UK) Ltd
National Agricultural Centre
Stoneleigh Park
Warwickshire CV8 2LZ

Federation of Tour Operators
170 High Street
Lewes
East Sussex
BN7 1YE

Holiday Care Service
Imperial Buildings
Horley
Surrey RH6 7PZ

Hospitality Association of Northern Ireland
108/110 Midland Building
Whitla Street
Belfast BT15 1JP

Hospitality Training Foundation
3rd Floor
International House
High Street
Ealing
London W5 5DB

Hotel Catering and Institutional Management Association (HCIMA)
191 Trinity Road
London SW17 7HN

Institute of Leisure and Amenity Management (ILAM)
ILAM House
Lower Basildon
Reading
Berkshire RG8 9NE

Institute of Sport and Recreation Management (ISRM)
Giffard House
36/38 Sherrard Street
Melton Mowbray
Leicestershire LE13 IXJ

Institute of Travel and Tourism
113 Victoria Street
St Albans
Hertfordshire AL1 3TJ

Museums Association
Clerkenwell Close
London EC1R 0PA

National Trust
36 Queen Anne's Gate
London SW1H 9AS

Tourism Concern
Stapleton House
277–281 Holloway Road
London N7 8HN

Tourism Society
26 Chapter Street
London SW1P 4ND

Travel Training Company
The Broadway
7/11 Chertsey Road
Woking
Surrey GU12 5AR

Youth Hostel's Association
Trevelyan House
8 St Stephen's Hill
St Albans
Hertfordshire AL1 2DY

Selected bibliography

Textbooks

Ashworth G and Goodall B 1990 *Marketing tourism places* Routledge, London

Bull A 1991 *The economics of travel and tourism* Pitman, Melbourne

Burkart A and Medlik S 1981 *Tourism: past, present and future* Heinemann, London

Burns P and Holden A 1995 *Tourism: a new perspective* Prentice Hall, Hemel Hempstead

Burton R 1995 *Travel geography* Pitman, London

Cambridge Training and Development 1996 *Advanced leisure and tourism* Oxford University Press

Cambridge Training and Development 1996 *Intermediate leisure and tourism* Oxford University Press

Cooper C et al. 1998 *Tourism: principles and practice* 2nd edition Longman, Harlow

Davidson R 1998 *Tourism in Europe* 2nd edition, Longman, Harlow

Davidson R and Maitland R 1997 *Tourism destinations* Hodder & Stoughton, London

English Tourist Board 1991 *Tourism and the environment: maintaining the balance* ETB, London

Gamble W 1989 *Tourism and development in Africa* John Murray, London

Gunn C 1994 *Tourism planning* Taylor & Francis, New York

Hall C M 1994 *Tourism and politics* John Wiley & Sons, Chichester

Hall D (ed.) 1991 *Tourism and economic development in Eastern Europe and the Soviet Union* John Wiley & Sons, Chichester

Hall M and Lew A 1998 *Sustainable tourism* Longman, Harlow

Holloway C 1998 *The business of tourism* 5th edition Longman, Harlow

Holloway C and Robinson C 1995 *Marketing for tourism* 3rd edition Longman, Harlow

Horner P 1996 *Travel agency practice* Longman, Harlow

Inkpen G 1998 *Information technology for travel and tourism* Longman, Harlow

Inskeep E 1991 *Tourism planning: an integrated and sustainable development approach* Van Nostrand Reinhold, New York

Jones C and Radcliffe M 1996 *Foundation GNVQ leisure and tourism* Longman, Harlow

Kemp K and Pearson S 1996 *Intermediate GNVQ optional units* Longman, Harlow

Krippendorf J 1989 *The holiday makers* Butterworth Heinemann, Oxford

Laws E (ed.) 1997 *The ATTT tourism education handbook* Tourism Society, London

Lea J 1988 *Tourism and development in the Third World* Routledge, London

Lickorish L 1991 *Developing tourism destinations* Longman, Harlow

Mathieson A and Wall G 1982 *Tourism: economic, physical and social impacts* Longman, Harlow

Middleton V 1994 *Marketing in travel and tourism* 2nd edition Butterworth Heinemann, London

Mill R and Morrison A 1992 *The tourism system* Prentice Hall International, Hemel Hempstead

Murphy P 1985 *Tourism: a community approach* Routledge, London

Outhart T et al. 1995 *Leisure and tourism for Intermediate GNVQ* Collins Educational, London

Outhart T et al. 1997 *Leisure and tourism for Advanced GNVQ* Collins Educational, London

Pearce D 1989 *Tourist development* Longman, Harlow

Pearce D 1995 *Tourism today: a geographical analysis* Longman, Harlow

Pompl W and Lavery P 1993 *Tourism in Europe: structures and developments* CAB International, Oxford

Ryan C 1991 *Recreational tourism: a social science perspective* Routledge, London

Sharpley S and Sharpley J 1997 *Rural tourism: an introduction* International Thomson Business Press, London

Smith V 1989 *Hosts and guests: the anthropology of tourism* 2nd edition University of Pennsylvania Press, Philadelphia

Swarbrooke J 1995 *The development and management of visitor attractions* Butterworth Heinemann, London

Van Harssel J 1994 *Tourism: an exploration* 3rd edition Prentice Hall International, Hemel Hempstead

Watt D 1998 *Event management in leisure and tourism* Longman, Harlow

Witt S, Brooke M and Buckley P 1995 *The management of international tourism* Routledge, London

World Tourism Organisation 1994 *National and regional tourism planning: methodologies and case studies* Routledge, London

Yale P 1993 *Tourism and leisure in the countryside* ELM Publications, Huntingdon

Yale P 1995 *The business of tour operations* Longman, Harlow

Youell R 1995 *Leisure and tourism Advanced GNVQ* 2nd edition Longman, Harlow

Youell R 1996 *Advanced GNVQ travel and tourism optional units* Longman, Harlow

Youell R 1996 *The complete A–Z leisure, travel & tourism handbook* Hodder & Stoughton, London

Youell R 1998 *Tourism: an introduction* Addison Wesley Longman, Harlow

Journals

Annals of Tourism Research

Insights (English Tourism Council)

International Journal of Tourism Research (John Wiley & Sons, formerly *Progress in Tourism and Hospitality Research*)

Journal of Sustainable Tourism (Channel View Publications, Bristol)

Journal of Travel and Tourism Marketing

Tourism (Journal of the Tourism Society, London)

Tourism Management

Periodicals

Attractions Management

Business Traveller

Leisure Management

Leisure Opportunities

Travel News

Travel Trade Gazette

Travel Weekly

Websites featured in the book

Website address	Organisation
www.world-tourism.org	World Tourism Organization
www.toursoc.org.uk	Tourism Society
www.visitbritain.com	British Tourist Authority
www.countryside.gov.uk	Countryside Agency
www.ccw.gov.uk	Countryside Council for Wales
www.24hourmuseum.org.uk	24 Hour Museum
www.eureka.org.uk	Eureka! Museum for Children
www.travelodge.co.uk	Travelodge
www.hoseasons.co.uk	Hoseasons Holidays
www.open.gov.uk	Open Government site
www.nationalexpress.co.uk	National Express
www.eurotunnel.co.uk	Eurotunnel
www.buzzaway.com	Buzz low-cost airline
www.portland-holidays.co.uk	Portland Holidays
www.airtours.com	Airtours
www.wallacearnold.com	Wallace Arnold Holidays
www.superbreak.com	Superbreak
www.bitoa.co.uk	British Incoming Tour Operators' Association
www.culture.gov.uk	Department for Culture, Media and Sport
www.centerparcs.com	Center Parcs
www.tttc.co.uk	The Travel Training Company
www.careercompass.co.uk	Careercompass
www.artscouncil.org.uk	Arts Council of England
www.ccc-acw.org.uk	Arts Council of Wales
www.englishtourism.org.uk	English Tourism Council
www.tourism.wales.gov.uk	Wales Tourist Board
www.ni-tourism.com	Northern Ireland Tourist Board
www.holiday.scotland.net	Scottish Tourist Board
www.british-airways.com	British Airways
www.fly.virgin.com	Virgin Atlantic Airways
www.thomson-holidays.com	Thomson Holidays
www.drivebudget.com	Budget rent-a-car
www.tourist-offices.org.uk	Tourist offices worldwide
www.world-tourism.org/tourworl.htm	World Tourism Organization link to tourist offices worldwide
www.yha.org.uk	Youth Hostels Association
www.nationaltrust.org.uk	National Trust
www.waveney.gov.uk	Waveney District Council
www.wttc.org	World Travel and Tourism Council

www.tourismconcern.org.uk	Tourism Concern
www.resort-guide.co.uk/purbeck/	Purbeck, Dorset
www.cambridge.gov.uk/leisure/	Cambridge City Council
www.wtg-online.com	World Travel Guide
www.travelocity.com	Travelocity
www.lonelyplanet.com	Lonely Planet guides
www.oag.com	Overseas Airways Guides
www.roughguides.com	Rough Guides
www.sabre.com	Sabre CRS
www.worldspan.com	Worldspan CRS
www.galileo.com	Galileo CRS
www.fco.gov.uk/travel	Foreign Office travel advice
www.cim.co.uk	Chartered Institute of Marketing
www.towerbridge.org.uk	Tower Bridge Experience
www.bestwestern.co.uk	Best Western Hotels
www.rank.com	Rank Organisation
www.warwick-castle.co.uk	Warwick Castle
www.firstchoice.co.uk	First Choice Holidays
www.teletext.co.uk	Teletext
www.lastminute.com	lastminute.com
www.ipr.org.uk	Institute of Public Relations
www.asa.org.uk	Advertising Standards Authority
www.hilton.com	Hilton Hotels
www.hilton.com/hotels/BFSHITW/	Hilton Hotel, Belfast
www.gner.co.uk	Great North Eastern Railway Company
www.hertz.co.uk	Hertz rent-a-car
www.havenholidays.co.uk	Haven Holidays
www.air2000.co.uk	Air 2000
www.english-heritage.org.uk	English Heritage
www.disability.gov.uk	Government's site on disability issues
www.thomascook.co.uk	Thomas Cook
www.englishtourism.org.uk/quality	English Tourism Council benchmarking
www.businesslink.co.uk	Business Link
www.cbc.org.uk	Business Connect Wales
www.london-marathon.co.uk	London Marathon Company

Please note that website addresses are subject to change. Use a search engine if you are experiencing difficulty accessing any of the above sites.

Index

Note: case studies references are in bold.